INTUITION IN KANT

In this book, Daniel Smyth offers a comprehensive overview of Immanuel Kant's conception of intuition in all its species – divine, receptive, sensible, and human. Kant considers sense perception a paradigm of intuition, yet claims that we can represent infinities in intuition, despite the finitude of sense perception. Smyth examines this heterodox combination of commitments and argues that the various features Kant ascribes to intuition are meant to remedy specific cognitive shortcomings that arise from the discursivity of our intellect, with intuition acting as the intellect's cognitive partner to make knowledge possible. He reconstructs Kant's conception of intuition and its role in his philosophy of mind, epistemology, and philosophy of mathematics, and shows that Kant's conception of sensibility is as innovative and revolutionary as his much-debated theory of the understanding.

DANIEL SMYTH is Assistant Professor of Letters, Philosophy, and German Studies at Wesleyan University, Connecticut. He publishes on Kant, philosophy of mathematics, and aesthetic theory and has translated numerous books and articles from German.

INTUITION IN KANT

The Boundlessness of Sense

DANIEL SMYTH
Wesleyan University, Connecticut

CAMBRIDGE
UNIVERSITY PRESS

CAMBRIDGE
UNIVERSITY PRESS

Shaftesbury Road, Cambridge CB2 8EA, United Kingdom

One Liberty Plaza, 20th Floor, New York, NY 10006, USA

477 Williamstown Road, Port Melbourne, VIC 3207, Australia

314–321, 3rd Floor, Plot 3, Splendor Forum, Jasola District Centre, New Delhi – 110025, India

103 Penang Road, #05–06/07, Visioncrest Commercial, Singapore 238467

Cambridge University Press is part of Cambridge University Press & Assessment,
a department of the University of Cambridge.

We share the University's mission to contribute to society through the pursuit of
education, learning and research at the highest international levels of excellence.

www.cambridge.org
Information on this title: www.cambridge.org/9781009330282

DOI: 10.1017/9781009330305

First published 2024
First paperback edition 2025

A catalogue record for this publication is available from the British Library

ISBN 978-1-009-33031-2 Hardback
ISBN 978-1-009-33028-2 Paperback

It is too little to call *Man* a *little World*; Except *God*, Man is a *diminutive* to nothing. Man consists of more pieces, more parts, than the world; than the world doeth, nay than the world is. And if those pieces were extended, and stretched out in Man, as they are in the world, Man would be the *Gyant*, and the World the *Dwarfe*, the World but the *Map*, and the Man the *World*.

—John Donne, *Devotions upon Emergent Occasions*, 1624, Meditation IV

Various predicates of space that one would otherwise regard as objective can now be explained through this concept [sc. of space] in view of its origin. 1. Space is unitary [einig], because it is the form of representations of every possible outer object in a unitary subject. 2. Space is infinite. For the capacity to suffer [Fähigkeit zuzulassen] various impressions of outer things, or receptivity [Empfänglichkeit], has no limitations [Schranken] in itself. 3. Space is necessary; for it is that upon which the possibility of the senses is grounded.

—Kant, R4673, 1774–1775, 17:641.14–21

When a man summoned to animated observation begins to do battle with nature, he initially feels a prodigious drive to subjugate its objects to himself. Yet it does not take long for them to intrude so violently upon him that he well feels how much cause he has to acknowledge their power and to admire their efficacy. No sooner has he convinced himself of this reciprocal influence than he becomes aware of a double infinity, in the objects the manifoldness of being and becoming and their lively criss-crossing relations, in himself, however, the possibility of an infinite development, as he refines his receptivity as well as his judgment to ever new forms of up-take and reaction.

—Goethe, "Apology for the Undertaking," Ideas on Organic Formation, 1806–1807, FA 24:389

Contents

Acknowledgments

This project began as a dissertation at the University of Chicago over a decade ago. No part of that dissertation survives in the present book, but the formative influence of my advisors and my fellow graduate students endures. Robert Pippin's breadth and savvy taught me the value of viewing issues against a wide historical horizon and of imaginatively inhabiting unfamiliar postures of thought. Jim Conant's capacity for slow, generous reading showed me the importance of attending closely to philosophical methodology. From Daniel Sutherland I learned to appreciate the fecundity of Kant's philosophy of mathematics and the acuity of its scholars. And Anat Schechtman introduced me to the profundity of Leibniz's and Descartes's views on infinity and helped me to see their relevance to Kant. I am forever discovering and re-discovering gems that they managed to slip into my pockets. I'm grateful to Nathan Bauer, Thomas Land, Justin Shaddock, and Clinton Tolley for discussing Kant with me before I knew what I was talking about. And I'm grateful to Simon Gurofsky, Joshua Mendelsohn, Andrew Pitel, Daniel Rodriguez-Navas, Jess Tizzard, and Andy Werner for continuing those discussions after I would not shut up.

I owe a great debt to the broader community of Kant scholars for cultivating an intellectual estuary for up-and-comers that is at once nurturing and rigorous. My views and habits of mind have improved immeasurably from being an active member of the North American Kant Society. For encouragement, intellectual camaraderie, and invaluable insights at various stages along the way, I am grateful to Matt Boyle, Emily Carson, Rosalind Chaplin, Andrew Chignell, Stephen Engstrom, Anil Gomes, Johannes Haag, Andrea Kern, Pat Kitcher, Michelle Kosch, Samantha Matherne, Colin McLear, Bennett McNulty, James Messina, Sasha Newton, Sebastian Rödl, Timothy Rosenkoetter, Ulrich Schlösser, Lisa Shabel, Nick Stang, and Rachel Zuckert. I have particularly benefitted from extended conversations with Ian Blecher, Thomas Land, and Tyke

Nunez. And I cannot begin to survey the debts I owe to my closest interlocutors about Kant (*auch allen Dingen überhaupt*), Till Hoeppner and Jess Tizzard. I shudder to think where I would be without their good sense and good humor.

I also benefitted from acute and constructive reports by two anonymous reviewers for Cambridge University Press. For finding such fantastic readers and for guiding me through the review and publication process with patience and practicality, I am grateful to Hilary Gaskin. Thanks are also due to Cameron Cook for creating the Index and to my department for paying for it.

The process of writing this book was no walk in the park, so I am especially grateful to my wonderful colleagues at Wesleyan University for advice, moral support, and walks in the park. My colleagues in the College of Letters, as well as my comrades in the Philosophy Department, worked to ensure that I felt valued and secure, actively protecting my time for research and family. For going above and beyond in different ways, I must single out Joe Fitzpatrick, Steve Horst, Tushar Irani, Katherine Kuenzli, Roger Matthew Grant, Uli Plass, Joe Rouse, Sanford Shieh, and Courtney Weiss Smith.

What writing this book has required more than anything else is time. I am grateful for Wesleyan's parental leave program, which enabled me to put research on hold during the precious early months of my children's lives. I am grateful to my mother-in-law, Kristin, for dropping everything when the pandemic hit in order to devote herself to her grandkids. I am grateful to the teachers at Neighborhood Preschool in Middletown for the care they practiced during the pandemic and for the love they practice always. I am grateful to my children, Fionn and Eva, for being relentlessly amazing. And I am grateful to my wife, Leigh Ann, for her resilience and forbearance when I have been absent or irritable, for the intensity and generosity of her attention, for her capacity for gentleness, and for her tenacity. It is to my family, not to Kant, that I owe my most vivid sense of the boundlessness of our human capacities.

Abbreviations, Citations, and Other Conventions

References to Kant

Translations of Kant are my own, but key terms accord with standard English editions. I underline text to signify my own emphasis, and note it parenthetically. I use bold typeface to express Kant's emphasis (where he would have used Sperrdruck), which I generally leave unremarked. I retain Kant's italics in quotations, though only to indicate foreign words, not to express emphasis.

References to Kant's writings follow standard practice with one refinement: the addition of line numbers. I provide volume, page, and line numbers from the Akademie Ausgabe of Kant's writings (Kant 1901–), except for the *Critique of Pure Reason*, where I cite the A (1781) and B (1787) pagination. The A/B page number is followed, after a period, by the line numbers of the Meiner Philosophische Bibliothek edition (Kant 1998). These line numbers track the pagination of the Meiner volume, not the pagination of the A, B, or Akademie editions. To locate cited passages, first find the A/B page in the Meiner edition and then look for cited line numbers within that A/B page.

Because an A/B page may extend across a page break in the Meiner edition, line numbers may sometimes appear to go backward. Thus, A53/B77f.34–06 refers to the sentence, "Sie hat also [...] gemeinen Verstandes." This sentence begins on line 34 of page 131 of the Meiner edition and ends on line 6 of page 132. For the same reason, some early portions of B77 have higher line numbers than later ones, since they appear before the page break: B77.30–34 precedes B77.2–4.

When no line numbers are specified, I mean to refer to an extended discussion in that area of the text. I do this only when I take my interpretation to be uncontroversial.

I supply Adickes's estimated dating of all Reflections and of all unpublished writings that fall outside the penumbra of Kant's "critical period" (1777–1792). I do not provide dates for texts within this period or for published writings.

I abbreviate Kant's works as follows:

A–	Anthropology lectures, followed by full title (e.g. A-Collins; A-Menschenkunde)
Anthropology	Anthropologie in pragmatischer Hinsicht (1798)
Critique	Kritik der reinen Vernunft (1781 = A / 1787 = B)
Directions	Von dem ersten Grunde des Unterschiedes der Gegenden im Raume (1768)
Discovery	Über eine Entdeckung, nach der alle neue Kritik der reinen Vernunft durch eine ältere entbehrlich gemacht werden soll (1790)
Dreams	Träume eines Geistersehers, erläutert durch Träume der Metaphysik (1766)
Groundwork	Grundlegung zur Metaphysik der Sitten (1785)
Inaugural	De mundi sensibilis atque intelligibilis forma et principiis (1770)
Judgment	Kritik der Urteilskraft (1790)
L–	Logic lectures, followed by abbreviated title:

Blom	Blomberg (early 1770s)
Bus	Busolt (c. 1789)
DW	Dohna-Wundlacken (1792)
Jäsche	Immanuel Kants Logik, ein Handbuch zu Vorlesungen (1800)
Ph	Philippi (1772)
Pö	Pölitz (1780–1782)
Wien	Wiener Logic (1780–1782)

M–	Metaphysics lectures, followed by abbreviated title:

DW	Dohna-Wundlacken (1792–1793)
H	Herder (1762–1764)
Mr	Mrongovius (1782–1783)
Pö/L_1	Pölitz / L_1 (1777–1780)
Pö/L_2	Pölitz / L_2 (1790–1791?)
Schön	von Schön (1789–1791)
Vi/K_3	Vigilantius / K_3 (1794/95)
Vo	Volkmann (1784/85)

Metaphysical Foundations	Metaphysische Anfangsgründe der Naturwissenschaft (1786)
On Kästner	Über Kästners Abhandlungen (1790)
Orient	Was heißt: sich im Denken orientieren? (1786)
Physical Monadology	Metaphysicae cum geometria iunctae usus in philosophia naturali, cuius specimen I. continet monadologiam physicam (1756)
Postumum	Opus postumum (c. 1796–1801)
Practical	Kritik der praktischen Vernunft (1788)
Prolegomena	Prolegomena zu einer jeden künftigen Metaphysik, die als Wissenschaft wird auftreten können (1783)
Proof	Der einzig mögliche Beweisgrund zu einer Demonstration des Daseins Gottes (1763)
R	Reflections, cited with Adickes's estimated dating
Teleological	Über den Gebrauch teleologischer Principien in der Philosophie (1788)
Tone	Von einem neuerdings erhobenen vornehmen Ton in der Philosophie (1796)

References to Major Historical Figures

I generally cite critical editions with the standard abbreviations indicated in my bibliography. I provide line numbers when available and useful. I depart from this practice only when I think it will be easier for readers to find the passage by section numbers or in a widely available collection. Thus, citations of Aquinas, Wolff, Baumgarten, and Meier employ section numbers, as do many citations of Leibniz.

Other References

All other references, including citations of secondary literature, employ the Chicago-style, name–date format. When a piece has been republished or translated, I cite the version I think is easiest to access, providing the original date of publication in square brackets for historical context. Thus, "Parsons (1992 [1969])" refers to his classic essay "Kant's Philosophy of Arithmetic" as it appears in Posy's invaluable collection, *Kant's Philosophy of Mathematics: Modern Essays.*

Other Conventions

I enclose words in angled brackets to mention the concepts they express. Thus <horse> and <*Pferd*> co-refer to the concept of the natural species *equus ferus*. I use these same angled brackets to refer to the judgment expressed by the sentence they enclose, which I also italicize. Thus <*horses are mammals*> is an analytic judgment.

I use single quotation marks to mention the words enclosed by them. Thus 'horse' has two vowels, but '*Pferd*' only one.

I use double quotation marks both to quote text and as "scare quotes", to call critical attention to a phrase or idea.

Introduction

From Infinity to Givenness: Kant's Apperceptive Faculty Psychology and His Top-Down Approach to Intuition

Distinguishing the sensible from the intellectual aspects of our knowledge is the keystone of Kant's critical enterprise. In his practical philosophy, it is our amphibious status as rational yet sensible beings that makes us subject to, and simultaneously authors of, ethical imperatives. And in his theoretical philosophy, Kant argues that a proper account of sensibility and understanding – and their associated representations, intuitions and concepts – reveals both the possibility of human knowledge and its inherent limits (*Critique* A44/B61–62, A271/B327). Now Kant is hardly the first to contrast "sense" with "intellect" or to distinguish "lower" from "higher" cognitive capacities. Yet the conclusions he bases on this distinction are so heterodox that his conceptions of its disjuncts must diverge significantly from traditional accounts.

Kant's most notorious heterodoxy is, of course, his "transcendental idealism": the twin claims that (a) spatiotemporal objects and properties are mere "appearances", i.e. mind-dependent or "transcendentally ideal" phenomena, and that (b) human knowledge is restricted to such appearances and does not extend to things in themselves. But the Kantian heterodoxy that precipitated the present project is even more unorthodox than his idealism: namely, his claim that we can represent the mathematically infinite not *despite* but *in virtue of* the sensible, intuitive aspects of our cognition.

This is a view unprecedented in the history of philosophy. Rationalists and empiricists alike agree that *if* we are capable of knowledge involving mathematical infinity, such knowledge cannot have a sensible foundation. They take this to follow from the undeniable finitude of human sense perception. Some phenomena are just too small or too faint, others too large or too intense for our sensory apparatus to register or perceptually discriminate. So empiricists such as Hobbes, Berkeley, and Hume argue that, since all knowledge must be grounded in sense perception, which is finite, cognition of mathematical infinity is impossible, and we should instead develop a strictly finitistic geometry based on *minima sensibilia*.[1] Inverting this reasoning, rationalists such as Descartes, Spinoza, and Leibniz point to the mathematical limitations of human sense and imagination as proof of a higher power of intellect, which they make responsible for infinitary cognition.[2] Kant is unique in denying their shared assumption: that sensible, intuitive representation must be finite.

Now Kant does recognize the obvious limits on sense perception. He insists, however, that "the form of possible experience has nothing at all to do with their [sc. the senses'] coarseness" (A226/B273). The mathematical properties of space and time, including their infinite divisibility, must be exhibited in our empirical intuitings (A165f./B205f.), even if these properties outstrip our sensory or phenomenological acuity. Indeed, Kant seems to treat the representation of mathematical infinity as a defining characteristic of intuition: "Space is represented as an infinite **given** magnitude. [. . .] <u>Therefore</u> the original representation of space is **intuition** and not **concept**" (B39–40, Kant's bold, my underlining).

This poses an interpretive puzzle: What conception of sensible intuition would allow for the intuitive representation of mathematical infinities, while respecting the undeniable finitude of sense perception and retaining the latter as the paradigm case of intuition? And what philosophical rationale could Kant have for rejecting the traditional, finitistic conception of sensibility in favor of one that makes a single capacity responsible for

1 Hobbes rejects the very idea of infinity on the grounds that our senses are finite (*Leviathan* 1.3, 11). He advocates a materialist (corpuscularian) geometry in his 1655 *De Corpore* and a variety of mathematical treatises (see Jesseph 1999, esp. chs. 4 and 6). Berkeley argues that no genuine ideas are communicated by infinitary terms in his 1707 essay "Of Infinities" and later attacks the foundations of infinitesimal calculus in *The Analyst* (1734). He outlines a finitistic geometry based on *minima sensibilia* in §§ 123–131 of the *Principles of Human Knowledge* (1710). Jesseph (1993) remains the authority on these aspects of Berkeley's philosophy of mathematics. Hume's finitism emerges in his treatment of our ideas of space and time in book 1, part 2 of *Treatise* (1739) and in *Enquiry* part 2, §12 (1748). Jacquette (2001) offers a sympathetic reconstruction of Hume's finitism.

2 In the sixth Meditation, Descartes distinguishes pure intellect from imagination by observing that our inability to form a distinct quasi-perceptual image of a chiliagon does not hinder us from mathematically demonstrating its properties (AT 7:72–73). On Descartes's notion of infinity, see Schechtman (2018, 2019). Leibniz deploys the chiliagon example to distinguish symbolic from intuitive knowledge in his 1684 "Meditations on Knowledge, Truth, and Ideas" (G 4:423, AG 24–25) and again in his 1705 *New Essays* to distinguish ideas from images (II.xxix.13, A 6.6:261–262). Similarly, for Spinoza, a principal source of confusion about infinity is the "failure to distinguish what we can apprehend only by the intellect and not by the imagination, and what can also be apprehended by the imagination" (Letter 12, G 4:53, SM 787; cf. *Ethics* 1p15s.). For Spinoza's influence on Leibniz's views about infinity and infinitary cognition, see Nachtomy (2011).

such contrary cognitive achievements – viz. the representation of infinitary structure and the production of finite sense perceptions?

Interpreters sometimes try to resolve this difficulty by "charitably" minimizing Kant's commitment to the intuitive representation of infinity. Intuitions, they suggest, exhibit only a *potential* infinity: We represent space merely as open-ended, not as actually endless; as indefinitely divisible, not as containing an actual infinity of distinct spaces. Moreover, what holds for mathematical abstracta need not hold for perceptible concreta or their representations.

Perusal of Kant's texts undermines these responses, however, as recent scholarship has shown.[3] Kant resolutely maintains that space and time, as forms of sensible intuition, are actually infinite in the large and in the small. Indeed, the potential infinities to which some commentators propose we retreat are possible, according to Kant, only insofar as they are grounded in actual infinities, of which we have an "original representation" in our form of sensible intuition.[4] And Kant insists that the mathematical properties of the form of intuition are inherited by all intuitive representations bearing that form (A165–166/B205–206). Thus, to come to grips with Kant's epistemology and philosophy of mind – based as it is in his distinction between sensibility and intellect, intuition and concept – we must recover a conception of sensible intuition for which the representation of mathematical infinities is a constitutive possibility, despite the undeniable sensory and phenomenological limits on the sensitivity, scope, and acuity of human sense perception.

[3] See, for example, Büchel (1987, 185–220); Carson (1997); Friedman (2000, 2012, 2020); Domski (2008); Posy (2008); Patton (2011); Onof and Schulting (2014, 2015); Smyth (2014, 2023 [2021]); Tolley (2016); Chaplin (2022); Rosefeldt (2022); and Winegar (2022). Kemp Smith emphasizes Kant's acceptance of actual infinity in his discussion of the first Antinomy (1992 [1918], 486–487). But his was a minority opinion. Kant's clearest endorsement of the actually infinitary character of intuition appears in *On Kästner*. And Kant's authorship of this text was discovered only in 1890, with Dilthey's analysis of the Rostock *Nachlass*. By then, finitistic interpretations of Kant were too entrenched to be overturned. The few *fin-de-siècle* scholars who even registered Kant's commitment to actual infinity dismissed it as an inconsistency in his position (Vaihinger 1892, 253–261) – a view that still has advocates today (Guyer 2018). The idea that actual infinity is a consistent and essential feature of Kant's conception of sensible intuition remained a minority view, especially in Anglophone discussions, well into the 1990s. It has many champions today.

[4] When Kästner (1790) challenges Kant on this point, arguing that geometry requires only potential infinities, not actual infinities, Kant responds: "[To claim that] a line can be extended into infinity amounts to saying that the space in which I describe the line is greater than every line that I can describe in it; and thus the geometer grounds the possibility of his task of enlarging a space (of which there are many) into infinity upon the original representation of a unitary, infinite, **subjectively given** space" (*On Kästner* 20:420, cf. 421). For discussion, see Smyth (2023 [2021], section 2) and Section 5.4.1.

My argument in *The Boundlessness of Sense* is that this heterodox, infinitary conception of sensible intuition arises from an aspect of Kant's philosophical method that has fallen into disrepute: his "faculty psychology", i.e. his approach to the mind as a seat of diverse but coordinated cognitive capacities.[5] A capacity is defined through its characteristic function, its contribution to a specified output or achievement. In the case of Kant's transcendental epistemology, the output relative to which capacities are identified and discriminated is human knowledge of objective reality.[6] Since cognitive capacities are defined by their function, i.e. their contribution to knowledge, any representation that fulfills the cognitive role of an intuition *just is* an intuition, whatever its intrinsic properties may be. This is the first step toward solving our interpretive puzzle. For it makes room for the possibility that a representation could play the distinctive cognitive role of an intuition without exhibiting the intrinsic limitations (sensory, phenomenological, or whatever) that are characteristic of human sense perception and incompatible with infinitary structure. I argue that, for Kant, our representations of space and time do just that: they fulfill the cognitive function of intuitions while surpassing the sensory and phenomenological limits associated with human sense perception.

So what is the defining cognitive function of sensible intuition for Kant? And how does he go about identifying it? What sorts of arguments, what sorts of evidence are dispositive in Kant's faculty psychology? Kant's Early Modern predecessors recognized two complementary methods for theorizing the mind and its powers: (i) "empirical psychology", which relied on

[5] I use the neutral term 'capacity' because Kant reserves 'faculty' for *spontaneous* capacities. Kant classifies sensibility not as a *faculty* (*facultas*, *Vermögen*) but as a *capacity* (*potentia*, *Fähigkeit*) and, specifically, as a passive capacity or *receptivity* (*receptivitas*, *Empfänglichkeit*). See R3588 (1773–1778) 17:75.

[6] Recent interpreters stress that Kantian cognition (*Erkenntnis*) cannot be identified with knowledge (*Wissen*); see Watkins and Willaschek (2017, 2020 [2017]). I agree that there are important distinctions here, but they are of a peculiar kind. Kant's aim in the *Critique* is to vindicate the possibility of human *Wissen* (and, ultimately, *Begreifen*: comprehension). It is in service of this goal that Kant introduces such terms as "*Erkenntnis*", "*Kenntnis*", "*Anschauung*", "*Sinnlichkeit*", "*Empfänglichkeit*", and so on. I take these terms to have a "focal meaning", expressing a more or less intimate relation to human knowledge in its highest form. Thus, I take all Kantian cognitive capacities and acts to be epistemic in that their essential function is to promote knowledge (*Wissen, Begreifen*). In characterizing a representation as an intuition, or as a cognition, Kant is highlighting the features of that representation that have the potential to contribute to *Wissen*. This is not to deny that the representation may have other, non-epistemic features or that the intrinsic properties that serve an epistemic function may also serve non-epistemic functions. Nor is it to deny that acts of cognition often fall short of the *Wissen* that is their defining aim. What it does mean is that it will not be necessary, for our purposes, to contrast cognition with knowledge in what follows. I regret that I cannot devote to this contentious issue the attention it deserves. The rudiments of my position are outlined in Sections 2.3 and 2.4.

"observation and analysis" (as in Wolff, Baumgarten, or Tetens), and (ii) "rational psychology", which applied antecedently established metaphysical first principles to the special case of the soul, as thinking substance (as in Leibniz, Wolff, or Baumgarten). I argue that Kant charts a third course. The principal claims of Kant's faculty psychology – and, in particular, the fundamental characterizations of sensibility and understanding that lead to some of Kant's most interesting and heterodox views – constitute a special sort of self-knowledge, akin to the first-personal knowledge one has of one's intention in performing certain kinds of intentional action.

In order to issue an apology, for instance, or bind one's troth in marriage, one has to enjoy an internal, first-personal awareness of what one is up to. This awareness is "internal" in that it is a constitutive part of performing the action: It is impossible to perform the action unawares. Nevertheless, my awareness of my intention may only be implicit, despite being internal to my performance. I needn't actively attend to my intention as I proceed in order for a first-personal awareness of it to inform what I am doing. Indeed, I may struggle to accurately characterize my true intention or to distinguish it from subtly different motives I might have had. But when I enjoy an internal awareness of my intention, I can, in principle, make that awareness explicit to myself through first-personal reflection. Doing this constitutes a special sort of self-knowledge. My suggestion is that the faculty psychology at the heart of Kant's transcendental epistemology is based on a similar sort of self-knowledge.

The similarity is not accidental. According to Kant, what enables me to have this special self-knowledge of my intentions is precisely the fact that intentional actions are exercises of practical *reason*. Kant conceives our intellectual powers to be essentially self-conscious or "apperceptive".[7] The self-conscious character of the intellect's operations means that the intellect acts only insofar as it can represent itself as thus acting. Acts of the intellect are like the kinds of intentional action that one cannot perform without a first-personal grasp on what one is doing. This implies that the intellect must possess some conception of the kinds of acts it can perform. For it can only engage in those acts insofar as it is able to *represent itself* as engaging in them. It is, for example, essential to any act of judging that one knows, at least implicitly, that one is *judging* (rather than, say, *musing*

[7] I use the term 'intellect' to cover all higher, spontaneous, cognitive capacities, including the faculties Kant calls *Verstand* and *Vernunft*. This, I take it, is the sense of the term 'Reason' in the title of the *Critique*.

or *hoping*). Yet I can represent myself as specifically *judging* (as opposed to *musing* or *hoping*) only if I know, at least implicitly, what judgment involves: i.e. only if I have a conception of the essential features that constitute a bit of mental activity as an act of judging. By reflecting on these implicit self-conceptions and gathering them into an explicit concept, which is susceptible to further analysis, the intellect can form a theory of its own cognitive functions: i.e. a faculty psychology. I call this Kant's "apperceptive method" and argue that it provides the basis for the accounts of our cognitive capacities he offers as part of his critical inquiry into the possibility and limits of human knowledge.[8]

It is not immediately clear, however, how this apperceptive method might yield a theory of *sensible intuition* as a cognitive capacity. Sense perception is inarguably a paradigm case of sensible intuition. Yet it is far from obvious that, in order to perceive something, I must be able to self-consciously represent myself *as perceiving*. But the interpretation I advocate does not require that our acts of sensible intuiting are essentially self-conscious (though it also does not rule this out). For the intellect's apperceptive grasp on its constitutive functions includes an appreciation that its activities are not, on their own, sufficient for full-fledged knowledge.

Implicit in my apperceptive knowledge of myself as *judging* is the recognition that merely judging that *p* does not generally guarantee that *p*. Judgers know, simply in virtue of being judgers, that judging is not (yet) knowing. The intellect is thus able to reflect on the cognitive functions it presupposes but cannot perform, such as the capacity to verify (e.g. by perceiving) that *p*. The theory of intuition that I reconstruct on Kant's behalf is, as it were, the shadow cast by the intellect's self-illumination, a byproduct of the intellect's self-understanding. In recognizing that there are specific prerequisites for knowledge – particular cognitive functions – that the intellect cannot fulfill, we posit a non-intellectual cognitive capacity to satisfy them. Intuition is introduced to pick up the intellect's cognitive slack.[9]

[8] Despite renewed interest in Kant's methodology, too few commentators emphasize the centrality of apperception to Kant's critical philosophy. This is because commentators tend to focus on the method of Kant's critical *metaphysics*, which he prominently contrasts with the method proper to mathematics (e.g. Marshall 2014; Gava 2015, 2018). Once we shift our attention to the methodology of Kant's critical *epistemology* (including his faculty psychology), the centrality of apperception is more evident (see Ferrarin 2019; Schafer 2020a; Land 2021 [2018]).

[9] The possibility of such an account has been remarked by Engstrom (2017, 36–37) and Schafer (2020a, 14–17). The present work is an attempt to realize these suggestions.

Somewhat paradoxically, then, the same apperceptive method that gives the intellect insight into its *own* cognitive functions also gives it insight into the functions of a distinct, non-intellectual cognitive capacity that must act as its partner in generating knowledge. The intellect's knowledge of *itself* thus includes an indirect cognition of intellect's *Other*. And it is this paradoxical aspect of Kant's methodology in theorizing the mind that accounts for the unprecedented features he attributes to sensible intuition. I thus trace Kant's doctrinal heterodoxy back to his revolutionary methodology.

Kant's apperceptive method leads to what I call a "top-down" approach to intuition – that is, one that theorizes the "lower" cognitive capacity of sensible intuition on the basis of an independent (viz. apperceptively grounded) account of the "higher" cognitive capacities of understanding (*Verstand*) and reason *(Vernunft*). This contrasts with the "bottom-up" approach to intuition that is typical of Kant's predecessors and that remains widespread among Kant's commentators. Bottom-up approaches start from fundamental premises about sensible intuition itself, such as claims about the physiology or metaphysics of sensation, the phenomenology of perception, or the semantics of direct reference or singular representation. While there is much to recommend these approaches both philosophically and interpretively, they tend to elevate finitistic truisms (e.g. about our sensory, perceptual, or phenomenological acuity) into theory-constraining criteria of intuitive representation, which makes a mystery of Kant's commitment to infinitary intuitions. And even when bottom-up approaches manage to leave room for the idea that intuition may be infinitary, they cannot explain Kant's conviction that it *must* be. Only a top-down approach that foregrounds the cognitive needs of the intellect and that construes intuition as its cognitive complement can capture Kant's rationale for treating infinity as a *constitutive* feature of intuition.

Kant's rationale is this: The hallmark of the intellect, as revealed through apperceptive reflection, is its "spontaneity" – that is, its ability to produce representations through its own activity, in the form of novel concepts, judgments, and inferences. But not all representational contents can be generated through the spontaneous activity of a *discursive* intellect such as ours. So the human mind must also possess a "receptive" cognitive capacity that accounts for the representations that our discursive intellect cannot spontaneously generate but which are required for objective knowledge (or that we de facto find ourselves with). This receptivity, conceived as the functional complement of discursive spontaneity, is sensible intuition. Representations that must be "given" to the mind in order to be thought at all are eo ipso intuitive. Spatiotemporal representations must be given in this sense. Indeed, they must be given precisely because they are infinitely complex. For discursive representations are structured in hierarchies of genera and species. Such hierarchies are always finitely complex, no matter how much one multiplies genera and species. So our discursive intellect cannot account for the infinitary features of representations. If we do enjoy infinitary representations – and Kant thinks pure mathematics and Newtonian physics requires us to – they must have their source in receptive, sensible intuition.

For Kant, therefore, representations of infinitary contents must be intuitive, since (i) they are essential to our knowledge of objective reality; yet, (ii) the apperceptively validated functions of our discursive intellect cannot account for them. Human sense perceptions will count as intuitive for the same reason: namely, because they present the mind with contents that the spontaneous powers of discursive thought cannot fully account for. This solves our interpretive puzzle about why Kant credits a single capacity – sensible intuition – with both the representation of infinitary structure and the essentially finite deliverances of human sense perception. Both types of representation satisfy the same fundamental criterion of intuitive cognition, as specified by the intellect's apperceptive reflection on its cognitive functions and, in particular, its cognitive needs. That criterion is *givenness*. Sense perceptions and infinitary representations each present the mind with contents that spontaneous, discursive thought cannot account for and that must therefore be *given* to the mind.

The infinitary features of Kantian intuition thus serve as the ratio cognoscendi of my interpretation: as our first clue to the strangeness of Kant's views and a helpful corrective in reading his texts. But the ratio essendi of my interpretation is Kant's faculty psychology and the apperceptive, top-down methodology it pursues. It is his revolutionary methodological approach to our cognitive capacities that accounts for Kant's doctrinal heterodoxies about human sensible representation. The bulk of my argument, therefore, does not focus on issues surrounding infinitary magnitudes and their representation.[10] Resolving our interpretive puzzle only takes center stage in Chapter 5. My abiding aim is rather to explore Kant's rationale for advancing such a peculiar and unprecedented conception of sensible representation.

[10] I address these topics in Smyth (2023 [2021]).

My title, *The Boundlessness of Sense*, is not quite true to the content of my argument: It is not *sense* that Kant thinks is infinite but *sensible intuition*. The title does, however, capture something important about my approach, inasmuch as I aim to provide a partial response to Strawson's pathbreaking study, *The Bounds of Sense* (1966). Strawson begins by distinguishing "Two Faces of the *Critique*". The first he approvingly terms an "analytic argument" – what we would now call a "transcendental argument". That is, a line of reasoning that premises a particular cognitive achievement or an accepted account of cognition and then "regressively" identifies certain necessary conditions as its presuppositions. In Strawson's words, "the investigation of that limiting framework of ideas and principles the use and application of which are essential to empirical knowledge, and which are implicit in any coherent conception of experience which we can form" (1966, 18, my underlining). The second "face" is one that Strawson famously derides as "the imaginary subject of transcendental psychology" (1966, 32). Kant's lucubrations about our cognitive faculties are, Strawson laments, unhappily and quite unnecessarily entangled with his more lucid, analytical reflections:

> It is true that Kant thought of himself as investigating the general structure of ideas and principles which is presupposed in all our empirical knowledge, but he thought of this investigation as possible only because he conceived of it also, and primarily, as an investigation into the structure and workings of the cognitive capacities of beings such as ourselves. The idiom of the work is throughout a psychological idiom. Whatever necessities Kant found in our conception of experience he ascribed to the nature of our faculties (1966, 19, my underlining).

I think Strawson is correct to distinguish Kant's analytical, transcendental arguments from the core claims of his faculty psychology. Strawson is also right that Kant views his faculty psychology as the "source" or explanatory ground of the "necessary general features of experience" identified in his transcendental arguments (Strawson 1966, 15). But I cannot agree that "there is no doubt that this doctrine [viz. that the necessary features of experience have their source in our cognitive constitution] is incoherent in itself and masks, rather than explains, the real character of Kant's inquiry" (1966, 15–16).

The Boundlessness of Sense aims to show that Kant's "capacities-first" approach to human cognition is neither incoherent nor obfuscatory, as Strawson contends.[11] I hesitate to say that I've hit upon "the real character

[11] I adopt the label "capacities-first" from Schafer (2020a). I owe countless refinements and reframings to Schafer's exceptional contributions.

of Kant's inquiry", but that is chiefly because I adopt a pluralistic interpretive stance toward Kant's corpus. Kant supports his signature doctrines in a variety of ways across his writings and even within a single text – apparently confident that this methodological and evidentiary diversity converges into a unified account. Different interpretive approaches emphasize different argumentative methods, respond to different sorts of considerations, and register different kinds of evidence. My aim in *The Boundlessness of Sense* is to highlight *one* line of argument in the *Critique* and related works – namely, Kant's apperceptive approach to our cognitive capacities and, in particular, his top-down approach to intuition. I argue that this is an underappreciated but important aspect of Kant's critical project and that it can yield remarkable results. But I claim neither that this dimension of Kant's thought exhausts his views on human sensible intuition, nor that I have identified the maximally illuminating, much less uniquely correct, way to interpret the texts I discuss. My aim is not to provide the last word on Kantian intuition, but an opening for a new conversation.

Even with this pluralistic caveat, however, the interpretation I advance suggests that Strawson's proposal to separate out Kant's "analytical argument" from his "transcendental psychology" is ill-conceived. By its very nature, an analytic, regressive, or transcendental argument presupposes a contentful conception of cognition or of a particular cognitive achievement. Otherwise, there is nothing to analyze. Yet Strawson devotes remarkably little attention to the "source" of the conception of cognition, or experience, that he proposes to analyze. Apart from disparaging Kant's "transcendental psychology", Strawson gives no positive account of the starting point for the "analytical argument" he finds so fruitful, nor does he explain our entitlement to presuppose it as the terminus a quo of our analysis.[12]

It is here that my account aims to improve on Strawson's by inverting it. Kant holds that we have an apperceptive grasp on the character of our discursive intellect. I argue that this gives us a special entitlement to certain kinds of a priori claims about the constitutive form of our intellect and suitably related cognitive capacities. These claims are well suited to serve as the basis *analysand* for subsequent "regressive" arguments about necessary and limiting conditions on experience. Far from undermining the respectable, "analytical argument" of the *Critique*, Kant's "transcendental psychology" is what generates and what legitimates the starting point of such

[12] For elaboration of this critique, see Cassam (2016).

analysis. To separate Kant's "analytic argument" from his "transcendental psychology", as Strawson proposes to do, is to render his inquiry dogmatic rather than critical. It is the essentially apperceptive character of our intellect that first furnishes us with a conception of the nature of our cognition. That is what enables us – and entitles us – to prosecute transcendental arguments that regressively identify and analytically exfoliate the latent presuppositions of our cognitive self-conception.[13]

Chapter Summaries

My account falls into two parts. Chapters 1 through 5 track the opening chapters of the *Critique* and interpret those texts as pursuing an apperceptive, top-down approach to human intuition. Chapters 6 through 8 take a step back to offer a synoptic account of Kantian intuition in the form of a *Stufenleiter* of the genera and species of intuition Kant discusses. Though they are in close conversation, these two parts of the work can be read independently and in either order. Within these two parts, the chapters are more interconnected.

Chapter 1 examines an analogy Kant repeatedly draws between pure general logic and his critique of human theoretical knowledge. The relevant similarity, I argue, is that both sciences appeal to the self-conscious nature of the intellect's operations in justifying their claims. They each express "reason's self-knowledge". They differ in that this self-knowledge remains merely *formal* in the case of pure general logic – that is, it adumbrates the form of *all* thought, regardless of its content – whereas the *Critique* specifically concerns the form of *material cognition*, i.e. knowledge of thought-independent objects. Despite this difference, the doctrines of both sciences are erected on the same sort of apperceptive justificatory basis. This is the starting point for my apperceptive, top-down approach to Kantian intuition, but it can also be read as a self-standing account of Kant's transcendental methodology.

Chapter 2 examines Kant's Introduction to the *Critique* and finds that it implicitly pursues a top-down approach to intuition. I argue that Kant's distinction between synthetic and analytic judgments can be read as an apperceptive reflection on the character of the intellect's constitutive functions, of the sort described in Chapter 1. I then argue that the sensibility/understanding distinction Kant draws at the end of the Introduction is a corollary of this analytic/synthetic distinction. This

[13] This paragraph attempts to compress the argument of Schafer (2020a, 9–14).

reconstruction yields an initial formulation of "givenness" as the fundamental criterion of intuition. This chapter involves significant discussions of analytic judgment as well as an overview of the "top-down" approach to intuition. It, too, can be read independently of the others.

Chapter 3 addresses Kant's first major discussion of intuition in the *Critique* – namely, the opening section of the Transcendental Aesthetic. I argue that the central features of Kant's account are, like the "givenness" criterion outlined in Chapter 2, grounded in apperception. The immediacy of intuition, the receptivity of our intuition, and the applicability of a form/matter distinction for any receptive intuition can all be established through apperceptive reflection. What cannot be established in this way, however, is that our intuition is not just receptive but *sensible* (affection-dependent). For this, I argue, we must appeal to further (e.g. phenomenological, or metaphysical) considerations. This chapter gets into the weeds of the Aesthetic and is best read in concert with Chapters 4 and 5.

Chapter 4 discusses the mode of argument Kant calls a "metaphysical exposition" and argues that apperception plays a central role in this special sort of conceptual analysis. In addition to close readings of the Aesthetic, this chapter discusses Kant's views on given versus made concepts, original acquisition, discursive marks, conceptual analysis, and definition, which may be of wider interest.

Chapter 5 applies the criteria identified in Chapter 3 and the methodology outlined in Chapter 4 to reconstruct Kant's argument for the intuitive origin of the concept <space> in the Metaphysical Expositions. When Kant says we represent space to have a holistic structure, I argue, he is echoing a Leibnizian account of its continuity (infinite divisibility) and boundlessness. It is these infinitary properties that imply that our original representation of space must be receptive and intuitive, rather than spontaneous and discursive. For discursive contents, in virtue of their classificatory structure, are incapable of exhibiting infinite complexity. This resolves our interpretive puzzle about the constitutive possibility of infinitary intuitions. Here readers will find discussions of various criteria of intuition (immediacy vs. singularity vs. givenness), the holistic character of intuitive representation, the infinitary structure of space, and the nature of discursivity.

Chapter 6 is a short rant about the logic and purpose of Porphyrian trees, or *Stufenleiter*, crucial features of which are often misunderstood. *Stufenleiter* are targeted analytical tools that reflect, in a variety of ways, the interests of the investigation to which they contribute. They are not "detail views" of a uniquely correct Great Chain of Being. This discussion prepares the way for my own *Stufenleiter* of Kantian intuition, but can be read on its own.

Chapters 7 and 8 elaborate the genera and species of Kantian intuition that I consider most significant to his thought and the specific differentiae that I consider most illuminating. I provide detailed commentary on the species I distinguish and the criteria that distinguish them, noting throughout the textual and philosophical grounds that support my classification. Chapter 7 discusses the genus *intuition überhaupt* and its defining criterion, *givenness*. It then divides this genus into the species *spontaneous intuition* and *receptive intuition* via the specific differentia, *cognitive spontaneity*.

Chapter 8 resumes this discussion by dividing the genus *receptive intuition* into the species *receptive non-sensible intuition* and *sensible intuition* via the specific differentia, *affection-dependence*. I then divide *sensible intuition* into the species *inner* and *outer intuition* via the specific differentia *self/other*. Under these fall, respectively, human (temporal) inner sense and human (spatial) outer sense – though these are instances, not species, of inner and outer intuition. In the course of this chapter, I highlight several underappreciated problems for Kant's accounts of causation and mind–body union.

One ambition of these final chapters is to show that Kant's discussions of intuition are often couched at different levels of abstraction. Sometimes his claims about our capacity for intuition turn on its *receptivity*; at other points, they depend on its more specific, *sensible* character; at still others, on its peculiar *spatial* character. I illustrate this by discussing the increasingly concrete guises that the singularity of our intuition assumes at these different levels of abstraction. By showing how different considerations and types of evidence come into view at different levels of abstraction, this classificatory exercise helps to place long-standing debates in new light and reveal ways in which participants are prone to talk past one another.

I

Reason's Self-Knowledge and Kant's Critical Methodology

> [The fashion of professing indifference to metaphysics] is a demand for reason to take on anew that most difficult of all her tasks, namely that of self-knowledge, and to institute a tribunal that will secure her in all her rightful claims, while being able to dispatch all her groundless pretensions, not through despotic decrees but through her eternal and unchangeable laws; and this [tribunal] is none other than the **critique of pure reason** itself.
>
> Axi–xii, original emphasis

Kant's *Critique of Pure Reason* is fundamentally an exercise in self-knowledge. Yet, the self-knowledge it seeks is of a peculiar sort. Kant ascribes this self-knowledge to reason itself, as a cognitive faculty. He figures our capacity for reason as an epistemic agent in its own right. It is far from clear how this sort of facultative self-knowledge relates to the more familiar kind that an individual person might have about her own thoughts, intentions, personal history, and so on. What does it mean for a cognitive faculty to enjoy self-knowledge? What is it that reason knows in knowing itself? And how does it come by such knowledge?

The aim of this chapter is to unpack Kant's idea of critique as "reason's self-knowledge". I will argue that one of the distinguishing features of such knowledge is that it demands a special philosophical methodology. The status of critique as the self-knowledge of reason turns not so much on *what* is known but on *how* it is known. What makes critique *facultative* self-knowledge is not merely that reason is the subject matter of the inquiry as well as the central means by which it is pursued. It is because the inquiry relies on a special sort of cognitive ground: namely, apperceptive insight into reason's constitutive norms. That is what makes critique the sort of self-knowledge that it makes sense to ascribe to a cognitive *faculty* rather than an individual person. For it exploits the essentially self-conscious character of reason in order to justify claims about the constitutive essence (i.e. the form) of that very faculty.

In this respect, Kant's conception of critique is closely analogous to his conception of pure general logic (PGL). Kant claims that both sciences embody reason's self-knowledge of its own form. Yet, while PGL concerns the form of reason in *all* its manifestations – practical as well as theoretical, empirical as well as pure – the *Critique of Pure Reason* is specifically concerned with the form of reason as it manifests itself in a priori theoretical cognition, just as the *Critique of Practical Reason* is concerned with the form of reason in its practical use, i.e. insofar as it is capable of determining the will. Critique is thus a formal science of the material use of reason – its use in cognizing objects a priori, either practically or theoretically. PGL, by contrast, is a formal science of reason *überhaupt* – reason "in general" or merely "as such" – without taking its various material uses into consideration.

A central challenge for this reading is to explain how an inquiry into the *material* use of reason can nevertheless count as *formal*. The form of reason, I contend, is that through which an activity is constituted as rational: The form of reason is its *essence*. In order for knowledge of this essence to count as *self*-knowledge in the relevant sense, the form of reason must not only be its topic but also its source. Critique is thus a rational investigation of the constitutive principles that make an investigation rational. This is why Kant associates the *formality* of such knowledge – in PGL and in critique – with the idea that the principles of the relevant science can be known exhaustively and with certainty: namely, because the inquiry is guided by the very principles it seeks to articulate, so that the task is just to make this implicit guidance explicit. Because critique and PGL manifest the very form they seek to characterize, rational self-reflection alone provides a sufficient cognitive ground for each science.

Making sense of the formality of critique is a significant step toward understanding it as the sort of self-knowledge that belongs to a faculty and not to individuals, as such. For knowledge of these principles is grounded in the nature of reason, as a self-reflective capacity, and not in any special endowment or experience. Of course, only individual persons are cognitive agents. So all knowledge, including knowledge of logic and of critical philosophy, is possessed by individual persons alone. But it is not *as* individual persons that we know such things. Rather, it is in virtue of being rational that we can enjoy reason's self-knowledge.

The chapters that follow will explore how specific doctrines of Kant's critical philosophy – in particular, his characterizations of human intuition – fit into this self-knowledge of reason. The peculiarly reflective, self-conscious methodology that Kant identifies as central to PGL and critique is not restricted to uncovering features of our "higher" cognitive faculties.

I will argue that Kant employs the very same methodology in articulating his critical theory of sensible intuition. Paradoxical as it may seem, part of what reason knows, in knowing *itself* (its own form), is the general character of a capacity *distinct* from it – a capacity for receptive intuition, on which reason depends in order to attain its constitutive cognitive ends.

1.1 Unfolding A Priori the Mere Concept of a Faculty of Knowledge

When the *Critique* first appeared, it encountered more incomprehension than opposition. This, at least, was Kant's view. In the appendix to the *Prolegomena*, Kant complains about one anonymous reviewer who "seems not at all to see what was really at stake in the investigation with which I (felicitously or infelicitously) occupied myself" (4:373.7–8; cf. 376.19–21, 261.9–11). The reviewer seizes on Kant's idealism but does not appreciate that this "so-called (actually critical) idealism is of a quite peculiar sort" (375.15–16). In particular, the reviewer fails to grasp the overarching problem for which Kant's critical idealism aims to provide a solution: namely, how we can enjoy synthetic knowledge a priori (377.19–31). Instead, the reviewer takes Kant to be engaged in just the sort of traditional metaphysics that the *Critique* calls into question. So what the reviewer is missing is the very idea of a critique of pure reason. His local misunderstandings stem from a general blindness to the special character of the critical enterprise, as reason's self-interrogation of its own capacity for a priori knowledge: "The reviewer thus understood nothing of my text and perhaps also nothing of the spirit and essence of metaphysics itself" (377.31–33).

Distressed by Kant's public castigation of his review, Christian Garve wrote to Kant, revealing himself as its author and conceding Kant's main objection: "I [Garve] believe that I rightly grasped the sense of most passages considered singly; I am not so sure that I had a proper overview of the whole."[1] Kant was mollified. His conciliatory reply to Garve is especially valuable, since it attempts to enlighten Garve about the central point the review missed, concerning the distinctive character of the critical philosophy and its method:

> Please be so good as to cast another quick glance upon the whole and note that what I develop in the Critique is by no means metaphysics but an

[1] Garve to Kant, 13 July 1783, 10:330.2–4. Garve shunts responsibility for the review onto the editors of the *Göttingische gelehrte Anzeigen*, claiming (inaccurately) that they "mutilated" his original text (332.31; cf. 330.29). On the Garve controversy, see Kuehn (2001, 250–252, 267–268).

> entirely new and hitherto unattempted science, namely, the critique of a reason that judges a priori. Others have admittedly touched on this faculty, such as Locke and also Leibniz, but always muddled together with other cognitive powers[.] [Y]et no one has even entertained the thought that this [faculty] may be an object of a formal and necessary and, indeed, quite extensive science, which (without departing from this restriction merely to assess the sole faculty of pure knowledge [*des alleinigen reinen Erkentnisvermögens*]) demands such a multiplicity of subdivisions and simultaneously (which is marvelous) can derive from its [the cognitive faculty's] nature all objects to which it extends and can enumerate them [and] prove their completeness through their interconnection in a whole faculty of cognition. This absolutely no other science is capable of doing, namely, unfolding a priori out of the mere concept of a faculty of knowledge (if it is determined precisely) all objects and everything that one can know of them [...]. Logic, which would most closely resemble this science, is in this respect infinitely beneath it. For it [logic] admittedly pertains to every use of the understanding whatsoever, but cannot at all indicate to which objects and how far intellectual cognition [*Verstandeserkenntnis*] will extend[.] (Kant to Garve, 7 August 1783; 10:340.2–25)

There is a lot to unpack here. Kant claims (1) that critique concerns "a [faculty of] reason that judges a priori"; (2) that it is "a formal and necessary science" of this faculty; (3) that this science analyzes ("unfold[s] a priori") "the mere concept of a faculty of knowledge (if it is determined precisely)"; and (4) that this analysis reveals "all objects and everything that one can know of them". Kant aims to elucidate these claims by comparing critique to logic. On the one hand, "[l]ogic [...] would most closely resemble this science" – presumably because both are "formal and necessary". On the other hand, what is "marvelous" about critique is that it "can derive from the nature [of the cognitive faculty] all objects to which it extends and can enumerate [and] prove their completeness"; whereas logic "cannot at all indicate to which objects and how far intellectual cognition will extend", since logic "pertains to every use of the understanding whatsoever".

I think this discussion of critique – and especially the comparison with logic – is a helpful guide to Kant's difficult but crucial conception of reason's self-knowledge. I will first outline the sense in which logic is "formal and necessary" (Section 1.2). With this in place, we can then unpack Kant's comparison of critique to logic (Section 1.3). This will clarify in what sense logic and critique embody reason's self-knowledge. It will also position us to appreciate what is "marvelous" about critique (Section 1.4): namely, its ability to "[unfold] a priori from the mere concept of a cognitive faculty (if it is determined precisely) all objects and everything that one can know [*wissen*] of them".

1.2 Pure General Logic as a *Selbsterkenntnis* of Reason

Kant's discussion of "logic" in his letter to Garve clearly refers to what he elsewhere calls "pure general logic" (PGL). For he tells Garve that logic "pertains to every use of the understanding whatsoever" (10:340.23–24). This recalls his description of general logic in the *Critique* and elsewhere as concerned with "the absolutely necessary rules of thinking without which no use of the understanding takes place at all".[2] By contrast, a "special" or "particular" ("*besondere*") logic concerns only "the rules for thinking correctly about a certain kind of object" (A52/B76.1–2). So the logic Kant describes to Garve must be general rather than special: It concerns all thinking, whatever its object may be.

In addition to being general, the logic Kant mentions to Garve must be pure. "General logic", the *Critique* tells us, "is either pure or applied":

> A **general** but **pure logic** has to do with pure principles [*lauter Prinzipien*] a priori and is a **canon of the understanding** and of reason, but only with respect to what is formal in their use[.] [...] A **general** logic is called **applied** when it is directed at the rules for the use of the understanding and the subjective empirical conditions that psychology teaches. It thus has empirical principles, even though it is general insofar as it pertains to the use of the understanding without distinguishing between its objects. (A53/B77.25–03)

An applied logic rests on empirical grounds and so is not a necessary science. Pure general logic, by contrast, promulgates its principles a priori and thus articulates necessary truths about "what is formal" in our use of the understanding and reason. Kant surely has such a pure logic in mind when he tells Garve that "logic [...] most closely resembles" critique (10:340.21–22), which he has just called a "formal and necessary [...] science" (340.9–10). So it is to PGL that Kant finds it instructive to compare the critical philosophy in order to bring out the distinctive status that Garve's review failed to register.

1.2.1 PGL as Selbsterkenntnis *with Respect to Subject Matter*

The generality of PGL consists in the fact that it "abstracts from all content of intellectual cognition [*Verstandeserkenntnis*] and the differentness

[2] A52/B76.33–35; cf. A131/B170.12–21; R1620 (1780s) 16:40.17–27; L-Jäsche 9:12.19–24, 13.27–14.1; L-Pö 24:503.15–22; L-Wien 24:790.22–28; L-DW 24:694.14–16.

[*Verschiedenheit*] of its objects, and has to do with nothing but the mere form of thinking".[3] But this does not mean that PGL is devoid of content or that it lacks a proper subject matter.[4] Pure general logic is not vacuous; it is formal. Its object is the form of thinking *überhaupt*. Pure general logic discloses "the absolutely [*schlechthin*] necessary rules of thinking, without which utterly no use of the understanding takes place" (A52/B76.33–35). These rules are formal in the sense that they concern the *essence* of thinking, the characteristics that constitute mental activity *as thinking* (rather than as *feeling pain*, say).[5] Such characteristics pertain to thought merely as an act of intellect,[6] regardless of its content, the sorts of objects it concerns, or how it relates to those objects. Because PGL investigates the form, the essence, of acts of thinking as such, it can be understood as an inquiry into the faculty of thinking itself:

> [PGL] is a rational science not merely [1.] with respect to form but [2.] with respect to matter, since [1.] its rules are not taken from experience and since [2.] it also has reason for its object. Logic is hence a self-cognition [*Selbsterkenntniß*] of the understanding and of reason, but not with respect to their capacities in regard to objects, but merely with respect to form.[7]

All correct exercises of the intellect, by definition, obey "the absolutely necessary rules of thinking": rationality is their *form*.[8] But not all correct

3 A54/B78; cf. Bvii.9–ix.21, A299/B355.25–28; *Groundwork* 4:387.8–12.

4 On the proper subject matter of PGL as a science, see Lu-Adler (2018a, 154–161). I am convinced by Tolley (2012) that transcendental logic (TL) is not a special logic, i.e. that it is not distinguished from PGL by having a narrower object domain. Both PGL and TL share the same object domain; they differ in that TL takes into account the relation of thinking to the objects in that domain, specifying that this relation must be possible a priori, whereas PGL abstracts from all relation of thought to its object, whether this relation can be established a priori or only on the basis of experience (cf. Lu-Adler 2018a, 157–160). Thus, PGL is more *abstract* than TL, but need not be more *general*, since the determinations from which it abstracts do not narrow the object domain. I will formulate my account in accordance with this view, though it is also possible to do so *mutatis mutandis* on the assumption that TL is a special logic concerned with thinking about the sort of objects that can be given in pure sensible intuition (cf. MacFarlane 2002, 42n.35). For instance, Merritt treats TL as a special logic (2018, 22–28) but develops an account of reflection that my interpretation echoes in numerous points (cf. Merritt 2018, chs. 1–3).

5 For this use of "formal" as meaning *essential*, see *Tone* 8:404.12–21; M-Mr 29:826.2–7, 847.9; *Postumum* (1800) 22:11.20–22. For discussion, see Graubner (1972, 37–45); Pollok (2017, ch. 4); Boyle (forthcoming-a).

6 I use "intellect" to refer generically to the spontaneous cognitive powers, understanding, and reason, as I take Kant to employ the term "reason" in the title "Critique of Pure Reason". See Willaschek (2018, 21–23).

7 L-Jäsche, 9:14.22–27; cf. R3939 (1769) 17:356; R1612 (mid 1770s) 16:36.5–9; L-Ph (1772) 24:315.5–14, 316.7–10, 316.21–317.2; L-Blom (early 1770s) 24:24.25–27, 24.38–39; L-Wien 24:791.30–32, 792.1–2, 792.6–14; L-DW 24:695.24–29.

8 I will not address the special sort of rational form that elevates merely correct cognition into science, i.e. into a systematic hierarchy of explanatory principles organized under a single idea. For an

exercises are *about* the formal laws of thought: Rationality is not their matter, is not the object or topic about which they entertain claims. Pure general logic, however, has rationality as both its form and its matter. Pure general logic is a "self-cognition of the understanding and of reason" in the sense that it brings to explicit consciousness – it "cognizes" as its "object" – the rules and principles that (consciously or unconsciously) inform every correct use of the intellect, merely as such.[9]

1.2.2 PGL as Selbsterkenntnis *with Respect to Cognitive Ground*

Pure general logic counts as a *Selbsterkenntnis* in a more specific sense as well – not merely with respect to the object it cognizes (namely, the form of thinking) but with respect to the *cognitive grounds* it relies on in cognizing this object.[10] Yet, apart from his repeated insistence that PGL is an a priori science and does not rely on experience, Kant provides no positive characterization of the cognitive grounds, the justificatory basis, we rely on in bringing to explicit consciousness the constitutive laws that in-form all thinking.[11] Indeed, he writes as though no special cognitive ground were necessary to move from an unconscious employment of the laws of thought in concreto to an explicit cognition of them in abstracto:

> For there can be utterly no doubt that we cannot think or use our understanding otherwise than according to certain rules. Now these rules we can, in turn, think in their own right [*für sich selbst*], i.e. we can think them without their application or *in abstracto*. (L-Jäsche 9:12.3–7, my underlining)

This suggests that our explicit consciousness of the laws of thought in abstracto relies on nothing – no further evidence, faculty, or other

illuminating discussion of insight (*Einsehen*) and comprehension (*Begreifen*) as central to Kantian scientific cognition, see Schafer (2022).

9 I use "self-cognition" and "self-knowledge" interchangeably, though I mostly leave "*Selbsterkenntnis*" untranslated. I agree with Schafer (2020a, 19–22) that the cognitive achievements embodied in Kant's critical epistemology are importantly different from those embodied in his critical metaphysics, but I do not think this requires us to contrast *Erkenntnis* with *Wissen* in the present case (cf. Watkins and Willaschek 2017, 2020 [2017]; Schafer 2022, 2023).

10 By "cognitive ground" I mean what Kant calls the "source" of a cognition (*Prolegomena* 4:266), i.e. what one would appeal to in justifying a particular judgment as knowledgeable: the evidentiary basis on which one stakes one's claim to know. I use "cognitive ground", "justificatory basis", and "epistemic warrant" interchangeably to get at this idea.

11 Maimon challenges Kant on this point and calls for a critique of logic to "determine those forms and make them complete by reflecting on the faculty of cognition" (Maimon to Kant, 2 December 1793, 11:471, my underlining; discussed in Lu-Adler 2018a, 161–169). Kant apparently felt it unnecessary to spell out the cognitive grounds of PGL, for reasons I will try to explain.

cognitive ground – beyond what we already rely on in "us[ing] our understanding" in the first place. This is true only of faculties that are essentially self-conscious. For it means there is a constitutive link between the faculty's first-order acts "in concreto" and its representation "in abstracto" of the principles governing those acts. Only an intellect that is intrinsically capable of both (i) representing its acts, in the first person, as its own and (ii) representing those acts as satisfying certain normative principles can form a representation in abstracto of the rules governing its acts solely on the justificatory, cognitive basis of the first-order acts that are so governed. Granted, one need not *actually* represent one's acts of thinking or the rules governing them in order to think at all. The cognitive acts in concreto merely make their *in-abstracto* counterparts possible. But it is essential to the first-order acts to do this. A mental episode cannot count as an act of thinking unless it provides a sufficient cognitive ground or epistemic warrant for an act of thinking (actual or only potential) about the constitutive formal principles governing that first-order act.[12] That's why an abstract cognition of the laws of thought, *if* it occurs, relies on no cognitive grounds beyond those contained in the first-order act, whose form it characterizes.

Pure general logic is thus a *Selbsterkenntnis* not merely in the sense that it takes the intellect's form as its object, but in the sense that it relies on the essentially self-conscious character of the intellect: its capacity for pure apperception. As Kant puts it in the *Anthropology*, "in logic we investigate according to what the intellectual consciousness offers up [*an die Hand giebt*]", clarifying that by "the intellectual consciousness" he means "the I as subject of thinking (in logic), which signifies pure apperception (the merely reflecting I)" (7:134.21–26; cf. 141.1–4).

This account of PGL as cognitively grounded in the essentially self-conscious character of concrete acts of thinking provides a richer understanding of the apriority of PGL. For such *Selbsterkenntnis* is a priori in the

[12] An acute reviewer asks, "What is Kant's justification for claims such as this one?" The only answer I think Kant can consistently give is this: Such claims are known and justified *through apperception*. It is perhaps frustrating that the snake eats its tail here. But accepting such claims is, I take it, part of what it means to treat the intellect as essentially self-conscious: namely, to treat its acts as licensing a representation of their own constitutive essence. This is a defining commitment of Kant's innovative, apperceptive method. Though there is no "further" justification to be had here, we can nevertheless elucidate such claims by elaborating Kant's theory of apperception. I can only gesture at such an elaboration in the present work (see Section 1.3.3). For more fulsome discussions to which I'm indebted, see Merritt (2009, 2011); Kitcher (2011, ch.9); Engstrom (2013, 2016); Dyck (2017); and Land (2021 [2018], section 2.2).

"cognition from grounds" sense of the term.[13] Although self-conscious reflection on concrete acts of thinking obviously depends on such concrete acts as an enabling condition, what we reflect on, in articulating the formal laws of thought in PGL, are not the particular acts of thinking themselves but the lawful cognitive disposition that expresses itself in them. And we reflect on this cognitive disposition not only as something general, unlike the concrete acts themselves, but as something that determines and, in that sense, grounds the particular acts on which we are reflecting *as* the specific type of acts they are – namely, as *thoughts*, as acts of intellect. In bringing the form of thinking to reflective consciousness, then, we cognize the formal ground of our acts of thinking. So the self-conscious reflection we are considering is cognition from grounds. In such reflection, we know the concrete acts through the form of the capacity that gives rise to them; we know the effect through the cause, not the reverse. As Kant puts it in one of his logical Reflections: "Logic thus does not predate the use [of the understanding], but its rules, once they are cognized [*erkant*] at all, are indeed clear through themselves [*aus sich selbst*], because they contain the ground of all judgments, namely, their form" (R1602, mid-1770s, 16:32.2–4).

This sort of reflective self-consciousness is also a priori in the negative sense that it does not appeal to experience as source of evidence or justification.[14] Pure general logic not only cognizes effects (acts of thinking) through their ground (their form) but also cognizes this ground without appealing to experience to justify its claims, relying instead on the intellect's ability to make its own activity and form into an object of thought. This capacity for apperception, according to Kant, cannot be derived from experience, for it is a precondition of all experience. So PGL is a priori not merely in the negative sense that its principles are not empirical generalizations, but in the positive senses that (i) they cognize the formal ground of all thinking, as such, and that (ii) they do so by exercising a capacity for self-consciousness that is essential to the intellect and, thus, not derived from experience.

[13] See especially M-Mr 29:747.34–748.24 as well as *Critique* A758/B786.30–4; *Metaphysical Foundations* 4:470.18–19. For discussion, see Smit (2009) and Melamedoff-Vosters (2023, sections 1–2). All empirical cognition is a posteriori in this sense because experience is itself a *consequence* (not a ground) of the thought-independent realities we seek to cognize. So cognition based on experience is not cognition from the grounds of what is cognized but from its consequences (M-Mr 29:748.17–19).

[14] See A2.20–23 and B2f.15–20. As Pippin helpfully puts it, "a priori does not mean 'not derived from experience' but 'known without appeal to experience'" (1982, 102).

This account of PGL's cognitive grounds as a pure *Selbsterkenntnis* of reason can initially seem rather obscure and mysterious. So it is important to register that this self-cognition of the form of thought in abstracto is not attained through some unmediated *Wesensschau* or a rarefied form of gnostic interiority, but through painstaking reflection upon, and reflective engagement in, concrete acts of thinking.[15] Kant emphasizes that although "the necessary and universal rules of thinking [...] can and must be cognized a priori independently of the natural use of the understanding and of reason in concreto", it is nonetheless true that "they can only first be found [*gefunden*] through observation of that natural use".[16] Reason's cognition of its own form is mediated through, though not justified by, "observation" of concrete exercises that manifest (because they are informed by) the laws in question. Clearly, such "observation" cannot consist in an empirical, inductive survey of de facto features we encounter in our thinking. Pure general logic is, as Kant likes to put it, "**abstracted** from the **empirical** use of the understanding, but not **derived** from it".[17]

The fact that the formal rules of thinking *can* "be found" – and, indeed, can *only* "be found" – by "observ[ing]" the natural use of reason implies that acts of thinking, as such, involve an implicit conception of the formal rules that constitute thinking as thinking. If a conception of the laws of thought were not contained in these acts, then it would be impossible to recover those laws merely by reflecting on those acts. Indeed, when we say that acts of thinking, as such, involve an "implicit" awareness of the formal, constitutive laws of thought, all we (can) mean is that an explicit (clear) consciousness of those laws can be attained and *justified* merely through self-conscious reflection on that act – through mere "observation" and "abstraction" – without the introduction of further cognitive grounds or "data" beyond what is already at hand in the relevant act of thinking. This, as we saw, is what distinguishes PGL as a kind of self-knowledge with respect to its cognitive grounds and not merely with respect to its subject matter.

The laws treated of in PGL are *internal* to the acts of thinking that they govern in the sense that they are *represented in* those acts, though typically

[15] See Section 4.4 for an elaboration of what I take this to involve.

[16] L-Jäsche 9:17.27–31; cf. L-Ph (1772), 24:316.21–317.2; L-Wien 24:791.30–32, 792.1–2; L-DW 24:697.10–19.

[17] R1612 (mid-1770s) 16:36.9, original emphasis. This is one of a series of mid-1770s Reflections expressing the same idea: R1602, 16:31.22–32.4; R1603, 33.10; R1607, 34.11. See also R1620 (1780s) 41.14–16; R1627 (1790s) 43.9–10; L-Wien 24:792.1–2; *Anthropology* 7:133.31–33.

unconsciously.[18] That is to say, every act of thinking, merely as such, must involve an appreciation – conscious or unconscious, explicit or implicit – of the formal laws that constitute it as an act of thinking, even if it only imperfectly satisfies the laws it represents (perhaps unconsciously) as constitutively normative for it. By "appreciation", I mean not only that these laws (or the cognitive disposition they characterize) exercise a de facto influence on our thinking, nor merely that our thoughts involve a representation of such laws, albeit unconscious. I mean that these laws exercise an influence on our thinking, though not an insuperable one, and that they exercise this influence *in virtue of* our representing them, albeit unconsciously, as binding on our thought.[19] Acts of thought are, in this sense, guided by an internal representation of the constitutive, formal principles of thinking. Such guidance manifests itself not only in a subject's disposition to assent to such principles when explicitly presented with them but also in her disposition to recognize the relevance to her thinking (or others') of certain kinds of questions or challenges – about, say, contradictions or logical entailments – and in her readiness to revise her thinking in response to such challenges (or to urge such revisions on others).[20]

This conception of internal guidance is compatible with the fact that particular acts of thinking may not perfectly satisfy the laws they internally, if only unconsciously, represent as unconditionally binding on themselves.[21] Similarly, acts of moral turpitude do not undermine Kant's claim that a representation of the moral law belongs to the form of practical reason, as such. For what it means to represent a law as unconditionally binding on one's act is to accept its authority as a standard of correctness against which one's act is to be assessed. This does not entail that every act meets the standard it sets for itself. Even when one adds that the logical laws are, like the moral law, formal and thus constitutive with respect to the acts they govern, logical blunders remain possible and explicable.

[18] On unconscious representations, see L-Jäsche 9:33–34; *Anthropology* 7:135–137; R176–177 (prior to 1770?) 15:64–66; A-Mrongovius 25:1221.16–21. For discussion, see La Rocca (2008a, 2008b) as well as the essays by Crone, Heidemann, Kitcher, Rockmore, and Schulting collected in Giordanetti et al. (2012).

[19] Compare Kant's remark that "[e]verything in nature operates [*wirkt*] in accordance with laws. Only a rational being has the capacity to act [*handeln*] in accordance with the representation of laws, i.e. in accordance with principles" (*Groundwork* 4:412). Though Kant makes this point specifically about the faculty of practical reason (i.e. the will), I take an analogous claim to hold for all rational capacities, as such. Here I follow Schafer (2020a).

[20] For elaboration of this idea, see Land (2021 [2018], esp. section 2.2).

[21] This is well-trodden ground (MacFarlane 2002, 37; Smit 2009, 214; Nunez 2018; Land 2021 [2018]; Boyle forthcoming-a).

Logical laws characterize the proper functioning of the *faculty* of thought.[22] They thereby set a standard of correctness for particular acts of thinking, as such. A mental act counts as an act of thinking just insofar as it is subject to this standard of correctness. But an act can be subject to a standard without perfectly satisfying it.[23] And in the case of essentially self-conscious capacities, it suffices that the act *represent itself* as subject to the relevant standard in order for it to *be* subject to that standard. Thus, the special character of reason's *Selbsterkenntnis* in PGL reflects not only the essentially apperceptive character of the intellect but also its essential *autonomy*, in that its acts are subject only to laws that they internally represent as binding on themselves.[24] Indeed, its acts constitute themselves as the types of acts they are – as acts of thinking, or as exercises of practical reason, say – precisely in promulgating, albeit unconsciously, the laws by which their own correctness is to be assessed. Even acts that fail to fully satisfy the formal principles that constitute them as the types of acts they are nevertheless represent those principles, albeit unconsciously, as unconditionally binding on themselves. Such acts, which are all too possible, are flawed by their own lights. That is why Kant characterizes such cases not as violating some independent principle or as conflicting with reality but as a failure of reason to agree *with itself*.[25]

1.2.3 The Internality of Selbsterkenntnis

We can get a more concrete sense of the internality of logical laws to all acts of thinking by considering a particular logical principle: the law of non-contradiction. It is partly constitutive of what it is to think that *p* that one's thought is, consciously or unconsciously, guided by the principle

[22] For a trenchant exploration of this point, see Boyle (forthcoming-a). Cf. also Smit (2009, 214, 222n.13); Land (2021 [2018], 7).

[23] Kant does seem to hold that some degree of actual compliance with the relevant standard is required for an act to count as the type of act that is constitutively governed by that standard. My point is just that perfect conformity is not required. Indeed, perfect compliance may be impossible or unverifiable for finite minds. See L-Blom (early 1770s) 24:93.28–94.20; L-Wien 24:825.33–826.5; L-DW 24:721.5–6, 722.6–8; L-Jäsche 9:54.22–28; as well as note 26.

[24] Apperception, Kant writes, is "*autonomia rationis purae*" (*Postumum*, 1800–1803, 21:81.30). The autonomy of reason is a consequence of Kant's view that reason is essentially self-conscious, because this implies that its acts are self-constituting. Kant claims credit for being among the first to recognize this consequence and grasp its significance, but if he is right, it is something all rational creatures – including Kant's predecessors – are implicitly (no doubt unconsciously) committed to. Compare Kant's clarification that his categorical imperative is not a new moral principle but a new *formulation* of a principle everyone already (and necessarily) accepts (*Practical* 5:8n.).

[25] B115.3–4; R1628 (1780s) 16:46.4–5; R1629 (1780s) 16:47.17–19. See Engstrom (2009, 131–134).

that one ought not conjointly think *not-p* (nor anything that would entail *not-p*).[26] That is to say, it would not so much as count as an act of thinking if the subject thinking *p* did not, in that very act, represent the principle of non-contradiction as unconditionally binding on her thought that *p* and suitably related contents. Part of what it *is* to think that *p* is to appreciate that one's thought is subject to the schema *<not (p and not-p)>*.

To claim that the law of non-contradiction must be internally represented in all acts of thinking is tantamount to denying that it is a distinct thought in its own right. According to Kant, the laws of logic cannot be conceived as a set of separate, if privileged, thoughts that stand alongside all our other thoughts, as Quine's "web of belief" would have it.[27] Now a Quinean account might preserve Kant's idea that a standing belief in certain logical principles is a normative, even constitutive, condition on one's status as a thinker. Its core idea is rather that these "logical beliefs" are distinct from a subject's day-to-day beliefs, such as her belief that meerkats bark.

What Quine's account fails to appreciate, from a Kantian standpoint, is the complete generality of logical laws as formal principles. The principle of non-contradiction governs the relations in which *all* thoughts may permissibly stand – including purportedly distinct thoughts about the laws of logic. If one treats logical commitments as distinct from other determinate acts of thinking, then a subject who simultaneously holds the belief that *p* and the belief that *not-p* is merely committed to an inconsistent triad, made up of this pair of contradictory beliefs along with her belief in the law of non-contradiction.[28] This makes it seem as though she could restore consistency to her web of belief by rejecting the law of non-contradiction, while retaining the beliefs that *p* and that *not-p*. What is absurd about this proposal is not that such a subject would, by rejecting the principle of non-contradiction, undermine her status as a thinker and, thus, cease to *think* the contents in question. There may be something tragic in a subject's self-exile from the space of reasons, but it is not incoherent. From a Kantian perspective, what is absurd in the Quinean scenario is that the subject's *reason* for rejecting the principle of

[26] In proscribing *anything* that would entail *not-p*, the principle of non-contradiction implicates an indefinite set of cognitions. It thereby imposes a sort of systematicity, a total classification, on one's thoughts, both actual and possible. This is analogous, I take it, to the universalizing import of the moral law, both in its "natural law" formulation and insofar as a finite agent is morally compelled to represent her maxims within a "kingdom of ends".

[27] Quine (1980 [1951]).

[28] Quine speaks of a web of beliefs, rather than of mere thoughts, but the point is the same.

non-contradiction could only be that *it contradicts* other beliefs she holds. So her rejection of the principle would, absurdly, manifest her allegiance to it. This enduring commitment to the principle of non-contradiction, even in the act of rejecting it, demonstrates the "internality" of logical laws to all her acts of thought – including the thought that the principle is false.

The subject's adherence to logical laws cannot be sequestered in a special set of beliefs, separate from the other thoughts she entertains. An implicit appreciation of the principle of non-contradiction will always insinuate itself into (or "in-form") her other acts of thinking. For if a subject is capable of appreciating that there is a contradiction between her belief in the principle of non-contradiction and her conjoint beliefs that *p* and that *not-p*, then she must have the more basic capacity to directly recognize the contradiction between her belief that *p* and her belief that *not-p*. She must have this latter capacity because the sentence letters we are using are purely schematic, so we can just rewrite the former scenario (the inconsistent triad) as the latter (the dyadic contradiction) by interpreting <*p*> to be her contradictory belief pair and <*not-p*> to be the principle of non-contradiction itself. Thus, even though it is possible, as Kant himself claims, for a subject to represent the principle of non-contradiction on its own and in abstracto, the ability to do so presupposes a more fundamental recognition of the principle that is internal to her capacity for thinking anything at all. That is to say, only a subject whose logical knowledge is internal to – that is, implicit in, but explicatable through mere self-conscious reflection on – her acts of thinking is in a position to frame and apply logical principles in abstracto as a distinct and privileged set of beliefs. The Quinean account of logical knowledge is otiose. For it presupposes just the sort of internal, apperceptive, autonomous grounding of the laws of logic that it proposed to supplant.

1.2.4 The Resulting Picture of PGL

What picture of PGL does this leave us with, so that we may return to Kant's comparison of logic to critique? Pure general logic has a proper subject matter, namely the formal rules governing all thinking, regardless of its object, its (empirical or a priori) relation to that object, or its content. This is what makes it a general logic. And it relies on a special sort of cognitive ground in cognizing this subject matter: namely, the essentially self-conscious character of the intellect. This is what makes it a pure logic, an a priori science. It is a priori both (i) in the sense that a self-conscious cognition of the form of thought is a cognition of what grounds all particular thoughts and (ii) in the sense that the capacity for such self-consciousness is not derived from experience. But this independence from experience merely concerns the justification or epistemic warrant of such self-conscious cognition. It does not mean that such self-consciousness is possible in the absence of experience. Quite the contrary. It means that the possibility of such a self-conscious representation of the form of thinking is inscribed into all acts of intellection, as such. The knowledge PGL presents in abstracto is distilled through painstaking reflection on particular acts of thinking in concreto – reflection that aims to bring to explicit consciousness the appreciation of the formal rules of thought that necessarily, if unconsciously, informs and guides those acts, thereby constituting them *as* acts of thinking. The underlying assumption of this reflective method is that all acts of thinking contain a conception of the essence of thought *überhaupt*. It may take great intellectual labor to isolate and unpack this conception. But such labor is fundamentally analytical in that its sufficient cognitive ground is contained in the acts whose form it seeks to characterize.

1.3 Critique as a *Selbsterkenntnis* of Reason

In what respects does critique resemble PGL and how, precisely, do they differ? We are helped toward an answer not only by Kant's letter to Garve but also by his various discussions of PGL, which present the same picture. Notably, the passages from L-Jäsche we have just been considering, where Kant characterizes PGL as reason's *Selbsterkenntnis* of its own form, draw the same comparison between logic and critique:

> [PGL] is a science of reason not merely with respect to form but with respect to matter, since its rules are not taken from experience and since it also has reason for its object. Logic is hence a self-cognition of the understanding and of reason, but not with respect to their capacities in regard to objects, but merely with respect to form. In logic I do not ask what the understanding knows [*erkennt*] and how much it can know or how far its knowledge extends. For that would be self-cognition with regard to its material use and thus belongs in metaphysics. In logic, there is only the question: how will the understanding cognize itself? (L-Jäsche 9:14)[29]

The "material use" of the intellect is its use in cognizing objects that do not depend, for their existence or inner constitution, on the acts through

[29] Cf. L-Wien 24:857.1–10; M-Mr 29:755.35–756.4; R5644 (1783–1784) 18:286.15–16.

which they are thought or cognized.[30] This material use comprehends the practical use of reason, in cognizing what is good (pursuit-worthy, what ought to be), as well as the theoretical use of reason, in cognizing what is true (belief-worthy, what is).[31] Kant mentions several questions one might raise about the material use of the intellect: namely, "what the understanding knows", "how much it can know", and "how far its knowledge extends". These are precisely the questions that define the critical project.[32] They correspond to Kant's claims to Garve that critique "derives, from the nature of [sc. 'the sole pure cognitive faculty' (10:340.11–12), i.e. 'a reason that judges a priori' (340.6)], all objects to which it extends" (340.14–15) and that critique can do this by "unfolding a priori out of the mere concept of a faculty of knowledge (if it is precisely determined) all objects and everything that one can know of them" (340.17–21).[33] So it is *critique* that L-Jäsche characterizes as "self-cognition [of the understanding] with regard to its material use".

L-Jäsche thus presents us with the same elucidatory comparison of PGL and critique as Kant's letter to Garve, but helpfully expands on the idea that these sciences are "formal and necessary" (10:340.9–10), adding that each is "a self-cognition of the understanding and reason" (9:14.25).[34] The difference is that PGL treats of reason in all its uses, whereas critique considers reason specifically in its pure but material use, i.e. in its a priori cognition of objects that exist independently of our acts of cognizing them. Critique is the *Selbsterkenntnis* of reason as a faculty of a priori yet synthetic cognition.[35]

[30] See B23.30–31, quoted subsequently. This is what I will mean by "thought independence". Of course, thought-independent objects may be mind-dependent in various other respects. In particular, they may depend *for their intelligible form* (i.e. for their cognizability), on the *capacities* of sensibility and understanding (though perhaps not on particular acts of those capacities), so that any knowable object must exhibit the forms of space and time as well as the forms of unity prescribed by the categories. I will not, however, address Kant's idealism in any detail.

[31] Bix-x.31–02; *Groundwork* 4:387.8–16; M-Mr 29:753.24–754.3.

[32] See, for instance, A3.18–8/B7.30–8. Kant admittedly says the answer to these questions "belongs in metaphysics" (9:14.30). But I take this to be a capacious use of the term, on which critique, as prolegomenon and canon, is both the first part and the complete idea of a scientific metaphysics. See especially A841/B869.20–29; cf. Bxxiii.11–xxiv.24; *Prolegomena* 4:365.25–28; *Metaphysical Foundations* 4:469.30–470.1; R4284 (1770–1775) 17:495.9–16.

[33] See also *Prolegomena* 4:365.17–25; *Metaphysical Foundations* 4:475n.37–42.

[34] Further characterizations of critique as the *Selbsterkenntnis* of reason include A735/B763.13–15, A763/B791.6–8, A849/B877.14–18; *Prolegomena* 4:328.20–25; *Tone* 8:390.30; R4892 (1776–1778) 18:21.2–5; R2667 (after 1790) 16:459.20–22; notes for *Metaphysics of Morals* 23:402.11–14; M-Mr 29:756.10, 783.21–22.

[35] Cf. A10.16–21, B19.28–02; *Prolegomena* 4:274.6–22; *Judgment* 5:289.3–5; R5133 (late 1770s or early 1780s) 18:101.

Now, the previous section argued that PGL is *Selbsterkenntnis* with respect to (i) its object (its subject matter) as well as (ii) its cognitive ground (its justificatory basis or epistemic warrant). Pure general logic (i) takes the form of the intellect as its object of inquiry and (ii) it bases its claims about this object on self-conscious reflection upon, and reflective engagement in, particular acts of intellection, merely as such. Pure general logic is *Selbsterkenntnis* in the special sense that has its sufficient cognitive ground in the essentially apperceptive character of the intellect, as realized in particular acts of thinking. If critique is likewise *Selbsterkenntnis* in this twofold sense, then it should be possible to adduce the principles of the critical philosophy through painstaking but a priori reflection on particular acts of material cognition. The principles of the critical philosophy ought to implicitly in-form all object-directed cognition, as such. Accordingly, if critique is *Selbsterkenntnis* in this twofold sense, the principles of the critical philosophy will be constitutive of what is to count as discursive knowledge of objects in the same way that the principles of logic are constitutive of what is to count as thought *überhaupt*. Here, too, it may turn out that particular acts of cognition fail to perfectly satisfy the principles that constitute them as material cognitions. But such cases will be flawed not with respect to some external standard but insofar as the intellect fails to agree with itself – insofar as its acts flout principles that they internally represent as binding on themselves.[36] This, I will argue, is precisely Kant's view.

1.3.1 Critique as Selbsterkenntnis *with Respect to Subject Matter*

Now, one might think this account of critique is a non-starter. For Kant is clear that PGL is a purely formal science, whereas he specifically associates critique with the material use of the intellect. However, critique can be *concerned with* the material use of the intellect without itself *constituting* a material use of the intellect. Kant is quite explicit about this:

> This science ["the critique of reason" (B23.21)] also cannot be terribly wide-ranging, because it does not have to do with objects of reason, whose variety is infinite, but merely with [reason] herself, with tasks that spring wholly from her own womb and are set for her not by the nature of things

[36] Axii.16–18, 21–22, A484/B512.24–25, A293f./B350.20–25; L-Ph (1772) 24:315.23–33. Such failures of self-agreement range from mild forms of heteronomy, in which sensibility exercises an undue influence on one's act of intellection (A294/B350f.4–9), to blatant antinomies, in which the intellect's own internal standards come into conflict through "subreptive" misapplication (A643/B671).

> that are distinct from her but through her own [nature]. For when she has already [*zuvor*] come to know completely her own capacity in regard to the objects that may crop up in experience, it must be easy to determine completely and with certainty the scope and the boundaries [*Grenzen*] of her attempted use beyond all bounds of experience. (B23)[37]

Critique is not concerned with "objects of reason" as its subject matter but "merely with [reason] herself". Now the faculty of reason that critique undertakes to study is, for its part, concerned to cognize "objects that are distinct from it" and to cognize them "beyond all bounds of experience". So critique is *indirectly* concerned with objects of reason. For it investigates the faculty of reason in its material use. But this does not make critique itself a material use of reason. It rather means that critique is not concerned with reason *überhaupt* but specifically with "a reason that judges a priori", as Kant writes to Garve (10:340.6). Such an investigation is still *formal* in the sense that it concerns reason's essence, its fundamental character. Critique addresses "tasks that spring wholly from [reason's] own womb", tasks that are set for it "through her own nature" (my underlining), rather than issues that may arise from "things that are distinct from her". Critique is reason's attempt to "come to know completely her own capacity in regard to the objects that may crop up in experience" (my underlining). And it is this concern with the fundamental nature of reason – its form – that enables critique "to determine completely and with certainty the scope and the boundaries of [reason's] attempted use beyond all bounds of experience".

Kant's initial attempt to distinguish his critical enterprise from traditional metaphysics draws a contrast between their respective subject matters.[38] The subject matter of metaphysics consists in thought-independent objects, which reason purports to cognize a priori. The subject matter of critique, by contrast, is the *faculty of reason* that aspires to such a priori cognition of thought-independent objects. Critique consists of what Kant calls "transcendental cognition", which "essentially concerns [*überhaupt beschäftigt*] itself not so much with objects [*Gegenständen*] but rather with our manner of cognizing [*Erkenntnisart*] objects, insofar as this [sc. cognition] is supposed to be possible a priori" (B25.1–5).[39] This distinction in subject matter applies to "critical" as well

[37] See also Aiv.20–28, Bxxiii.11–01, A12.27–A13.3/B26.28–4; *Prolegomena* 4:274.27–35.

[38] See also *Progress* 20:343.29–31; M-Mr 29:750.18–751.10, 752.11–18, 756.1–17, 779.24–37, 780.27–31; M-Vi/K_3 (1794–1795) 29:949.14–24.

[39] Cf. A11–12.1–4, A56/B80.11–19; A751/B779.10–16; *Judgment* 5:176.19–23. Kant's hedge "not so much with objects" suggests that this distinction may not be exclusive. Indeed, it turns out that

as "dogmatic" metaphysics.[40] Critical metaphysics consists of those synthetic a priori judgments that are genuinely knowable, in light of the faculty analysis prosecuted by critique. But metaphysics and critique proper (which I will call "critical epistemology") nevertheless have different topics, and Kant accordingly treats them in different sections of his critical texts.

The core of Kant's critical epistemology is established in the Transcendental Aesthetic and the Analytic of Concepts. It is there that claims directly addressing the nature of our cognitive faculties are concentrated: for example, that sensibility and understanding are the two stems of human knowledge (A15/B29.7–12), that intuition involves an object's being given to the mind (A19/B33.5–10), that objects are given to us only insofar as they affect us (A19/B33.9–12), that the understanding is spontaneous (A51/B75.1–6), that it can be regarded as a capacity to judge (A69/B94.19–26), that the "I think" must be able to accompany all my representations (B131.4–132.8; A107.25–29, A118n.18–32), and so on. This critical epistemology vindicates the possibility of a genuinely knowledgeable metaphysics of nature, which is subsequently outlined in the Analytic of Principles. Here we encounter claims that are directly concerned with thought-independent objects, such as the principle that all appearances are extensive magnitudes (B203.18–19), that real properties are continuously gradable (B211.6–11), that substance endures throughout all change (A182.23–25, B222.4–6), and so on. The Dialectic, of course, is likewise preoccupied with claims about thought-independent objects, though Kant's aim there is to expose them as illusory, insofar as they are incompatible with the critical epistemology, and to diagnose our temptation to believe them. Here we encounter traditional metaphysical dogmas, e.g. that the soul is a substance (A344/B402), that the world has a beginning in time (A426–8/B454–6), and so on.

With respect to subject matter, then, critical epistemology is no less a *Selbsterkenntnis* of reason than is PGL. Critique does not exhibit the thoroughgoing formality of PGL, since it is concerned with the material

an investigation of our *faculty* for a priori cognition yields an a priori account of the *objects* such a faculty can cognize. But this move requires Kant's signature idealism: "a priori cognition can attribute nothing to objects except what the thinking subject takes from within herself" (Bxxiii). Only within such an idealistic framework can transcendental philosophy, as a science of the faculty of speculative reason, amount to an ontology, as a science of being (A247/B303.17–23; cf. A845/B873.29–02).

[40] Kant's use of the term "metaphysics" varies somewhat, but its core meaning is the material use of reason a priori, i.e. the pure rational cognition of thought-independent objects. This comprehends the constitutive principles of practical reason, the subreptive speculations of traditional metaphysics, and the immanent principles of transcendental ontology. See *Groundwork* 4:388.4–8.

use of the intellect, but neither is it a sort of material cognition. In both sciences, reason investigates its own form. Their difference lies in the degree of abstraction with which they consider their common subject matter, namely reason's form.[41] Reason has just one form, of course, but it can be characterized more or less abstractly. Pure general logic characterizes this form in abstraction from all material use of the intellect, whereas critique takes account of reason's use in cognizing objects a priori and thereby offers a more concrete, but still formal, account of what reason most essentially is.[42] Now there are, Kant says, just two ways that material cognition can relate to its object: namely, (i) theoretically, by "merely **determining** it" through concepts, and (ii) practically, by "also **making** it **actual**" (Bix–x, Kant's emphases). So there will be a critique of theoretical reason as well as a critique of practical reason. And these critical inquiries into the form of reason in its theoretical and its practical applications are specifically concerned with reason's capacity to cognize its object a priori – that is, with reason's character as a "pure faculty of knowledge [*reinen Erkenntnisvermögen*]" (Kant to Garve, 10:340.12).[43] So while both PGL and critique are a priori inquiries into the form of the intellect, PGL abstracts from both the *objects* of thought and the *manner* in which thought relates to its objects – empirically or a priori, theoretically or practically. Critique abstracts from the former but not the latter. Pure general logic is reason's *Selbsterkenntnis* of its form as a faculty of *thinking*; critique is reason's *Selbsterkenntnis* of its form as a faculty of *a priori cognition*, either practical or theoretical.

1.3.2 Critique as Selbsterkenntnis *with Respect to Cognitive Ground*

Thus far, we have fleshed out the idea that critique is a *Selbsterkenntnis* of reason with respect to its subject matter: Critique is reason's investigation

[41] This reading is controversial (see note 4). Others hold that critique – and, in particular, Transcendental Logic – has a different subject matter from PGL. The approach I am sketching can accommodate this. My main point is not that PGL and critique have the very same faculty as their object, but that, whatever faculty each has as its object, each embodies a *Selbsterkenntnis* of that faculty with respect to subject matter and cognitive ground. The core of my interpretation is that, as a *Selbsterkenntnis* with respect to cognitive ground, the claims of Kant's critical epistemology are justified through apperceptive reflection on (self-conscious engagement in) material cognition of objects.

[42] Kant calls critique a "formal science" in *Prolegomena* 4:262.5; cf. *Tone* 8:404.3–21.

[43] For reasons that do not affect the present argument, Kant prefers to speak simply of a critique of practical reason, not of *pure* practical reason. Kant argues that, if reason can determine the will at all, it must do so a priori. So the critical question comes down to whether reason can be practical *at all*, i.e. whether our will is free (*Practical* 5:15.16–16.2).

of its own essential principles, as a faculty of a priori material cognition. Whether critique is also a *Selbsterkenntnis* with respect to its cognitive ground or justificatory basis is a more difficult question. For, as in the case of PGL, Kant provides almost no positive characterization of the epistemic warrant enjoyed by critique, beyond repeatedly insisting that it is an a priori science. But some of his remarks are quite suggestive.

For instance, Kant claims that we can reasonably "hope to complete such a system" of critical epistemology because:

> the object here is not the nature of things, which is inexhaustible, but rather the understanding, which makes judgments about the nature of things – and the understanding [is the object] only with respect to its cognition a priori – the advantage of which is that, since we clearly need not seek for it externally [*ihn doch nicht auswärtig suchen dürfen*], [the understanding] cannot remain hidden from us[.] (A13/B25)[44]

Kant's first point is familiar to us: Critique has a special "object" (i.e. subject matter) – namely, "the understanding [. . .] with respect to its cognition a priori". But he now adds that the nature of this subject matter is such that "it cannot remain hidden from us" because the understanding is not something that we must seek out "auswärtig" – "externally", or "elsewhere". This recalls Augustine's dictum: "Let not the mind, therefore, seek itself as though it were absent, but let it take care to discern itself as present."[45] Kant contrasts "seek[ing] elsewhere" with the epistemic procedure of critique, which, by implication, need not seek, since its object is already manifest: its object is not "elsewhere" but *here* in what already lies before it. And what already lies before us, in critique, are precisely the understanding's "judgments about the nature of things". That is why the

[44] See also Kant's remarks in the A-edition Preface: "Nothing can escape us here, because what reason produces entirely of herself cannot conceal itself but will be brought to light by reason herself as soon as one has only discovered the common principle of it [sc. what reason produces of itself]." (Axx.14–18) Again: "[In the Critique] I have solely to do with reason herself and her pure thinking, for extensive acquaintance [Kenntnis] with which I need not search far beyond myself, because I encounter her in me myself, and common logic already provides me an example of how to completely and systematically enumerate all her [sc. reason's] simple acts" (Axiv.18–25).

[45] *De Trinitate* 10.9.12, cited in Boyle (2011). Augustine continues:

> Let it not know itself as though it did not know itself, but [let it know] how to distinguish itself from that which it knows to be another thing. When it hears the command "Know thyself", how will it be able to carry it out if it does not know what "know" means, and what "thyself" means? If, however, it knows what both mean, then it also knows itself.

It is customary to align Augustine with Descartes (e.g. Menn 1998; Matthews 2003); yet Kant's conception of critical epistemology also bears suggestive similarities to Augustine's account of intellectual self-inquiry. A direct influence of Augustine or Augustinianism is doubtful, however.

understanding "cannot remain hidden from us": because it is already manifest *in our judgments about objects.*

This is not to say that we might not overlook important features of our understanding or that we are immune to error in our characterizations of it. As Kant stresses early in the Introduction, it is only "once long practice has made us attentive to it and adept at separating it out" that we come to appreciate "what our own faculty of cognition (merely occasioned by sensible impressions) provides [*hergibt*] of itself" (B1f.21–26). The sense in which the understanding "cannot remain hidden from us" is rather that everything we require to give a correct and complete account of its form is already open to view in our intellectual judgments (*Verstandesurteile*) about objects. If the nature of the understanding is hidden, it is hiding in plain sight.

Critique, then, is a *Selbsterkenntnis* of the understanding with respect to its cognitive ground. Its claims, like those of PGL, are based on the essentially apperceptive character of the understanding, for what they bring to light is already contained in the exercises of the faculty whose form they characterize. The claims of critique are established through mere reflection upon, and reflective engagement in, concrete acts of judgment.[46]

Kant makes a similar point in the B-edition Preface, which likewise indicates that critique is distinguished not merely by its subject matter but by a special epistemic relation to that subject matter:

> [The critique of pure speculative reason] is a treatise on method, not a system of the science [sc. of pure speculative reason] itself; but it nevertheless outlines the entire structure of that science, with respect to both its boundaries and its internal articulation. For pure speculative reason has this particularity: that she can measure out [*ausmessen*] her own capacity, according to the different manners in which she selects objects for thought [. . .]; because, with respect to the first point [sc. that reason can measure out her own capacity], nothing can be attributed [*beigelegt*] to the object in a priori cognition except what the thinking subject takes from within herself [.] [. . .] Accordingly, metaphysics has the rare fortune, which redounds to no other rational science that has to do with objects (for **logic** busies itself only with the form of thinking in general), that, once critique has set it upon the sure path of a science, it [sc. metaphysics] can [. . .] complete its work [. . .] for it has to do merely with the principles and limitations of her [sc. pure speculative reason's] use, which are determined through [reason] herself. (Bxxii–xxiv, Kant's emphasis; cf. A467f./B504f.; *Prolegomena* 4:366.12–22)

46 For discussion of how such reflection proceeds, see Section 4.4.

Kant is again claiming a principled completeness for critique – and, by extension, for the reformed metaphysics that critique exhaustively "outlines". Kant links this completeness to his claim that a priori cognition of objects can only concern "what the thinking subject takes from within herself" (my underlining). Thus, the content and extent of metaphysics, as a priori cognition of objects, will be determined by the nature of the thinking subject, viz. by the essential character of reason. The task of critique, then, is to explicate the essence of speculative reason, the constitutive principles that characterize its form. This much is familiar. What is new is the suggestion that we are in a position to explicate these principles – to prosecute a critique of pure speculative reason – precisely because they "are determined through [reason] herself".[47] This is an expression of reason's autonomy – of the fact that reason's exercises are governed by principles that they internally represent as binding on themselves.

We have already seen that the purely formal laws of PGL are self-legislated in this sense (Section 1.2.2). Kant is now claiming that the same autonomy is involved in *material* uses of reason. Reason "determines" for herself "the principles and limitations" of her own use "according to the different manners in which she selects objects for thought". This is her autonomy. Accordingly, the epistemic basis of critique, which delivers a cognition of the form of reason in its material use, will consist in self-conscious reflection on, and reflective engagement in, concrete acts of material cognition – the acts through which its constitutive principles are self-legislated. Its aim is to bring to explicit consciousness the principles that such acts internally, if unconsciously, represent as binding on themselves, insofar as they stem from an autonomous rational faculty – a faculty that "determines" its own principles of operation.

1.3.3 The Immanence of Critique as Selbsterkenntnis

These discussions in the introductory sections of the *Critique* are merely suggestive, but they are reinforced by the accounts of apperception, synthesis, and judgment that Kant subsequently develops in the

[47] Cf. *Prolegomena* 4:349.31–38; *Critique* A751/B779.20–21. See also Kant's remark in the *Anthropology*:

> If by the word "understanding" is meant the faculty of cognition by means of rules (and thus through concepts) in general, so that it comprehends the entire higher faculty of cognition, then these rules are not to be understood as those through which nature guides the human being in his conduct [. . .] but only those that he [the human being] himself makes (7:197, my underlining).

Analytic.[48] Consider Kant's well-known claim that "[t]he **I think** must **be able** to accompany all my representations" (B131, Kant's emphases). This says that I can, in principle, become explicitly conscious of any of my representings and can do so without relying on empirical observations. The power to do this is called pure apperception, which Kant considers an essential characteristic of rational faculties, as such.[49] As Kant emphasizes, however, apperceptive consciousness need not actually accompany all my representations.[50] Some of my representations may remain unconscious – indeed, Kant thinks the vast majority do.[51] What is essential to them, as representations belonging to a rational faculty, is that it is *possible* for me to become explicitly conscious of them.[52] Now, on the interpretive approach I've been sketching, the principles of critical epistemology are supposed to emerge through apperceptive reflection on material uses of the intellect. So the question we now face is whether Kant takes acts of material cognition to essentially involve a *representation*, albeit unconscious, of the constitutive principles governing material cognition, as such. If he does, then critique can explicate those principles through pure apperception.

Kant's discussions of synthesis and judgment in the B-edition Transcendental Deduction suggest that he does indeed take acts of material cognition to essentially involve a representation of the general principles that constitute them as material cognitions – just as acts of thinking are, as such, guided by an appreciation of the laws of logic that constitute them as thoughts. Material cognition, as opposed to mere thought, is based on synthesis: i.e. the combination (*Verbindung*) of a manifold that is given independently of the act of thinking and combining it (B130.19–24).[53]

48 I can offer nothing approaching an adequate treatment of these matters here. My aim is not to defend this reading against all alternatives but to outline an account of Kant's critical methodology that is intelligible and plausible. The more important test of my interpretation is the light it sheds on Kant's actual prosecution of the critique, not the degree of credence it can compel in advance and in abstracto. What I say here is indebted to and supported by the more detailed discussions of Engstrom (2009, ch. IV; 2013; 2016); Merritt (2009; 2011; 2018, ch. 3); Land (2021 [2018]); and Schafer (2019; 2020a; 2021 [2018]; 2022).

49 See B134n.35–38, A114.32–02, A117n.30–32; *Anthropology* 7:127.4–14.

50 Cf. A117n.27–32; Kant's letter to Beck, 4 December 1792, 11:365.6–8.

51 See note 18.

52 Precisely *how* we are to become conscious of them (i.e. what is involved in actually exercising our power of pure apperception) is a question we will touch on in Sections 2.5 and 4.4. A full account would take us too far afield.

53 I do not mean to suggest that thinking does *not* involve combination, but merely that PGL takes no account of this. Because PGL abstracts from the origin of our representations, it ignores whether the concepts combined in a judgment are "given" independently of that act of combination or whether they are "made" through that act. Accordingly, the laws of PGL hold for every intellect whatsoever, whether discursive (i.e. dependent on receptivity) or intuitive (i.e. spontaneously productive).

Material cognition, for Kant, is not a passive absorbing of information but an active sense-making and stance-taking that involves the forging of rule-governed connections. As Kant says later in the Dialectic, "the senses cannot err [...] because they do not judge. Thus truth as well as error [...] are only to be met with in judgment" (A293/B350). One of Kant's pivotal claims early in the Deduction is that combination is an act of spontaneity, which he takes to entail that "we can represent nothing as combined in the object [*Objekt*] without having previously combined it ourselves" (B130). But the act of synthesizing or combining a manifold, Kant claims, always involves a representation of the unity that is to result from such synthesis:

> Combination is the representation of the **synthetic** unity of the manifold. The representation of this unity cannot therefore arise out of the combination, rather it makes the concept of the combination possible in the first place by being added to the representation of the manifold. (B131, Kant's emphasis)

What is important here for our purposes is that combination involves a representation of unity – some concept of oneness that guides the synthesis of the manifold.[54] Since I can, through pure apperception, become explicitly conscious of any of my representings, it follows that I can, in principle, become explicitly conscious of the representation of unity that guides my synthesis in a given act of material cognition.

Now, most such representations of unity are not candidates for constitutive, formal principles of material cognition, because they are not common to all acts of material cognition. The concept <rattlesnake>, for instance, is a representation of unity that may guide the synthesis of an intuited manifold in a particular act of material cognition (cf. A141/B180.25–30). But most material cognitions (thankfully) do not involve representing a rattlesnake. There is, however, one representation of unity that Kant argues is essential to all synthesis and, thus, to all material cognition. This is the synthetic unity of apperception, which expresses itself in the pure concepts of the understanding – in "the category" (singular), as Kant often puts it.[55] This suggests that a theory of "the category" can be elaborated on the basis of pure apperception, since "the category" is a

By contrast, Kant's doctrine of synthesis and the associated account of material cognition pertain only to a discursive intellect (B135.20–27, B138f.3–14, B145.27–15, B153.7–18, B159.16–20).

54 A few pages later, Kant offers an example: The concept of a line gives unity to the act of combining a particular spatial manifold into a determinate one-dimensional segment (B137f.16–22).

55 B131.22, B144.6–7, B145.21, B146.24, A139/B179.15–16, A181/B224.15–17, A253.1–2, 5, A326/B383.20–23, B423n.17–18, A409/B436.5–6, A770/B798.23–25.

representation of unity that is essential to all material cognition. Such a theory would set out constitutive principles governing all material cognition, as such. These principles will be internally represented in any act of material cognition, since they characterize the unity that is represented as the aim of all synthesis. This is why an apperceptive consciousness of those principles would be "pure": because it would rely only on what is contained in any act of material cognition, as such. And insofar as the synthesis it investigates is an "act of the understanding" (B130.23, B130.17–19), this apperceptively grounded theory of the category will be "essentially concerned not so much with objects as with our manner of cognizing objects" (B25.2–4, cf. A11f.11–13). So what we have described is a transcendental account of the constitutive principles of material cognition – a critique of speculative reason – based on pure apperception, in the sense of analytical reflection upon, and reflective engagement in, concrete acts of judgment about thought-independent objects.

Much the same picture emerges from Kant's discussion of judgment in the B-Deduction.[56] Judgment is the root of all material cognition, for Kant, because it is only in judging that one claims *objective validity* for one's thought:

> **Judgment** [is] a relation [of representations] that is **objectively valid** and that sufficiently distinguishes itself from the relation of the same representations in which there would be merely subjective validity, e.g. in accordance with laws of association. For in accordance with the latter I can only say, "when I carry a body, I feel a pressure of heaviness", but not, "it, the body, **is** heavy", which amounts to saying that these two representations [sc. <body> and <heavy>] are combined in the object [*Objekt*], i.e. regardless of differences in the state of the subject, and not merely compresent [*beisammen*] in perception (however often it [sc. the perception of them together] may be repeated). (B142, cf. B168.33–15)

Truth, Kant says, consists in "the agreement of cognition with its object [Gegenstande]" (A58/B82). Objective validity, by contrast, consists in a *claim* to truth. A judgment not only represents an object, with which it may or may not agree; it also represents *itself* as agreeing with its object. Judgment, for Kant, involves a kind of "taking condition".[57] Even an association of representations that does in fact agree with the object – as some subjective associations no doubt will – falls short of judgment and,

[56] The picture I sketch here agrees with Aquinas's view of rational judgment, according to Coope (2013, esp. 8–10); cited by Land (2021 [2018]).

[57] The term "taking condition" is due to Boghossian (2014), but the idea is widespread and can be fleshed out in a variety of ways; see Valaris (2020).

thus, of material cognition. To cognize an object, one must also *take* one's combination of representations to indicate the state of the object. That is, one must represent one's own act of synthesizing the representations as grounded in the object to which they refer. Otherwise one is not really making a *claim* about the object, even if one's mental state contains information about the object and this information is accurate. This means that a judgment, as a vehicle of material cognition, essentially involves a representation of the standard of correctness against which that very act of judgment is to be assessed: namely, the standard of agreeing with its object. For a judgment intrinsically represents itself as *satisfying* this standard. Indeed, representing itself as subject to this standard of correctness is, for Kant, precisely what constitutes a combination of representations as a judgment in the first place: "That is the aim of the connective term [*Verhältniswörtchen*] 'is' in [judgments]: to distinguish the objective unity of given representations from the subjective" (B141f).[58]

Kant takes judgment to essentially involve a representation of the standard of correctness that governs all material cognition. Therefore, since (i) the "I think" must be able to accompany all my representations and (ii) it is constitutive of all material judgment to represent the standard of correctness that characterizes the form of all material cognition, pure apperception must suffice to bring this standard to explicit consciousness. Critique consists in performing just this apperceptive task. In thus spelling out the standard of correctness that is internally represented in every act of potentially knowledgeable judgment, critique elaborates the form (the essence) of material cognition.

Though they are couched in different terms, this account coincides with the previous discussion of combinatory synthesis. Recall, first, that any act of combination presupposes some representation of unity that guides it and, second, that Kant takes "the category" to be a representation of unity that is common to all acts of synthesis concerned with thought-independent objects. This led us to describe critique as a theory of "the category" that can be elaborated on the basis of pure apperception. We then turned to judgment and sketched a view of critique as an apperceptive explication of the constitutive standards of correctness governing all material cognition, based on Kant's view that it is essential

[58] This is why the senses do not judge (A293/B350.18–20). Though acts of sensing are, of course, subject to certain standards of correctness – namely, regarding the senses' proper (healthy) operation – an act of sensing does not, merely as such, involve representing itself as satisfying any such standard. Sensations convey information only about the current state of the sensing subject (cf. A320/B376.26–28).

to all potentially knowledgeable judgment to represent itself as agreeing with its object.

These accounts coincide because Kant conceives of the categories as "concepts of objects in general [*überhaupt*]" (A93/B126.2–5, cf. B128.8–11). Kant puts the same point the other way around when he says that an "**object** is that in the concept of which the manifold of intuition is **united**" (B137.22–02, Kant's emphasis). The categories are those concepts of the object with which all judgment, as a vehicle of material cognition, essentially takes itself to agree. That is why Kant can say that "the principles of the objective determination of all representations" – that is, the standards of correctness for all material cognition – "are all derived [*abgeleitet*] from the principle of the transcendental unity of apperception" – that is, the unity that finds expression in the categories (B142.21–24). And it is why a theory of the category amounts to an account of the constitutive standards of correctness governing all material cognition – and why such an account can be epistemically based on pure apperception alone.

1.4 Prosecuting a Critique via Pure Apperception

This account of critique raises several questions, two of which are especially pressing for my project in this book. First, the idea that the constitutive principles of material cognition can be known via pure apperception can seem mysterious, in much the way that calling PGL a *Selbsterkenntnis* of reason may seem to generate more heat than light. This worry is not allayed by reassurances about what apperceptive reflection is *not* – for example, that it is not an unmediated *Wesensschau*, not a mystical form of introspection, not an infallible or exhaustive form of self-omniscience. What one wants, in order to assess the textual and philosophical plausibility of the proposal, is a positive account of what it *is* to prosecute a critique of speculative reason via apperception, accompanied by concrete illustrations of such a procedure, with running commentary on how and why it unfolds as it does.

A second pressing question for my project in this book is how pure apperception could yield insight into the character of *sensibility*, even if one grants that it can somehow explicate the form of *the intellect* in its pure material use. After all, the accounts of synthesis and judgment sketched in the previous section suggest that pure apperception only enables a kind of "maker's knowledge" of my spontaneous intellectual activity. I can apperceive only what I enact. Or, more precisely, I can apperceive only those representations that guide me in my spontaneous synthetic activity, i.e. the representations that manifest the self-activity of my intellect, the autonomy and self-determination of reason in its material use. So apperception can perhaps yield knowledge of the principles essential to all combination – that is, a theory of the category (or categories). But Kant is explicit that "**combination** [. . .] can never come into us through the senses and thus also cannot be contained in the pure form of sensible intuition" (B129.14–15). Indeed, Kant appears to hold that sensible representations do not require combination:

> The manifold of representations can be given in an intuition that is merely sensible, i.e. nothing but receptivity, and the form of this intuition can lie a priori in our faculty of representation, without being anything other than the manner [Art] in which the subject is affected. (B129.9–13, cf. B132.8–9)

This seems to place sensibility, as a capacity for representation, outside the scope of what we can cognize through pure apperception. And this is reflected in Kant's division of the Doctrine of Elements into (i) a Transcendental Aesthetic, which treats of sensibility insofar as it helps make synthetic a priori knowledge possible, and (ii) a Transcendental Logic (TL), which treats of the intellect insofar as it purports to cognize thought-independent objects a priori. It is therefore tempting to think that what is properly analogous to PGL, as a *Selbsterkenntnis* of reason, is not critique per se but TL to the *exclusion* of Transcendental Aesthetic and the theory of sensible intuition it elaborates.

The chapters that follow attempt to answer these worries. Chapter 2 reconstructs a series of arguments from pure apperception that support conclusions about the nature of receptive intuition. These arguments are located in the Introduction to the *Critique* and establish Kant's *Vorerinnerung* about the two "stems" of human cognition: (i) a receptive capacity for intuition (termed "sensibility") through which objects are given and (ii) a spontaneous faculty of thought (termed "understanding") through which they are cognized. Chapter 3 turns to the opening section of the Transcendental Aesthetic (A19–A22/B33–B36) and identifies apperception-based arguments for key elements of Kant's theory of sensible intuition: in particular, his claims that (iii) intuitions, as object-giving representations, relate immediately to their objects and that (iv) any *sensible* intuition must involve not just particular sensible affections but also an affection-independent "form" that enables these to be ordered in determinate relations. These claims are based on an apperceptive grasp on the nature of our own cognitive powers combined with very general conceptual considerations. It is only with the claim that human intuition is based on *sensible affection* (B33.10–12) that Kant must appeal to a different sort of evidence, such as phenomenological reflection or empirical observation.

These discussions address the first worry by illustrating in detail how critique can be prosecuted via pure apperception. But they do less to allay the second worry, since they only establish *that* we possess a non-intellectual capacity for intuition and that any sort of receptive intuition must have a *pure form*, without delving into the determinate character of such representations or how these might, in virtue of specifiable features, contribute to synthetic, a priori cognition of thought-independent objects. I take up that challenge in Chapters 4 and 5, which present an interpretation of the Metaphysical Expositions at the heart of the Aesthetic. I argue that Metaphysical Exposition is a special sort of conceptual analysis, in which apperceptive reflection plays a central role. The Metaphysical Expositions aim to show that our representations of space and time originate in pure intuition. Kant does this by making claims (i) about the marks of our concepts, <space> and <time>, and (ii) about the essential characteristics of pure intuitions. Apperception plays a leading role in establishing both kinds of claims. The first arise from conceptual analysis as described in Chapter 4; the second from the reflections on our cognitive capacities outlined in Chapters 2 and 3.

This addresses the second worry, by illustrating how specific features (givenness, immediacy, infinity, singularity) can be established as essential to human intuition on the basis of apperceptive reflection. But it is only to be expected that, in the Transcendental Aesthetic and elsewhere, Kant blends together considerations that I want to ascribe to pure apperception with considerations of a phenomenological, metaphysical, mathematical, or even broadly empirical character. The argument from apperception that I aim to trace is not the only sort of argument Kant offers. But it is one that rewards our scrutiny.

2

Synthetic Judgment and Intuition
The Sensibility/Understanding Distinction in the "Introduction"

> The starting point [*Das erste*] [in rational psychology] is the consciousness of my Self, the I; it is the first *actus* of the Psyche: the faculty to cognize oneself as representing subject and also as object of our own representation. This apperception [. . .], insofar as I myself am determinative [*bestimmend*], is called *intellectualis, apperceptio pura*. It is very difficult to grasp. [. . .] This pure consciousness already comes up in logic. – (All judgments are representations, of whose unity we are conscious.) This faculty [sc. of pure apperception] contains the ground of the distinction between sensibility and understanding (faculty of rules – higher cognitive faculty)
>
> M-DW, 1792/93, 28:670.28–671.5, my underlining

Kant begins both editions of the *Critique* with claims he takes to be beyond doubt:

> Experience is without doubt the first product that our understanding brings forth in processing [*bearbeitet*] the raw material of sensible sensations. It is thereby our first instruction and, in its progression, so inexhaustible of new lessons, that the interconnected lives of all future generations would never lack for new information that can be gathered on this basis. (A1)

And:

> There is no doubt whatsoever that all our knowledge begins with experience. For how else should the faculty of cognition be awakened to exercise, if not through objects that rouse our senses and effect [*bewirken*] representations partly on their own and partly bring our intellectual activity into motion to compare these, to connect or separate them, and to thereby work up [*verarbeiten*] the raw material of sense impressions into the cognition of objects that is called experience? (B1)

I will argue that these claims, and others like them, characterize the form (the essence) of the human *Erkenntnisvermögen* and that the account they present is based on pure apperception. Indeed, it is precisely because they are grounded in pure apperception that Kant can treat these claims as beyond doubt. For, as I argued in Chapter 1 (Section 1.3.3), a mental act counts as an act of cognition (an act of objectively valid judgment) only insofar as it represents itself as normatively bound by certain constitutive principles that characterize the form of material cognition. No one with the relevant capacity for cognition can consistently doubt these principles, since exercising her capacity for knowledge already commits her to their truth. (She may, of course, fail to recognize that she is so committed, or mischaracterize the content of those commitments, but that is another matter.[1]) Thus, my interpretation is built around the following line of thought: (i) We possess the very capacity for knowledge whose form we are attempting to characterize. (ii) This capacity for knowledge is essentially self-conscious or apperceptive. So (iii) possessing and exercising this capacity equips us with (or puts us in a position to obtain through reflection) a concept of the features and principles that are constitutive of this faculty and its acts. And (iv) many pivotal doctrines of Kant's critical philosophy consist in bringing to explicit consciousness this apperceptive concept of our *Erkenntnisvermögen* and rendering it distinct through conceptual analysis. I call Kant's account of these constitutive, formal features his "critical epistemology", in contrast to his "critical metaphysics" (see Section 1.3.1).

One of the principles to which we are, in this way, ineluctably, if unreflectively, committed is the distinction between sensibility and understanding, which Kant presents at the end of the Introduction (A15/B29.6–12). In this chapter and Chapter 3, I will argue that the conception of sensible intuition articulated in the Introduction and in the opening sections of the Transcendental Aesthetic is, in the aforementioned sense, an apperceptively grounded self-cognition of reason. Mere self-conscious reflection on principles that are implicit in and constitutive of all objective cognition reveals that our capacity for knowledge must exhibit (i) a receptivity to representations that are (ii) object-giving (A15/B29.10–15; A19/B33.9–10, 14–16), and (iii) immediate (A19/B33.7–9). Though such apperceptive reflection does not, on its own, establish Kant's further claims that our intuition (iv) depends on sensible affection (A19/B33.10–12) and (v) contains a multiplicity of sensations (A19f./B34.23–01), it *does* show that (vi) an intuition that is receptive (i.e. affection-dependent in the

[1] One might wonder: If so many doctrines of the critical philosophy are evident merely through self-conscious reflection, how is it that all philosophers prior to Kant have failed to recognize them? The short answer is: because self-knowledge is the "most difficult of [reason's] occupations" (Axi.20–21). For a fuller answer, see Section 4.4.

broadest sense) must be conditioned by an a priori form, within which the representational results of such affections can be ordered in determinate relations (A20/B34.7–16).

Now, apperceptive reflection need not be the *only* way in which these aspects of our mindedness are manifest to us. There may arguably be alternative routes to these conclusions, such as metaphysical reasoning, semantic and epistemological considerations, phenomenological introspection, empirical anthropological study, and so on. I do not wish to suggest that the tapestry of Kantian philosophy is woven from a single thread. My goal is just to show that there is at least one thread that runs throughout Kant's critical epistemology – namely, reason's *Selbsterkenntnis*. My aim is to follow this thread into sections of the *Critique* where one might not expect it to surface, such as the Introduction and the Transcendental Aesthetic.

2.1 Knowledge that Comes to Be

The *Critique* begins by asserting that there is a beginning to our knowledge. Human knowledge is not "always already" actual; it is something that must come to be. It is part of our nature, as humans, to pass from ignorance to knowledge, from innocence to experience, from potentiality to actuality. This is a version of Aristotle's claim that the mind is a *tabula rasa*, i.e. something whose essence and original state is a certain *capacity* or *potentiality* for knowledge but not yet actual knowledge of anything determinate.[2] The need to transition from mere potentiality to actuality

[2] Aristotle writes that mind "can have no nature of its own, other than that of having a certain capacity. Thus that in the soul which is called mind (by mind I mean that whereby the soul thinks and judges) is, before it thinks, not actually any real thing" (*De Anima* III.4, 429a21–24). Aristotle likens the mind to a *tabula rasa* at 430a1: "What [the mind] thinks must be in it just as characters may be said to be on a writing tablet on which as yet nothing actually stands written: this is exactly what happens with mind." This is, of course, only half of Aristotle's account of the intellect, which comprises not only the receptive *nous pathetikos*, "which is what it is by virtue of becoming all things", but also the productive *nous poietikos*, "which is what it is by virtue of making all things" (*De Anima* III.5, 430a14–16). Aristotle likens the way *nous poietikos* "makes" all things to the way light "makes" color: namely, by actualizing the disposition of colored objects to be seen as having some determinate color. The precise import of the analogy depends on Aristotle's views on optics and color perception, which require considerable parsing (see Lindberg 1976, 6–9, 43–57; Code 2008). But Aristotle is clear that the mind *acts* (and thus "makes" in the relevant sense) both in "thinking of the simple objects of thought", where neither truth nor error is possible, and in "putting together objects of thought in a quasi-unity", "where the alternative of true or false applies" (*De Anima* III.6, 430a26–28). These are the first two of the Aristotelian "*tres operationes mentis*" – namely, the *simplex apprehensio*, the act of judgment (*judicium*), and the act of inferring (*ratiocinium*). For discussion of the *tres operationes mentis* in relation to Kant, see Dyck (forthcoming, section 1). Despite suggestive resonances, it is doubtful that Kant's views were shaped by close study of the Aristotelian corpus or

is the mark of a *nous pathetikos*: that is, a passive or receptive intellect – the *Aql Bil Quwwah* of the Arabic tradition and *intellectus possibilis* of the Latin.[3] Even an arch rationalist such as Leibniz agrees that human knowledge is receptive in the minimal sense that it intrinsically involves a transition from potentiality to actuality.

Consider the Preface to Leibniz's *New Essays on Human Understanding*, which Kant is generally thought to have studied at the outset of his "silent decade".[4] Leibniz writes: "This is how ideas and truths are innate in us – as inclinations, dispositions, tendencies, or natural potentialities, and not as actualities [*actiones*]" (A VI.6:52). Leibniz prefers to figure the passivity or receptivity of the mind through "the analogy of a veined block of marble, as opposed to an entirely homogeneous block of marble, or a blank tablet – what the philosophers call a *tabula rasa*", since the latter are "entirely neutral as to whether it [sc. the marble, the tablet, the mind] assumes this shape or some other" (A VI.6:52). Yet Leibniz, too, insists that "the senses are necessary for all our actual knowledge [*connoissances actuelles*]" (A VI.6: 49, my underlining). Indeed, we can hear in Kant's own introductory remarks echoes of Leibniz's claim that "the soul originally contains the sources of various notions and doctrines, which external objects merely awaken [*réveillent*] on suitable occasions" (A VI.6: 48, my underlining):

> For how else should the cognitive faculty be awakened [*erweckt*] to exercise, if not through objects that rouse [*rühren*] our senses [...]? (B1.7–9, my underlining)

And:

> It could well be that even our experiential knowledge is a composite of that which we receive through impressions and that which our own cognitive faculty (merely occasioned [*veranlaßt*] by sensible impressions) brings forth [*hergibt*] out of itself[.] (B1.19–23, my underlining)

Human knowledge must doubtless involve a transition from mere potentiality to actuality, even if certain ideas and principles have their source in the mind's own innate dispositions.[5]

its Arabic and Latin receptions. His Aristotelianism is of a later vintage. See the excellent collection edited by Gobsch and Land (forthcoming).

[3] I am grateful to Robert Pippin for pressing me, long ago, to address the place of a *nous pathetikos* in Kant's epistemology.

[4] See Look (2022, 21–26), who also cites Vaihinger (1881, I:48); Tonelli (1974, 437); and Schmucker (1976).

[5] Indeed, Kant argues the forms of sensibility, the categories, the principles, and the ideas of reason have just such a source. Kant admittedly denies that any representations are innate in the sense of being "implanted" – "eingepflanzt" (B167.23–24, B168.2) or "anerschaffen" (*Discovery* 8:221.26;

All knowledge that must come to be – all knowledge that essentially involves a transition from potentiality to actuality – requires a sort of receptivity. For a cognitive capacity that is not "always already" actualized is not realized in all conditions. It is realized (or realized in a determinate way) under certain conditions but not others. It must therefore involve a sensitivity to the conditions that obtain, such that it is actualized (at all or in a determinate way) in certain conditions but not others. This sensitivity must be a receptivity to conditions external to the faculty. For if the conditions that trigger its exercise were internal to the faculty, it would always be actualized and would never be in a state of mere potentiality and, thus, never transition from potentiality to actuality.

This shows that the human mind must possess the receptivity of a *nous pathetikos*. But it does not yet show that it must exhibit the receptivity that Kant attributes to sensible intuition. Sensible intuition, for Kant, is not just the mind's susceptibility to be "roused" into intellectual activity. It is a receptivity to *representations* – representations that make a positive contribution to cognition by "giving objects to thought". Intuitions are supposed to positively contribute to cognition in the sense that they account for the determinacy of thought-contents and secure thought's status *as* cognition in establishing thought's connection with knowable objects.[6] Yet for all that has been said thus far, sense experience might serve, like oxygen and other necessities of life, as an external and merely enabling condition for the mind to realize its own innate cognitive dispositions and to unfold contents that arise from its own activity. To invert Kant's formulation, human knowledge might be "merely occasioned by sensible impressions" (B1.22–23) without "on that account [...] arising **from** experience" (B1.18–19). Such receptivity is compatible with even the most cartoonish picture of the Leibnizian monad as a cognitive coil that, once triggered (either through sensory stimulus or divine caress), unspools the entirety of its mental life from its own complete notion in an extended

M-Vi/K_3, 1794–1795, 29:959.11) – a position he associates with Leibniz (*Discovery* 8:223n.34–36; M-Vi/K_3 29:959.9–14; cf. B167.27). Yet a charitable reading of Leibniz and close attention to Kant's account of "original acquisition" suggests that their views largely coincide; see Vanzo (2018) and Jauernig (2019, 65–67). Kant introduces original acquisition in *Discovery* 8:221–225; cf. M-Vi/K_3 (1794/95) 29:949–954; letter to Kosmann, September 1789, 11:82.1–21. I discuss original acquisition in Section 4.2.

[6] I do not mean to suggest that sensible intuitions can perform these cognitive feats on their own, independent of intellectual activity. The point is just that (i) we must appeal to something beyond our powers of intellection and the receptivity of a *nous pathetikos* to explain the determinate content and objective validity of material cognition and (ii) what we must appeal to involves a *further* sort of receptivity that Kant ascribes to sensible intuition.

spasm of self-activity. The receptivity of a *nous pathetikos* need only provide an *occasion* on which we acquire knowledge (perhaps from our own internal resources), whereas sensibility is supposed to be a *source from which* knowledge can be acquired.

To establish a form of specifically *cognitive* receptivity – a receptivity internal to the process of cognizing and not merely an enabling condition for its exercise – we must look to Kant's distinction between analytic and synthetic judgments. This is not altogether surprising, since Kant touts this distinction, along with his sensibility/understanding doctrine, as one of his greatest contributions to philosophy and since sensible intuition is central to his account of how synthetic judgments are possible (cf. A158/B197.4–7). There is a rich literature on the development and import of Kant's analytic/synthetic distinction, but the features of Kant's discussion that will concern us are uncontroversial.

2.2 Analyticity and Intellectual Grounds of Truth

Kant holds that a subject-predicate judgment, <*A is B*>, is analytic just in case "the predicate B belongs to the subject A as something that is contained (in a hidden manner) in this concept A" (A6/B10.13–15).[7] The judgment is synthetic, by contrast, just in case "it adds to the concept of the subject a predicate that is not at all thought in it and which no analysis could extract from it" (A7/B11.28–01). What is significant about this distinction for our purposes is that the truth of an analytic judgment is cognized through the subject concept of the judgment itself. This is why all analytic judgments are a priori:

> For it would be wrongheaded [*ungereimt*] to base [*gründen*] an analytic judgment on experience, because I may not [*darf nicht*] go outside my concept in order to formulate [*abzufassen*] the judgment, and therefore need no testimony of experience to do so. That a body is extended is a proposition that holds a priori and no judgment of experience. For before I go to experience, I have all the conditions for my judgment already in the concept, out of which I only extract the predicate in accordance with the principle of contradiction, and by this means I can at the same time become conscious of the necessity of the judgment, which experience would never even teach me. (B11f.15–25; *Prolegomena* 4:268.1–10)

[7] I follow Kant in focusing on affirmative, categorical judgments. Though it is non-trivial to extend Kant's account of analyticity to other forms of judgment, such complications do not affect my argument here.

This passage concerns not just how we come to *know* an analytic judgment is true but also what *makes* it true in the first place. That the subject concept contains the predicate concept not only provides me an epistemic means to verify *that* the proposition is true – namely, analysis "in accordance with the principle of contradiction" – it also constitutes the underlying reason *why* the proposition is true.[8] Analytic judgments contain the grounds of their own truth.[9] The reason bodies are extended is that corporeality partly *consists in* extension: Being extended is part of what *makes* something a *body*. That is to say, <extended> is one of the criterial marks in virtue of which the concept <body> applies. The predicative combination of these concepts in the judgment is grounded in the fact that they are already combined in the concept itself as hierarchically nested discursive marks.

Now, it may be tempting to interpret this passage as making the principally epistemological point that analytical truths can come to be known by "extract[ing] the predicate in accordance with the principle of contradiction". This reading is attractive because there is so little discursive distance between the concept <body> and the concept <extended>. But Kant's examples of analytic judgments involving empirical concepts make this reading difficult to sustain. Consider the judgment, *<air is an elastic fluid, whose elasticity is not eliminated by any known degree of cold>*, which Kant identifies as analytic (*Prolegomena* 4:273.25–26). One is hardly likely to frame this thought by "extract[ing] the predicate" from one's pre-theoretical concept of air! Rather, if the concept <air> analytically contains this complex of predicates, that is surely because we have adapted our concept <air> in response to the sorts of experimental findings for which Kant praises Torricelli (Bxiif.2–7; cf. *Prolegomena* 4:267.20). This does not mean that the *judgment* is empirical, however. It means that we have

[8] Kant calls the grounds of analytic judgments "logical grounds", which he distinguishes from the "real grounds" that support synthetic judgments. See M-Mr 29:807.12–26; M-Vo 28:402.28–403.39; M-Pö/L_2 28:548–550; M-Schön 28:486–487. Kant's logical grounds differ from Crusius's "ideal grounds" in that they are not mere grounds of cognition (as Crusius would have it) but also grounds of truth. See M-H (1762–1764) 28:12 and M-Mr 29:809.19–24. For discussion, see Stang (2016, ch. 3), and Melamedoff-Vosters (2023). Heidegger also frames the analytic/synthetic distinction in terms of grounds of truth – albeit only in his 1926–1927 lectures (GA 25:48–51), not in the resulting Kant book.

[9] In claiming that analytic judgments contain the grounds of their own truth, I do not mean to be taking a position on whether analytic judgments are true in virtue of agreeing with their objects (per Lu-Adler 2013; cf. Paton 1936, 84–86, 213–221) or whether they are purely formal and enjoy a special, syntactic sort of truth (per Tolley 2007, 418–439) or no truth value at all (Rosenkoetter 2008). The objective purport of analytic judgments will, however, become relevant later (Section 4.3); see also note 31 of the present chapter.

determined to treat certain empirical properties as criterial marks for the proper application of the concept <air>.[10] Accordingly, it means that the analyticity of the judgment reflects the fact that the subject concept <air> constitutes a ground of truth, not merely a ground of cognition. The *reason* air is an elastic fluid (etc.) is because being air partly *consists in* elastic fluidity (etc.) – that is, <elasticity> and <fluidity> are among the criterial marks in virtue of which the concept <air> applies.

So the analyticity of a judgment amounts to more than the epistemological criterion that we can verify a proposition through conceptual analysis in accordance with the principle of contradiction. For such analysis may be quite impractical, as in the case of <*air is an elastic fluid*> and similar analytic truths about natural kinds. What is special about an analytic judgment is that the concepts in the judgment themselves constitute the ground of the truth of the proposition and the source of its necessity.

This is the core insight I want to draw from Kant's discussion of analyticity. In an analytic judgment, the ground of truth is provided by the intellect itself, qua faculty of concepts. This helps to explain the otherwise curious formulation that Kant repeats in the present discussion of analytic judgment: "I may not [*darf nicht*] go outside my concept in order to formulate the judgment" (B11.16–17; my underlining, cf. A7.2–3, B11.3–4). Translators tend to give this the sense of "I *need not* go outside my concept", and this is certainly a possible reading.[11] But

10 Kant outlines how we can reform given empirical concepts in light of experience in various places, including the Discipline (A728/B756.25–15; I discuss this in Section 4.4, note 31). This has suggested a "recuperation strategy" for making certain empirical judgments analytic. In the wake of Quine's attack on analyticity (Quine 1980 [1951]), Lewis White Beck (1965 [1955]) generalizes this into a threat to the analytic-synthetic distinction itself, as does Anderson (2015, 29–32, 141–142, 189–195), both of them citing pre-critical Reflections (viz. R3920, 1769, 17:345.7–19 and R2928, 1769, 17:350.2–20). I think this threat is overblown. Schultz's 1790 response to Eberhard and Maaß (20:408–409), which was written in close consultation with Kant, as well as Kant's exchange with J. S. Beck (3 July 1792, 11:347.2–26) show that this recuperation strategy provides no succor to the rationalist who wishes to reduce all synthetic judgments to analytic ones, nor to the Quinean empiricist who wishes to reduce all judgments to empirical claims. First, not all synthetic judgments can be "recuperated" in this manner: mathematical judgments, existential judgments, and judgments employing "given" (as opposed to "elective [*willkürliche*]") concepts cannot. Second, a "recuperated" analytic judgment presupposes the prior availability of synthetic judgments that supply the content of the relevant subject concept and secure the objective validity of that content. The recuperation strategy is a peripheral curiosity in Kant's system – a consequence of our ability to spontaneously contrive new concepts as we "compel nature to answer [our] questions" (Bxiii). Nonetheless, the possibility of converting (some) synthetic judgments into analytic ones helps to underscore that a judgment is analytic, in the fundamental sense, when its ground of truth lies in the *concepts* it employs.

11 Kemp Smith, Pluhar, and Guyer and Wood all pursue this line.

I think Kant may intend the stronger claim: "I *ought not* go beyond my concept." For in an analytic judgment, my concept is not only a ground of *cognition*, i.e. a *sufficient* means by which I can verify the proposition. It is the ground of the *truth* of the proposition, and thus the *exclusive* source (i.e. a necessary condition) of the validity and necessity of the judgment. The concept is at once a ground of cognition *and* a ground of truth. To look beyond the subject concept, therefore, is not only unnecessary but "wrongheaded [*ungereimt*]". The reason that "I may not go outside my concept" is because there is no other way that "I can at the same time become conscious of the necessity of the judgment" (B12.23–24).

Though Kant's discussions of analyticity tend to focus on judgments that have the affirmative and categorical form, <*A is B*>, he clearly intends his account to generalize to analytic judgments of any logical form (e.g. <*if A is BC, then A is C*>; <*A is B or A is not B*>, and so on). It is difficult to see how Kant's remarks about conceptual containment, which apply so naturally to categorical judgments, might be adapted to capture the analyticity of non-categorical judgments.[12] But our core insight into the

[12] Hypothetical judgments are especially tricky, since the antecedent and consequent may not have any concepts in common, in which case the conceptual-containment criterion of analyticity cannot apply. But some hypothetical judgments may yet turn out to be containment-analytic. For instance, <*if there is perfect justice, the obstinately wicked will be punished*> (A73/B98.22–24) might plausibly spell out a containment relation between the concept <perfect justice> and the concepts <obstinately wicked> and <punishment>. Certainly, this is not much harder to accept than the containment-analyticity of <*air is an elastic fluid whose elasticity is eliminated by no known degree of cold*>. Hypothetical judgments that do not hold in virtue of conceptual containment must either be synthetic, or analytic in some other sense – for example, true in virtue of the laws of PGL or, as I have suggested, in virtue of containing the grounds of their own truth. In his unmatched account of containment-analyticity, Anderson (2015, 99–107) argues that it is a shortcoming of Kant's conception of containment-analyticity that it cannot capture the formal validity of hypothetical syllogisms. Here I think Anderson overestimates the ambition of Kant's analytic/synthetic distinction and underestimates the power of his (Anderson's) own reconstruction of containment-analyticity. It is not obvious to me that Kant shares the contemporary view that a valid inference can always be re-formulated as an analytic hypothetical judgment, with the conjunction of its premises as antecedent and the conclusion as consequent. Thus, Kant's recognition (e.g. L-Jäsche 9:129) that hypothetical *syllogisms* do not have a middle term and therefore do not rest on conceptual containment but on the principle of sufficient reason, need not pose a "dilemma" for his account of analytic judgments. For if he is not committed to the idea that a valid syllogism can always be expressed as a complex analytic judgment, he need not grant that there are analytic judgments (viz. those that re-formulate valid hypothetical syllogisms) that are not containment-analytic. Though Kant does regard PGL as analytic in some sense (cf. A76/B102.10–14), the fact that the analytic/synthetic distinction is concerned with the *content* of concepts suggests that it has no significant role to play in PGL (cf. *Prolegomena* 4:266.15–23, 270.5–8; L-Jäsche §§ 18–19 and 36, 9:101, 111). So Anderson's demand that containment-analyticity should provide a criterion of logical validity for inferences strikes me as excessive. I think it is plausible that Kant would regard as synthetic any hypothetical or disjunctive judgment that is not containment-analytic, as Anderson reconstructs this notion. At any rate, it is natural for Kant to treat conceptual containment as a privileged form of analyticity in an

nature of analyticity should still hold: A judgment is analytic just in case it contains the ground of its own truth, i.e. just in case the ground of its truth is provided by the intellect. When Kant claims that analytic judgments are cognized through the principle of identity or the principle of contradiction, his point is that anyone who has mastered the concepts deployed in the judgment is in a position to recognize the judgment as true. For those concepts, mediated by the relevant logical forms, ground the truth of the proposition. So anyone who understands those concepts and is suitably adept in formal logic can acquire a consciousness of the necessity of the judgment solely by drawing on her powers of intellection – that is, her capacity to frame concepts and to manipulate them according to logical principles. Analytic judgments are, in this sense, conceptual truths, purely intellectual cognitions. In an analytic judgment, the understanding – as a faculty of concepts and their logical manipulation – is a self-sufficient source of knowledge.

2.3 Synthetic Judgment and Intuition

To distinguish synthetic from analytic judgments, then, is to identify a class of truths for which our understanding, qua faculty of concepts, is *not* a self-sufficient source of knowledge. In particular, it is to claim that the ground of truth for some judgments is not provided by the concepts employed in the judgment. Such judgments are not true merely in virtue of the concepts they employ. Accordingly, we cannot know them to be true merely by exercising our faculty of conceptual understanding. Rather, knowledge of synthetic truths requires, in addition, a cognitive capacity that gives us epistemic access to extra-conceptual grounds of truth, i.e. a capacity for intuition. This, I submit, is the rationale underlying Kant's distinction between the "two stems of human cognition" at the conclusion of the Introduction.[13] As Kant puts it in the A edition, commenting on the analytic/synthetic distinction:

epistemological context such as the *Critique*, since categorical judgments are the ultimate constituents of all complex judgments (A73/B98.19–22; *Prolegomena* 4:325n.31–32). And if one demands a more general account of analyticity than conceptual containment can provide, one can always look to the logical principles that Kant associates with categorical, hypothetical, and disjunctive syllogisms: respectively, the principle of contradiction (or identity), the principle of sufficient reason, and the principle of excluded middle. An analytic judgment, in this more capacious sense, is one that can be cognized through those principles of PGL.

[13] Though Kant labels one of these stems "sensibility" (A15/B29.10), I think we must regard this designation as anticipatory. What he actually describes is a capacity for *intuition* (see my discussion

> Now it is clear from this (1) that our cognition is not extended through analytic judgments [. . .] and (2) that in the case of synthetic judgments I must have, apart from [*außer*] the concept of the subject, something else in addition (X), on which the understanding relies [*sich stützt*] in order to cognize a predicate that is not contained in that concept as nevertheless belonging to it. (A8.13–20; cf. A9.28–03, B13.2–6)

Kant's claim here is that the very idea of synthetic judgment points up a cognitive function that the faculty of concepts cannot fulfill. Kant describes this function in conspicuously indirect and schematic terms. Knowledge of synthetic truths requires "something else in addition (*X*)".[14] About this *X*, we know only that (i) it is not my concept of the subject (nor, presumably, any other concept employed in the judgment) and (ii) it is something that the understanding can "rely on" in justifying its judgment, i.e. in "cogni[zing]" the relevant combination of concepts. So *X* is a ground of truth for the proposition and, though not itself a concept, it is also a cognitive ground – something on which the understanding can base its cognition. Whatever provides this *X* will therefore be a cognitive capacity – a source of cognitive grounds – that is distinct from the understanding, as the faculty of concepts. And its role will be to provide the understanding with cognitive access to grounds of truth for judgments in those cases when the concepts employed in the judgment do not themselves provide such grounds of truth. On this account, then, the fundamental role of intuition, as a cognitive capacity, is to pick up the understanding's cognitive slack.[15]

I will call this the "baseline account" of human intuition, in order to indicate (i) that it is the central conception with which the *Critique* operates but also (ii) that Kant refines and enriches this conception as his argument progresses. Intuition is a capacity that enables us to cognize

of "top-down" approaches in Section 2.4). That our capacity for intuition is sensible is one of Kant's early claims in the Aesthetic, which I discuss in Chapter 3.

[14] See also Kant's characterizations of synthetic judgment as relying on a "third thing", in addition to the subject and predicate concepts: A155/B194.28–32, A157/B196.13–17, A216f./B263f.9–32, A259/B315.29–33, A732/B760.26–30, A733/B761.4–11, A766/B794.3–10; *Prolegomena* 4:269.34–37; *Discovery* 8:245.14–21. This "third thing" is, I take it, an intuitive representation.

[15] Intuition, on this account, is an essentially epistemic notion, defined in terms of its function in enabling our knowledge of synthetic judgments. It is this defining function that constitutes intuition as a *cognitive* capacity. There is, of course, a difference between Kantian cognition (*Erkenntnis*) and knowledge (*Wissen*). But the former constitutively aims at, and should be understood in terms of its contribution to, the latter. Our acts of intuiting do not, as such, count as knowledge, since they do not involve judgment. Yet intuitings do count as cognition insofar as they are capable of promoting knowledgeable judgment. This aligns with the cognition/knowledge distinction drawn in Watkins and Willaschek (2017, 2020 [2017]), but challenges their conception of intuition as serving a merely semantic role.

synthetic propositions. This capacity cannot be our faculty of concepts, since concepts do not constitute grounds of truth for synthetic propositions. So intuition is a cognition-enabling capacity distinct from the understanding that provides us epistemic access to grounds of truth for synthetic propositions.

This baseline account is a direct consequence of Kant's distinction between analytic and synthetic judgments. Kant makes this explicit in responding to Eberhard's attacks on both distinctions:

> For the term 'synthetic' clearly indicates that something outside the given concept must be added as a substratum that makes it possible to go beyond it [the given concept] with my predicates; accordingly the investigation of the possibility of a synthesis of representations aimed at promoting cognition in general must soon lead to [*bald dahin ausschlagen mußte*] the acknowledgment of intuition – and, for a priori cognition, pure intuition – as the indispensable conditions of the same [sc. synthesis]. (*Discovery* 8:245.14–21)[16]

It is thus a direct corollary of the analytic/synthetic distinction that "there are two stems of human knowledge". This helps to explain Kant's almost perfunctory formulation of that monumentally important distinction at the end of the Introduction:

> The only thing that seems necessary by way of introduction or preliminary [*Vorerinnerung*] is that there are two stems of human knowledge, which perhaps spring from a common but to us unknown root, namely sensibility and understanding, through the first of which objects are **given** to us, while they are **thought** through the second. (A15/B29.6–12, Kant's emphases)

Kant's casual tone and the brevity of his discussion hardly seem consonant with the profound significance of the sensibility/understanding distinction for his critical philosophy or with the fact that, as Kant himself is keen to emphasize, his version of the distinction diverges from the foremost contemporaneous accounts of the higher and lower cognitive faculties (A271/B327.15–23). But if Kant viewed this distinction as a direct consequence of the analytic/synthetic distinction, he is merely highlighting an implication of something he has just discussed at length (viz. A6–A10, B10–B22). Though much remains to be determined about what cognitive access to extra-conceptual grounds of truth involves (what it means for "objects" to be "given") and whether we humans actually possess such a

[16] Kant makes this same move from the possibility of synthetic judgment to the need for intuition at *Prolegomena* 4:281.14–21; *Progress* 20:339.19–21; R4275 (1770–1771) 18:492.3–4.

capacity (whether "objects are given to us"), the *idea* of such a capacity is implicated in the idea of knowledgeable synthetic judgment. Thus, an account of this capacity for intuition – a Transcendental Aesthetic – is an indispensable part of explaining how synthetic judgments a priori can be knowable for us humans.

2.4 Features and Advantages of This Interpretation

Before we consider the apperceptive credentials of this baseline account of intuition, it is worth pausing to highlight some distinctive features and interpretive advantages of the present approach.

First, it provides a new way of understanding Kant's standard formulation that sensibility is the capacity through which "objects are given to us".[17] This formulation has led to debates about whether and in what sense intuitings are object-dependent.[18] For Kant appears to hold that mathematical constructions, imaginings, and hallucinations are (or involve) intuitions; yet such mental acts need not entail the real existence of their objects.[19] And if the relevant objects do not exist, it is hard to make out in what sense they can be "given" to the mind or how being "given" in that way can enable cognition. By characterizing the contribution of intuition in terms of providing cognitive access to grounds of truth, however, we can make some headway on these questions.

On the present account, the "object" that is given is the ground of the truth of the relevant synthetic proposition(s), and its being "given" consists in one's having cognitive access to that ground of truth – that is, in its being a ground of cognition, its providing one with an epistemic warrant for the relevant synthetic judgment. This enables us to acknowledge that the "objects" we intuit and the manner in which they are "given" to us can be as varied as the grounds that make synthetic judgments true and that justify us in formulating such judgments. This account is agnostic about the phenomenological character of givenness and about the ontological status and ontic character of the objects that are thus given. It remains an open question whether having a cognitive ground (an epistemic warrant)

[17] A15/B29.10–11, A19/B33.9–10, A50/B74.8–15; cf. *Prolegomena* 4:281.32–282.03.

[18] For instance, Stephenson (2015, 2017); Chignell (2017); Grüne (2017); McLear (2017).

[19] Indeed, Kant often seems to define imagination as intuition in the absence of the object or without the presence of the object. Stephenson (2015) cites *Anthropology* 7:153.21–23, 167.20–21; R225 (1783–1784) 15:86.4–5; M-Mr 29:881.14–16; M-DW (1792/93) 28:673.36–37; M-Pö/L_1 28:230.8–24; M-Pö/L_2 28:585.1–4; L-DW 24:701.33–702.2, 705.9–12.

requires a certain sort of phenomenological experience, and whether grounds of truth must enjoy a certain ontological status. Those are matters for further argumentation; they play no part in the baseline conception of human intuition. The baseline conception states only that knowledge of synthetic propositions requires a capacity that provides cognition-enabling access to extra-conceptual grounds of truth.

Many problem cases for object-dependent interpretations of intuition can be captured in these terms. For instance, it should be uncontroversial that a mathematical construction, such as a geometrical diagram, can provide us with cognitive access to a ground of truth for the proposition that it demonstrates, regardless of the ontological status we may assign to "mathematical objects". Similarly, imaginings can, in the right circumstances, provide grounds of truth about what is not just logically but really (metaphysically) possible, even when it is obvious that the object one is imagining does not actually exist.

It is also important to note that grounds of truth are proposition specific. So a mental state may count as intuitive in certain respects but not in others, inasmuch as it provides grounds of truth for some propositions but not others. For instance, a hallucinatory episode may provide cognitive access to grounds of truth for synthetic propositions concerning one's own mental state or one's recent pharmacological intake, even if it fails to provide grounds of truth for various synthetic propositions about its intentional objects. In short, the baseline conception of intuition offers us a plausible and univocal account of intuitive givenness – in terms of cognitive access to grounds of truth for synthetic judgments – that can accommodate the problem cases that vex object-dependent interpretations.

A second significant feature of the present interpretation is that it is couched at the level of the cognitive *capacity* rather than at the level of its acts. Just as the analytic/synthetic distinction pertains to general classes of judgments, the sensibility/understanding distinction pertains to the general cognitive functions that must be met if such judgments are to be knowledgeable. In order to be knowledgeable, analytic judgments need only draw upon a cognitive faculty of concepts and their logical combination and manipulation in judgments, whereas synthetic judgments implicate a further capacity for cognitive access to extra-conceptual grounds of truth.

Now, as we saw in Chapter 1 (Sections 1.2.2 and 1.3.2), it is a familiar feature of the logic of capacities that particular acts may fail to fully realize the function that defines the capacity from which they spring. On a capacity-level approach, the nature of human intuition does not reside in the "greatest common factor" that particular acts of intuiting actually share but in the fully elaborated cognitive function with reference to which they are identifiable as exercises of human intuition, qua cognitive capacity. Thus, the failure of particular acts of intuition to exhibit certain features is not, in itself, evidence that those features are inessential to intuition. Rather, the features that are essential to intuitions, as such, are determined by the cognitive role that the *capacity* is to play in enabling synthetic knowledge. To identify a particular act as an intuition is to understand it in light of the cognitive role that defines intuition as a cognitive capacity. Even if the act in question does not fully satisfy its cognitive obligations, its status as *failing to do so* is itself intelligible only with reference to the cognitive role that defines the capacity to which it belongs.

This provides us with a further line of response to the problem cases that object-dependent interpretations struggle to account for. In order to qualify as an intuition, a mental act only needs to be recognizable as an exercise of the relevant cognitive capacity. While this does mean characterizing the act in light of the cognitive function that defines that capacity, it does not mean the act must fully satisfy the relevant function. Hallucination is arguably a case in point. Only a mind capable of veridical perception is capable of hallucination.[20] Indeed, a mental episode counts as hallucinatory only insofar as it *purports* to satisfy the function that defines the capacity for perception. That is what justifies one in characterizing it as a case of sensible intuition, i.e. as an act of the very same capacity whose defining function is to provide veridical sense perceptions. So while it is important to highlight those cognitive functions that a given act does satisfy, and which are essential to its status as an intuition, it is equally important not to take a particular act's failure to satisfy other functions as proof that the latter are inessential to sensible intuition.[21] For the essence

[20] Note that the baseline conception of human intuition does *not* include the idea of veridical perception. This is a characterization of sensibility that first comes into view in the Aesthetic and whose vindication requires both the Transcendental Deduction and the Analytic of Principles (notably, the Anticipations of Perception and the Refutation of Idealism). I am invoking veridical perception only to illustrate the interpretive advantages of a capacity-level account of intuition over an act-level account.

[21] Thus, Stephenson's account of Kant on hallucination provides valuable insights into the role of sensation and imagination in sensible intuition (2015, esp. 496–505). But the case-based reasoning he employs, couched as it is at the level of particular *acts*, cannot deliver the general conclusion about the *essence* of sensible intuition that Stephenson wants. Stephenson succeeds in showing that some *acts* of intuition are not object-dependent in the strong sense demanded by interpreters who regard Kant as a naïve realist or relationalist about perception (e.g. Hanna 2005, 2008; Allais 2009). But this does not settle whether Kant conceives of sensible intuition as a *capacity* for representations that are object-dependent in this strong sense. Though I agree with many of Stephenson's

of intuition is to be sought at the level of the capacity, in the cognitive function it must perform to enable synthetic knowledge.

Third, by treating the sensibility/understanding distinction as a corollary of the analytic/synthetic distinction, we develop what I will call a "top-down" approach to our lower cognitive capacity, human sensible intuition. The baseline conception is couched in terms of intuition's contribution to cognition and, more specifically, in relation to the cognitive functions of the understanding, as a faculty of concepts. It is with reference to this prior conception of what cognition is and of what the understanding can contribute to cognition that we frame the baseline account of intuition. We thus proceed *from* an account of the higher cognitive faculty – namely, the understanding as a faculty of concepts and their logical employment in judgments – *to* an account of the lower cognitive capacity – namely, the human capacity for sensible intuition. This top-down orientation is a matter of conceptual dependence and need not be directly reflected in the order of exposition.[22] The account of the higher faculty "comes first" not in the sense that it has to be articulated before one can turn to consideration of the lower capacity but in the sense that the account of the lower cognitive capacity is couched in terms that are only intelligible by reference to the higher faculty with which it contrasts and cooperates. This often results in merely "negative" or "indirect" formulations, such as the description of intuition as providing the "something else in addition (X)" required for synthetic judgments to be knowledgeable (A8.17–18). A top-down approach thus contrasts with a bottom-up account that would characterize sensible intuition in positive terms that are intelligible independent of any reference to cognition or to the understanding – for

conclusions about the nature of intuition, I do not think his arguments are pitched at the appropriate level to establish them. I think this sort of casuistical, case-based reasoning similarly undermines the avowed commitment to a "capacities-first" approach in McLear (2016).

[22] In order of exposition, of course, Kant's account of sensible intuition in the Transcendental Aesthetic precedes his account of the understanding in the Transcendental Logic (cf. A16/B30.15–20). But Kant was apparently untroubled by J. S. Beck's proposal to "reverse the method of the critique": namely, by beginning with the principle of apperception (the possibility of self-attributing any of my representations) and the deduction of the categories and only then "leading [the reader] to the adjudication of the Critique of p[ure] r[eason] in its Introduction, Aesthetic, and Analytic" (Beck to Kant, 17 June 1794, 11:510.24–34; cf. Beck 1796). Kant indicates his tacit approval by saying that he has "at the moment nothing to reply" to the proposal "apart from the following [two] brief remarks", neither of which addresses the reversed order of presentation (Kant to Beck, 1 July 1794, 11:514.29–515.2; see also Kant's comments about Beck, drafted for Tieftrunk, October 1797, 13:493). My present claim is that, regardless of order of exposition, there is a privileged line of thought in Kant, on which an account of the understanding is conceptually prior to an account of intuition: namely, a line of thought that draws on pure apperception to develop the idea of a cognitive capacity for sensible intuition.

example, when sensible intuition is introduced as a capacity for representing particulars, or for phenomenologically vivacious representations, or for having one's representational state modified through sensory affection, or for veridical perception.

One way to bring out the significance of this top-down orientation is to reflect on the fact that the terms 'sensibility' and 'intuition' suggest quite different concepts, both on their face and in the philosophical tradition.[23] If Kant seems at times to use the terms interchangeably, he is thereby expressing a substantive philosophical position, and he is nonetheless aware of the conceptual distance between them. (If he considered the terms synonymous, his myriad references to intellectual intuition would make no sense.) Sensibility has to do with sensation and sense perception, sentience and embodiment. It is a capacity that alienates us from the angels and affiliates us with the brutes.[24] Intuition, by contrast, is an intrinsically cognitive notion, indicating an especially intimate epistemic relation to an object of knowledge.[25] These capacities need not coincide. For instance, Kant says that Plato "posited a pure intuition of the non-sensible or = a supersensible intuition and assumed that the soul, before it fell into its corporeal state, possessed the capacity for intuition of the divine".[26] The

[23] This point is well emphasized by Hintikka (1969, 40–42, 46–47). Hintikka's ensuing attempt to drive a wedge between Kantian intuition and sensibility is, however, quite contrary to the interpretation I am developing.

[24] Philosophical *theories* of sensibility and sensible representation can, of course, vary considerably, since they implicate a variety of theoretical issues – concerning causation, the mind–body relation, consciousness, and so forth. My point is that all such theories, however diverse, seek to explain (or explain away) the same *explanandum*: the bodily mediated awareness of their environs and corporeal states that embodied sentient creatures seem to enjoy.

[25] As Allais rightly insists, "the fundamental contrast between intuitions and concepts is epistemological (it concerns different kinds of mental representations and the roles they play in cognition)" (Allais 2015, 146, my underlining). This point is often neglected in discussions of Kant's views on animal minds. Commentators often ascribe intuitions to non-rational animals on the grounds that they have sensible representations – or, more precisely, sensible representations that represent particulars in a phenomenologically immediate manner (e.g. McLear 2011, 2020; Golob 2020). The interpretation of Kantian intuition I am developing suggests this is a mistake. If non-human animals are incapable of cognition and knowledge, as Kant clearly holds, then they cannot enjoy cognitive access to grounds of truth for synthetic judgments – that is, they lack a capacity for intuition. To my knowledge, the term "Anschauung" appears in connection with non-human animals just four times in Kant's corpus. The only passage in Kant's own hand is ambiguous (*Postumum*, c.1801, 21:82.30–32). Two passages from student lecture notes are inconclusive: One is ambiguous (M-Vo 28:449), the other a likely student interpolation (L-DW, 1792, 24:702.12–14). The only unambiguous attribution I can find is M-Pö/L_2 28:594.32–33. For discussion of these passages, see the Extra Materials section on my website: https://wesleyan.academia.edu/DanielSmyth.

[26] M-Vi/K_3 (1794/95) 29:950.25–29, cf. 953.36–954.18, 957.25–29; R4449 (c. 1771) 17:555.18–20; cf. R4446 (1771?) 18:554.1; M-Pö/L_1 28:232.23–27, 241.15–24. Kant consistently glosses Plato's theory of ideas in terms of an *intuition* of intellectualia or

conceptual difference between a capacity for sensibility and a capacity for intuition comes out quite clearly in Kant's 1782/83 lectures on metaphysics:

> [O]ur intuition is sensible. – It rests on receptivity, on openness [*Empfänglichkeit*] to being affected by things. We can think of a being that intuits through spontaneity of its own power, through itself without being affected by objects, as one imagines God; we cannot comprehend [*einsehen*] how this is possible except perhaps through the cognitive power's producing things, for he [God] affected them, not they him; but we have no concepts of this: our intuition is receptivity. (M-Mr 29:800.9–17, cf. 759.36–760.10, 796.39–797.21, 880.30–35, 888.10–17; A252.11–13)

Intuition is a cognitive capacity that "gives objects" to the mind in the sense that it provides cognitive access to grounds of truth. This is as true of divine intuition as it is of sensible intuition. Sensibility, by contrast, is a passive capacity (a receptivity) for having one's representational state modified through sensory affection. In interpreting Kant's position, therefore, we must distinguish several substantive philosophical theses: (i) Humans have a capacity for intuition. (ii) Human sensibility is a capacity for intuition. And (iii) Sensibility is our sole capacity for intuition. Kant is careful to track these distinctions in the opening of the B-edition Aesthetic:

> [Intuition] only takes place insofar as the object is given to us; but this, in turn, is only possible, for us humans at least, through the object's affecting the mind [*das Gemüt*] in a certain way. The ability (receptivity) to receive representations through the manner in which we are affected by objects is called **sensibility**. (B33.9–14; underlined phrase added in B-edition)

We will consider this passage at length in Chapter 3. For now, my aim is to clarify what is distinctive about a top-down approach to sensible intuition by invoking this notional distinction between sensibility and intuition. A top-down approach begins with a conception of intuition – which is an intrinsically cognitive notion – and proceeds to identify those features that give human intuition a specifically sensible form. A bottom-up approach, by contrast, begins with a conception of sensibility – which is *not* an

supersensibles. Note, however, that the "mystical" intuition he finds in Plato is not the spontaneous or productive mode of intuition that Kant attributes to an *intellectus archetypus* or intuitive understanding. It is a non-sensible but still *receptive* mode of intuition, of the sort Kant sometimes suggests we may enjoy after death, when the soul is separated from the body (M-Pö/L$_1$ 28:297.30–298.17; M-Mr 29:919; M-Vo 28:445 f.). On the receptivity/sensibility distinction, see Chapter 8.

intrinsically cognitive notion – and then seeks out those features that would elevate it into a sort of intuition. The baseline account of sensible intuition we have been developing belongs to a top-down approach in this sense. As a corollary of the analytic/synthetic distinction, the baseline conception is a fundamentally cognitive notion: It describes a capacity for gaining epistemic access to extra-conceptual grounds of truth. This is, in the first instance, a conception of intuition and not (i.e. not *yet*) a conception of sensibility. It is a conception that emerges from a general consideration of what cognition involves – namely, epistemic access to grounds of truth – and what the understanding can supply – namely, epistemic access to *analytic* grounds of truth, in the form of concepts that can be combined into judgments and manipulated according to certain logical rules.

In advocating a top-down reading of Kant's account of sensible intuition, I am not denying the presence or importance of bottom-up arguments in his corpus. Kant has a multidimensional and mutually buttressing vision of how things, in the broadest sense of the term, hang together, in the broadest sense of the term. My aim is to identify one line of force within this structure and to argue that it has special significance for Kant's critical philosophy, insofar as it exemplifies a special form of reason's self-knowledge.

2.5 Self-Consciously Tracking the Truth

Thus far, I have argued that intuition, as a cognitive capacity, is what makes synthetic judgments possible by providing "that on which I rely [*mich stütze*] and through which the synthesis is possible" "when I am supposed to go beyond [A9.13: outside] the concept *A* in order to cognize another concept *B* as combined with it" (A9/B12f.19–22). Kant's baseline conception of intuition is a direct consequence of his analytic/synthetic distinction. But we have yet to consider Kant's arguments for applying these distinctions and conceptions to our (human) mind – that is, his reasons for thinking that we actually make irreducibly synthetic judgments and thus possess a capacity of intuition. In particular, we have yet to consider how our possession of such a capacity might come to light through pure apperception: through mere reflection on the principles that are constitutive of and implicit in any act of objective cognition as such.

Now, Kant presents a variety of considerations in defending the validity and irreducibility of the analytic/synthetic distinction, which commentators have reconstructed and refined in marvelous detail.[27] But even if it were possible to rehearse those arguments here, that would not directly address the issue that defines the reading I propose: namely, whether and in what sense Kant's account of sensible intuition belongs to reason's apperceptive self-knowledge of the form of material cognition. So my present aim is not chiefly to reconstruct Kant's arguments but to show that they have a certain status: namely, that they are based in apperception. And this is best done, I think, not by retracing long chains of argumentation but by directly illustrating how the baseline conception of intuition can come into view merely by reflecting on what is implicit in all our acts of potentially knowledgeable thought.

We can begin with the idea that theoretical cognition aims at truth.[28] This is surely part of theoretical reason's self-knowledge – that is, a principle that we intrinsically (if only unconsciously) represent as normatively binding on our mental activity insofar as we purport to be theoretically cognizing something. If I do not represent my mental act as aiming at truth – that is, as truth evaluable and subject to correction in light of how things stand – then I am ipso facto not engaged in an act of theoretical cognition. I may be engaged in a variety of other intelligent activities, such as fantasizing, flattering, bullshitting, or what have you, but cognition is not on the cards. Further, my act must intrinsically represent itself as actually meeting this standard. Doubts, guesses, and musings are self-consciously truth evaluable, but they do not intrinsically represent themselves as true and thus are not candidates for cognition. Moreover, I must take myself to have sufficient reason for thinking I have got hold of the truth. I must represent my act as warranted, as having a cognitive ground. Hunches and hypotheses, for instance, represent themselves as true, but not as sufficiently warranted to demand the assent of others. Finally, I must take the cognitive ground on which I self-consciously (if implicitly) base my claim to be a ground of *truth*, not just a sufficiently compelling consideration. Certain articles of faith, such

27 Foremost among these reconstructions is Anderson (2015), who identifies two main strands of argument: one based on the inadequacy of traditional logic to express the claims and inferences of mathematics (chapters 8–9) and another based on the idea that conceptual containment can never commit us to the extra-conceptual existence of objects (chapter 10). I cannot improve on these accounts and defer to them for explication and defense of the analytic/synthetic distinction, from which the baseline account of intuition follows.

28 Some considerations in this paragraph implicitly track Kant's discussions of *Fürwahrhalten* in the Canon. But I take them to be independently plausible as apperceptively grounded characterizations of cognition. I will not address the interpretive issues raised by the Canon, which are nicely outlined in Chignell (2007a, 2007b).

as Kant's practical postulates or "pragmatic beliefs" (A824/B852.17–18), are truth claims for which we may have a sufficient warrant. But they are not theoretical cognitions because the cognitive grounds on which they are based are practical rather than theoretical: They are believed for reasons concerning what is good rather than reasons concerning what is true.[29] That we are intrinsically, if only implicitly, conscious of the distinctively practical grounding of such acts is evidenced by our tendency to shield them from counterevidence and to segregate them from other, evidence-based convictions.

We can shorthand these reflections by saying that theoretical cognitions are constitutively and self-consciously "truth tracking". Indeed, the fact that they intrinsically represent themselves as truth tracking is part of what constitutes them as theoretical cognitions. A mental act is a candidate for theoretical cognition only insofar as it represents itself (albeit unconsciously) as tracking the truth: as normatively bound by the standard of truth, as actually meeting this standard, and as warranted by reasons bearing on why the asserted proposition is indeed true. That theoretical cognition tracks the truth is therefore something that we know through pure apperception. For the "I think" can accompany all my representations, including my intrinsic (if implicit) representation of my acts of theoretical cognition as truth tracking.

With the idea of essentially truth-tracking cognition emerges the idea of a faculty of theoretical knowledge – that is, a faculty that provides epistemic access to grounds of truth. In some cases, our faculty for thinking – for framing concepts and combining them in judgments – qualifies as such a faculty for knowledge. Some thoughts are self-verifying in the sense that they contain their own ground of truth. Analytic judgments are a prominent example. For in an analytic judgment, as Kant says, "I already have all the conditions for my judgment in the concept from which I only extract the predicate in accordance with the principle of contradiction, and I can thereby simultaneously become conscious of the necessity of the judgment" (B12.21–24).

[29] A practical postulate, for Kant, is "a **theoretical** proposition, though one not demonstrable [erweislich] as such [sc. as theoretical], insofar as it is inseparably attached [anhängt] to an a priori unconditionally valid **practical** law" (*Practical* 5:122.23–25, Kant's emphases). Tizzard (2020) presents a compelling account of the postulates of practical reason. Though practical postulates are theoretical propositions, they are at root practical cognitions – not merely because they are endorsed on practical grounds but because their principal role is to contribute to our practical cognition, by securing objective validity for, and specifying the content of, our concept of the highest good (*Practical* 5:132.13–34).

When a judgment contains its own ground of truth in this way, we are apperceptively aware that it does. When I make an analytic judgment, it is essential to my act that I represent it as already containing a sufficient ground of its truth. That is what makes me conscious of the *necessity* of the judgment. And it is why it would be "ungereimt" (B12.15), not merely superfluous, to look beyond my own thought for evidence or confirmation of its truth. To begin inspecting bodies to confirm their extendedness would betray a fundamental misunderstanding of the thought, <*bodies are extended*>. In particular, it would threaten the mental act's candidacy for theoretical cognition, just as much as would a failure to represent it as susceptible to correction in light of the facts. This indicates that representing one's act as tracking the truth – and, in particular, representing certain acts as containing their own grounds of truth – is essential to that act's status as theoretical cognition and is therefore a feature of theoretical cognition that we can establish through apperception.

It is equally true – and for the same reason – that we intrinsically represent other judgments as tracking a truth that is independent of our present act of thinking.[30] It is not generally the case that merely thinking something makes it so – and an awareness of this essentially (if implicitly) informs all our pursuits of theoretical knowledge.[31] The idea of thought-independent grounds of truth is, in fact, implied in the very idea of truth tracking. For in representing our judgments as normatively governed by the standard of truth, and thus as subject to *correction* in light of how things stand, we are leaving open the possibility that our thought may *fail* to agree with its object.[32] And this would not be an open possibility if all our thoughts were self-verifying in the way analytic judgments are.

[30] The type of thought-independence at stake here merely concerns the particular act of thinking that is a candidate for theoretical cognition. It does not imply that the relevant ground of truth is independent of *all* my acts of thinking, or that it is fully mind-independent.

[31] This includes our self-consciously analytic judgments. Though analytic judgments represent themselves as already containing their own grounds of truth, they also have objective purport (see Lu-Adler 2013). That is, the concepts they employ intrinsically purport to apply to objects. And these objects are, and are represented as being, grounds of truth for possible *synthetic* judgments, even if the claim one is currently entertaining about those objects is true merely in virtue of the concepts that apply to them. For on the critical, transcendental conception, an object *just is* a ground of truth for a synthetic judgment (cf. B137.20–08). Nothing in what follows turns on this point, however.

[32] This is not to say that the concept of error, or even the concept of thought, is prior to the concept of knowledge. For Kant, the capacity to think *is* the capacity to know. It is only to say that it is a constitutive and apperceptively available aspect of all cognition that we mark a distinction between (i) thinking something and (ii) its being so. But as Engstrom argues (forthcoming), this distinction marks a merely logical possibility. It is not apparent through pure apperception that error is a *real* possibility for a mind like ours. That unhappy realization stems from empirical misadventures.

An appreciation of this feature of our theoretical knowledge – the fact that there are thought-independent grounds of truth – is essential to any act that is a candidate for cognition, even if this appreciation typically remains implicit. Someone for whom it is an open question whether *all* her acts of thinking are self-verifying – whether merely thinking them guarantees their truth – is not engaged in potentially knowledgeable mental activity but flirting with solipsistic madness. Just as it is essential to certain acts of judgment – those Kant will classify as "analytic" – that one represent the ground of the judgment's truth as *internal* to one's very act of thinking, it is equally essential to other acts of judgment – those Kant will classify as "synthetic" – that one represent the ground of the judgment's truth as *independent* of one's current act of thinking. Thus, we must take ourselves to possess a cognitive capacity that provides us with cognitive access to thought-independent grounds of truth insofar as judgments of the latter sort present themselves as potentially knowledgeable – something that, as we have seen, all judgments essentially do. The idea of a capacity for intuition, and an appreciation of its distinctness from our faculty of thought, is therefore available to us through pure apperception – that is, by reflecting on what we essentially, if only implicitly, represent in making potentially knowledgeable theoretical judgments.

Now it might be objected that this line of reasoning begs the question against Leibniz. For it simply takes for granted that some judgments are irreducibly synthetic (as Kant would put it) and that truth does not consist in the containment of the predicate in the subject (as Leibniz would put it). Leibniz would readily grant that it is not always possible to "extract the predicate [from the subject concept] in accordance with the principle of contradiction", as Kant formulates it (B12.22–23). But this does not imply, for Leibniz, that the concept of the subject (its "complete notion") is not a sufficient ground of truth. Nor, by extension, does it imply that knowledge of such truths requires a cognitive capacity *distinct* from the intellect qua faculty for conceptualization, judgment, and inference. It merely implies that, in such cases, the intellect operates in accordance with a different (but still intellectual) principle: namely, the principle of sufficient reason.[33]

[33] This response is available to Leibniz but not to Wolff or his followers, since, as Kant observes, Wolff attempts to derive the principle of sufficient reason from the principle of contradiction (see M-Mr 29:788.25–789.02). If synthetic truths are not demonstrable in accordance with the principle of contradiction, they cannot be demonstrable in accordance with a mere corollary of the principle of contradiction.

This is an important objection but not one that directly imperils my interpretation. It was not my aim to provide a decisive argument against Leibniz and in support of Kant's analytic/synthetic distinction – a challenge that has been ably taken up by others (most prominently, Anderson 2015). I was rather illustrating how we might view the analytic/synthetic distinction as expressing essential and apperceptively available aspects of theoretical cognition. It namely reflects the idea that judgment must track the truth, that there are thought-independent grounds of truth, and that a capacity for gaining epistemic access to such grounds is a condition on our judgments being knowledgeable. These ideas are internal to every act of theoretical cognition as such. Representing some grounds of truth as independent of my act of thinking is part of what constitutes that act as one of theoretical cognition. If one is not alive to this distinction between thinking something and its being so, then, whatever else one may be doing, one is not engaging in potentially knowledgeable theoretical cognition. This gives us good reason to think that Kant's analytic/synthetic distinction is grounded in pure apperception. Because the sensibility/understanding distinction is a corollary of the analytic/synthetic distinction, this would mean that Kant's two-stems doctrine likewise enjoys an apperceptive grounding. Though Kant's two-stems doctrine stands with the analytic/synthetic distinction, it need not fall with it. There could be other ways of justifying the understanding/sensibility distinction – either by appealing directly to the apperceptively available notion of truth-tracking judgment or, of course, by appeal to non-apperceptively available considerations. My aim, again, is not to provide a uniquely correct account of *the* rationale for Kant's theory of human intuition, but to trace one line of thought that I think deserves more attention than it has received.

2.6 Intuition and Receptivity

I would like to conclude this chapter by tying the foregoing discussion of truth tracking to Kant's language in distinguishing the "two stems of human cognition". Kant says that sensibility and understanding differ in that "through the first of them [sc. sensibility] objects are **given** to us, but through the second [sc. understanding] they are **thought**" (A15/B29). A central implication of this distinction, I take it, is that the act of thinking about an object does not suffice to "give" it to the mind.[34] Kant often

[34] It may also suggest that objects can be given to the mind without being thought (cf. B30.17–20, B129.9–13, B132.8–9), but I will not pursue that implication here.

seems to understand this point in terms of ontological independence. Merely thinking about an object does not guarantee its existence, its actuality, or its real possibility. For instance, Kant writes:

> **To cognize** an object requires that I can prove its possibility (whether through its actuality, on the testimony of experience, or a priori through reason). But I can **think** whatever I want, if only I do not contradict myself, i.e. if only my concept is a possible thought, even if I cannot attest whether in the sum total of all possibilities an object [*Objekt*] corresponds to this [sc. concept] or not. (Bxxvii.27–33)

This is an ontologically inflected version of the idea that there is a difference between my thinking something and its being so. My acts of thinking are not ontological grounds of the objects at which they are directed. Whatever the ontological status of the objects I think about may be – whatever their existence, actuality, or real possibility consists in – they enjoy that status independently of my particular acts of thinking about them. Yet genuine cognition is ontologically demanding. For an act to count as a cognition it need not itself contribute to (ground) the ontological status of its object but it must enable me to prove (as appropriate) the existence, actuality, or real possibility of the object cognized.[35]

Kant frequently clarifies this point by contrasting our specifically human mode of thought and cognition with a hypothesized divine mind. In his famous 1772 letter to Herz, for instance, Kant describes "the key to the whole mystery of metaphysics, which has hitherto remained hidden from itself":

[35] The qualifier "as appropriate" reflects the fact that different sorts of synthetic propositions require different sorts of grounds of truth, since the objects we cognize may vary in ontological status. A geometrical theorem, for instance, is demonstrated through construction, by exhibiting the relevant concept *in concreto* in pure intuition. The constructed object is actual as a formal intuition, i.e. as a determinate aspect of the form of our sensibility, and is therefore really possible as a way in which our sensibility may be affected. But the object need not *exist* in the sense that phenomena or sensible objects do (cf. R6324, 1790–1793, 18:647.20–27). The "objects" of geometry are grounds of truth for geometrical propositions, and they are "given" to us in whatever ways we can gain cognitive access to those grounds of truth. Similarly, certain empirical concepts may require only proof of real possibility, if we have sufficient information about the relevant natural laws. For instance, I can prove it is really possible to carve a pink ice cube into bust of Kant in advance of the sculpture's actually existing. I need only show that a skilled sculptor can carve just about anything out of blocks of ice, that it is possible to dye ice pink without seriously affecting its physical properties, and that we have sufficient materials on hand (water, freezers, dye, chisels). In other cases, however, where our knowledge of or ability to manipulate the relevant physical factors is shaky, only ostensive demonstration of an existing specimen will suffice. McLear (2016) is surely correct that the concept <platypus> is like this, as is Kant's own example of a marine chronometer (A729/757.8–15). But I am not convinced that this generalizes to all empirical concepts. The decisive criterion in all cases, I submit, is what it takes to provide a ground of truth for the relevant synthetic proposition.

> I asked myself namely this: upon what grounds rests the relation [*Beziehung*] of that in us which one calls representation to the object? [...] If that in us which is called representation were active with respect to the object, i.e. if the object were produced [*hervorgebracht*] through [the representation] itself, the way one imagines divine cognitions as the archetypes of things [*Urbilder der Sachen*], then the conformity of the representation with objects could be understood. Thus the possibility of both the *intellectus archetypi*, upon whose intuition things themselves are grounded, and of the *intellectus ectypi*, which draws the *data* of its logical activity [*Behandlung*] from sensible intuition of things, is at least intelligible. Yet our understanding is, through its representations, neither the cause of the objects (apart from in morality, in the case of good ends) nor is the object the cause of the representations of the understanding (*in sensu reali*). (Kant to Herz, 21 February 1772, 10:130)

As we saw in his 1782/83 metaphysics lectures, Kant is operating here with a generic conception of intuition that admits of both divine and human species. Intuition *überhaupt* is a capacity for enjoying cognition-enabling representations, in which the actuality of the representation is intimately connected with the actuality (or real possibility, or existence) of the object cognized, so that the object grounds the representation, or vice versa.[36] It is in virtue of this ontological entanglement of representing and represented that intuition enables cognition in the ontologically demanding sense of Bxxvii. From the actuality of an intuitive representation, one can prove (as appropriate) the existence, actuality, or real possibility of its object. Whether the representation grounds the object or vice versa, the actuality of the representation permits one to infer the actuality of its object.

Kant deploys this conception of intuition *überhaupt* in arguing that the human intellect is not a faculty of intuition. In so doing, he tacitly assumes that spontaneity, or self-activity, is the defining characteristic of the intellect. He first argues that "[t]he passive or sensible representations have a comprehensible relation to objects" (10:130.12–14) in order to raise a puzzle about representations that are, by contrast, *active* and therefore *intellectual*. Both the *intellectus archetypus* and the *intellectus ectypus* are, by definition, spontaneous insofar as they are *intellectual* powers. Yet the

[36] In the 1772 letter to Herz, Kant conceives the intimate connection between intuition and object in causal terms. Longuenesse (1998, 18–26) argues that, by 1781, Kant develops a non-causal account of this connection as a "making possible" relation. But whether it is understood causally or non-causally, the relation between representing and represented that is distinctive of intuition is one of ontological dependence: grounding with respect to existence, actuality, or real possibility. Kant appears to retain causal formulations at least in his 1782/83 lectures (cf. M-Mr 29:796.39–797.21, 880.30–35), but the present discussion does not turn on this.

intellectus archetypus is "active with respect to the object", whereas an *intellectus ectypus* is active merely with respect to "its logical activity [*Behandlung*]" but not with respect to the *data*, or the objects, at which this logical activity is directed.

The representations of an *intellectus archetypus* would actively produce their objects and would therefore be both (i) intellectual, in virtue of being spontaneous, yet also (ii) intuitive, in virtue of the intimate ontological connection between representing and represented. Now, because an *intellectus archetypus* would produce the very objects it cognized, it would never transition from ignorance to knowledge, from cognitive potentiality to actual cognition. The knowledge of an *intellectus archetypus* is always already complete, since the objects it has the *potential* to cognize only exist insofar as it *actually* cognizes them. Even if we suppose that there are objects beyond its ken – objects whose existence and actuality does not depend on its acts of intellection – the *intellectus archetypus* would have no way of coming to know those objects and so could not pass from potential to actual knowledge with respect to them. So the knowledge of an *intellectus archetypus* is always already complete, even if it is not omniscient.[37]

By contrast, the representations of an *intellectus ectypus*, though spontaneous by definition, are not intuitive. And human knowledge is clearly ectypal rather than archetypal. As Engstrom puts it, echoing Housman's poem: "The world we seek to know is a world we never made."[38] What I would like to emphasize is that the ectypal, non-intuitive character of our intellect is evident to us through pure apperception. We have an intrinsic, if often implicit, conception of human knowledge as the sort of thing that comes to be – as involving a transition from mere potentiality to actuality. For it is an essential and self-conscious aspect of our cognition that we seek to *expand* our knowledge, that learning is essential to our pursuit of knowledge. This is a formal self-cognition of reason. And this is what justifies Kant in claiming not only that "all our knowledge begins with experience" but that "there can be absolutely no doubt" about this

[37] I am assuming here that intuitive intellection exhausts the cognitive power of the mind in question. Were it also endowed with a mode of *receptive* intuition and a coordinated faculty of *ectypal* (discursive) intellection, it might indeed be able to cognize objects that are ontologically independent of its acts of cognition. The point is that it would know those objects not as an *intellectus archetypus* but as an *intellectus ectypus*. One might imagine a welter of divine minds, each with perfect knowledge of its own created world, but each irremediably ignorant of the others' worlds. For elaboration of this point, see Section 7.3.1.

[38] Engstrom (2006, 6).

(B1.6–7).[39] Further, since our need to pass from cognitive potentiality to actual cognition forecloses the possibility that our intellect might be intuitive, we can likewise establish through apperceptive reflection that "human knowledge has two stems": namely, (i) a faculty for thinking and (ii) a capacity for intuition – that is, for securing cognitive access to extra-conceptual grounds of truth.

This enables us to draw a further conclusion about our capacity for intuition. Because spontaneity is the defining characteristic of the intellect, and because we know (on the basis of pure apperception) that our intellect is non-intuitive, we can conclude (again on the basis of pure apperception) that our capacity for intuition is not spontaneous but *receptive*.[40] For if our capacity for intuition were spontaneous, it would be a faculty of intellect – namely, an *intellectus archetypus*. And this contradicts our intrinsic, if implicit, self-understanding of human knowledge as something that comes to be. The apperceptive, top-down approach to intuition that we have traced through Kant's arguments in the Introduction to the *Critique* thus yields a conception of our (human) cognitive faculty as comprehending both (i) a spontaneous faculty of concepts and their logical combination in judgments and (ii) a receptive capacity that provides cognitive access to extra-conceptual grounds of truth for judgments.

In sum, the top-down approach to human intuition via pure apperception that I attribute to Kant goes like this. Tracking the truth is an essential and essentially self-conscious aspect of our cognition. In self-consciously representing our acts of (would-be) cognition as tracking the truth, we represent some judgments as self-verifying and others as dependent on thought-independent grounds of truth. Thus, insofar as we take our judgments to be potentially knowledgeable, we implicitly represent ourselves as possessing a cognitive capacity for representing (epistemically accessing) thought-independent grounds of truth. We have, that is, an

[39] Ian Blecher once observed to me that Descartes's meditator pursues a similar line of thought:

> But perhaps I am something greater than I myself understand, and all the perfections which I attribute to God are somehow in me potentially, though not yet emerging or actualized. For I am now experiencing a gradual increase in my knowledge, and I see nothing to prevent its increasing more and more to infinity. [. . .] But all this [sc. the idea that I might be or become God] is impossible. First, though it is true that there is a gradual increase in my knowledge, and that I have many potentialities which are not yet actual, this is all quite irrelevant to the idea of God, which contains absolutely nothing that is potential; indeed, this gradual increase in knowledge is itself the surest sign of imperfection (AT 7:47).

[40] The receptivity of our intuition does not yet entail that it is sensible (i.e. dependent on sensory affection). The "mystical" intuition Kant finds in Plato is receptive but non-sensible (see note 26 as well as Section 8.1.1). It is only in the Transcendental Aesthetic that Kant argues for the specifically sensible character of human intuition (see Section 3.4).

apperceptive understanding of ourselves as possessing a capacity for intuition. Moreover, since spontaneity is the hallmark of the intellect, we can establish through apperceptive reflection that our capacity for intuition must be receptive. For we just stated that our intuition is a capacity for *thought-independent* grounds of truth. Yet any spontaneous cognitive faculty is eo ipso a faculty of thought (an intellect) and thus cannot be a capacity for entertaining thought-independent grounds of truth.

The receptivity of our intuition can be helpfully illustrated by contrasting the human mind (as we conceive of it via pure apperception) with what we suppose a divine mind would be – though no such illustration is strictly required for the foregoing argument. A divine mind would possess an *intellectus archetypus*: a faculty of thought that is, at the same time, a faculty of intuition – that is, a faculty of spontaneous intuition. Such a mind would always already know everything it could possibly know. It would never pass from mere potentiality to cognitive actuality: Its knowledge would not come to be. Yet it is an essential and essentially self-conscious aspect of our cognition that human knowledge comes to be – that it involves learning, passing from cognitive potentiality to actual cognition. So we know – and know via pure apperception – that our capacity for intuition cannot be spontaneous, since we know (via pure apperception) that it is of the essence of human knowledge to come to be. Indeed, this is implicit in the idea of truth tracking. In representing our cognition as normatively governed by the standard of truth, we represent it as an open question – as a logical possibility – that our thoughts may fail to be true. And this could not be the case if our capacity for intuition were spontaneous.

This baseline characterization of human intuition, as a receptive cognitive capacity for representing thought-independent grounds of truth (or, equivalently, grounds of truth for synthetic judgments), follows from apperceptive reflection on the nature of cognition and the nature of the intellect, as a spontaneous cognitive faculty of concepts and their logical concatenation in judgment. Thus, part of what reason knows, in knowing its own form, are the limits of its own cognitive powers and, thereby, the general cognitive functions that its partner-in-cognition must perform, if knowledge is to be possible for us humans. In knowing this, reason has a formal *Selbsterkenntnis* that human knowledge involves two stems: a receptive cognitive capacity through which objects are given and a spontaneous cognitive faculty through which they are thought.

3

An Apperceptive Approach to the Transcendental Aesthetic

The Transcendental Aesthetic can be divided into four main parts: three stages of argumentation, followed by a commentary meant to clarify the preceding argument and answer some objections (Table 3.1).

Kant first lays out, in an apparently programmatic or stipulative fashion, some general criteria concerning intuition, sensibility, sensation, and a form/matter distinction, which is, in turn, used to ground a pure/empirical distinction (§ 1, A19–22/B33–36). Call this first stage the "Preliminaries".

Next, Kant presents a series of considerations to show that the concepts <space> and <time> originate in pure sensible intuition, presumably in light of the criteria concerning *purity*, *sensibility*, and *intuition* just laid down in the Preliminaries. In the B-edition, which will serve as our point of reference for all headings and section numbers, these considerations are presented as a four-part "Metaphysical Exposition" (ME) of the concept of space (§ 2, A23–25/B37–40), followed by a "Transcendental Exposition" (TE) of that same concept (§ 3, B40–41). The concept of time is then subjected to a roughly parallel ME (§ 4, A30–32/B46–48) and TE (§ 5, B48–49, referring back to § 4.3, A31/B47.23–07). Call this second stage of the argument the "Expositions", namely, the parallel MEs of each concept, with their four numbered "moments", together with the two TEs.

The ME and TE of each concept is immediately followed by a section of "Conclusions from the above concepts". Here Kant argues that, since space and time are the forms of our outer and inner sensible intuition, spatiotemporal determinations are (a) transcendentally ideal in that they do not pertain to things in themselves (A26/B42.19–26; cf. A32/B49.22–08), yet (b) empirically real in that they necessarily pertain to inner/outer appearances as subjective conditions of their possibility (A26/B42.27–08; cf. A33/B49.9–25).

The Aesthetic wraps up with two numbered sections (§ 7 and § 8, A36–49/B53–73) that clarify the preceding argument by answering some

Table 3.1 *Outline of the Transcendental Aesthetic*[a]

1. Preliminaries	§ 1 [No Title]	A19–22/B33–36		
2. Expositions	§ 2 *ME of <Space>* § 3 *TE of <Space>*	A23–25/B37–40 B40–41	§ 4 *ME of <Time>* § 5 *TE of <Time>* cf. § 4.3, A31/B47	A30–32/B46–48 B48–49
3. Conclusions	[no § #] *Conclusions from the above concepts*	A26–30/B42–45	§ 6 *Conclusions from these concepts*	A32–36/B49–53
4. Commentary	§ 7 *Elucidation*	A36–41/B53–58	§ 8 *General Remarks on Transcendental Aesthetic*	A41–49/B59–73

[a] This table elaborates the outline in Merritt (2010, 8).

prominent objections, contrasting Kant's position with alternative views and teasing out some of its implications. These final sections of "Commentary" are of great interpretive value, but the structure of the text indicates that §§ 1–6 constitute Kant's argument proper – namely, for the claims that (i) space and time are forms of our sensible intuition and, therefore, that (ii) they are transcendentally ideal insofar as spatiotemporal determinations do not pertain to things in themselves, yet (iii) are empirically real in that they necessarily pertain to inner/outer appearances as subjective conditions of their possibility.

This outline of the Aesthetic suggests a series of related questions that any interpreter of the *Critique* must face: about the status of the Preliminaries, about the relation of the Preliminaries to the Expositions, about the status of the claims in the Expositions themselves, and, finally, about the relation of the Expositions to the Conclusions.

First, where do Kant's Preliminaries come from, and what is their evidentiary status? Are they stipulations that are justified only retroactively, in the subsequent elaboration of Kant's theory of knowledge? Or, if they are not stipulations, what sorts of claims are they, and what is Kant's entitlement to them? Are they contentious, synthetic propositions? Made on what basis? Or are they analytic? If so, what concepts do they analyze, and what is our epistemic entitlement to those concepts?

Second, how are the Preliminaries implicated in the Expositions? How do the various considerations presented in the Expositions even purport to show, much less succeed in demonstrating, that space and time satisfy the relevant criteria presented in the Preliminaries such that they qualify as (i) *forms* of (ii) *sensible* (iii) *intuition*?

Third, what is the evidentiary status of Kant's claims in the Expositions? In the B-edition, Kant tells us an Exposition is "the clear (albeit not exhaustive) representation of what belongs to a concept" (B38). But again, we must ask: What is our entitlement to the relevant concept? And on what basis do we determine what "belongs" to it? Do these analyses appeal to specific mathematical results? To phenomenological evidence? To thought experiments? To common usage, i.e. to our ordinary understanding of judgments that deploy the concept?

Finally, there are the usual questions about how to interpret Kant's Conclusions – that is, about the nature of his idealism – and whether these conclusions are valid implications of the Preliminaries and Expositions, or whether (and which) further premises are needed to establish them.

The present chapter will address the first question, about the evidentiary status of the Preliminaries. Chapter 4 will take up the second and third questions, about the way the Expositions implicate the criteria put forward in the Preliminaries, the sorts of considerations the Expositions rely on, and whether the resulting argument for the formal intuitive status of space is cogent. I will not, however, address the move from the Expositions to the Conclusions, since a treatment of Kant's transcendental idealism would demand a book-length project of its own.[1]

3.1 Apperception and the Preliminaries

Most commentators do not worry overmuch about the Preliminaries. Because their readings are not centrally motivated by a conception of Kant's methodology in the *Critique*, the evidentiary status of the Preliminaries is not an urgent question for them, and they have considerable latitude in addressing it. They are free to read the Preliminaries as stipulations, or anthropological generalizations, or results of phenomenological reflection, or claims that Kant argues for elsewhere, or what have you. I have no such latitude. The interpretation I am developing places severe constraints on the evidentiary status the Preliminaries can enjoy, if Kant is to adhere to the philosophical method I attribute to him. My central contention in this book is that the core of Kant's theory of sensible intuition can be established on the basis of pure apperception.

[1] Allais (2015) and Jauernig (2022) are recent testaments to the complexity of this interpretive project and to the philosophical and philological acumen required to execute it. I take some comfort in Kant's declaration that transcendental idealism "does not by a long shot constitute the soul of the system" (*Prolegomena* 4:374.11–12).

This is not to deny that Kant's characterizations of sensible intuition can be, and often are, supported by other forms of evidence as well. My claim is rather that apperceptive reflection provides one argumentative route – and, I suggest, a privileged route – to Kant's central claims about sensible intuition.[2] Kant's Preliminaries are especially significant for this reading because they are one of the few places where Kant directly addresses the nature of sensible intuition. So if his Preliminary claims cannot be plausibly interpreted as somehow grounded in apperception, my reconstruction becomes little more than a revisionist curiosity. On the other hand, if it is plausible to read Kant's Preliminaries as setting forth an apperceptively grounded conception of receptive intuition, then my account offers unique and appealing answers to pressing questions about the Aesthetic.

A brief note to forestall misunderstanding: My argument about the status of the Preliminaries will draw on texts beyond the Aesthetic. This is common interpretive practice, since the discussion in the Aesthetic is often too lapidary to support one reading over others. It is important to register, however, that I invoke these extra-textual resources only to reveal the epistemic status of Kant's claims, not to provide evidence for their truth. My aim is not to shore up Kant's argument by importing premises that he articulates only later in the *Critique* or in other writings. Rather, I cite extra-textual claims about our intellect in order to explain the conspicuous *absence* of premises in the text as written. It is not that Kant entitles himself to his Preliminary claims only later in the text. Rather, we can come to understand his (and our) entitlement to those claims – an

[2] To briefly recapitulate, the idea is this. Because the intellect is essentially self-conscious, we can form a conception of the nature of our capacity for reason and understanding by reflecting on the acts that issue from these faculties. In reflecting on our acts of intellection, however, we come to recognize that our intellectual powers are not generally sufficient for knowledge of objects, viz. for synthetic, ampliative, cognition. As I argued in Chapter 2, we have an apperceptive grasp on the fact that our cognition must track the truth. In order to be a candidate for theoretical cognition, an act of intellection must represent itself as tracking the truth. Yet we also have an apperceptive grasp on the fact that our intellectual powers do not typically provide us with grounds of truth. Our judgments are not generally self-verifying, as analytic judgments are. This realization enables us to form the conception of a non-intellectual capacity, whose defining function is to provide us with epistemic access to grounds of truth for synthetic judgments. We can form this conception merely on the basis of apperceptive reflection – that is, on the basis of the understanding's intrinsic, self-conscious grasp on its constitutive aim (cognition of objects), on its own operations, and on the insufficiency of those operations to attain that aim. But a non-intellectual capacity for representing grounds of truth just *is* a capacity for receptive intuition – "receptive" because it is non-intellectual (i.e. non-spontaneous) and "intuitive" because it provides epistemic access to truth-makers for synthetic judgment, i.e. because it "gives" objects to the mind, in Kant's transcendental sense of "object". This has the surprising implication that the essentially apperceptive character of our *intellectual* faculty enables us to form an indirect and schematic but nonetheless contentful conception of our *non-intellectual* cognitive capacity – namely, receptive intuition.

entitlement we already possess early in the text – only once we come to understand the nature of our intellectual faculties – something we cannot (or anyway do not) grasp until later in the text or in the course of other investigations.

In Section 3.2, I analyze the opening of the Aesthetic and its conspicuously teleological language. I then show that the apperceptive approach I outline in Chapter 2 neatly accounts for the teleological cast of Kant's thought and prepares the way for a compelling reconstruction of Kant's argument for the immediacy of intuitive representation (at A19/B33.18–22).

I provide that reconstruction in Section 3.3. Kant's account of conceptual representation as mediated through discursive marks entails that, for a discursive intellect, any object-giving representation must be immediate and, hence, non-intellectual. Since intuition is just defined, in the tradition, as *immediate* cognition, it follows that the only mode of *object-giving* representation that a discursive mind can enjoy is intuitive. Our basis for applying this conclusion to our own, human, intuition is pure apperception. For it is through apperception that we appreciate the discursive character of our own intellect. And similarly, it is through apperception that Kant purports to establish his theory of discursive marks, as a doctrine of pure general logic.

In Section 3.4, I show that it is a short step from this apperceptive account of the immediacy of intuition to the claim that our capacity for intuition is *receptive* and that its representations are object-giving in virtue of being *affection-dependent*. For if our capacity for intuition and object-giving representation were spontaneous, it would also be intellectual. Since we have an apperceptive appreciation of the discursive and, thus, non-object-giving character of our intellect, our grasp on the non-intellectual character of our intuition is likewise based in apperception. But the claim that our intuition is *receptive* must be distinguished from the claim that our intuition is *sensible*, i.e. that it depends on the affection *of sense organs*. Awareness of the embodied, animal, sensory constitution of human intuition can perhaps be attained phenomenologically, or perhaps only through empirical anthropological study, but it cannot be established through pure apperception.

In Section 3.5, I explore how this receptivity/sensibility distinction complicates Kant's form/matter distinction as it applies to human intuitings and I address the role of sensation (*Empfindung*) in Kant's account. I argue that Kant's main line of thought in the Aesthetic requires only that we distinguish between the matter (the manifold) of intuition and its form.

This distinction necessarily applies to any intuition that is receptive. It does not presuppose that the manifold of intuition is realized in or essentially conditioned by an embodied sensorium. Further, because Kant holds that the form/matter distinction is "inseparably bound up with every use of the understanding" (A266/B322.12–15), it is a notion that is apperceptively available to us as a "concept of reflection". So we can preserve Kant's main line of thought, including his crucial distinction between the form and matter of intuition, while drawing solely on what is apperceptively available to the mind.

Taken as a whole, then, this chapter shows that pure apperception can justify the chief criteria that Kant must invoke in the Expositions, in arguing that <space> and <time> must have their origin in the (i) *form* of our (ii) *sensible* (or, more properly, *receptive*) (iii) *intuition.* On my reading, the Preliminaries comprise an analysis of concepts such as <intuition>, <spontaneity>, and <form/matter>. These concepts are what Kant elsewhere calls "original acquisitions": namely, concepts that we come to possess merely by exercising our cognitive capacities. By reflecting on these concepts, we bring to light the criteria on which Kant's arguments in the Expositions will turn: namely, *givenness* as criterion of intuition, *affection-dependence* as criterion of receptivity, and *holistic coordination* as criterion of form. The present chapter thus prepares the way for my reconstruction of Kant's arguments in the Expositions in Chapters 4 and 5.

3.2 Kant's Teleological Language in the Preliminaries

Kant opens the Aesthetic by claiming that intuition is responsible for any immediate relation of cognition to objects. For his intended audience, this would have been uncontroversial. That intuitive cognition is immediate in some important sense is a truism in the Early Modern philosophical tradition.[3] Yet Kant formulates this commonplace in a way that is curiously convoluted both conceptually and grammatically. Especially striking is Kant's alignment of terms expressing immediacy of reference with teleological vocabulary denoting means-end relations. These are underlined in the passage:

[3] Contemporaneous critical dictionaries register this (e.g. Adelung 1793, 1:354, *vide* "Anschauen" and "anschaulich"). Hintikka's résumé of the traditional philosophical usage remains valid (1969, 40–42). Falkenstein is quite right that "the study of Kant needs to begin with a recollection of the traditional meanings assigned to his terms by ancient and medieval philosophy" (1995, 31, cf. 29–32).

> In whatever way and through whatever means [*Mittel*] a cognition may relate to [*beziehen auf*] objects, the one [*diejenige*] through which it immediately relates [*unmittelbar bezieht*] to these, and toward which all thinking as a means aims [*als Mittel abzweckt*], is **intuition**. (A19/B33)

Rather than simply saying (uncontroversially) that intuitive cognition relates to its object immediately and then arguing (more controversially) that all thought and cognition must ultimately relate to intuition if they are to relate to objects, Kant imports teleological language into his discussion of mediated and immediate reference.[4] Thinking is characterized "as a means [*als Mittel*]" that "aims at" intuition. This plays on the double meaning of "*Mittel*": figuring the referential *mediatedness* of thought as a teleological *means*-end relation. It suggests that the relation of referring (*beziehen*) should be understood as a relation of purposive aiming, as at a telos (*abzwecken*). What does Kant mean – and what does he gain – by this teleological inflection?[5]

To say that "all thinking as a means aims at [*abzweckt*]" intuition strongly suggests that intuition is the telos (the *Zweck*) of thinking, not merely the final link in a chain of object-reference. I will challenge this reading presently, but let us first consider what it might mean for intuition to be the telos at which thought aims. It could mean that thinking is instrumental in promoting acts of intuiting. Or it could mean that thinking aims to become intuitive – that intuition is the regulative paradigm to which discursive thought aspires to be adequate.

The first option fits Kant's language but conflicts with his other views. Thinking about something does not make that content *more intuitive* to us. Indeed, Kant holds that the reverse is often true. Kant distinguishes

[4] Commentators tend to ignore the teleological import of this passage. Not even Vaihinger's obsessive commentary mentions it (cf. Vaihinger 1892, II:3–5); nor do the other major commentators I've surveyed: cf. Watkins and Willaschek (2017, 89–91), Allais (2015, 145–163), Allison (2004, 462n.9), Brandt (1998, 83–84), Falkenstein (1995, 28–29, 61), Parsons (2012 [1992], 6–11), Guyer (1987, 345–350), Paton (1936, I:93–99), or Kemp Smith (1992 [1918], 79–80). One notable exception is Heidegger, since Kant's teleological language fits nicely his reading of the *Critique* as a "groundwork of metaphysics" and a *Wesensbestimmung* (determination of the essence) of human cognition in its finitude (GA 3:20). The present section is an abridged version of a longer analysis that engages more extensively with Heidegger's reading. See the Extra Materials section on my website: https://wesleyan.academia.edu/DanielSmyth.

[5] It may be tempting to dismiss the passage as yet another instance where Kant's thought is confuddled by artless rhetoric. But there is reason to think that the teleological language and hypotactic formulation are well considered. They could not enjoy a more prominent placement in the text, as the opening sentence of the Doctrine of Elements and our entrée into the critique proper. And Kant leaves the passage unchanged in the second edition, even as he makes changes elsewhere on the page (viz. B33.10–11 and B33.19–20) and inserts marginal comments on other aspects of the A-edition passage (viz. 23:21.22–28, 44.16–18).

intellectual clarity and distinctness ("logical perfection") from intuitive clarity and distinctness ("aesthetic perfection").[6] Elegant formulations or beautiful representations can exhibit both; yet Kant warns that "[i]n general, there always remains of course a sort of conflict between the aesthetic and the logical perfection of our cognition that cannot be fully removed".[7] Far from promoting intuition, discursive thinking is prone to inhibit it.

Moreover, the distinguishing feature of intuition, as Kant tells us in the very next sentence of the Aesthetic, is that it obtains "only insofar as the object is given to us" (A19/B33.9–10). Yet discursive thinking in no way contributes to giving cognizable objects to the mind. Kant's slogan, "**being** is not a real predicate" (A598/B626.17; cf. *Proof* 2:72.2–3), entails that no amount of discursive thinking can evidence the reality of the object of cognition. This idea appears in various guises throughout his critical corpus:

> To **cognize** an object requires that I be able to prove its possibility [. . .]. But I can **think** anything I want, if only I do not contradict myself, i.e. if only my concept is a possible thought, though I admittedly cannot guarantee whether or not in the sum total of possibilities an object corresponds to this [sc. thought]. In order to attribute objective validity (real possibility, for the former was merely logical) to such a concept, something more is required. (Bxxvii.27–35; cf. A50/B74.8–19, A51/B75.1–23)

Kant consistently treats discursive thought as ontically sterile and, thus, as dependent on intuition for its modal force.[8] So precisely where it counts – namely, in giving knowable objects to the mind – thinking cannot promote or be instrumental for intuition, however else it may facilitate our sensible representations. The first option is a non-starter.

[6] R179, 1769–1770?, 15:67.11–13; L-Jäsche 9:35 and 62; L-Pö 24:511–512; L-Wien 24:805–808; M-Mr 29:878.26–31. See also Kant's discussion of the need for judgment in recognizing instances of discursive representations (A132f./B171f.) as well as his rejection of intellectual confusion as a mark of sensibility (A43f./B60.23–62.25).

[7] L-Jäsche 9:37.23–25; cf. 62.13–18 as well as L-Wien 24:807.30–32, 808.23–25.

[8] Kant writes: "Our concept of an object may contain whatever and however much it will, we must still go out beyond it [sc. the concept] in order to attribute existence to the latter [sc. the object]" (A601/B629.19–21). Or, again: "However the understanding may have arrived at this concept, still the existence of its object [Dasein des Gegenstands] nevertheless cannot be analytically found in it, because cognition of the **existence** of the object [Existenz des Objekts] precisely consists in [cognizing] that this [sc. object] is posited in itself **external to** [außer] **the thought**" (A639/B667.7–12). See also A598/B626.30–04; A599/B627.13–19. For discussion of how modal considerations figure in Kant's view that cognition requires intuition, see Hogan (2013); Chignell (2014); Stang (2016, ch. 6.6); Blecher (2018).

What about the second option – that intuition is a cognitive paradigm to which discursive thought aspires? One version of this idea observes that it is a hallmark of intuition to be able to present a concrete individual to the mind as maximally – perhaps infinitely – determinate across a variety of dimensions (e.g. volume, shape, duration, color, texture, etc.).[9] Similarly, extended thinking involves making ever more numerous and more specific determinations of an object. This increasing richness and determinacy of content might asymptotically approach the profuse manifoldness-in-unity that Kant associates with intuitive representation in concreto. All thinking would then "aim at" intuition in the sense that thinking is an ongoing activity of conceptual enrichment and growth, the ultimate goal of which is to adequately capture the full determinacy of its object.[10] Since intuition is the paradigm of what such full determinacy amounts to in a representation, it would serve as the telos, the standard of adequacy, for all thought, insofar as the latter is a means to cognition of objects.

But this proposal runs into the same problem as the first. No matter how determinate or information-rich a thought becomes, it comes no closer to *giving* an object to the mind. So if this is the central feature of intuition – as I argue it is – thought cannot even *approach* intuition. It makes no sense to speak of thought "aiming" at a goal toward which it is constitutively incapable of making any progress.

[9] Compare Jauernig's provocative account of the singularity of intuition:

> That intuitions are the only completely determinate representations that we are capable of is a direct consequence of the nature of completely determinate representations and the nature of our cognitive faculties, sensibility and the understanding. On the assumption that "individuality involves infinity," to use a memorable formulation from Leibniz, that is, on the assumption that all individuals have infinitely many determinations and that, in order to represent an object in its individuality, infinitely [many] determinations must be specified – which is an assumption that Kant quite clearly endorses – it follows that every completely determinate representation is infinitely complex in the sense of comprising infinitely many representations in it. [...] [I]ntuitions are completely determinate, according to Kant, and, thus, directly represent individuals, which is reflected in their infinite complexity (Jauernig 2021, 208–209).

While I largely agree with the claims Jauernig makes for Kantian intuition in this passage, she seems to treat this characterization as a central *premise* in Kant's argument in the Expositions, whereas I understand the infinitary character of intuitive content to be something that emerges from those reflections and which, in turn, entails the singularity of intuition. I make this case in Chapter 5.

[10] Compare Kant's description of "the ideal of pure reason" as "the unique case [in which] an intrinsically general concept of a thing is thoroughly determined through itself and cognized as the representation of an individual" (A576/B604.15–18). That is to say, the ideal of reason is an intellectual representation that approximates to an intuition in its singularity and concreteness of content.

There is another way of developing the idea that intuition is a cognitive paradigm for all thinking that would allow us to embrace the constitutive inadequacy of discursive thought per se: namely, if we read the relevant concept of cognition not as *human* cognition but as cognition in an unqualified sense. This view is heir to the rationalist tradition, exemplified by Leibniz, which holds that our primary concept of cognition – our concept of cognition *simpliciter* – is the concept of *divine* cognition and that it is with reference to this cognitive standard that all knowledge, including human knowledge, is to be characterized and assessed.[11] Thus, the intuition that would be paradigmatic of cognition *überhaupt* would not be *human* intuition but the ontically generative representations of a divine mind. It is no objection to this view that human mental life cannot begin to approach this cognitive standard. For it may still furnish us with evaluative criteria for assessing human cognitive achievements as more or less perfect in a variety of respects (clarity, distinctness, adequacy, simplicity, generality, etc.), even if complete perfection is out of the question.

The problem with this reading is that breaking with just this rationalist lineage is one of the central commitments of Kant's critical philosophy. Kant is happy to discuss the cognitive capacities of minds that are "higher" than our own, as well as those belonging to "lower" minds. Yet he consistently portrays such speculation as an analogical projection from *our own case.*[12] Our fundamental concept of cognition, the paradigm from which all our notions of alternative modes of cognition must derive, is a concept modeled on the workings of our own minds (as we understand them). For Kant, our concept of divine cognition is derivative, not fundamental. To form this concept, we begin with our concept <human cognition> and then specify particular features (*Merkmale*) of this concept to modify (to omit or negate) in order to frame the new concept. Thus, we might abstract from the sensible dependence of human cognition to frame the concept <spirit (i.e. non-sensibly-dependent mind)>, or negate the

[11] At times, Engstrom seems to attribute to Kant the view that "intellectual intuition is the archetype (cf. A695/B723)" of cognition *überhaupt*, from which we then derive our notion of finite cognition (Engstrom 2006, 9, 23n.14; cf. Engstrom 2013, 43n.3). I think this is a misreading. In calling the divine mind "*intellectus archetypus*" (A695/B723.30), Kant is not claiming that <*intellectual intuition*> is our fundamental concept of cognition but that the representations of a divine mind are archetypes of their objects. See *Judgment* 5:408.18–23; L-Blom (early 1770s) 24:125.32–35.

[12] For instance, *Critique*, B71–72.12–04, B139.13–19, B148.12–17, A256/B311–312.10–17; A287/B343.27–344.02; *Prolegomena* 4:355 f.; *Practical* 5:131n.26–30; *Judgment* 5:407–408; *Religion* 6:64n.35–65.08; *Prominent Tone* 8:400n.20–27; R2835 (mid-1770s) 16:537.8–9; M-Mr 29:888.6–17, 906.21–38, 953.36–954.10, 978.1–7; M-Vo 28:449; M-Pö/L_2 28:594.12–39, 606.15–607.8; M-DW (1792/93) 28:667.34–668.6, 668.15–30, 689.35–690.21.

ontic sterility of human thinking to frame the concept <productive intellect>. Note that forming such concepts is a necessary concomitant of rendering distinct (*deutlich*) our concept, <human cognition>. For to become explicitly conscious of two marks as distinct from one another involves being conscious of the logical possibility of a concept that contains one mark but not the other. Thus, Kant sometimes argues that, in order to fully appreciate a certain feature as belonging to the peculiar constitution of our own minds, we must think – that is, must be able to frame the concept – of a mind that differs (or would differ) from our own in precisely that respect.[13] But our ability to frame such a thought, necessary though it may be, can offer us no insight into the real possibility or positive constitution of such alternative forms of mindedness. For the concept it deploys consists in our concept of our own mode of cognition, modulo the *Merkmale* it negates or omits.

Concepts of other modes of cognition may enable us to identify various respects in which our own cognition is less perfect than we might wish. But this does not imply that such concepts function as a cognitive standard against which our own mental acts should be assessed. For these concepts of "higher" minds derive from our concept, <human cognition>. Thus, using the new concept(s) as a standard for assessing human cognition is just a roundabout way of measuring human cognition against itself. This is one of the radical innovations of Kant's critical philosophy: to treat human cognition, in its theoretical as well as its practical forms, as *autonomous* – as answerable to its own endogenous norms and self-legislated principles and to no others.[14] Though venerable, epistemologies *ad imaginem Dei* are fundamentally heteronomous and anathema to Kant's critical project.

Here is my alternative reading of Kant's teleological formulation. Kant says that thinking "aims at [*abzweckt*]" intuition and that, in doing so, thinking serves "as a means". This does not strictly imply (and Kant does not say) that intuition is the telos (*Zweck*) that thinking serves, in functioning as a means. Kant does not identify the telos for which thinking is a means. I propose that this telos is *cognition.* The passage admittedly does not spell this out. But it comports well with the baseline account of intuition outlined in Chapter 2.

[13] For instance, B71f.12–22; A256/B311f.; *Prolegomena* 4:316n.31–35; *Judgment* 5:408; *Religion* 6:65n.

[14] Though framed in different terms, my argument here agrees with Allison (2004, 27–38) and Pollok (2017, ch. 1).

We developed the baseline account by reflecting on the fact that theoretical cognition, by its essence, aims at truth. Truth is the constitutive telos of theoretical cognition, just as the good is the constitutive telos of practical cognition. But acts of theoretical cognition do not merely aim at truth; they represent themselves as attaining this aim. Nor is this just a default, self-congratulatory posture. An act of theoretical cognition represents itself as having adequate *grounds* for representing itself as true: It represents itself as warranted. Yet acts of thinking generally do not constitute – and generally represent themselves as not constituting – adequate grounds of truth for the proposition they entertain. When I engage in potentially knowledgeable thought, I represent my act of thinking as non-self-verifying and as depending, for its truth, on some ground beyond itself. Thus, while cognition constitutively aims at truth, thought, in aspiring to the status of theoretical cognition, aims at securing epistemic access to non-intellectual grounds of truth. And the idea of a cognitive capacity that provides epistemic access to non-intellectual grounds of truth *just is* the baseline conception of receptive intuition outlined in Chapter 2. Insofar as cognition aims at truth, then, all thought must aim at intuition, since that is what provides us epistemic access to grounds of truth. That is, since cognition aims at truth, and since objects are truth-makers for thought, all potentially knowledgeable thought must aim at objects. But objects, in the transcendental sense, are just grounds of truth for synthetic judgments. Thus, all potentially knowledgeable thought is directed at intuition, as the source of such grounds.

On this account, it is both the case that thinking is a *means* for promoting cognition and that it serves as such a means just insofar as it *aims at* intuition, as the source of all non-intellectual grounds of truth. This explains why Kant might want to embed the traditional view of intuition's immediacy of reference within a teleological structure. For he is concerned with the constitutive essence, the intrinsic, formal *aim* of theoretical cognition. Cognition aims at truth. And objects are what make judgments true. Thus, it is precisely because intuition *refers immediately* to objects – that is, to grounds of truth, to truth-makers – that thinking, insofar as it aspires to be cognition, *aims* at, and therefore refers to, intuition. The relations of reference track teleological relations.

Why all this sound and fury about Kant's teleological language at A19/B33.5–9? Whatever scholarly itch it may scratch to decode Kant's teleological language, it does not alter the criterion of intuitive representation that is evident on a first reading – namely, that intuitions refer immediately to their objects. Yet the announced purpose of this chapter is to elucidate the criteria of *intuition*, *sensibility*, and *form* that Kant lays down in the Preliminaries and later deploys in the Expositions. What, then, was the point of this excursus?

The point was not to adduce new criteria but to trace a clue about the evidentiary status of the immediacy criterion and the method underpinning Kant's argumentation. What accounts for the teleological cast of Kant's thought, I suggest, is his engagement in a functionalist investigation of our cognitive capacities and their associated exercises. Kant prosecutes this functionalist – and therefore teleological – investigation using a specific method: namely, apperceptive reflection and conceptual analysis. Kant holds that we can acquire special concepts of our own cognitive faculties by bringing to explicit awareness the constitutive principles that guide us in our concrete exercises of them. We can subsequently analyze these "originally acquired" concepts by asking how one capacity, in virtue of falling under a certain concept (i.e. as defined by a certain cognitive function, a certain constitutive aim), enables, requires, or excludes another capacity, insofar as the latter falls under a certain concept (i.e. is defined by a certain cognitive function).

The concepts and cognitive functions we have discussed thus far fit this picture. The notion of truth-tracking judgment, of analytic and synthetic truths, of a non-intellectual (non-spontaneous) capacity for representing grounds of truth for synthetic propositions – all these notions can be adduced (for subsequent analysis) by reflecting on the constitutive features of our intellectual activity. These are features of our mental acts that we can bring to explicit consciousness in virtue of the essentially apperceptive character of intellection. I am arguing that it is on the basis of such apperceptive reflection and conceptual analysis that Kant ascribes certain features to our cognitive capacities and establishes certain relations among them.

I emphasize the teleological cast of Kant's thought because it is a conspicuous and puzzling aspect of the Aesthetic that my interpretation naturally accounts for, while other readings must sweep it under the rug. This does not yet address Kant's *argument* for the claim that only intuitions – that is, non-intellectual representations of grounds of truth for synthetic judgments – refer immediately to their objects. It is rather a reading of A19/B33 that indicates what status the *premises* of such an argument will have – namely, insights based on apperception and conceptual analysis. For the argument itself, we must turn to the continuation of the opening paragraph of the Aesthetic.

3.3 Discursivity and Generality; Immediacy and Givenness

I have been trying to make plausible the idea that the Preliminaries are part of a functionalist account of our cognitive powers – an account framed by a teleological conception of cognition as truth-tracking judgment and fueled by conceptual analysis of apperceptively available concepts. It is in this light I propose we read the explicit, albeit compressed, argument for the immediacy of intuition that concludes the opening paragraph of the Aesthetic:

> All thinking, however, must ultimately relate [*beziehen*], whether straightaway (directly) or circuitously (indirectly), *by means of certain marks*, to intuitions and thus, in our case, to sensibility, because no object can be given to us in any other way. (A19/B33, italicized phrase added in B)

Kant presupposes here an account of thinking as fundamentally discursive: as relating to intuitions (and, thus, to objects) "by means of certain marks".[15] A mark, for Kant, is "a partial representation insofar as it is regarded as a ground of cognition of the whole representation".[16] To regard a partial representation as a ground of cognition of the whole representation is to represent it as something that could be shared by other (whole) representations, since what is part of one representation may also be part of another. Thus, marks are intrinsically general: They are "representations that make what is common to many things into a ground of cognition".[17] Marks denote features that may be shared by an indefinite

[15] In his own copy of the A-edition, Kant writes in the margin: "Intuition is opposed to the concept, which is merely the mark of intuition" (R X, 23:21.23–24, my underlining). So he clearly has in mind his theory of discursive marks. The remark continues: "The general must be given in the singular. That's how it has meaning [Bedeutung]" (21.25–26). I discuss the idea that discursive representations depend, for their meaning, on their instances in Section 5.4.2.

[16] L-Jäsche 9:58.16–17; see also A320/B377.30–33; R2280–2286 (mid-1770s) 16:298–300. Kant employs the term *Merkmal* promiscuously – much as he does the term *Vorstellung* – applying it both to partial representations and to the features of objects denoted by those partial representations. I will implicitly track the represent*ing*/represent*ed* distinction by calling partial representations "marks" and their objective correlatives "features".

[17] L-Jäsche 9:58.10–11. On the intrinsic generality of *Merkmale*, see also L-Jäsche 9:58.14–19, B39.22–40.1, B133.24–134.35; *Progress* 20:273.33–274.5; *Judgment* 20:211.30–33. Many commentators now follow Wolff (1995, 66) and Smit (2000) in distinguishing discursive marks, which are general and multiply instantiable, from intuitive marks, which are singular and unrepeatable, like tropes. Fruitful accounts of Kant's views on reflection, abstraction, and cognitive content can be developed in these terms (see Hoeppner 2021, 30–37, 82–92; Sutherland 2021b, 127–130), but I am skeptical that intuitive marks actually figure in Kant's thought. The idea appears in just a single Reflection (R2286, 1780s, 16:299.15–300.2), jotted in the margin of Meier's *Auszug aus der Vernunftlehre*, Kant's textbook for his logic lectures. The Reflection comments on § 116, which distinguishes between immediate and mediate marks. So Kant may well be glossing *Meier's* views, not voicing his own (cf. L-Blom, early 1770s, 24:108–110;

plurality of objects and instances, actual or merely possible.[18] This is the source of the double-edged power and impotence of discursive representation.

The power of discursive representation expresses itself through generality. Because marks only ever convey part of a "whole representation", they have the power to relate to an indefinite multiplicity of objects – namely, to any object that can be cognized through that partial representation – any object that shares the feature denoted by the mark. This enables thought to range beyond the contingencies of the present moment, to represent things past or merely possible, and to limn the necessary by weighing counterfactuals. In representing an object through a mark, I place it in relation to all conceivable objects that share a certain feature. The cognitive power of discursive representation is further realized in judgment, when thought combines two or more coordinate[19] marks as belonging together in an object (state of affairs, instance): The judgment

L-DW 24:725–726). To my knowledge, the notion of intuitive marks never reappears in Kant's writings or student lecture notes. Anyway, the present discussion of the immediacy of intuition in the Preliminaries is exclusively concerned with discursive marks.

[18] Marks are general by definition, and concepts consist solely of marks. But it does not follow that concepts are invariably general. One can also combine marks in such a way that it is logically, metaphysically, or mathematically impossible for more than one object to instantiate those marks. This uniqueness of reference is not always due to the concept's being put to "a singular use" (cf. L-Jäsche 9:91). Nor does it always happen, so to speak, behind the back of the concept, as an accident of extension or instantiation. A consciousness that the concept refers uniquely can be part of the intensional content of a discursive concept. A case in point is <*ens realissimum*>, which Kant describes as both "an intrinsically [an sich] general concept" and as "the representation of an individual" (A576/B604.15–18). I take this to mean that the marks making up the concept, which determine what the concept is "an sich", are general, but that, as a matter of metaphysical (perhaps even logical) necessity, those same marks have a unique conjoint instantiation. And consciousness of this necessity is part of the concept itself. A similar point holds for concepts such as <sum of 7 and 5> (B15.17–18, B16.7–8), which has a unique referent as a matter of mathematical necessity, and concepts such as <coldest known temperature> (cf. *Prolegomena* 4:273.25–26), which has a unique referent as a matter of logical necessity. This helps to explain why the *Stufenleiter* does not characterize concepts as "general", but instead says that concepts are "mediated by means of a mark that can be common to many things" (A320/B377.32–33; cf. L-DW 24:752.11–12). For discussion of cases where discursive concepts fail to be general despite consisting of general marks, see Smyth (2014, 554–556 and associated notes). A signal virtue of Jauernig's account of intuitive singularity (2021, 207–209) is that it does not reduce to uniqueness of reference and can thus acknowledge these atypical cases of discursive representation.

[19] That is, marks that are neither subordinate nor superordinate to each other (L-Jäsche 9:59.6–28). For instance, <fragrant> and <warm> are coordinate marks, since neither is a species of the other. Marks remain coordinate even if one is much more concrete (many more steps removed from their common genus) than the other (e.g. <armadillo> and <invertebrate>). (Kant holds that all concepts share a common genus.) Asserting the compresence of super- or subordinated concepts yields an analytic judgment. Kant often seems tempted by the view that all objects (or at least all *sensible* objects) exhibit infinitely many coordinate features (e.g. L-Blom, early 1770s, 24:109.1–15; L-Wien 24:834.26–29; L-DW 24:728.28–29).

<F is G> says that what has mark *<F>* also has mark *<G>*.[20] Just as concepts refer to objects through the mediation of marks, Kant conceives of judgments as doubly mediated: "Judgment is therefore the mediated cognition of an object, hence the representation of a representation of it" (A68/B93.2–4). And this discursive mediation can ramify still further, as judgments concatenate into syllogisms.[21] Every judgment functions as a rule: *If x has mark <F>, then x has mark <G>*. In this sense, every judgment is the major premise of possible syllogisms, just as every concept is a predicate of possible judgments (cf. A69/B94.24–25). For Kant construes the syllogism to consist of three elements:

> (1) a general rule, which is called the major premise (*propositio major*),
> (2) the proposition that subsumes a cognition under the condition of the general rule and which is called the minor premise (*propositio minor*), and finally
> (3) the proposition which affirms or denies the predicate of the rule of the subsumed cognition: the conclusion (*conclusio*). (L-Jäsche 9:120)

The conclusion of a syllogism is cognition thrice mediated: through the inferential relation between the premises, through the predicative relation within each premise, and through the marks that make up the concepts in each premise.[22] Discursive cognition is mediated representation *par excellence*. And with each form of further discursive mediation – conceptual, judgmental, inferential – cognition acquires greater generality and greater opportunities for growth.[23]

20 I am setting aside here complications related to the quantity of the judgment. It is also worth noting that this implies the convertibility of concepts and judgments. If the judgment, *<Some G is F>*, is warranted, then concept <F-ing G> is objectively valid. Conversely, if a concept is valid of some object (actual or really possible), then a corresponding judgment involving the coordinate marks of that concept is warranted. See R3045 (1776–1779) 16:630.5–8 and 630.17–18; Kant's letter to Beck, 3 July 1792, 11:347.2–26; as well as Schultz's 1790 defense of Kant's position against Maaß and Eberhard (20:408–409). Due to this convertibility, Kant sometimes refers to judgments as "concepts": "A judgment is the representation of the unity of the consciousness of various representations, or the representation of their relation insofar as they constitute a concept." (L-Jäsche 9:101.5–7, my underlining; cf. L-Ph, 1772, 24:461)

21 On the proleptically syllogistic character of judgment, see Longuenesse (1998, 90–95). Indeed, the present paragraph can be viewed as a summary of key points in Longuenesse (1998, ch. 4).

22 It is tempting to extend this a step further, as syllogisms are organized into theories, sciences, and, ultimately, a system of knowledge. It is not clear to me, however, that the architectonic systematization of arguments principally expresses the *discursivity* of cognition, rather than other essential aspects of reason.

23 This is one way of understanding Engstrom's characterization of judgment as "self-enlarging" (Engstrom 2006, 16) or "self-productive" (Engstrom 2016, 44). The idea is that discursive mediation fosters the growth of knowledge by multiplying points of possible connection – conceptual, predicative, and inferential – among cognitions. This growth is "*self*-enlarging"

As I intimated, however, this power of discursive mediation is complemented by a peculiar impotence. A discursive mark applies indifferently to every object that shares the relevant feature, regardless of whether those objects actually exist.[24] This is what enables thought to range beyond the contingencies of the present moment, into the realms of the possible and the necessary. By the same token, however, a discursively mediated representation cannot evidence the existence of an object. For many of the objects that can be cognized through it precisely do *not* exist. Generality is purchased at the expense of givenness. Kant tends to express this point by claiming that the human mind is not ontically creative, that it cannot spontaneously generate ex nihilo genuine existents as objects of possible cognition.[25] The underlying reason for this ontic impotence, I am suggesting, is provided by Kant's theory of discursivity.

This is what justifies Kant in saying that "no object can be given to us in any other way" than in intuition (A19/B33.21–22). For discursive cognition is mediated through marks that are intrinsically capable of representing nonexistent objects. As such, discursively mediated cognition cannot guarantee the existence of its object. So any cognition that *can* ensure the existence of its object cannot refer to its object through the mediation of discursive marks. It must therefore refer to its object immediately – presenting the object to the mind in a way that implicates its existence. Yet any cognition that relates to its object in this way is, ipso facto, intuitive. For such immediacy is the hallmark of intuitive cognition in the Early Modern tradition. This is the truism about immediacy of reference with which the Aesthetic opens and which Kant glosses by saying that "[intuition] takes place only insofar as the object is given to us" (A19/B33.9–10).[26] It follows, therefore, that a mind whose principal cognitive

because judgment is both the primordial site of discursive mediation as well as the paradigmatic product of such mediation: Judgment makes more of itself.

[24] Whenever I speak of the existence of an object, I mean its existence in the relevant ontological register. Tickles and trapezoids exist just as much as stones and salinity, but they are all quite different sorts of things and arguably occupy different categories of being. Thus, it is appropriate to grant existence to Sherlock Holmes's brother but to deny it to his daughter, because, whatever the ontological status of the fiction inhabited by Holmes, he has a male sibling but no children. I take this sort of ontological plasticity to be built into the notion of a "ground of truth". See Section 2.4.

[25] For example, Kant to Herz, 21 February 1772, 10:130; M-Mr 29:759 f., 796 f., 800.9–17, 880.32–36.

[26] Though they are sometimes run together, the truism is the *converse* of the claim for which Kant argues. The truism says that intuition, as such, must involve the givenness of its object: It makes givenness a *necessary* condition of intuition. The claim for which Kant argues is that givenness, for us humans, is also a *sufficient* condition of intuition – that is, that givenness, for us, must involve intuition. The latter claim follows only if we premise a certain conception of the discursivity of our intellect.

faculty is a discursive intellect must also possess a cognitive capacity for intuition, if it is to be capable of cognizing real existents. For genuine cognition requires grounds of truth for synthetic judgments. Yet a discursive intellect cannot supply such grounds, since its representations are mediated through marks. Such grounds must therefore be supplied by a non-intellectual capacity, whose representations relate to them immediately. But intuition just is a capacity for immediate cognition of grounds of truth. Thus, grounds of truth for synthetic propositions can only be given to us in intuition: "for no object can be given to us in any other way" (A19/B33).

3.3.1 The Evidentiary Status of Kant's Theory of Discursive Marks

In outlining this interpretation of A19/B33, I have appealed to an account of discursive marks and conceptual representation that is, at most, only gestured at in three words added to the B-edition: *vermittelst gewisser Merkmale* (B33.19–20). Because this theory of discursive mediation cannot, by any reasonable standard, be found in the Aesthetic, I need to address the role it plays in Kant's argument and in my interpretation. Is it permissible for Kant to presuppose this theory in putting forward his claims in the Aesthetic? And if not, how can it be permissible for me to appeal to it in interpreting the Aesthetic?

On the one hand, Kant's doctrine of discursive marks is neither elaborated nor justified in the Aesthetic. Indeed, the view seems to be simply taken for granted the various times it surfaces in the *Critique*.[27] If one had to identify a relatively self-contained argument for the doctrine in the *Critique*, the most plausible candidate would be Kant's discussion of predication and judgment in the *Leitfaden*.[28] But considerable interpretive work would be required to extract the doctrine of discursive marks from Kant's lapidary remarks on predication. The need for so much interpretive work suggests that Kant's account of discursive marks is far from self-evident, even if his contemporaries would not have regarded it as especially contentious. So it appears that Kant's argument in the Aesthetic, as I have reconstructed it, relies on an assumption that stands in need of justification and yet receives none. My reading seems to saddle Kant with a premise to

[27] For instance, A8/B12.2–5, B40.22–25, B133f.24–35, B192.20–23, A241.31–06, A320/B377.30–33, A727f./B755f.20–15, A730/B758.6–13, A732/B760.16–22.

[28] Namely, A67–69/B92–94. On the connection between this discussion and Kant's doctrine of marks, see Wolff (1995, 65–67, 75); Longuenesse (1998, 85–93); and Hoeppner (2021, 96–117).

which he is not entitled and thereby undermines his entitlement to his conclusions (i) that, for us humans, intuition alone is immediate and object-giving and (ii) that all thought must therefore relate to intuition if it is to have cognitive significance. Surely it is more charitable to read Kant as other commentators do: as stipulating the meanings of key terms, as laying down certain assumptions as quasi-axiomatic, or as mooting hypotheses that will be retroactively justified by the overall fruitfulness of the view.[29]

On the other hand, Kant takes his account of discursive marks to belong to pure general logic (PGL). Accordingly, his most detailed discussions of discursive marks and their role in conceptual representation occur in his logic lectures and, secondarily, in the sections of the *Critique* most immediately concerned with logic.[30] But as I argued in Section 1.2, Kant takes our knowledge of PGL to be based in pure apperception. Pure general logic is reason's self-knowledge of its own form. So even if Kant's argument in the Aesthetic does presuppose his account of discursive marks, that is quite consistent with the idea that the *Critique* "presupposes nothing as given apart from reason itself [. . .] without relying on any fact" (*Prolegomena* 4:274.32–33). In light of this special status as a doctrine of PGL, the theory of discursive marks is not exactly an unjustified assumption, since it is something every rational person is already committed to nolens volens, simply in virtue of exercising her cognitive powers.

Now, this is not to say everyone will regard the doctrine as obvious, or even accept it as true. Just as Kant disputes various doctrines in the logical teachings of his predecessors, it is possible to dispute Kant's account of discursive marks.[31] The point is that the standard of correctness here, what any proposed doctrine of PGL is attempting to adequately capture, is

29 For instance, Jauernig argues that Kant's "ontological uncreativity thesis" – that is, the claim that the spontaneity of the human mind is incapable of generating knowable objects and, hence, incapable of giving them to the mind for cognition – is a "rock-bottom commitment" that "itself does not need any justification in Kant's eyes" (Jauernig 2021, 316; cf. Jauernig 2019). I agree that, for Kant, the thesis stands in need of no further justification in the sense that it is not derived from premises that are more epistemically fundamental. But I do think we can say a bit more about *why* human intellection is ontically sterile (namely, because it is discursively mediated) and about *how* it is that we know this (namely, through apperception). Still, these elucidations do not amount to a justification in the sense of an argument from independent premises.

30 See L-Jäsche 9:58–61; L-Bl 24:106–115; L-Wien 24:834–839; L-DW 24:725–728.

31 Kant's challenges to logical tradition cover issues big and small: from his lifelong opposition to the doctrine of the four syllogistic figures, to his nit-picking insistence that confusion (*Verwirrung*) cannot be the opposite of distinctness (*Deutlichkeit*), since simple representations cannot be confused but can be indistinct (e.g. R178, 1769–1770?, 15:67.5–7; *Anthropology* 7:138.6–10; L-Jäsche 9:34.29–35.12; L-Blom, early 1770s, 24:41.19–42.3; L-Wien 24:805.28–35). On Kant's relation to the logical tradition, see Lu-Adler (2018a, ch. 4).

nothing other than our apperceptive consciousness of the form of reason, which we enjoy in virtue of exercising our reason. What we are attempting to give voice to, in formulating the tenets of PGL, is the formal character of reason. Thus, it is *by our own lights* that our proposed doctrines will be true, if they are true, or false, if they are false. It is humbling that our rational self-accountings can be such a struggle and that they so often end in failure. But such is our lot. It may require extensive elucidation to bring us to recognize a particular doctrine as a true characterization of the formal character of our own rational activity. But courting such conviction is not a matter of adducing evidence to which we did not previously have access. It does not, in that sense, consist in justifying or giving an argument for the doctrine.

Where does this leave us? It is fair to say that, when Kant appeals to the theory of discursive marks in the Aesthetic, he does not make clear what our entitlement to that theory is. But that is not quite the same thing as failing to justify the theory or being unentitled to invoke it. For the only thing that could make clear our entitlement to the theory, as Kant understands it, would be an elaborate logical discussion of the nature of discursive conceptualization, judgment, and inference. Such a discussion has its proper place in PGL. Including it in the Aesthetic would confuse the composition of the *Critique* just as much as omitting it occludes his local line of argument. In light of the special evidentiary status Kant attributes to his account of discursive marks, as a doctrine of PGL, it is at least understandable, though not without its dangers, that Kant should treat it as a presupposition requiring no explicit justification. But this does not make it a stipulation laid down as axiomatic nor an assumption to which we are not entitled at that point in the text. We *are* entitled to this self-characterization of the nature of our intellect at the outset of the Aesthetic. For it is in the nature of PGL as an apperceptively grounded science that we are always already entitled to assert its doctrines. What we may not yet be in a position to do, at that point in the text, is appreciate *that* we are warranted to appeal to the theory.

The upshot of my interpretation, then, is that Kant's characterization of human intuition as our sole capacity for immediate and object-giving representations is grounded in a pure, apperceptive consciousness of the formal character of our own intellectual powers. Givenness is a necessary condition of all intuition, human or otherwise. That much is part of the traditional definition of intuitive representation as immediate cognition. Kant then argues that givenness is also a sufficient condition of any intuition that is paired with a discursive understanding. This claim is based on an account of discursive representation through marks that Kant takes to be apperceptively grounded as a doctrine of PGL. Accordingly, his claim that human intuition is our only object-giving representation (A19/B33.18–23) is grounded in pure apperception.

3.4 Receptivity and Sensibility

It is a short step from the claim that intuitions are the only object-giving representations that humans can enjoy to the claim that human intuition must be *receptive*. For Kant everywhere assumes that only intellectual representations can be spontaneous. And he also holds, as we have just seen, that *human* (i.e. discursively mediated) intellectual representations cannot give objects to the mind. So, for a discursive mind, object-giving representations must be non-intellectual and, thus, non-spontaneous (i.e. receptive).[32] Human intuition, as object-giving, must therefore be a *receptive* capacity.

It should be uncontroversial that this line of argument is Kantian in spirit, for it involves premises he endorses in many places. What does stand in need of discussion and defense, however, is (i) its relation to the text of § 1 in the Aesthetic and (ii) its relation to my contention that Kant's argument is grounded in apperception.

After introducing intuition as that representation through which cognition relates to objects immediately, Kant writes:

> [Intuition] only takes place insofar as the object is given to us; yet this, in turn, is only possible, *for us humans at least*, through its [sc. the object's] affecting the mind in a certain way. The ability (receptivity) to acquire [*bekommen*] representations through the manner in which we are affected by objects is called **sensibility**. By means of sensibility, therefore, objects are **given** to us and it alone delivers us **intuitions**; through the understanding, however, [objects] are **thought** and from it **concepts** arise. (A19/B33.9–18, italicized phrase added in B, original emphases in bold)

Sensibility is not the same as receptivity: It is a particular *species* of receptivity. It is a receptivity to enjoy representations (here, intuitions) on account of objects' physically affecting one's sensory organs. In Chapter 8, I will discuss the place of receptive yet non-sensible intuition in Kant's framework. What I want to point out here is that Kant appears to argue for the sensible character of human intuition on the basis of a direct

[32] Here I'm assuming, as an analytic truth, that all cognition is either spontaneous or receptive. See Section 7.3 for discussion.

claim about its affection dependence: "[Intuition] is only possible, *for us humans at least*, through its [sc. the object's] affecting the mind in a certain way." This argumentative strategy runs counter to the top-down approach I am ascribing to Kant. Rather than starting from claims about the "higher" cognitive faculty (intellect) – and, in particular, from claims that are knowable through pure apperception – and then arguing to conclusions about our "lower" cognitive capacities, Kant here takes as his starting point a direct characterization of our "lower" cognitive capacity: For us, intuiting involves being affected. Whatever the source of this claim may be – whether phenomenological reflection or empirical observation – it clearly is not knowable via pure apperception.

Indeed, the *Groundwork* appears to credit *feeling* (*Gefühl*) with such consciousness of the affection-dependent character of our intuition:

> Here is an observation that requires no subtle reflection, but which one can assume even the commonest understanding can make, though in its own manner, through an obscure discrimination of judgment [*Urteilskraft*] that it calls feeling: that all representations which come to us without our choice (such as those of the senses) give us objects to cognize only as they affect us, while we remain ignorant of what they may be in themselves[.] (4:450.35–451.04, my underlining)[33]

The context of this passage is Kant's effort to elucidate the distinction between appearances and things in themselves. His aim is to clarify this distinction by tracing it back to a more basic observation, one "even the commonest understanding" can make – namely, that some of our representations "such as those of the senses" "come to us without our choice". Our immediate awareness of the involuntary character of certain representations leads us, "through an obscure discrimination of judgment", to regard these representations as affection-dependent, as "giv[ing] us objects to cognize only as they affect us".[34] This pursues what I call a "bottom-up" approach to Kantian intuition.[35] It suggests that we have a direct

[33] Kant goes on to refer to "the distinction observed between representations given to us from elsewhere and in which we are passive [leidend] and those we produce simply from ourselves and in which we demonstrate our activity" (*Groundwork* 4:451.9–12). Kant clearly takes us to have a fairly unproblematic ability to distinguish the representations that we passively receive from those that we produce through our own spontaneous cognitive activity. The question is on what epistemic basis we identify representations as the one or the other.

[34] Haag (2007, 94) and Willaschek (2001, 223–227) appear to read Kant in this way: basing our consciousness of the receptivity of intuition on our consciousness that we have no voluntary control over the occurrence or the specific content of a given intuition.

[35] For my distinction between "top-down" and "bottom-up" approaches to intuition, see the Introduction.

consciousness of our passivity in the face of sensible representations and of the *sensible* character of all our intuitive representations – or, if not a *direct* consciousness of this sensible character, then at least a consciousness of it that does not derive from an independent, apperceptive grasp on the nature of our "higher" intellectual powers.

I grant that Kant sometimes engages in such bottom-up argumentation and that A19/B33.9–14 is an important strand of bottom-up argumentation in the Aesthetic. But I also want to emphasize the philosophical limitations of this line of argument; for I think its shortcomings justify us in looking for other, top-down strands of argumentation in the Aesthetic as well.

Kant is not the first to propose that the *involuntariness* of a representation might betoken a provenance independent of the mind. Descartes's Meditator reflects:

> But here I must inquire particularly into those ideas that I believe to be derived from things existing outside me. Just what reason do I have for believing that these ideas resemble those things? Well, I do seem to have been so taught by nature. Moreover, I do know from experience that these ideas do not depend on my will, nor consequently upon myself, for I often notice them even against my will. Now, for example, whether I will it or not, I feel heat. It is for this reason that I believe this feeling or idea of heat comes to me from something other than myself, namely from the heat of the fire by which I am sitting. (*Meditations* AT 7:38, my underlining)

The Meditator then asks "whether these reasons are powerful enough" and swiftly concludes they are not – and for very Kantian reasons:

> Again, although these ideas do not depend on my will, it does not follow that they necessarily proceed from things existing outside me. For just as these impulses about which I spoke just now seem to be different from my will, even though they are in me, so too perhaps there is also in me some other faculty, one not yet sufficiently known to me, that produces these ideas, just as it has always seemed up to now that ideas are formed in me without any help from external things when I am asleep. (*Meditations* AT 7:39, my underlining)

The reason involuntariness is not a reliable indicator of mind independence is that our mind could well harbor faculties that generate ideas (representations) without involving our will and, further, without making us aware that we are the source of those ideas. This is no fanciful supposition spawned by the radical doubt that animates the *Meditations*. Kant himself maintains that we are often unaware of our mind's activities and, in particular, that we are prone to misidentify spontaneous representations as receptive. For instance, Kant boasts that "no psychologist" before him had even entertained the thought "that imagination is a necessary ingredient in perception itself" (A120n.28–29).[36] Apparently, generations of psychologists had misidentified as passively received representations that are actually products of the spontaneity of productive imagination. Similarly, Kant describes imagination, whose synthetic and, hence, spontaneous activity "first brings forth a cognition" (A77/B103.14), as "a blind yet indispensable function of the soul" (A78/B103.23–24). The activity of imagination is "blind" in the sense that its activities are typically unconscious as well as involuntary. Yet they are nonetheless spontaneous, not passively received or merely suffered. So if Kant's argument in the Aesthetic appeals to some direct awareness we have of our passivity vis-à-vis our intuitive representations, it stands on unstable ground by his own accounting. For we are often not aware of the spontaneity of spontaneous representations (B130.19–20). And this can easily be mistaken for an awareness of their non-spontaneity.

This points to a graver difficulty for this argumentative strategy – namely, to account for the intuitive status of other offspring of the productive imagination – especially mathematical constructions. It is crucial to Kant's critical epistemology that such representations are intuitive. Yet they are quite obviously products of our mind's spontaneous activity. Moreover, Kant maintains that we have a direct awareness of them as produced by our own mental activity: "<u>We also observe this in ourselves at all times</u>: we cannot think of a line without **drawing** it in thought, of a circle without **describing** it, [...] even of time itself without attending, in the **drawing** of a straight line [...] merely to the act of synthesis of the manifold" (B154, Kant's bold, my underlining; cf. B137.16–138.22). We represent time, Kant says, by attending to our spontaneous synthetic activity in drawing a line – and, in particular, to the successiveness of that activity in generating ever-larger parts of the line. Moreover, the fact that we attend to the successiveness of our own spontaneous activity is itself something that "we observe in ourselves at all times". Here we are *not* blind to the spontaneity of the representation. Rather, Kant alleges that we are directly aware of our spontaneous activity in generating the representation. Yet the representation in question is an *intuition*: of a line, of a circle, of

[36] This boast is obviously an exaggeration – Berkeley's theory of vision is a relevant counterexample. Nevertheless, Kant is prudent to frequently remind the reader that combination cannot be given through the senses (B129f., B134.6–135.14, *et passim*), since this idea runs contrary not just to tradition but to the folk psychology of perceptual experience.

time (viz. successiveness). So awareness of our passivity vis-à-vis a certain representation is not merely unreliable as a *sufficient* criterion of intuition, since so much of our mind's spontaneity expresses itself unconsciously; it also fails as a *necessary* criterion, since it would rule out a host of representations that Kant counts as intuitive.

I do not pretend that these difficulties are insuperable. But they are real. And it is troubling that they should arise at so early and so prominent a part of the text. An interpretation of Kant's opening characterizations of intuition that clashes with key critical doctrines – for example, about the nature of imagination or mathematical constructions – leaves something to be desired. Can a top-down reading do any better?

Here I would emphasize that the passage from the Aesthetic quoted previously (A19/B33.9–18) contains not only a direct characterization of human intuition as affection-dependent but also a comparison of intuition to thought: "By means of sensibility, therefore, objects are **given** to us and it alone delivers us **intuitions**; through the understanding, however, they [sc. objects] are **thought** and from it **concepts** arise." One dimension of this contrast is that we *receive* representations (viz. intuitions) through sensibility, whereas the understanding itself *produces* representations (viz. concepts). Clearly, both sides of this contrast – the receptivity of sensibility and the spontaneity of understanding – are to be understood together. But that does not mean that they enjoy the same epistemic status. I propose that, for Kant, we have a special appreciation of the spontaneous character of our intellectual representations that is not matched in the case of sensible intuition. Kant admittedly says little to emphasize the spontaneity of the intellect in the Aesthetic, apart from claiming that "from it concepts arise [*entspringen*]".[37] And the Introduction contains only a few vague remarks to the effect that "I can think what I want" (Bxxvii.29–30). Nevertheless, Kant might reasonably have thought himself entitled to this premise, not as a received truism but as an insight based in pure apperception.

For let us suppose that the intellect is essentially apperceptive, i.e. that its acts are such that it is, in principle, possible for us to become conscious of them. Now, to be conscious of something, such as a mental act, is inter alia to represent it. So the essentially apperceptive character of the intellect entails that we can, in principle, represent any of its acts. But we obviously do not have an actual consciousness of every act of intellect, even if it is

[37] This is an expression of cognitive spontaneity as characterized in the Transcendental Logic: "the capacity to itself bring forth representations" (A51/B75.4).

essential to each act to ground the possibility of such consciousness. So we must distinguish between the act and the representation of (the consciousness of) that act, since ex hypothesi some acts go unrepresented. It follows, then, that becoming conscious of an act of intellect involves the generation of a representation that would not otherwise have arisen. But the ability to generate representations just is spontaneity in a cognitive capacity. Therefore, an essentially apperceptive cognitive faculty must be spontaneous. For it would not otherwise be able to generate representations of its acts and, thereby, become conscious of them. And that would contradict the supposition that it is essentially apperceptive.[38] Apperception entails spontaneity.[39]

This gives us a different route to the desired conclusion. Instead of starting from a direct characterization of human intuition as affection-dependent and therefore sensible, we can start from a direct characterization of *intellect* as spontaneous, which will lead us to an *indirect* characterization of human intuition as receptive. The linkage is this. We have already seen that discursive mediation renders human intellection incapable of giving objects to the mind. But intuition *überhaupt* – and, thus, human intuitions, if there are any – are object-giving. So, in humans, intuition is a non-intellectual capacity. Thus, if spontaneity is the hallmark of intellect *überhaupt*,[40] then human intuition must be non-spontaneous (i.e. receptive) precisely insofar as it is object-giving.

This indirect, top-down argumentative route to the receptivity of human intuition also yields a subtler version of that doctrine that is not subject to the difficulties I raised for direct, bottom-up readings. On those readings, human intuition is passive, full stop. And this is hard to square

38 What are Kant's grounds for claiming that intellect is essentially apperceptive? Though the details of Kant's view on this question may be obscure and disputable, it is clear what his ultimate answer must be: It is through apperception that we know that our intellect is essentially apperceptive. Here the snake eats its tail. This is one ramification of Kant's claim that "the synthetic unity of apperception is the highest point to which one must affix all use of the understanding, even the whole of logic and, after it, Transcendental Philosophy; indeed this faculty is the understanding itself" (B134n.).

39 For further discussion, see Section 7.3 as well as Boyle (2015).

40 Indeed, Kant appears to regard spontaneity as a defining criterion of intellect. Thus, he will call a productive (i.e. object-generating) intuition "intellectual" precisely in virtue of its spontaneity. So spontaneity pertains to intellect at the highest level of abstraction (i.e. to intellect *überhaupt*), just as immediacy and the giving of knowable objects pertains to intuition *überhaupt*. Discursive mediation is a more specific feature that pertains to the *finite* (and, in particular, *human*) intellect, but not to intellect merely as such, just as receptivity is a more specific feature that pertains to finite (and, in particular, *human*) intuition, but not to all intuition merely as such. These are the first of several distinct levels of abstraction that we must distinguish in order to track Kant's argument. For elaboration, see Chapter 7.

with the evident spontaneity of the intuitive representations that Kant places at the heart of mathematical demonstration – namely, formal intuitions – or those that arise from the productive imagination. On the top-down approach, by contrast, human intuitions must be receptive *insofar as they give objects to the mind.* That is to say, it is only the object-giving aspects of human intuition that must be receptive. The receptivity of human intuition specifically compensates for the ontic sterility of discursive spontaneity. This does not require that every intuition *in its entirety* is passively received. It allows that discursive spontaneity may account for various aspects of our intuitive representations. What it does require, however, is that the object-giving character of these intuitive representations is due to their ultimate dependence on affection and *not* to whatever spontaneity contributes to their production.

Now it must be admitted that, on my "top-down" reading of A19/B33, not every clause in Kant's discussion does essential argumentative work and, contrariwise, some essential argumentative work is compressed into just a few words or even left to the reader to fill in. But this is not incompatible with the larger picture I am painting of Kant's procedure in the *Critique.* I think Kant pursues multiple lines of thought at once. Though these lines of thought often overlap in their premises and (of course) in their conclusions, they appeal to different types of evidence and do not have the same epistemic status. Kant's critical epistemology is a rich tapestry. My contention is not that it consists of a single thread, but that one of its many threads has a special status – namely, as grounded in apperception. I argue that this thread, if traced carefully, will be found to run through crucial facets of his theory of intuition.

One of the textual strands that my reading does not pick out is the specifically *sensible* character of human intuition and the embodied, *sensory* character of the affection to which we are receptive. We can know through apperception, albeit indirectly, that our intuition must be receptive insofar as it is object-giving, but we cannot in this way know that our receptivity is realized in embodied sense organs. The specifically sensible character of human intuition is not available to us via apperception, though its merely receptive character is.

Significantly, however, the sensible character of human intuition does virtually no argumentative work in the Aesthetic.[41] It is the notion of receptivity that does the heavy lifting. This is not to say that Kant uses

[41] The only place where I think the sensible character of our intuition plays a significant role is in the first ME of <space>, where Kant speaks of "[referring] certain sensations to something outside of

"sensibility" when he only means receptivity – though it is telling that this pretty nearly exhausts his gloss on the term (A19/B33.12–14) and on "sensation" (A19/B34.23–01; see Section 3.4). Kant's topic in the *Critique* is, quite appropriately, *human* knowledge. And so his vocabulary naturally gravitates toward terms that apply to human cognitive capacities as such. Yet many of the points he wishes to make about human knowledge do not turn on parochial features of our minds but on more generic, or more abstract, features that might be shared by quite different kinds of minds. That is, many of the aspects of human cognition that interest Kant obtain not in virtue of the specifically human character of our minds but in virtue of some more abstract characterization (for example, the affection-dependent character of our intuition, or the spontaneous character of our intellect, etc.). To follow Kant's arguments often involves shifting between subtly different levels of abstraction.[42] And these shifting levels of abstraction are not always reflected in Kant's language, which remains, appropriately enough, focused on the human case, even when the aspects of the human case that interest him apply more broadly to other types of finite minds.

Kant's discussion of sensation is a particularly instructive case of this misalignment between Kant's vocabulary, which typically suggests specificity to the human case, and the levels of abstraction at which his arguments are actually prosecuted, which typically invoke quite abstract features that are not unique to the human mind. Let us turn, then, to Kant's notion of *Empfindung* and his correlated distinction between the matter and the form of intuition.

me (i.e. to something in another place in space from that in which I find myself)"(A23/B38.5–6). Kant portrays the cognizing subject as located at a particular place in space, where "I find myself". This strongly suggests that the cognizing subject is united to a particular body that occupies the space where it is located to the exclusion of other bodies (see Section 8.2.3 for discussion). And the ensuing discussion suggests that the embodied, sensible character of human intuition plays a role in grounding the representation of chiral orientation – that is, our ability "to represent [things] as outside of *and next to* one another" (A23/B38.8–9, italicized phrase added in B). (See Smyth MS for elaboration of this reading.) But I do not see that the specifically sensible (as opposed to merely receptive) character of intuition plays a role in establishing Kant's main conclusions in the Aesthetic – namely, that space and time are forms of our intuition and, therefore, that they are (a) transcendentally ideal in that spatiotemporal determinations do not pertain to things in themselves, yet (b) empirically real in that they necessarily pertain to inner/outer appearances as subjective conditions of their possibility.

42 We have already tracked several such shifts. The spontaneity of our intellect is a maximally abstract feature, for it characterizes all intellect *überhaupt*; whereas the discursivity of our intellect is more specific, though perhaps not unique to us. Similarly, the immediacy of our intuition is a maximally abstract feature, which pertains to all intuition *überhaupt*; whereas the receptivity of our intuition is more specific, its sensible character yet more specific, and its spatiotemporal character more specific still.

3.5 Sensation in the Abstract: Matter and Form of Intuition

The opening paragraph of the Aesthetic establishes (i) that intuitive representations alone can give objects to the human mind (see Section 3.3) and (ii) that such givenness is ultimately grounded on our receptivity to affection by objects (see Section 3.4).[43] In the next two paragraphs, Kant analyzes this relation of affection, which obtains between objects and the cognizing subject, so as to bring to light a form/matter distinction that will govern all subsequent argument in the Aesthetic.

He begins by introducing sensation (*Empfindung*) as the subject-side relatum of the affection relation: "The effect of an object on the capacity for representation [*Vorstellungsfähigkeit*], insofar as we are affected by it [sc. the object], is called **sensation**" (A19/B34). This is a remarkably bloodless characterization of sensation. It says nothing about the force and vivacity of sensory experience, nothing about the subjective *pour-soi* character of perceptual qualia, nothing about the embodied materiality of the sensory organs and their integration in a multi-modal nervous system. Kant eschews the rich and concrete descriptors of phenomenology, materialism, and anatomy, which are favored by other early modern thinkers, in favor of quite schematic and abstract metaphysical terminology.[44] Indeed, Kant seems to go out of his way to avoid even the implication that sensation must be realized in a material body by employing the dualism-friendly term "*Vorstellungsfähigkeit*" rather than more obvious and more obviously materialistic vocabulary such as *Sinnen* (senses), *Sinnlichkeit* (sensibility), *Wahrnehmungsvermögen* (perceptual faculty), or even *Gemüt* (mind). Sensation is characterized in merely causal terms, as the influence of an object on the subject's representational state. We should not, of course, conclude from this that Kant advocates an immaterialist conception of sensation, as other critical works make clear.[45] It does, however, suggest that the argumentative use of <*sensation*> in the Aesthetic will trade on

43 I cannot consider here whether the object-side relatum of this affection relation is occupied by things in themselves, appearances, or both but considered under different aspects. I touch on this issue in Chapter 8.

44 Contrast this with the attention to the vivacity of sensory experience one finds in Descartes, Leibniz, Hume, or Tetens; the sensitivity to the subjective phenomenology of sensory experience in Descartes, Berkeley, and others; the interest in the anatomy of the human sensorium in Descartes or Locke; and the emphasis on the material and embodied character of human sensibility and affect in Descartes, Spinoza, or Condillac.

45 See, in particular, *Anthropology* §§ 15–16, 21, 24, (7:153ff, 161 f.); cf. *Discovery* 8:208.33. Falkenstein (1990) makes a strong case for the view that Kantian sensations are conscious bodily states.

the highly abstract features highlighted in Kant's gloss and not on the phenomenology of sensations or their essentially embodied character. The Aesthetic is concerned with sensation in the abstract: representations that result from affection by objects.

Kant is careful to register that the representation that ultimately results from an object's affecting the cognizing subject may depend not only on the character of the object and the circumstances in which it is encountered but also on the character of the cognizing subject herself. This, I take it, is the significance of the qualification, "insofar as we are affected by it [sc. the object]". All causal action is *inter*action; all influence is commerce. When one thing affects another, the resulting effect reflects not only the action of the agent but also the constitution of the patient.[46] So if the cognizing subject has an abiding constitution that remains constant throughout the various affections it suffers, then the features of its representational state that are due to this subjective constitution will not count as sensations. For while these features may indeed be part of the overall effect that an object has upon the subject's *Vorstellungsfähigkeit*, they do not obtain "insofar as [the subject is] affected by it [sc. the object]" but insofar as the subject's own constitution conditions the result.

The underlying idea here is that receptivity to affection is not a thoroughly protean potential to take on any determination whatsoever: It is not an open door through which any accident may "wander over" into the mind (cf. *Prolegomena* 4:17–20).[47] Rather, a receptivity is a positive inner characteristic that a subject (or substance) can possess or lack. It is a

[46] During Kant's "silent decade", he pens the following reflection on Baumgarten's capacity metaphysics: "The *principium generale commercii* is: all influence in the world is **in part** the effect of the active in the passive, **in part** the resistance of the latter. This resistance of the inner condition and determination of the substance is the action, through which the accident of the influence is actuated (apprehension)." (R4704, 1773–1777, 17:681) The idea is that the transeunt action of one substance on another always involves a *re*action (resistance) on the part of the patient. So influence always involves *inter*action, even if one party to the interaction is dominant and thus counts as agent rather than patient. Kant is not simply smuggling Newton's third law into his ontology – not least because the reaction is not assumed to be equal to the action. The claim is rather that external influences, in Wuerth's apt gloss, "work *through* a substance's own powers to help bring about accidents in it" (2014, 75, original italics). Not every sort of accident can obtain in every sort of substance: Plants cannot be sassy, stones cannot be ill (cf. R3581, 1769–1771, 17:71.7–12) So the accidents that do obtain in a given substance, receptively or otherwise, are partly determined by (grounded in, explained by) the inner character of that substance (cf. M-Pö/L_1 28:207.21–25). For elaboration of this argument, see Wuerth (2014, ch. 3.2), to which the present discussion is indebted.

[47] Watkins and Willaschek aptly write, "sensibility cannot be *purely* passive or receptive, because it must *produce* representations in response to being acted on from without. External objects do not generate representations that the human mind simply receives; instead, an object acts on the mind and the mind creates a sensible representation in response" (2017, 90–91, original emphases).

genuine capacity (*Fähigkeit*) to take on specific kinds of determinations (e.g. to entertain sensible representations) when subjected to specific kinds of external influence. In this sense, *any* effect of an object on a subject's *Vorstellungsfähigkeit* is, of necessity, partly grounded in the nature of the subject/patient herself. For it is only in virtue of possessing the relevant receptivity that an effect or determination of the relevant sort can obtain in the subject/patient in the first place. Not even God can affect a fencepost in such a way that it receives a sensation.[48] The very possibility that a certain effect – in our case, a certain sort of representation – should be able to obtain is partly grounded in the intrinsic character, the inner constitution, of the subject in which it actually does obtain (when it does). And this remains true when the subject receptively suffers the effect in question by being affected from without. Any exercise of receptivity reflects, to some extent, the inner constitution of the thing in which the relevant property comes to inhere.

Once one grants that a receptivity is an enduring positive characteristic of the affected subject/patient, not a pantomorphic plasticity to whatever comes, then the possibility emerges that a receptivity could, in principle, play not just an *enabling* role in opening up the subject to suffering a particular range of predetermined effects but a positive *determining* role in shaping the effects to which the subject is receptive. It is conceivable that, for certain receptive capacities, this determining role may be minimal or even nil. But for every receptive capacity, it is a live question whether (and which) specific aspects of its exercises are due to the inner constitution of the subject and which are due to external influence. Investigating a receptive capacity – say, as part of a science of sensibility (an Aesthetic) (A21/B35.1–2) – will crucially involve distinguishing, within its exercises, endogenous features that are positively determined by the abiding inner constitution of the capacity – *nota bene*: there may be few or none – from adventitious features that are due to affection from without.

Kant's abstract conception of sensation thus anticipates his distinction between the *matter* and the *form* of sensibility and sensible representations. For the idea that a certain receptive capacity plays a determining role

48 Compare M-H: "**Every subject** in which an **accident inheres must itself be a ground of the inherence of the latter** [sc. the accident]. [. . .] Thus the inherence of an accident in A requires its [sc. A's] own power [Kraft], and a merely foreign power, even a divine power, is not sufficient. Otherwise, I could bring forth thoughts in a mere post, if it were possible to do so through a merely foreign power." (1762–1764, 28:52.8-16, original emphasis)

vis-à-vis its exercises is just the idea that it has a form. This follows from the very concepts of <form> and <matter>:

> **Matter and Form**. These are two concepts which underlie all other [concepts of] reflection, so much are they inseparably connected with every use of the understanding. The first [sc. <matter>] signifies the determinable *überhaupt*, the second [sc. <form>] the determination of it [sc. the determinable] (both taken in the transcendental sense, since we are abstracting from any difference in what is given and from the manner in which it is determined). (A266/B322)

What is determinable is subject to various possible determinations. It is changeable, mutable, variable. So the matter of a sensible representation will consist of all those aspects that can differ from representation to representation (in the same subject). These features vary with changes in the object and in the manner in which it affects the subject. They are the features of the representation that are due to affection by the object, those that reflect the influence of the object and its affection of the subject. Accordingly, sensation just *is* the matter of sensible representations. The form of a sensible representation, by contrast, is what remains constant from representation to representation. For it reflects the influence of the inner constitution of the capacity and is thus a necessary feature of all its exercises, as such: "Accordingly, the pure form of sensible intuitions *überhaupt* will be met with in the mind [*Gemüte*] a priori" (A20/B34.19–21; cf. A20/B34.13–16). Form is "the determination of the determinable" not in the sense that *maroon* is a determination of the determinable *red* but in the sense that *Mary mourning Jesus* is the determination that marks out all pietàs as such, however they may otherwise differ from one another, i.e. leaving all other aspects of them determinable but as yet undetermined. The form of sensibility is the "determination of [the determinable]" in the sense that it is what constitutes sensations *as sensible representations*. It is, as it were, the common grammar that structures sensations as well-formed expressions in the language of sensible representation.

Various aspects of this line of argument are bound to raise worries. First, it may appear that Kant is just building into his conception of sensation the assumption that sensibility will have (must have) a pure form that is necessarily exhibited by all its exercises. Second, and worse, it appears that this assumption is born of some highly speculative metaphysics of substances, capacities, and causation that properly belongs to Kant's precritical rationalism and should not survive his critical turn. Third, even if something like this metaphysical account of causal interactions between capacity-endowed substances does survive into the critical period, it is surely not something that could be plausibly known through apperception, as my proposed interpretation dictates it ought to be.

To the first point, I do think that Kant's conception of sensation in the abstract already takes for granted that sensibility, as a receptive capacity, must have a form. Now, Kant does offer an argument for the claim that sensibility has a form distinct from its matter:

> Since that in which alone sensations can order themselves and can be placed in a certain form cannot in turn be sensation, the matter of all appearance can admittedly only be given a posteriori, yet its form must as a whole already lie ready for them [sc. sensations] in the mind [*Gemüte*] a priori and, hence, must be able to be regarded separately from all sensation. (A20/B34)

Kant's thought seems to be that, whatever one identifies as sensation, there must always be something that is responsible for the orderability of sensations. And just as the order of the elements in a manifold cannot itself be an element in the manifold, this factor, which first enables sensations to be ordered with respect to one another, cannot itself be sensation. So it must be form, not matter. Form does not order the sensations but rather "makes it that the manifold of appearance [which 'corresponds' to sensation; A20/B34.5–6] can be ordered in certain relations" (A20/B34.6–8).

There is surely something plausible about the idea that what accounts for the orderability of sensations cannot itself be a sensation. But this thought is really a conditional: *If* there is something that accounts for the orderability of sensations, *then* that thing cannot be a sensation. Yet the text provides us no reason to accept the antecedent. It simply presupposes that there is a single factor that accounts for the orderability of sensations. The argument slides from a truism that relations among elements are different in kind from the elements that are their relata to a contentious claim about the ground of the possibility of certain elements standing in relations at all. Kant simply assumes that there must be such a ground and, moreover, that it must constitute an invariant structure inherent in all sensible representations. This begs the question. For the distinction between form and matter just *is* the distinction between the invariant features of sensible representations and the variable (determinable) ones. Kant takes for granted that sensible representation must have a constitutive form. I can find no justification for this claim in the text.[49]

[49] Commentators who scrutinize this argument tend to agree that it fails: Guyer (1987, 341 f., 351f, cf. 110); Falkenstein (1995, 135–137); Merritt (2010, 4–5). Characteristically, Allison (2004, 14–15, 126 f.) is more sanguine.

How problematic is this for Kant's overall argument in the Aesthetic? Not very. Kant's discussion does anticipate his transcendental idealist conclusion that spatiotemporal determinations are subjectively grounded relational properties.[50] But he does not need to *assume* that sensibility has a form to proceed with his investigation. All he needs is the claim that, whenever a receptivity is in play, it is crucial to draw a hylomorphic distinction between those features of its exercises that reflect the inner constitution of the subject/patient (if there are any) and those that are due to affection from without. The former features (if there are any) will be as invariant as the inner constitution that grounds them. This gives us criteria for identifying features as formal. Because they are *grounded in* the constitution of the subject, they are *necessary* aspects of every exercise of her receptive capacity, as such. That certain features of our sensible representations actually satisfy these criteria is not something Kant simply assumes in the Preliminaries. It is something he explicitly argues for in the first two Metaphysical Expositions, where he contends, first, that space and time, respectively, ground ("*zum Grunde liegen*") all representations of outer and of inner sense (A23/B38.10–11; A30/B46.9–10) and, second, that *because* they ground all sensible representations, they are themselves *necessary* sensible representations (A24/B38.16–17; A31/B46.14–15). That is, Kant provides a direct argument for the claim that sensible intuition has a form by positively identifying what that form is – namely, spatiotemporal structure.

Yet even if Kant's larger argument does not trade on an unwarranted assumption (the first line of objection), is not the hylomorphic conception of sensible intuition I have presented tainted by its origins in a pre-critical, rationalist metaphysics of capacities and causation (the second line of objection)? And doesn't that violate the epistemic strictures imposed by my top-down approach to intuition (the third line of objection)?

There are, no doubt, echoes of Kant's pre-critical metaphysics in the Transcendental Aesthetic and elsewhere in the *Critique*. But there are also indications that Kant takes these echoes to have been transposed into a critical key.[51] Recall that Kant identifies <form> and <matter> as concepts of reflection that are "inseparably connected with every use of the understanding" (A266/B322). It would appear, then, that he views

[50] See B66f., A284/B340.8–9. On Kant's relationalism, see Brittan (1978, ch. 4); Langton (1998, ch. 5); Setiya (2004); Messina (2018).

[51] For an outline of this "transposition" of pre-critical doctrines into a critical register, see Smyth (2015, Sections 2.4 and 2.5).

them as concepts that can be acquired merely by attentively reflecting on our employment of the understanding. That is to say, he takes the form/matter distinction to be knowable through pure apperception. How, precisely, Kant understands this to work is a difficult question that I cannot take up here.[52] But it seems overwhelmingly likely that it is his considered view.

This does not entirely deflect the second line of objection, however. For even if we accept that <form> and <matter> are available through pure apperception as critically sanitized concepts of reflection, something more is involved in applying this hylomorphic distinction to the notion of a receptive capacity of sensible intuition. The conception of sensation that is operative in the Aesthetic may be abstract, but it contains more than the mere idea of determinability and determination (cf. A266/B322.16). In particular, it involves a notion of causal interaction. And it is indeed implausible that we can know through pure apperception that we stand in causal relations or even that we have the capacity to do so.[53]

A top-down, apperceptive approach can establish that our intuition is *receptive* (i.e. dependent on determination from without) but not that it is *sensible* (i.e. dependent on causal affection). Accordingly, there is a significant strand of Kant's argument in the Aesthetic that my apperceptive account cannot capture – namely, his conception of the a priority of space and time in terms of their independence from *sensation* and, correlatively, his account of them as forms of *sensibility*.[54]

I would emphasize, however, that Kant's arguments in the Expositions do not turn on the specifically sensible character of our intuition. To argue that the original representations of space and time are forms of intuition

[52] I am tempted by a reconstruction along the following lines. The concepts of reflection, <form> and <matter>, appeal to a notion of determination and determinability that is sufficiently abstract to apply equally well to the determination involved in syllogisms, cognition, judgments, and intuitions, as well as to causal interactions and the properties of material substances. So the question whether <form> and <matter> are inseparably connected with all uses of the understanding is tantamount to the question whether all uses of the understanding involve the representation of determination and determinability in this abstract sense. It is plausible that Kant thinks they do. For all thought, even the framing of analytic judgments (B131n.28–32), involves a synthesis of representations. The crucial step, which I do not pretend to be able to demonstrate, would then be to show that synthesizing representations involves or is tantamount to representing determination in the relevant abstract sense. For an illuminating discussion of the concepts of reflection in general and their kinship to the categories, see Boyle (forthcoming-b).

[53] I am grateful to an anonymous referee for pressing me on this point.

[54] Though a top-down approach cannot establish that the forms of *sensible* intuition are a priori in the "sensation-independent" sense, it can establish that the forms of *receptive* intuition are a priori in the "from-grounds" sense. For these forms are still *grounds* of the possibility of all experience. See Section 1.2.2, note 13.

does require showing that they pertain merely to the form and not to the matter of intuition. But this need not involve reference to sensations. For the distinction between matter and form – between the determinable and its determination, between variable, adventitious features and invariant, necessary ones – applies to any receptive intuition, merely as such. A receptivity is not a simple openness to properties that wander over into the mind from without (cf. *Prolegomena* 4:282.17–20). A receptivity belongs to the intrinsic constitution of the subject/patient and, as such, it can in principle exert a positive, determining influence on the exercises that are passively wrung out of it. This is enough to underwrite the criterion of *formality* that Kant appeals to in the Expositions. And by showing that our original representations of space and time satisfy this criterion, Kant shows that they must be a priori representations – that is, that they must be independent of *whatever* matter happens to "fill out" our intuitions, whether it is sensation or something else.

3.6 Conclusion

Kant's overall argument in the Aesthetic can be divided into four main parts. (1) The Preliminaries lay out criteria of *intuition*, *sensibility*, and *form* so that (2) the Exposition can argue that space and time are (i) forms of (ii) sensible (iii) intuition. This serves as the basis for (3) the Conclusions that spatiotemporal features (a) are not determinations of things in themselves but (b) do necessarily apply to all appearances. Finally, (4) a Commentary clarifies these arguments and conclusions.

The present chapter focused on the Preliminaries. I argued that my apperceptive, top-down approach to Kantian intuition was particularly well suited to capture the teleological cast of Kant's thought (Section 3.2). I then proceeded to provide an apperception-based account of the principal criteria to which Kant must appeal in the Expositions.

In Section 3.3, I examined Kant's proposed criterion of human *intuition*. Kant starts with the traditional conception of intuition as *immediate cognition*. Intuitions are, by definition, object-giving. Kant then argues that, for us humans, intuitions are the *only* object-giving representations. To do so, he appeals to a theory of discursive marks. Insofar as intellectual representations are essentially mediated in their reference to objects by discursive marks, it follows that they cannot give objects to the mind for cognition. Accordingly, the only object-giving cognitions that a discursive mind can frame are non-intellectual and, hence, non-spontaneous. Because this theory of discursive marks belongs to pure general logic, it is knowable through pure apperception. We therefore have a criterion of human intuition as the cognitive complement of discursive intellection: Intuition is the ultimate source of all *given* objects and, in particular, of anything the intellect cannot account for due to its discursively mediated character.

In Section 3.4, I argued that the receptivity of intuition follows from the fact that spontaneity is the defining feature of the intellect and the previously established fact that human, discursive intellection is not object-giving (see Section 3.3). Since human intuition is object-giving, as all intuition by definition is, it cannot be intellectual and thus cannot be spontaneous. This argumentative route to the receptivity of our intuition is not as prominent in the text as other bottom-up readings. But it is not without textual support, and it avoids serious pitfalls to which bottom-up readings fall prey. For the most part, Kant's claims about our mode of intuition hold not in virtue of its specifically *sensible* character but merely in virtue of its *receptive* character, which is knowable via pure apperception.

Finally, Section 3.5 explicated Kant's notion of sensation in the abstract and his associated form/matter distinction. Though pure apperception cannot, of course, anticipate the specifically sensible character of human intuition, it does license a hylomorphic account of all receptive intuition, as such. Variable, adventitious features of receptive representations reflect the vicissitudes of external influences, whereas the intrinsic constitution of the cognizing subject grounds features that are invariant and necessary to its exercises as such.

To show that space and time are (i) forms of (ii) sensible (or, rather, receptive) (iii) intuition, therefore, Kant must argue that they exhibit features (i) that are necessary to all representations of outer or of inner sense, (ii) that discursive spontaneity cannot account for, and (iii) that involve objects being given to the mind. In the following chapters, I will argue that these are just the elements we find in Kant's Expositions.

4

Exposition, Conceptual Analysis, and Apperception

Chapter 3 argued that the "Preliminaries" in § 1 of the Aesthetic articulate criteria of intuition, sensibility, and form that Kant will exploit in the "Expositions", i.e. the metaphysical exposition (ME) of the concept <space>, the transcendental exposition (TE) of the concept <space>, and the parallel ME and TE of <time>. Applying these criteria to the considerations put forward in the Expositions is supposed to justify certain "Conclusions from the above Concepts" – in particular, that space and time are forms of outer and of inner sense, respectively, and therefore (a) do not pertain to things in themselves, but (b) necessary pertain to appearances.

Just as Chapter 3 highlighted the apperceptively grounded aspects of Kant's arguments in the Preliminaries, this chapter and Chapter 5 pursue an apperception-based reading of the Expositions. The present chapter argues that apperception is central to Kant's technical notion of *exposition* and, in particular, *metaphysical* exposition. Chapter 5 analyzes Kant's specific arguments for the intuitive origin of <space>.

I first address Kant's own characterization of his arguments, as "isolating" the form of sensibility (Section 4.1) and as "expositions" of a special sort of concept – namely, one that is given a priori (Section 4.2). I explain Kant's distinction between given versus made concepts and connect the notion of concepts that are given a priori with Kant's later account of the "original acquisition" (*Discovery* 8:221.29) of a priori representations. I then turn to Kant's conception of exposition as a form of conceptual analysis (Section 4.3) and argue that apperceptive reflection is the principal vehicle of conceptual analysis and, thus, the *modus probandi* of Kant's arguments in the Expositions (Section 4.4). This yields a general picture of the Expositions as pursuing the critical project of reason's self-knowledge (Section 4.5). The Expositions analyze, via apperceptive reflection, a concept that we come to possess merely by self-consciously exercising our cognitive faculties.

4.1 Isolating Sensibility: Elimination versus Abstraction

Kant closes § 1 of the Aesthetic with a suggestive description of how the subsequent investigation will proceed:

> In the Transcendental Aesthetic, therefore, we will first **isolate** sensibility by separating out [*absondern*] all that the understanding thereby thinks through its concepts, so that nothing but empirical intuition remains left over [*übrig bleibe*]. Second, we will partition off [*abtrennen*] all that belongs to sensation, so that nothing but pure intuition and the mere form of appearances remains left over, which is the sole thing that sensibility can deliver a priori. (A22/B36)[1]

It is natural to interpret this as a multi-stage process of elimination or removal, where various kinds of elements in a complex are filtered out and dispensed with until all that remains is the desired element one wishes to inspect – namely, pure intuition and mere form of appearance. There are, however, two fatal problems with this reading.[2]

First, it does not accurately describe how the Aesthetic actually unfolds in §§ 2–8. If anything, the ME proceeds in the opposite direction: arguing first that our representation of space is not empirical and, thus, cannot derive from sensation (moments 1 and 2); and *then* that it must originate in intuition and, thus, cannot derive from the understanding (moments 3 and 4). Moreover, the focus of these arguments is our *concept* <space>, not a pure intuition evacuated of all sensation and unadulterated by any intellectual activity. At no point in the Aesthetic does Kant discriminate those aspects of experience or cognition that are due to the understanding, so as to isolate intuition in a pre- or non-conceptualized state. If he did,

[1] This "isolation passage" elaborates an idea that was already floated at the outset of both Introductions:

> Now what is quite remarkable is that it turns out that even among our experiences cognitions are mixed in [*sich mengen*] that must have their origin a priori[.] [...] For when one removes [*wegschafft*] from the former [sc. experiences] all that belongs to the senses, there still remains left over certain original concepts and judgments generated out of them[.] (A2, my underlining)

And in B:

> Experiential cognition is a composite [*Zusammengesetzes*] of that which we receive [*empfangen*] through impressions and that which our own faculty of cognition (merely occasioned by sensible impressions) brings forth out of itself, which addition [*Zusatz*] we do not distinguish until long practice has made us attentive to it and skilled at separating it out [*zur Absonderung desselben geschickt*]. (B1, my underlining)

Kant doubtless aims to "isolate" the a priori elements of experience. The question is what doing this involves and what it produces (or what remains left over) as its result.

[2] Here I am indebted to the perceptive analysis of Falkenstein (1995, 148–151).

there would be no room left for debate over Kant's intellectualism or sensibilism about intuition (cf. McLear 2014). One could just point to the advertised discussion of empirical intuition shorn of "all that the understanding thereby thinks through its concepts" and plump for a sensibilist reading. Nor does Kant ever pinpoint and factor out the sensory element of empirical intuition, so as to exhibit pure intuition in the buff. If he did, it would bankrupt the cottage industry devoted to interpreting the distinction between a form*al* intuition and a form *of* intuition (B160n.). While the Aesthetic certainly purports to identify aspects of our cognition that can only be attributed to pure intuition, it does not do so by eliminating seriatim those aspects of cognition that are due to the understanding and to sensation.

Second, it would be a serious inconsistency for Kant to hold that intuitions (or, indeed, any cognitively significant representation) would still be accessible to conscious inspection or investigation once we remove "all that the understanding thereby thinks through its concepts". Recall Kant's famous slogan, "thoughts without content are empty; <u>intuitions without concepts are blind</u>" (A51/B76.13–15, my underlining). This need not imply that intuitions without concepts are nonexistent or impossible, but it surely implies that, without the contributions of the understanding, an intuition would be "nothing for me" (B132.8) – that is, "it would admittedly be an intuition lacking thought [*gedankenlose Anschauung*], but never cognition, and therefore for us as good as nothing" (A111.23–24). Kant holds that cognitively significant representations are available to conscious reflection only in virtue of the synthetic unity of apperception, which he identifies with the understanding itself (B134n.35–39). So, even if we grant that there are intuitions that reflect no input or influence from the understanding, they must, by Kant's lights, be obscure to us. They would not be susceptible to direct inspection or phenomenological investigation, for they would not be available to consciousness at all. Any characterization of them would have to be indirect – that is, inferred from observations about representations that are directly available to conscious reflection.[3] So the "isolation" of sensibility in the Aesthetic cannot involve the removal of all contributions of the understanding, even if this were possible. For once these are removed, there is nothing left that we might investigate, inspect, or consciously reflect upon.

[3] This is Falkenstein's positon (1995, 55–61, 82–83, 99). For Falkenstein, the understanding merely brings to consciousness features that already obtain in intuitions that are intrinsically unconceptualized and therefore unconscious.

Rather than describing successive steps in the Aesthetic's order of presentation, the isolation passage is better understood as enumerating distinct criteria that its arguments must satisfy. The task is to identify any features of our cognition that (i) cannot be attributed to the intellect and (ii) cannot be attributed to sensation – that is, to the influence of an object in affecting the mind (cf. A19f./B34.23–01 and Section 3.4). This fits Kant's actual procedure in the ME, which argues that the concepts <space> and <time> contain marks that cannot derive from sensation (moments 1 and 2) nor from the intellect (moments 3 and 4). The spatiotemporality of experience, therefore, can only reflect the intrinsic constitution of the mind's capacity for intuition: that is, the a priori form of our sensibility. Kant arrives at this conclusion not by eliminating the contributions of the understanding and sensation from our experience and describing what remains, but by showing that analysis of the *concepts* <space> and <time> involves abstracting from these contributions to experience.[4]

4.2 Original Acquisition and A Priori, Given Concepts

As if in response to these worries, Kant inserts into the B-edition a new characterization of the numbered paragraphs that precede – and, presumably, justify – his "Conclusions from the above Concepts":[5]

> I understand under **exposition** (*expositio*) the distinct [*deutliche*] (even if not exhaustive) representation of that which belongs to a concept; an

4 This picture is confirmed in *Discovery*, where Kant distinguishes abstract (i.e. abstract*ed*) representations from an abstract treatment of them:

> One does not abstract a concept as a common mark, rather one abstracts in the use of a concept from the differentness of that which is contained under it. The chemists alone are capable of abstracting something, when they extract [*ausheben*] a liquid from other materials, in order to retain it separately; the philosopher abstracts from that which he wants to leave out of account in a certain use of the concept. (8:199n.18–23)

It is this sort of abstraction – mere selective focus, not isolating extraction – that Kant employs in the Aesthetic:

> But if I say: space and time, considered in abstraction, i.e. prior to all empirical conditions, exhibit this or that property, then it at least remains open to me to regard these [sc. properties] as cognizable independent of experience (a priori), which I am not free to do if I regard time as a concept that has merely been abstracted from it [sc. experience] (8:199n.32–37).

5 In keeping with this clarification, Kant restructures the Aesthetic by adding section-numbers and partitioning the section "On Space" into "§ 2. Metaphysical Exposition of this Concept [sc. <Space>]" and "§ 3. Transcendental Exposition of the Concept of Space" and making parallel adjustments to the section "On Time". These changes do not represent a revision of Kant's arguments but only greater clarity about their inner workings. For the A-edition already contained a section titled "Conclusions from the above Concepts" in the Space section (and its complement in the Time section). So Kant was already conceiving of the numbered paragraphs that would become the ME and TE as some sort of conceptual analysis.

> exposition is **metaphysical**, however, when it contains that which exhibits [*darstellt*] the concept **as given a priori**. (B38)[6]

An exposition is a perspicuous account of (some of) the content of a concept. Kant's use of the Latin *expositio* signals, however, that he has in mind a technical notion, which we will examine in subsequent sections. Similarly technical is his specification that an exposition is "metaphysical" when it reveals a concept to be "given a priori".[7] The modifier "given" here is a term of art and means something quite different from the object-implicating immediacy distinctive of intuition (see Section 3.3 and Section 7.2).

In eighteenth-century German logics, it was standard to classify concepts according to their origin (i) from experience, (ii) from abstraction, or (iii) from "elective [*willkührliche*] combination".[8] Kant emends this tripartite classification in multiple ways. First, he advances a hylomorphic account of concepts. The matter of a concept consists in the marks that make up its intension. This matter constitutes its identity conditions and distinguishes it from all other concepts. Yet all concepts have the same form – namely, universality. This form is, in every case, due to the understanding's activities of comparison, reflection, and abstraction, as exercised on representations it already possesses.[9] Abstraction, then, is not a distinctive source of a special class of concepts, as tradition holds, but part of what accounts for the form common to all concepts.

Concepts can, however, be sorted into different classes according to the source of their content or matter. Here Kant follows tradition in holding

6 Similarly, the TE of <space> begins: "By a **transcendental exposition** I understand the explanation [*Erklärung*] of a concept as a principle from which the possibility of other synthetic cognitions a priori can be recognized [*eingesehen*]." (B40) The present section (Section 4.2) addresses the nature of exposition in general. The next (Section 4.3) addresses specifically metaphysical exposition. The nature of transcendental exposition will play a small role in the final section (Section 4.5).

7 Kant's distinction between metaphysical and transcendental expositions roughly parallels his distinction between metaphysical and transcendental deductions. A metaphysical exposition, like a metaphysical deduction, aims to demonstrate the a priori origin of a certain representation. A transcendental exposition, like a transcendental deduction, aims to demonstrate the possibility of synthetic a priori cognition through a certain representation. This involves demonstrating that the representation is necessarily valid of objects, as appearances. Thus, Kant argues in the TE of <space> that geometry is genuine synthetic a priori cognition *only if* <space> originates in the form of our outer sense. As the form of outer sense, however, it is necessarily valid of all outer objects valid of appearances (A27/B43.17–12). Merritt (2010) observes that this latter argument, which appears in the Conclusions, not in the TE itself, constitutes a transcendental *deduction* of <space>; cf. A87f./B119.20–120.2.

8 Meier *Auszug* § 254 *et seq.*; cf. Wolff, German Logic, §§ 5–6, 26–27, 33. Daniel Sutherland is responsible for the felicitous translation of *willkürlich* as "elective". "Arbitrary" is apt only if its root *arbitrium* dominates.

9 L-Jäsche 9:93–95; L-Wien 24:907–910; L-Bus 24:654.17–28; cf. L-DW 24:753.

that the content of some concepts is due to our "elective combination" of representations (viz. marks) already available to us.[10] Concepts whose contents are not curated in this deliberate, elective manner Kant calls "given".[11] Calling a concept "given", then, does not yet determine the source of its content. It merely implies that the content of the concept does not depend on my *Willkür* (*arbitrium*, choice) in selecting exactly which marks will constitute its intension.[12] Pure general logic has nothing more to say about given concepts, since it abstracts from all content of cognition and a fortiori from the source of that content. But as a matter of transcendental philosophy, Kant agrees that experience is one source of the content of given concepts. That it is not the only source is, of course, a central claim of his critical epistemology. The content of some concepts has an a priori source.

Now, if "a priori" here just means "independent of experience", then this is another merely privative characterization, like the modifier "given". It rules out one possible source (viz. experience) just as "given" rules out a different possible source (viz. choice). What we want is a positive characterization of the source of a priori conceptual contents. One option, of course, is to declare our spades turned: We could regard the content of a priori concepts as a brute given, i.e. something innate. But Kant is vocal throughout his career in rejecting nativism, which he understands as the view that some representations – as actual (if unconscious) states of the

[10] Mathematical concepts are paradigmatically *willkürlich*, as are the theoretical terms of natural science, with which we formulate questions that we then "compel nature to answer" (Bxiii.11; cf. L-Jäsche 9:63.28–64.4). In both cases, the content of the concept is utterly distinct (*deutlich*) and exhaustively specified, since it is deliberately selected. But only in the first case is a genuine definition possible, since only mathematics is capable of demonstrating the objective validity of its concepts in the very act of defining them. This is because mathematical definitions are genetic: They construct the object that falls under the concept in the act of defining that concept (see Heis 2020). So a well-defined mathematical concept cannot fail to have an object. By contrast, the theoretical concepts of natural science are mere "declarations" of one's project to cognize and explain natural phenomena (A729/B757.8–15). Their objective validity can only be settled empirically, through experience. And this is less a definition of the concept than a confirmation of its cognitive fruitfulness.

[11] L-Wien 24:914; L-Blom (early 1770s) 24:131.33–132.10, 252 f., 256, 262.8–12; L-DW 24:752.38, 756.27–37; R2852, 2853, 2855 (early 1770s) 16:546f.; R2867 (early 1770s) 16:552 f.; R2908 (1769–1770) 16:570.11–16; R2947 (1780s) 16:584; cf. A730/B758; L-Jäsche 9:93.19–26.

[12] Because they are fabricated from marks already available to the subject, made concepts are posterior to and explanatorily grounded in their marks, while the reverse is true of given concepts (see Section 5.2, notes 7 and 8). This difference between given and made concepts has not been adequately appreciated. Many commentators assume that all discursive marks exhibit part-to-whole priority over the concepts that contain them; some even claim that a "piecemeal" or successive, part-to-whole synthesis is distinctive of discursivity as such (e.g. McLear 2015, 89–93; Jauernig 2019, 63 f., 69). I contest this conception of discursivity in Section 5.4.2.

mind (i.e. particular exercises of its capacities) – are inborn.[13] Kant cannot treat a priori given concepts as innate ideas of the sort countenanced by (Kant's version of) Plato. He instead proposes that a priori contents arise through "original acquisition":

> The Critique allows for absolutely no implanted or innate representations: it treats one and all of them as acquired, whether they belong to intuition or to concepts of the understanding. Yet there is also an original acquisition (as the teachers of natural right phrase it) and, accordingly, also [an acquisition] of that which previously did not yet exist at all, and hence belonged to no thing [*keiner Sache*] prior to this action. The Critique claims that the form of things in space and in time is of this sort, as is the synthetic unity of the manifold in concepts. For our cognitive faculty derives [*hernimmt*] neither of these from objects, as something given in them [sc. the objects] in themselves, but rather brings them about a priori out of itself [*bringt sie aus sich selbst a priori zu Stande*]. Now there must, however, be a ground for doing this in the subject that makes it possible for the relevant representations to arise thus and not otherwise and for them to be able to be referred to objects that are not yet given, and this ground at least is innate. (*Discovery* 8:221 f.)

This view resembles, to a first approximation, the nativism about *dispositions* to form certain concepts that Leibniz advances in the *New Essays* as an answer to Locke.[14] The idea is that, although no actual

[13] See M-Pö/L_1 28:232–233; M-Mr 29:760–764; M-Vi/K_3 (1794/95) 29:949–950; M-Schön 28:467 f. Kant's discussions of nativism tend to focus on Plato rather than, say, Crusius, Wolff, Leibniz, or Descartes.

[14] Another nativist about dispositions is Crusius, who holds that such dispositions are implanted (*eingepflanzt*) in us by God at our creation: They are not just *angeboren* but *anerschaffen* in that we are *created* possessing them. Kant objects that this view is (i) unduly speculative, (ii) methodologically suspect, and (iii) not fit for purpose. First, speculating about the details of God's creation is bootless and unphilosophical (*Discovery* 8:222.2–7; cf. *Encyclopedia* 29:16.12–24; *Innaugural* 2:406.13–15; R4473 (1772) 17:564.25–29; M-L_1 28:233.24–26). Second, such a *deus ex machina* (or rather *machina ex deo*) proves too much. Once we grant that God implants *some* such dispositions in us, we must allow that *any* of our ideas might have arisen from divinely implanted dispositions (see B167.28–30, A772–774/B801f.9–24; *Prolegomena* 4:319n.; letter to Herz, 21 February 1772, 10:131.31–36). But the final, decisive objection to Crusius, which also cuts against Leibniz, is that dispositional nativism cannot account for the *necessary objective validity* of originally acquired representations unless one adopts Kant's transcendental idealism (B167f.31–15; M-Schön 28:467.1–4). For Leibniz and Crusius, God is responsible for the agreement of our originally acquired representations with their objects, as things in themselves. This makes their objective validity a matter of divine wisdom and grace, not a matter of objective necessity. To be *necessarily* valid of objects, our representations would have to *themselves* make their objects possible, not just share a common ground in God (or natural selection, or whatever). But insofar as these objects are things in themselves, it is God, not our representations, that makes them possible. Kant's Copernican turn corrects this, at once cutting God out of the epistemological picture and cutting us off from things in themselves. Our originally acquired representations make their objects, qua *appearances*, possible. They are, *in themselves*, necessarily

representations are innate, certain dispositions to form representations are. Experience then serves to activate or trigger these dispositions. Experience is thus a sine qua non for such representations, but it is not the source of their content, which is due to the character of the innate dispositions themselves. It is the peculiar intrinsic constitution of these innate dispositions, as "ground" that determines the contents of a priori given concepts by determining that they "arise thus and not otherwise" (8:221.37–222.1).[15]

When Kant says that an ME "exhibits the concept as given a priori" (B38.2–3), therefore, he is saying that the concept is revealed to derive its content from the intrinsic constitution of the mind and its innate capacities as "grounds" for representations. Though the reader is, of course, in no position to appreciate this, Kant is anticipating the following account of our "original acquisition" of <space> as a concept that is "given a priori".

First, there "lies ready in the mind" (A20/B34.14) a "ground" – namely, an innate capacity with a distinctive intrinsic constitution. This is, I take it, our sensibility, i.e. our capacity to receive representations insofar as we are affected by objects. Using the standard Aristotelian vocabulary, this ground is our sensible capacity in *first potentiality*.[16] When we are affected by objects, in experience, this capacity gives rise to empirical intuitions, enmattered with a particular manifold of sensations, due to affection, and bearing a distinctive form, due to the intrinsic constitution of our sensibility as innate "ground". These empirical intuitions are the *second actuality* of our sensibility, i.e. the fully actualized manifestation of that capacity. But between the bare capacity, as first potentiality, and its full-fledged exercise, as second actuality, we can distinguish an intermediary logical "moment". For in actualizing the bare capacity, as first potentiality, we not only acquire particular empirical intuitions, as second actualities, we also acquire a further, though related, potentiality – namely, the ability to represent the form common to all empirical intuitions, as second actualities – i.e. the form that is due to the intrinsic character of their

valid of objects – but only because they are restricted to appearances. For discussion of this dialectic, see Section 8.1.1, as well as Callanan (2013), Shaddock (2015), Lu-Adler (2018b).

[15] In tracing a priori contents to an innate "ground", the doctrine of original acquisition traces the *independent-of-experience* sense of "a priori" back to the *from-grounds* sense. Oberhausen (1997) offers the most detailed treatment of this Kantian retooling of the a priori.

[16] The *locus classicus* of this tripartite distinction – between first potentiality, first actuality = second potentiality, and second actuality – is *De Anima* II.5, 417a22 *et seq.*; cf. II.1, 412a8–11. Menn (1994) observes that this commonplace of Aristotelianism rests on surprisingly scanty textual evidence. I am, of course, using it only as an elucidatory tool.

sensible ground, as first potentiality.[17] This common form – considered on its own, in abstraction from the sensations that may enmatter it – is the second potentiality (= first actuality) of our sensibility. And it is this form – "the form of things in space and time" (8:221.32) – that Kant officially terms the "original acquisition". The concept <space> counts as "given a priori" precisely insofar as this form – the second potentiality (= first actuality) of our sensibility – is the source of its content (its matter).

We might compare the capacity for sensibility to the capacity for language. The bare capacity, as first potentiality, is like the ability to acquire and speak a natural language. Particular empirical intuitings are analogous to particular competent utterances in some natural language, as second actualities of the respective capacities (for sensible intuition, for language). Now all competent utterances in a particular natural language share a common grammar, just as all sensible intuitings exhibit a common form. Mastery of this grammar – considered on its own, in abstraction from its various exercises in particular utterances – is the second potentiality (= first actuality) of the capacity for language: It is the ability to speak, say, *German*, regardless of whether one is currently doing so. Likewise, the form of sensible intuitings is the second potentiality of that capacity: It is the ability to enjoy representations with specific constitutive features (for us, spatiotemporal properties).

Now, in rational creatures, the ability to produce competent utterances in a natural language is necessarily accompanied by an ability to reflect on those utterances, as we will see in detail in the following section. Thus, mastery of a grammar, as the ability (second potentiality = first actuality) to produce competent utterances in a particular natural language, can develop, through reflection, into an articulable knowledge of that grammar – that is, an ability to express, in language, the form common to all competent utterances in the relevant language. I submit that something analogous holds for the form of sensibility. Rational reflection can make the form of sensibility itself into an object of sensible representation. This yields particular intuitings that are purely formal, in that they abstract from all sensation and represent, in intuition, the constitutive features common to all sensible intuitings as such. Kant's notorious distinction between form *of* intuition and form*al* intuition (B160n.28–30) thus tracks the

[17] Assigning the form of sensibility this "intermediary" status as second potentiality (= first actuality) comports well with Kant's inclusion of it in the Table of Nothing: "The mere form of intuition, without substance, is not in itself an object, but merely the formal condition of one (as appearance), just as pure space and pure time are admittedly something, as forms of intuiting, but are not themselves objects that get intuited (*ens imaginarium*)." (A291/B347.26–32, my underlining)

distinction between second potentiality and second actuality. Formal intuitions are, alongside empirical intuitings, a further sort of second actuality of the capacity for sensibility (cf. B146f.7–13) – one that specifically draws on the rational capacities with which our sensibility is paired.[18]

Taking stock, then: A metaphysical exposition is concerned with concepts that are given a priori. A concept is "given" when it is not made through elective synthesis of pre-available marks. It is given a priori when it owes its content to some innate ground in the mind. Thus, when Kant re-describes the numbered paragraphs preceding the Conclusions as "Metaphysical Expositions", he is effectively reiterating the aim of the entire Aesthetic – namely, to uncover "the mere form of sensibility in the mind" (A21/B35.32–33; cf. A20/B34.13–14 A22/B36.14–05) that serves as the "ground" of certain a priori representations. The task of the MEs is to show that the content of <space> and <time> could only have arisen from such a ground.

4.3 Exposition as Conceptual Analysis

We now have a sense of the telos that ME pursues – namely, to show that a certain concept derives its content from the peculiar constitution of an innate cognitive capacity as ground. But by what *means* does it pursue this telos? Here we must explore Kant's technical notion of *Erörterung* (*expositio*).[19] The *Critique* mentions that an exposition renders explicit the marks that constitute the intension of a concept yet without purporting to exhaust that content (B38.28–01; cf. A730/B758.32–13). Kant elaborates on this notion of exposition in his logic lectures:

> Not all concepts can be defined, but neither do they all need to be. [¶] There are approximations to the definition of certain concepts; these are partly expositions (*expositiones*), partly descriptions (*descriptiones*). [¶] The expositing of a concept consists in the mutually dependent [*an einander hängend*] (successive) representation of its marks, insofar as these are found

[18] This implies that any form*al* intuition depends on intellectual synthesis but is silent about whether the form *of* intuition does. Even sensibilists should be able to accept this by arguing that such intellectual activity merely "brings to concepts" the intrinsic structure of human outer intuition, which *obtains* independently of such intellectual synthesis. See Falkenstein (1995, 98–100, 245–252). On interpreting B160n., see Onof and Schulting (2015); Friedman (2020).

[19] My discussion of metaphysical exposition in this and the following section builds on the illuminating analysis of Messina (2015). Falkenstein (1995, 148–150) and Merritt (2010, 8–11) also emphasize the Aesthetic's reliance on conceptual analysis.

> through analysis. Description is the exposition of a concept insofar as it [sc. the exposition] is not precise. (L-Jäsche § 105, 9:142.25–143.3)[20]

Let us postpone for the moment the claim that certain concepts – in particular, concepts that are given (not made) – do not admit of definition. Where definitions are, for whatever reason, impossible or unnecessary, expositions serve as "approximations to definitions". More precisely, an exposition provides (i) a non-exhaustive but (ii) distinct and (iii) successive (iv) representation of marks belonging to the intension of a concept, (v) where these marks are adduced through analysis.

A definition, for Kant, involves the clear and complete presentation of a concept's marks.[21] Expositions merely approximate to definitions in that they do not purport to exhaustively account for all the marks of a concept. But like definitions, expositions render explicit (i.e. represent clearly) the marks they do address, thereby rendering the concept more distinct. Expositions further resemble definitions in that they are not haphazard lists of any old marks that belong to the concept. An exposition is rather a "successive" account, in that its treatments of various marks are "dependent on one another [*an einander hängend*]" (L-Jäsche 9:143.1–2). When approaching the MEs in the Aesthetic, therefore, we should not assume that the numbered "moments" are discrete, self-standing arguments. We should instead expect that the marks of <space> highlighted in one moment will be intimately related to those examined in another. Indeed, as we shall see, it is no great exaggeration to say that all four moments are centrally focused on one essential mark of <space> – namely, that we conceive of space as an all-encompassing whole that conditions its parts as mereological components. The various moments of the ME can be thought of as foregrounding different aspects of this central feature – describing it from different points of view, as it were.[22] This

[20] Kant works toward this account in R2920–2996 (16:576–608). It reappears in L-DW 24:758–759; L-Pö 24:572; L-Bus 24:657–658; cf. L-Wien 24:918–919. And it clearly informs the Discipline of Pure Reason (A728–730/B756–758). These distinctions are not original to Kant, though he draws them in his own distinctive manner. Meier's *Auszug*, which Kant used as a textbook in his logic lectures, contrasts definition with description (§§ 268–270 et seq.) and, though it does not use the label "exposition", also distinguishes a form of non-exhaustive analysis that closely resembles Kantian *Erörterung* (§ 151).

[21] Kant lays down further criteria for definitions, but they will not concern us. See A727/B755.15–18, B755n.26–32; cf. L-Jäsche 9:140.22–34, 144.18–145.31; L-DW 24:756.14–25; cf. L-Pö 24:570–571; L-Wien 24:912.27–913.30.

[22] Here I follow Merritt and Jauernig. Merritt argues that "[t]hroughout the Metaphysical Exposition, a basic fact about our usage of the concept of space is continually under consideration: that we speak of representing things *in* space" (Merritt 2010, 14, original italics; cf. 33–34n.24). Jauernig goes so far as to say that all four moments explore a single "fundamental feature" "of our ordinary

interconnectedness of moments will be an important datum in Sections 5.3 and 5.4 when we examine the details of Kant's argument for the intuitive origin of <space>.

So much for the manner in which an exposition presents the marks of a concept – (i) not exhaustively, but (ii) distinctly and (iii) successively. But what does it mean to (iv) represent a mark as belonging to a concept in the first place? And how are these marks (v) "found through analysis" (L-Jäsche 9:143.2–3)? Marks are the partial representations that make up a concept's intension, that constitute its content. By distinguishing and explicitly attending to (representing with clarity) a concept's marks, one renders the concept more distinct and thereby increases the qualitative logical perfection of one's cognition through the concept. This is not a quantitative extension of one's cognition to new objects but an increase in the qualitative intensity or depth of one's knowledge of the same object(s). It thus involves the curious kind of "learning" that consists in becoming more aware of what one already knows:

> When I make a concept distinct, my cognition does not grow at all with respect to its content. This [sc. the content] remains the same, only the form is altered, in that I learn to better distinguish what already lay in the given concept or to cognize it with clearer consciousness. Just as merely illuminating a map adds nothing to it, merely clarifying a given concept through the analysis of its marks does not increase that concept itself in the slightest. (L-Jäsche 9:64)[23]

The judgments that express such increases in the distinctness of one's cognition are thus "elucidatory judgments [*Erläuterungsurteile*]" – as contrasted with "ampliative judgments [*Erweiterungsurteile*]" (A7/B11.23), which increase the quantitative logical perfection of one's cognition. To represent a mark as belonging to a concept, therefore, is to make an analytic judgment: Marks just are "logical grounds" for analytic judgments.

Now analytic judgments, for Kant, are not (or not just) about the concepts they involve.[24] They are also about the objects that fall under

representations of space" – namely, that "we necessarily conceive of and present any spatial determination as delineated in, and any determinate space, that is, any determinate figure and any determinate spatial volume, as a 'cut out' part of the same all-encompassing space" (Jauernig 2021, 204). I agree that this feature, which I call the "holistic mereological structure of space", is crucial to all four moments; I examine it in detail in Section 5.3; see also Section 5.5.

23 See also L-Blom (early 1770s) 24:41–42, 118–125, 131; L-Wien 24:840–843, L-DW 24:702, 709; L-Pö 24:538.

24 Recall Kant's admonition that "analysis must not go so far that in the end the object [*Gegenstand*] itself disappears" (L-Jäsche 9:64.25–26; cf. L-Wien 24:845.12–14). For discussion of the objective purport of analytic judgments, see Section 2.2 and Lu-Adler (2013).

those concepts, if any do. Suppose marks <F> and <G> belong to the intension of the concept <FG>. It may be a contingent fact whether any objects fall under <FG>: Some possible worlds may be devoid of FGs. Moreover, if an object *o* does happen to fall under <FG>, it may be FG only contingently: *o* may be FG in our world but not in other possible worlds where *o* exists. Nevertheless, that *FGs are G* remains a necessary, because analytic, truth. In that sense, object *o* is *necessarily* G insofar as it is *actually* FG (whether contingently or necessarily). Thus, analytic judgments express necessary, if hypothetical, truths about objects: Necessarily, if *x* is FG, then it is G.[25] This has two salient consequences for us.

First, it helps explain Kant's promiscuous use of the term *Merkmal* to refer to both the *partial representations* that constitute the intension of a concept and the *features of objects* that are denoted by those partial representations.[26] In the ME, for instance, Kant moves quite freely between claims about the marks of <space> and claims about features of space. These sudden semantic ascents and descents can be disorienting, but they are innocuous. For Kant is proceeding on the assumption that the object in question (i.e. space) falls under the concept he is analyzing (i.e. <space>). And on this assumption, the marks of <space> are *necessarily* predicable of space, i.e. they denote *de dicto* necessary features of space. For it is trivial that, if object *o* falls under <FG>, then *o* is FG. So, by assuming that the object in question falls under the relevant concept, Kant entitles himself to make not only representation-level claims of the form, *if x falls under <FG>, then it falls under <G>* and not only object-level claims of the form, *if x is FG, then it is G*, but also level-shifting claims of the form, *if x falls under <FG>, then x is G*, and of the form, *if x is FG, then x falls under <G>*. In sliding between representation talk and object talk, Kant is exploiting a commonplace modal feature of analytic judgment.[27] This suggests that many worries about whether the ME is

[25] For instance, <brother> contains the marks <sibling> and <masculine>. It is an analytic truth that I am *necessarily* a sibling insofar as I am a brother. This necessity holds even though there are possible worlds devoid of brothers and worlds in which I exist but am not a brother.

[26] It appears that this dual use of *Merkmal* is deliberate; see L-Jäsche 9:58.14–17; R2282 (1780s?) 16:298.16–20; as well as Section 3.3, note 16.

[27] It is important to recall here that Kantian hypothetical judgments are not truth-functional conditionals. Rather, they assert a ground-consequence relation between two facts. On a truth-functional account, the proposition, <*if pigs grunt, then 2 + 2 = 4*>, is necessarily true because its consequent is. Yet Kant would regard it as false, since there is no connection between antecedent and consequent. In the hypothetical licensed by an analytic judgment, what is necessary is the *connection* between being FG and being G. Kant understands the judgment as a necessary and universal rule whose condition is fulfilled precisely when the antecedent is satisfied. When the antecedent is satisfied – in, say, the minor premise in a hypothetical syllogism – Kant holds that "the

concerned merely with representations or (also) with objects may be misplaced: As a conceptual analysis, it is concerned with both.[28]

Second, because analytic judgments license necessary but *hypothetical* claims, we can identify marks and test proposed analyses by weighing counterfactuals and appealing to our modal intuitions.[29] In particular, we consider the negation of the hypothetical necessity licensed by an analytic truth: <*It is possible that x is G but not FG*>. And we weigh this against the contrapositive form of that hypothetical: <*Necessarily, if x is not G, then x is not FG*>. These modal musings are ubiquitous in the practice of conceptual analysis, because they provide a test for markhood that we can apply in particular cases.

We need a test for markhood because concepts do not wear their marks on their sleeves, as the trivializing notation 'FG is G' might suggest. Analysis of a concept is called for precisely because there can be uncertainty about whether a particular mark belongs to its intension. So how does analysis actually proceed? There is no universal recipe,[30] but the obvious test is to consider whether something could conceivably lack a proposed mark while falling under the relevant concept. By showing that it is incoherent to deny the mark of an object without eo ipso denying the concept of it, one vindicates the contrapositive associated with the analytic judgment.

4.4 Competent Use as the Criterion of Markhood

Now assessing these contrapositives often involves consideration of counterfactual scenarios. Yet our assessment of these counterfactuals is not

conclusion [i.e. the consequent] is always accompanied by the consciousness of necessity and thus has the dignity of an apodictic proposition" (L-Jäsche 9:122.9–10). Since it is usually trivial to select an object for which the antecedent is satisfied (i.e. an object *o* that falls under <FG>), the conclusion <*o is G*> holds *with necessity*. That is what I mean by claiming that they ascribe *de dicto* necessary features to the object. Provided that object *o* falls under <FG>, the mark <G> denotes a *de dicto* necessary feature of *o* (cf. M-Pö/L_2 28:559.10–18).

28 Either slides between representation talk and object talk are innocuous, or Kant's discussion displays a truly cringeworthy confusion. But if Kant is engaged in the sort of conceptual analysis I claim, such slides are legitimate.

29 I owe to Messina (2015, 428–429) the insight that there is an intimate connection between exposition qua conceptual analysis and reliance on modal intuitions (in the ordinary sense, not *Anschauungen*). As will become clear, however, I do not share Messina's view that analysis – even when directed at *given* (as opposed to made) concepts – must traffic in *de re* (as opposed to merely *de dicto*) necessities, nor that it yields insight into the real (as opposed to merely logical) essence of the concept under analysis.

30 L-Blom (early 1770s) 24:121.35–36. Kant suggests that a good way to proceed is to consider concrete cases about which some elementary judgments (analytical mark-attributions) can be made. See L-Blom 24:131.11–23, 272.17–19; L-Ph (1772) 24:457.16–458.4; L-Wien 24:843.38–844.05.

based on some fundamental insight into *de re* necessities, or the proximity of possible worlds, or the architecture of real possibility. Rather, what guides us in our consideration of concrete cases (even outlandish ones) is our capacity to competently employ the concept under analysis.[31] We think up a scenario in which an object lacks the proposed mark and ask whether, under those circumstances, we might still competently apply the relevant concept to the object – or whether doing so would betray an incomplete mastery of the concept in question. Thus, the standard we rely on in conceptual analysis is our competent *use* of the relevant concept.[32] So even though analysis is concerned with universal concepts and marks, it largely consists in considering particular cases, i.e. applying the concept to concrete scenarios:

> Philosophers and jurists, e.g., have never yet been able to develop and separate from one another [*auseinander setzen*] the concept of justice [*Recht*] and [that of] fairness [*Billigkeit*]. But we need only give one of them an instance in concreto and he will soon say to what extent it is just and to what extent it is fair. Thus, in my concept of fairness there must lie something that is different from my concept of justice, and I make use of this mark, which is shrouded in obscurity, in the case. (L-Wien 24:843.38.–844.5)[33]

[31] I am assuming, of course, that competent possession of the relevant concept is prerequisite for analyzing it. Otherwise, one's reflections would involve *acquiring* the concept, not just elucidating it. Kant has a place for this, too, but he distinguishes it from analysis: *Making a concept distinct* means increasing the qualitative logical perfection of a concept one already possesses, whereas *making a distinct concept* involves synthesizing clear marks into a representation one did not previously possess. See L-Jäsche 9:63.17–27; R2355 (1770?) 16:330.12–17; R2358 (1770s) 16:331.18–20; L-Wien 24:845; L-Blom (early 1770s) 24:130 f., 269 f.33–03; L-Ph (1772) 24:409 f.32–05, 417.5–29. The first procedure is analytic, the second synthetic. Each has its purpose, and the two can even be combined, "insofar as one is not yet satisfied with the marks that are already thought in a given concept" (L-Jäsche 9:64.18–20). This often happens when one closely examines ordinary empirical concepts – that is, the pre-theoretical conceptions of the "manifest image", such as <solid> or <heavy>, as well as various natural-kind concepts, including Kant's favorite examples, <gold> and <water>. As concepts – albeit concepts that are given, not made – they are subject to analysis. But as *empirical* concepts, which aim to capture natural phenomena, analysis of their de facto content is of limited interest. They are instead subjected to *synthetic* revision and conceptual engineering on the basis of new empirical findings and novel theories of the natural world: what Kant terms the exposition *of appearances* (L-Jäsche 9:141.14–17). Thus, while Kant deems the judgment, <*gold is a yellow metal*>, to be analytic (*Prolegomena* 4:267.16–21), we would nowadays consider it *false*, having revised our concept <gold> to exclude marks such as <yellow>. This is how I understand Kant's discussion of given empirical concepts in the Discipline (A728/B756.25–15; cf. L-Jäsche 9:141.22–27) .

[32] R1697 (1770s) 16:86; R2964 (1780s) 16:588; Merritt (2010, 12–19) is exceptional among commentators in emphasizing the centrality of concept use to analysis.

[33] One has to dig a bit to find discussions of the practice of conceptual analysis in Kant's corpus, but they present a consistent picture:

> By means of analytical distinctness, we do not cognize any more in a thing than we have already thought in it previously; rather, we cognize only what we already actually knew better, i.e. more

The idea here is that possessing a concept involves a basic ability to discriminate concrete cases where it applies from those where it does not – for example, to recognize a certain action as just or as fair.[34] A central strategy of analysis, then, is to contrive cases that lay bare the differences in one's use of similar concepts – for example, cases that are recognizably *fair* but not *just*. The conceivability or incoherence of such differences will determine whether one of these concepts is a mark of the other.

An analogy may help. Analyzing a given concept is like trying to explicitly formulate a rule that one has mastered without study and now follows fluently without deliberation. For instance, native English speakers can, from a young age, identify word pairs as rhyming or non-rhyming and can discern subtle differences between exact rhymes and near rhymes. But few can accurately articulate offhand the rule for when words rhyme. This is what it means for one's concept or grasp of a rule to be clear but indistinct (partly obscure): One can reliably discriminate cases, but without being able to specify the criteria one is tracking in doing so.[35]

> distinctly, more clearly, and with more consciousness. E.g. with the concept of perfection, I will first direct someone to the cases in which he makes use of the expression [']perfection['], in order thereby to instruct him what he really understands by perfection, what sort of concept he makes of it, and what he thinks when he utters the word [']perfection['] and ascribes it to a thing. (L-Blom, early 1770s, 24:131.12–21, my underlining)

See also L-Bus 24:617.4–30; L-Ph (1772) 24:457.16–458.4; L-Wien 24:843 f.38–05; 926.34–38, 927.3–5.

34 The more finely this discriminatory capacity is attuned to subtle differences, the *clearer* one's conception of the concept is (see note 35). The basic capacity to recognize particular instances of universals is *Urteilskraft* (A132/B171.18–21; *Judgment* 5:179.19–20). Kant argues that *Urteilskraft* is a special talent that can be cultivated but not inculcated (A133/B172.1–3). Accordingly, some may be more adept at case-based conceptual analysis than others (A134/B173). But everyone must appeal to the same criterion of markhood – namely, competence in the use of the concept. The membership of any particular mark in the intension of a certain concept is ultimately a function of that (whole) concept's cognitive contribution to potentially knowledgeable judgments (cf. L-Jäsche 9:64.13–15, 95.27–29, 96.5–13; *Critique* A69/B94.24–26, B133–134n.24–35, A728/B756.15–26).

35 This account of clarity and distinctness follows Leibniz rather than Descartes. For Leibniz, clarity manifests itself in one's ability to distinguish similar cases; distinctness in the ability to say what distinguishes such cases ("Meditations on Knowledge, Truth, and Ideas", G 4:422, AG 24). Thus, Justice Potter Stewart's "I know it when I see it" account of <obscenity> betrays a clear but indistinct concept. This Leibnizian account appears in both Wolff (German Logic, §§ 9, 13) and Meier (*Auszug*, §§ 13–14). By contrast, Descartes's account makes no mention of differences or differentiation: Clarity is consciousness of a representation as a whole; distinctness is clarity in all respects (*Principles* I, § 45, AT 8:21.30–22.9). These accounts do not coincide, but neither must they conflict. Kant often defaults to the Cartesian formulation in his logic lectures (L-Jäsche 9:33, 35; L-Blom, early 1770s, 24:119; L-DW 24:725; L-Wien 24:834). But the *Critique* defends the Leibnizian account:

> Clarity is not, as the logicians say, the consciousness of a representation; for a certain degree of consciousness [...] must be met with even in some obscure representations, since, absent all

Rendering a given concept distinct through analysis, then, is analogous to sussing out the rule for rhyming. One has a basic capacity to recognize rhymes, near rhymes, and non-rhymes. One contrives some particular cases on which to exercise this capacity and then compares them, reflecting on commonalities and differences. One then proposes a hypothesis that captures these results (e.g. *words rhyme when their final syllables sound the same*). And one tests the hypothesis in further cases, correcting it in light of one's basic capacity to follow the rule one is trying to articulate. This is not an empirical procedure of induction, because the inquiry is not directed at the cases themselves but at the *capacity* they serve to elicit. Whether one is formulating a rule or analyzing a concept, the standard of correctness and *Leitfaden* of one's inquiry is the basic capacity to recognize concrete instances as satisfying, nearly satisfying, or violating the rule or concept in question.

The capacity to competently *use* a concept in concrete cases is thus the lodestar of conceptual analysis. Competent use is the criterion of markhood.[36] This is significant for our understanding of the MEs in two ways. First, it explains why an exposition of given concepts can never purport to be *exhaustive*. For no capacity can be reduced to a finite set of its exercises. Second, it shows that analysis fundamentally consists in reflecting on one's own acts and dispositions to act. Thus, exposition is an exercise in apperception.

> consciousness, we would not make any distinction in the connection of obscure representations, which we are, however, capable of doing with the marks of some concepts (such as those of justice and fairness [. . .]). Rather, a representation is clear in which the consciousness suffices for **consciousness of its difference** from others [sc. representations]. If it [sc. the consciousness] suffices for distinguishing but not for consciousness of the distinction [*des Unterschiedes*], the representation must still be called obscure. (B414–415n.; cf. M-Pö/L$_1$, 28:277 f.; M-Mr 29:878–880; *Anthropology* 7:137 and associated Reflections, 15:66ff.; A-Collins 25:20–25; A-Friedländer 25:479–482; A-Busolt 25:1439–1441)

A clear consciousness of the marks of a concept is precisely a consciousness of what distinguishes it from other concepts. The concept remains partly indistinct so long as consciousness of these marks is lacking, however competent one's use of the concept may be (however clear one's concept may be).

36 There is reason to think that, for purposes of analysis, uses of the concept in *false* judgments may be less helpful. In principle, however, it should not matter whether the judgments guiding our analysis are true, false, analytic, synthetic, a priori, or empirical, so long as they competently employ the concept and perspicuously exhibit its cognitive contribution to the judgment and to inferences in which it may figure. Carson has objected that the ME of <space> cannot appeal to claims of geometry (as she alleges Friedman 1992 does), since that would "[go] against Kant's explicit assertion in the *Prolegomena* § 4 that in the *Critique*, he is pursuing the 'synthetic method' which is 'based on no data except reason itself' [Ak. 4:274]" (Carson 1997, 495). Though I agree that the ME, unlike the TE, cannot legitimately appeal to geometrical principles as objectively valid and necessarily true cognitions, I do think it can invoke them as competent (merely thinkable) uses of the concept <space>.

The first point is a kissing cousin of several well-known philosophical issues. It resembles the idea that certain powers, capacities, and dispositions cannot be reduced to their actualizations.[37] A genuine capacity is a source of a potential infinity of exercises, though it is only actually exercised finitely many times. And even if it could engage in infinitely many exercises, we could only ever consider finitely many of them. We therefore cannot survey the full expression of a capacity and thus can never prove, by reflecting on a subset of its exercises, that a particular analysis captures it exhaustively. So if the standard of adequacy for conceptual analysis is our *capacity* to competently employ a concept (and to recognize uses of it as apposite, inapt, etc.), then no conceptual analysis will be conclusive, for no capacity can be fully expressed in (or reduced to) the finite number of cases we can consider.

This point about the limits of conceptual analysis may also recall the problem of induction. In both cases, we consider only a finite set of instances yet form conclusions that extend beyond those instances to encompass unexamined cases – conclusions that are thus underdetermined by the considerations that motivate them. That is why analysis is open-ended and always subject to revision in light of competent uses of the concept that have yet to be considered. This echoes aspects of Quine's arguments for the indeterminacy of translation and Davidson's adaptation of similar lines of thought in support of the indeterminacy of interpretation. For here, too, an account of the meaning of a concept is informed by a limited set of observed behaviors (i.e. uses of the concept).

There is, however, a critical difference here. For Kant, conceptual analysis is not an empirical investigation, as translation is for Quine and interpretation is for Davidson: It is an exercise in a priori reflection. In Kantian conceptual analysis, the concrete cases of a concept's use do not serve as *evidence* for one hypothesis or another. They rather serve as occasions on which to exercise one's capacity for competently using the concept and, in particular, as occasions to *bring to reflective consciousness* aspects of that competency – namely, the criteria (*Merkmale*) that it tracks.

[37] I am obviously painting with very broad strokes here. I take for granted that Kant is a realist about our cognitive capacities (for defense, see Tolley 2021, esp. 251–260). Treating some powers and capacities as metaphysically basic has a venerable and complicated history, especially in the Platonic and Aristotelean traditions from antiquity through the early modern period. On this history, see the collections edited by Perler (2015) and Jorati (2021). The view persists in contemporary epistemology of a notably Kantian orientation (e.g. McDowell 2011; Kern 2017) as well as in analytic metaphysics of a quite different bent (e.g. Molnar 1999, 2003; Mumford 2009; Vetter 2015).

Kantian conceptual analysis is fundamentally unlike Quinean translation or Davidsonian interpretation in that one already *grasps* the meaning of the concept under analysis: Possessing a *clear* concept is the starting point and basic presupposition of Kantian analysis. Analysis intensifies clarity into greater distinctness: It does not bring light into darkness.[38]

In this respect, Kantian conceptual analysis more closely resembles the rule-following paradox Kripke finds in Wittgenstein (Kripke 1982). Though it is our own competency in using the concept that guides our analysis, we can only ever exercise (and, a fortiori, reflect on) that competency in a certain number of cases. Yet there will always be conflicting accounts of the content of the concept that capture these cases equally well. Since we have no other standard to which we can appeal, we are fundamentally unable to know our own minds, to fathom our own meanings and capacities. The concepts we possess and our capacity to competently employ them regularly outrun our reflective understanding of them.[39] Kripke takes this to threaten the idea that we enjoy a *clear* consciousness of the concept in the first place (1982, 55). But for Kant it merely places a principled limit on the degree of distinctness we can expect to achieve.

This brings us to the second lesson that should inform our understanding of the MEs. Because analysis chiefly consists in reflecting on our uses of a concept, it is fundamentally an exercise in self-knowledge. Analysis depends not only on our capacity to *use* the concept but crucially on our ability to explicitly reflect on our uses of it. Analysis thus trades on the

[38] A related difference is that, for Kant, there is a fact of the matter about the content of given concepts: Their meaning is not indeterminate as it is for Quine and Davidson. In the case of empirical given concepts, this fact of the matter is of little interest, of course, so analysis swiftly gives way to the synthetic activity of explicating appearances and amending our concepts accordingly (see note 31). The content of given a priori concepts is, however, of profound interest to philosophy. But the fact of the matter about the content of a priori given concepts is ultimately a fact about *ourselves*, about the constitution of our own minds (see Section 4.2). So our inability to conclusively determine the contents of a priori given concepts through analysis is fundamentally a failure of self-knowledge. The underlying nature of our own mind is itself one of the troubling questions that reason "cannot dismiss, since they are imposed on it by the nature of reason, but which it also cannot answer, since they outstrip every capacity of human reason" (Avii.2–7). Though we are rationally compelled to assume (as an idea of reason) that our cognitive capacities *have* a determinate constitution, we can never discover with certainty what this constitution is. This, I take it, is an implication of Kant's discussion of the merely regulative status of the idea that all our cognitive capacities stem from a single underlying *Grundkraft* (A648–650/B676–678; cf. M-Pö/L_1 28:261.34–262.31).

[39] Quine and Davidson, of course, also intend for their reflections on translation and interpretation to implicate our understanding of our *own* meanings and native tongue. But the fundamental difference with Kant persists: Kantian analysis begins with an indistinct yet clear, first-personal grasp on the concept in question. Quine and Davidson begin with the *absence* of such a grasp, which they seek to remedy through the empirical procedures of translation and interpretation.

essentially apperceptive character of our rational faculties and, in particular, of our understanding as the faculty of concepts. For it is a condition of engaging in an act of understanding that one is, in principle, able to accompany it with the "I think". This is what guarantees that we will be able to reflect on the uses we make of our concepts, thereby ensuring that concepts are susceptible to analysis in the first place. The practice of conceptual analysis is fundamentally an exercise of our capacity for apperception. Exposition, as Kant understands it, is therefore apperceptively grounded elucidatory cognition.

That conceptual analysis is an exercise in apperceptive self-knowledge and yet doomed to fall short of its goal is a persistent theme of Kant's discussions of analytical distinctness. He accordingly connects the project of conceptual analysis with a Socratic conception of philosophy as an ongoing effort at self-knowledge:

> It is with this sort [sc. of logical distinctness] that philosophy preeminently busies itself, e.g. through morals I do not nourish my cognition but only set it in a better light. Socrates said that he was the midwife of his interlocutors, i.e. he made it so that they reflected [*nachdenken*] better upon what they already knew [*wüßten*] and became better conscious of it. If we always knew what we know, namely in the use of certain words and concepts that are so subtle in application, we would be astonished at the treasury of our cognition. (L-Wien 24:843.30–38)[40]

The humbling implication here is that, because we can never be certain of the completeness of an analysis, neither can we fully appreciate the richness of our own knowledge. And, indeed, when Kant figures the Critique as an exercise in self-knowledge, he describes this as "that most difficult of all [reason's] occupations" (Axi.20–21).

Ironically, giving voice to this humility about our capacity for self-knowledge can often come across as arrogance, as Kant is well aware. In advancing quite novel accounts of our cognitive capacities – e.g. his analytic/synthetic distinction or his account of space and time as forms of sensibility – while at the same time presenting his critical epistemology as grounded in mere apperception, as I am arguing he does, Kant is effectively accusing his interlocutors of a failure of self-knowledge, indeed a failure of

[40] See also R1696 (1775–1778) 16:86.16–21; L-Blom (early 1770s) 24:122.12–13 and 131; L-Bus 24:617.21–25; L-Jäsche 9:64.27–28. Such passages call to mind the lines from *Faust I*: "Was du ererbt von deinen Vätern hast / Erwirb es, um es zu besitzen." (v.682–683) Literally: "What you have inherited from your fathers / Earn it, in order to possess it." On Kant's view, given concepts are a kind of cognitive inheritance that we come to fully possess only through analysis.

enlightenment.[41] On the one hand, he claims that his critical faculty psychology merely articulates our self-conscious grasp on the nature of our cognitive faculties – i.e. something we are always already in a position to know – insofar as it emerges from an analysis of concepts we cannot fail to possess, since they arise from (and derive their content from) the constitutive activities of our essentially self-conscious faculties. On the other hand, he claims that no one before him has gotten this analysis right – that, despite our inalienable apperceptive appreciation of the constitutive form of our cognitive faculties, generations of incisive thinkers have consistently managed to misapprehend and mischaracterize it.

Kant is aware that this can sound outrageous and that it risks provoking in the reader "an indignation mingled with contempt over such apparently boastful and immodest claims" (Axiiif.10–11; cf. *Prolegomena* 4:256.24–31). This indignation, however, is just the counterpart of the indignity one feels upon recognizing such a failure in oneself. What is peculiarly humbling about such failures of self-knowledge is that one has failed *by one's own lights*, since the refutation of one's view is already contained (albeit implicitly) in what one already knows. One is thus left feeling foolish, having committed an error that one could, in principle, have avoided through more extensive or attentive reflection. To impute this sort of failure to past luminaries rankles because it sounds like accusing them of carelessness. But this is a misconception. Acknowledging the risk – indeed, the inevitability – of such a failure of self-knowledge is a mark of humility, not arrogance. For it takes seriously the difficulty and tenuousness of any degree of self-knowledge and the impossibility of complete self-understanding. The task of apperceptive reflection, like the Delphic maxim *know thyself* or Kant's Enlightenment injunction *dare to know*, is simple, but that does not make it easy. Quite the contrary: It is the most difficult of reason's occupations (Axi).[42]

4.5 Conclusion

We now know what to expect from the metaphysical expositions in the Aesthetic. As an analysis of <space>, the ME will likely invoke particular uses of the concept, often in counterfactual constructions about what is

[41] See A593/B621.23–24; L-Blom (early 1770s) 24:121.4–13, 122.12–13, 123.8–13; L-Bus 24:617.21–30; letter to Plücker, 26 January 1796, 12:57.7–14. Merritt offers characteristically illuminating discussions of Kant's conception of enlightenment in relation to his notions of spontaneity (2009) and apperception (2011, esp. sections 2 and 7).

[42] I am grateful to an anonymous reviewer for prompting me to address this issue.

possible or necessary, conceivable or incoherent. In reflecting on these uses of the concept, the discussion may shift back and forth between (i) ascribing to the concept various marks, as partial representations, and (ii) ascribing to the object various features, denoted by those marks. The aim of examining these uses of the concept is to throw particular marks into sharper relief, thus providing us with a clear representation of those marks and, equivalently, a more distinct consciousness of the concept to which they belong. These concrete uses of the concept do not function as empirical evidence for the presence or absence of a mark but as solicitations of our capacity for self-reflection in using the concept: provocations or reminders that bring us to notice certain aspects of the concept that (already) inform our use. These solicitations can be effective precisely because the intellect, as a faculty of concepts, is essentially apperceptive. What justifies us in ascribing a mark to a concept is a self-reflective consciousness of the form: "Ah, I now see that this criterion does indeed inform my use of the concept, as consideration of the mooted case has brought me to appreciate." Accordingly, the claims put forward in a ME are justified a priori via apperceptive reflection. As an exposition, these apperceptively grounded claims do not purport to exhaust the content of the concept. They do, however, present a successive, interconnected ("*an einander hängend*", L-Jäsche 9:143) account of its contents in that they highlight how certain marks are intimately related. And every reader ought to be able to verify this account for herself by appealing to her own competency in employing the concept. For in a *metaphysical* exposition, every reader is, of necessity, possessed of the concept in question. Because the concept is an "original acquisition", a concept given a priori, that every human being acquires (or is in a position to acquire) simply in virtue of exercising the cognitive capacities that provide it (the concept) with content. The ME of the concept <space> therefore purports to show, via pure apperception, that certain *Merkmale* of this concept could only derive from the abiding form, the essential constitution, of our capacity for sensible (or receptive) intuition. Let us now consider that analysis.

5

Infinity, Discursivity, Givenness
The Intuitive Roots of Spatial Representation

> The mathematical properties of matter, e.g. infinite divisibility, proves that space and time belong not to the properties of things but to the representations of things in sensible intuition.
>
> (R5876, c. 1783–1784, 18:374.27–30)

Chapters 1–4 have argued for a particular understanding of Kant's criteria for sensibility, receptivity, form, and intuition, as laid out in the Preliminaries, and for a particular approach to the Metaphysical Expositions as conceptual analyses, which presumably invoke these criteria. In the present chapter, the rubber meets the road. Kant argues in ME3 and ME4 that our original representation of space must be intuitive, and he does so on the basis of a conceptual analysis of <space>. I will argue that the primary upshot of this analysis is that our original representation of space is infinitely complex in content. Since no discursive content can be infinitely complex, our original representation of space cannot be the product of discursive spontaneity but must rather be given to the mind in order to be thought at all. It is intuitive and, moreover, receptive.

In Section 5.1, I describe the central challenge in interpreting ME3 – namely, that it does not specify which criteria of intuitive representation support its conclusion that <space> originates in intuition. Section 5.2 considers various criteria and argues that the best option is the criterion of *givenness*, identified in the Preliminaries (see Section 3.3). Section 5.3 examines the marks that ME3 attributes to <space> and argues that the holistic structure Kant describes is meant to evince the *continuity* and, thus, the infinite complexity of space. Section 5.4 shows that a criterion of discursive representation, as finitely complex, is advanced in ME4, and argues that this criterion should be permitted to "bleed up" into ME3. With these criteria in hand, the argument of ME3 is straightforward: Our original representation of space is infinitely complex, since we represent space to be continuous (Section 5.3). But discursive representations can only be finitely complex (Section 5.4). Thus, our original representation of space cannot be discursive. It must therefore be given to the mind independently of its spontaneous activities. That is to say, these marks of <space> must originate in receptive intuition (see Section 3.4). Because this account can sound suspiciously like an interpretation of ME4, not ME3, I conclude in Section 5.5 by clarifying how these arguments differ. ME3 is concerned with the cardinality of elements we represent space to contain, whereas ME4 is concerned with the type of mereological relations that obtain among those elements. This interpretation enables us to see that the MEs do not presuppose the singularity of intuitive representation, as many commentators assume, but rather establish that human intuitions are singular in the strong sense that they represent particulars and their parts in their infinite individuality.

5.1 Approaching the Third Metaphysical Exposition

The argumentative portion of ME3 runs as follows:

> Space is no discursive or, as one says, universal concept of relations of things in general but rather a pure intuition. For, first, one can represent only one unitary [*einigen*] space, and when one speaks of many spaces, one understands by this only parts of one and the same solitary space. These also cannot precede [*vorhergehen*] the unitary all-encompassing space as, so to speak, its component parts (out of which a composition [sc. of it] would be possible), but can only be thought **in it**. It is essentially unitary [*wesentlich einig*], the manifold in it, and hence also the universal concept of spaces in general, rests solely on limitations. It follows from this that, with respect to it, an intuition a priori (which is not empirical) serves to ground [*zum Grunde liegt*] of all concepts of it. (A24f./B39)

This passage offers two considerations in support of its conclusion, each of which is supposed to capture an essential aspect of our concept of space. First, we can represent but one single space: Any thoughts we may entertain about a plurality of spaces must be understood to refer to mere parts of that single space. Second ("also", A25/B39.7), these spaces, as parts, cannot be conceived as "prior" to the all-encompassing whole that contains them, as though it resulted from assembling them. For to think of a space at all – and a fortiori to think of a plurality of spaces – is to think of it as *contained in* a unitary, all-encompassing whole. (Just what sort of "priority" is involved here will concern us in Section 5.3.3.)

Kant's evidence for these claims is an analysis of our use of the concept <space> – that is, a reflection on what "one understands" "when one speaks of many spaces" (A25/B39.5). That all spaces belong to a unitary, all-encompassing whole is supposed to be an analytic judgment, articulating an essential mark of the concept <space>. It is likewise analytic that thinking of a space involves representing it as part of the whole of space.[1] Moreover, these marks of the concept are connected, as befits the "successive" analysis distinctive of exposition (see Section 4.3). The first mark indicates that space is a single whole containing a plurality of parts, while the second specifies the relevant relation of parthood. These reflections are then summarized in the remark that "[space] is essentially unitary [*einig*], the manifold in it [...] rests solely on limitations" (A25/B39.10–13). It is at this point that Kant draws his conclusion: "it follows from this that [...] an intuition a priori [...] serves to ground all concepts of [space]" (A25/B39.13–15). This conclusion makes two claims about our concept <space>: (1) its ground is a priori, and (2) its ground is *intuitive* – and, presumably, *receptive* rather than spontaneous.

That <space> is an a priori representation should not be too contentious at this point in Kant's argument, since ME1 and ME2 were devoted to establishing this. It is worth observing, however, that the present discussion provides materials for a further apriority argument (cf. McLear 2015, 87). The central premise is (i) that particular spaces "can [...] be thought only **in it** [sc. all-encompassing space]" (A25/B39.7...10). A representation of all-encompassing space cannot derive from representations of particular spaces, since representing a particular space already presupposes a representation of the whole of space, i.e. of *that in which* one thinks the particular space as situated. We can supplement this with the implicit and plausible assumption (ii) that experience only ever presents us with particular, finite spaces. That is, no set of sensations discloses to us the whole of all-encompassing space (cf. A291/B347.26–31). From these two premises, the apriority of <space> follows. For <space> is the concept of an all-encompassing whole. This is an essential mark of the concept, identified via conceptual analysis. Yet by premise (ii), no particular experience can be the source of such a content, since no particular experience presents us with the all-encompassing whole of space. But neither can the representation of such a whole derive from a collection of experiences of particular, finite spaces, since, according to

[1] One can, of course, dispute Kant's claim by offering an alternative analysis of <space> based on competent uses of that concept in potentially knowledgeable judgments. Kant is clear that we are liable to mischaracterize the contents of our own concepts, despite our mastery in employing them. My point is just that the premise is supposed to be analytic and should be disputed on the grounds of conceptual analysis.

premise (i), each of these already presupposes the former representation. Thus, the concept of an all-encompassing whole of space cannot derive from experience, either particular or collective. It is therefore a priori and, according to the doctrine of original acquisition, must derive its content from an innate "ground" in the mind – that is, from the intrinsic constitution of one of our cognitive capacities (see Section 4.2). This satisfies the criterion for *form* that we identified in the Preliminaries (see Section 3.5). Anything that is not due to experience – i.e. due to sensation as the influence of affection on the capacity for representation – must be due to the intrinsic character of the mind and thus belong to the form of appearance rather than the matter that corresponds to sensation. So this secures part of Kant's ultimate conclusion: <space> reflects the *form* of some innate cognitive capacity.

The question now is how ME3 is supposed to show that this a priori "ground" of <space>, which contributes to the form of experience, must be *intuitive* and *sensible* (or at least receptive) rather than discursive and spontaneous. This is difficult to see. For though the conclusion must obviously rely on some criteria of intuitive and discursive representation, the passage does not indicate what the relevant criteria are supposed to be. So any reconstruction of the argument must supply a suppressed premise stating the relevant criteria of discursive and intuitive representation. It must then explain how the considerations Kant puts forward – about singularity and whole-to-part priority – demonstrate that spatial representation satisfies (or flouts) these criteria. Obviously, these two dimensions of an interpretation are mutually informing. But it is still helpful to consider them separately. I will first address the question of suppressed criteria (Section 5.2) and then turn to the considerations Kant advances (Section 5.3).

5.2 Criteria of Intuitive and Discursive Representation

The standard interpretation of ME3 seizes on the singularity of space as the lynchpin of Kant's argument. The suppressed premise, it claims, is that intuitions are essentially singular representations, whereas discursive representations are invariably general. Therefore, <space> must originate in intuition, since it belongs to its content to refer to a unique and essentially unitary whole.[2] This is a very natural reading, bolstered by many texts in

[2] Versions of this interpretation can be found in Vaihinger (1892, II:211 f., 223); Kemp Smith (1992 [1918], 103, 105); Paton (1936, I:115); Strawson (1966, 64); Pippin (1982, 64–66); Guyer (1987,

which Kant claims that intuitions are essentially singular. But I find it unsatisfying in a couple of ways. First, Kant does not mention, much less argue for, singularity as a criterion of intuition anywhere in the Preliminaries or in the Introduction to the *Critique*. Second, many *discursive* representations are singular in a variety of plausible and strong senses.[3] So there is no easy move from the singularity of <space> to its intuitive origin. Now, I do think there is a special sort of singularity that is essential to all and only intuitions. But characterizing this sort of singularity and establishing that it uniquely accrues to (sensible or receptive) intuition takes significant philosophical work.[4] It is not the sort of claim that Kant would be within his rights to presuppose as self-evident, nor is it a commonplace of the philosophical tradition to which he is heir.[5] These textual and philosophical problems should lead us to consider alternative readings.

The most popular alternative locates the crux of ME3 in the claim that we represent space as a whole that is somehow prior to its parts. I think this is the right move, but it is often made for the wrong reasons. The standard interpretive strategy is to claim that holistic containment structure, as I will call it, is distinctive of intuitive representation; whereas all discursive representations exhibit what I will call an atomic containment structure, in which partial representations (marks) are always prior to the whole representation (the concept).[6] Thus, discursive representations are

346–348); Parsons (2012 [1992], 14–15); Falkenstein (1995, 218); Carson (1997, 494–498); Allison (2004, 109–110); Shabel (2010, 100–102). I criticize this approach in Smyth (2014, 554–556).

[3] I have in mind discursive representations (i) that refer to exactly one object, (ii) that purport, as part of their content, to pick out exactly one object, and (iii) that refer to exactly one object as a matter of logical, mathematical, or metaphysical necessity. For instance, <coldest known temperature>, <even prime number>, <natural world>, or <*ens realissimum*>. For elaboration, see Section 3.3, note 18, as well as Smyth (2014, 554–556).

[4] Thus, while I agree with Jauernig's account of intuitive singularity as the concrete, completely determinate representation of an individual in its infinite complexity, I do not think Kant is in a position to premise this conception in ME3, as she suggests (Jauernig 2021, 206–210). The infinite complexity of intuition is something that emerges from considerations put forward in the MEs (see Section 5.3), as is the singularity of intuitive representation as the representation of infinitely individual particulars (see Section 5.5).

[5] The traditional paradigm for intuitive cognition in humans is knowledge of mathematical principles and theorems. (See Spinoza *Ethics* 2p40s2; Leibniz "Meditations on Knowledge, Truth, and Ideas" G 4:423 f., AG 25.) But such mathematical cognition is typically (and was traditionally understood to be) a knowledge of *universal* truths, not a singular representation of an individual, as such. So singularity is not part of the received or traditional concept of intuition and cannot be presupposed on those grounds (cf. Falkenstein 1995, 66–71).

[6] Versions of this interpretation can be found in Falkenstein (1995, 230, 234 f.); Carson (1997, 494–498); Allison (2004, 110); McLear (2015, 89–93); Jauernig (2019, 63 f.; 2021, 206–210).

assembled or composed (*zusammengesetzt*) out of their marks in just the way that Kant says is *not* true of spatial representation (A25/B39.9). So spatial representation must have an intuitive origin. This, too, is a tidy reading with some textual support.[7] But, again, Kant says nothing about the holistic structure of intuitive representation or the atomic structure of discursive representation in the early sections of the *Critique*. More importantly, Kant does not in fact hold that the marks of a concept are invariably prior, in the relevant sense, to the concept that contains them. Indeed, this is the exception rather than the rule. The concepts that are of greatest concern to philosophy exhibit a *holistic* containment structure of just the sort ME3 ascribes to our representation of space.

Recall Kant's distinction between concepts that are *made* and those that are *given* (see Section 4.2). Kant calls made concepts *willkürlich* because they depend on one's choice (*Willkür*, *arbitrium*) in selecting the marks that constitute their content. Made concepts are put together (*zusammengesetzt*) out of marks that are already available and intelligible to the subject. That is why they can be defined in the strict, exhaustive sense: "I can always define my concept in such a case [i.e. when it is *willkürlich*/made]; for I must surely know what I wanted to think, since I deliberately [*vorsätzlich*] made [the concept] itself" (A729/B757.2–5). The marks of a made concept are "prior" to it in two related senses. First, the marks are cognitively available to the subject independent of being thought through the made concept. The subject must have a clear grasp of these marks and understand their meaning independent of the *willkürlichen* synthesis that combines them into a novel concept. Second, the meaning of the made concept that results from this synthesis of pre-given marks – its content, its contribution to potentially knowledgeable

[7] The strongest support for this reading is the final ME of <time> in the A-edition: "But where the parts themselves and every magnitude of an object can only be determinately represented through limitations, there the entire representation cannot be given through concepts (for there [i.e. in concepts] the partial representations are prior)" (A32.32, my underlining). However, Kant changes this parenthetical phrase in the B-edition to read "(for they [sc. concepts] contain only partial representations)" (B48.26–27). If his argument really turned on the contrast between holistic versus atomic containment structure, this revision would be a serious mistake. It is more plausible that Kant gained a clearer sense that this distinction did *not* in fact track the contrast he was arguing for. His emendation suggests that, whereas concepts "contain only partial representations", intuitions contain *whole* representations. Or, as he later puts it: "space and time and all their parts are **intuitions**" (B137n.23–24, my underlining). That is, intuition allows for a dense ordering, an infinite nesting of spaces and times as wholes whose parts are wholes in turn. Conceptual contents, by contrast, exhibit a discrete, classificatory structure that cannot accommodate such infinite complexity. Thus, the concept/intuition distinction does not turn on the *priority* of part versus whole, but on the kind of *relation* that obtains between container and contained, as I argue in Section 5.5.

cognition – is determined by the fact that precisely these marks are included in it.

The opposite is true of given concepts and their marks. First, a subject may possess a given concept without enjoying a clear or independent grasp of some of its marks. Indeed, this is the typical case. One's grasp on the concept as a whole must be clear enough for one to competently employ it in potentially knowledgeable judgments, but this does not require (and often will not involve) a distinct grasp of the concept, i.e. a clear representation of its constituent marks. For this reason, it may be the case that the *only* cognitive grasp one has on certain marks is the clear but indistinct grasp one has on a complex conceptual whole that contains them. The mere possibility of given concepts that are clear but indistinct – which is, of course, the typical case – shows that their marks are not cognitively prior to the whole.

Second, a given concept, as a whole, enjoys not just cognitive but semantic and explanatory priority over its marks, as partial representations. Recall that concepts are "predicates of possible judgments" (A69/B94.24–25). It is the competent use of the concept – that is, its cognitive contribution to potentially knowledgeable judgments and cogent inferences – that constitutes its meaning, that determines its content. This is why conceptual analysis appeals to our competent use of a given concept *in judgments* as the criterion of markhood (see Section 4.4). And it is our clear grasp on the concept *as a whole* that guides us in our use of it – not least because that is often the *only* grasp that we have on the concept. Here the whole concept is semantically and explanatorily prior to its marks, as partial representations, in that the marks have the meaning they do, and belong to the given concept they do, in virtue of the fact that we use this concept in certain ways, i.e. in virtue of the contribution it (the concept) makes to potential cognitions. So it is not in virtue of containing such-and-such marks that a given concept has a certain content; rather, it is in virtue of having a certain content – that is, in virtue of making a certain contribution to possible cognition, which is borne out in the use we make of it in potentially knowledgeable judgments – that such-and-such marks belong to its intension. Of course, the whole concept cannot exist without the partial representations that make it up. Entertaining the whole *involves* entertaining its marks (if only obscurely). But the fact that the concept "already" contains certain marks, prior to analysis, does not mean there is some further fact of the matter about what marks belong to a given concept *apart from* our competent use of it. Talk of marks is really just a shorthand for an account of the proper use of a concept. Since it is our grasp on the whole concept that guides us in its use, given concepts exhibit a holistic containment structure.

All discursive representations aspire to be distinct, but Kant's contrast between concepts that are made and those that are given shows that discursive distinctness can be achieved in two ways: through the *willkürliche* synthesis of marks into novel, made concepts, as in mathematics, and through the analysis of given concepts into clear representations of their marks, as in philosophy.

> To the synthesis [of made concepts] belongs the rendering-distinct of objects [*Objecte*], to the analysis [of given concepts] the rendering-distinct of concepts. In the latter, the whole precedes the parts, in the former the parts precede the whole. The philosopher only makes given concepts distinct. (L-Jäsche 9:64.13–16, my underlining)[8]

It is a mistake to draw a tidy contrast between the holistic character of spatial representation and the containment structure of discursive concepts.[9] Kant's argument for the intuitive status of spatial representation must appeal to some other criterion of intuitive and discursive representation.

But what criteria of discursive and intuitive representation are left? Well, I argued in Chapter 3 that the Preliminaries put forward specific criteria of intuition, receptivity (and sensibility), and form. These are the only criteria to which I think Kant may legitimately appeal at this point in the *Critique*. The criterion of intuitive representation outlined in the Preliminaries is *givenness*, as object-implicating immediacy (see Section 3.3). By this criterion, a content must originate in intuition if that content would be cognitively unavailable unless a corresponding object (in the sense of a ground of truth for synthetic judgments) were given to the mind. I do not take the criterion of *sensible* representation outlined in the Preliminaries to be relevant to ME3, though the idea of *receptivity* is (see Section 3.4).

[8] The holistic containment structure of given concepts vis-à-vis their marks is also evident in L-Wien 24:845.21–29; L-Ph (1772) 24:457.34–458.04; L-Blom (early 1770s) 24:153.5–16; R2289 (early 1770s) 16:300 f.; R2400 (1770s) 16:345 f. It is also implicit in Kant's claim that distinctness in given a priori concepts is achieved through *analysis*, which breaks complexes into their components and thus proceeds from whole to part, whereas *willkürliche* concepts and empirical concepts are made distinct through a *synthesis* that combines elements into complexes and thus proceeds from part to whole. See, for instance, R2916 (late 1760s) 16:574.22–575.03; R2920 (early 1770s) 16:576.21–577.03; R2928, 2929 (early 1770s) 16:579; R2936 (early 1770s) 16:581; R2942–2945 and R2947 (late 1770s–1780s) 16:583 f.; R2949–R2953 (1780s) 16:584 f.

[9] This tidy contrast is often motivated by the view that, for Kant, discursive mental activity is, as such, *successive*, proceeding from part to part, and *piecemeal*, in proceeding from part(s) to whole (see McLear 2015; Jauernig 2019). I argue against this view in Section 5.4.2.

By this criterion, a content must originate from a *receptive* capacity if it cannot be accounted for by discursive spontaneity. So, on my reading, Kant's claim in ME3 is that the essential unity and holistic structure of spatial representation shows that space could only be given to the mind, since any representation with such a content could not be a product of our own discursive mental activity. The task now is to explain why Kant claims this.

5.3 Holistic Containment Structure and Continuity

I will argue that the holistic containment structure Kant highlights in ME3 is meant to signify the *continuity* of space – or, strictly speaking, its dense ordering or infinite divisibility.[10] The underlying contention of ME3 is that discursive spontaneity cannot account for continuous contents, because they are infinitely complex. Such contents must rather be given to the mind if they are to be entertained at all. That holistic containment structure is a mark of continuity is made clear both by discussions later in the *Critique* and also by the way Kant's language echoes Leibniz's well-known account of the "labyrinth of the composition of the continuum".

5.3.1 Holistic Structure and Continuity in Kant

Consider Kant's account of the continuity of magnitudes in the Anticipations of Perception:

> The property of magnitudes, according to which no part of them is the smallest possible (no part is simple), is called their continuity. Space and time are quanta continua, because no part of them can be given without being enclosed within boundaries [*Grenzen*] (points and instants), hence only in such a way that this part itself is in turn a space or a time. Thus space consists only of spaces, time of times. Points and instants are only boundaries, i.e. mere sites [*Stellen*] of their limitation [*Einschränkung*]; sites,

[10] Like his contemporaries, Kant does not clearly distinguish continuity from mere infinite divisibility (the fact that no part is simple) or its equivalent, denseness (the fact that between any two points there is a third). This distinction will not affect our discussion. I believe Kant has continuity in mind even when his official characterizations imply only denseness. For he repeatedly gestures toward a Newtonian, kinetic conception of continuity as the *flowing* character of a magnitude, which makes gaplessness (indeed differentiability) a primitive notion that Kant expresses in metaphorical terms. See *Inaugural* 2:399.33–35; A170/B211.30; *Metaphysical Foundations* 4:494.31; *Postumum* 22:171.13–17; R5382 (late 1770s) 18:167.19–20. On this Newtonian heritage, see Kitcher (1992 [1975], 122); Friedman (1992, 74–80); Sutherland (2021a). Prior to Bolzano, Cauchy, and Weierstrass, however, no such distinction was in circulation, notwithstanding some suggestive gestures in Leibniz (see Levey 1999, 2021).

however, always presuppose those intuitions that they are supposed to delimit or determine, and neither space nor time can be composed [*zusammengesetzt*] out of mere sites, as out of component parts that could be given prior to space or to time. (A169f./B211.16–29)

Here we find the same language we encountered in ME3: Space cannot be "composed [*zusammengesetzt*]" out of "component parts [*Bestandteilen*]" that are "prior [*vor*]" to space, because a "part [*Teil*]" of space is only given through the "limitation [*Einschränkung*]" of a greater whole that contains it. Now, unlike ME3, the present passage does not emphasize the all-encompassing character of space or its consequent singularity. Indeed, by noting that every *part* of space "is itself in turn a space" (A169/B211.21–22), the passage suggests that finite spaces are determined not only by imposing "limitations" on *all-encompassing* space but also by imposing limits on *other finite spaces* of greater magnitude or dimensionality. That is the sense in which "no part is simple" (A169/B211.17) – namely, because every part is subject to further "limitation", which reveals it to contain a plurality of proper parts in its turn. The present passage focuses our attention on the densely ordered, Matryoshka-doll containment relation that nests parts within wholes and, thus, on the holistic dependence that this structure involves insofar as it is articulated by the function of "limitation". Kant's central claim in the passage is that this holistic mereological structure is a mark of *continuity*: It is "because [*weil*]" space and time have this structure that they count as "quanta continua" (A169/B211.18–19).

This is not an isolated passage. Kant repeatedly emphasizes that every finite space necessarily "rests on" – that is, is determined through – limitations placed on a greater whole and, ultimately, on all-encompassing space. And he consistently presents this holistic mereological structure as a mark of continuity or infinitely divisibility, i.e. a dense ordering of parts.[11]

So when Kant identifies holistic mereological structure as a mark of <space> in ME3, what he means is that *continuity* is a mark of <space>. It is an analytic judgment not just that "space consists of spaces" (A169/B211.22–23) but that *any* space harbors infinitely many subspaces nested within it. This belongs to our very concept <space> – it is part of "what one understands" "when one speaks of many spaces" (A25/B39.5).

[11] *Inaugural* 2:403n.32–33; R4424 (c. 1771), 17:540 f.; R4979 (c. 1771) 18:48.22–49.6; R5299 (1776–1778) 18:147.21–30; R5728 (1780s) 18:338; R5869 (late 1770s to mid-1780s) 18:372.23–29; R5882 (1780s) 18:375 f. See also B137n.23–28; R5510 (1771?) 18:150.

But could Kant have reasonably expected a philosophically educated reader to pick up on this connection between the holistic containment structure he emphasizes in ME3 and the continuity of magnitudes, which goes unmentioned? I think so. Kant's formulations in ME3 echo not only his account of continuity later in the *Critique* but Leibniz's well-known solution to one of "the two labyrinths of the human mind", namely the composition of the continuum.[12]

5.3.2 Holistic Structure and Continuity in Leibniz

In the *New Essays*, Leibniz writes:

> The true infinite, strictly speaking, is only in the **absolute**, which is prior to all composition and is not formed by the addition of parts. (2.17.1, A6.6:157, G5:144, original emphasis)

And:

> I [sc. Theophilus, Leibniz's spokesperson] believe that we have a positive idea of each of these [sc. of infinite duration and infinite extension]. This idea will be true provided that it is conceived not as an infinite whole but rather as an absolute, i.e. as an attribute without limits [*bornes*]. In the case of eternity [i.e. infinite duration] [. . .] there is no dependence on parts, nor is the notion of it formed by adding times. (2.17.18, A6.6:159, G5:146)

By "absolute" here Leibniz means the opposite of "relative". The absolute is what serves as the standard or benchmark with reference to which all relative determinations of the relevant sort must be made. It is thus "an attribute without limits" insofar as limits are relative determinations, made with reference to something else qua absolute. Naturally enough, "true infinity" is found only in the absolute (i.e. in what lacks limits), whereas the finite results precisely from introducing limits into the absolute.[13] It is because finite parts only result from placing limits on the absolute that the absolute involves "no dependence on parts" but "is prior to all composition and is not formed by the addition of parts". Leibniz's notion of the "absolute", then, corresponds to what Kant terms the "essentially unitary" character of space.

[12] "On Freedom", AG 95.

[13] This conception of infinity as an absolute from which the finite results through the introduction of limits is echoed in Wolff (*German Metaphysics* § 54, § 109) and Baumgarten (*Metaphysica* § 248, § 261 – see also Kant's Reflection on § 248: R4428, early 1770s, 17:542). Significantly, however, the labyrinth of the continuum, which is so central to Leibniz's thought, plays no notable role in theirs (see Wilson 1995, 449) – as is evident e.g. in *German Metaphysics* § 61 and § 604.

To appreciate the relevant similarity, however, we must bracket some significant differences between Leibniz's account and Kant's. First, Leibniz calls the absolute an "attribute", i.e. a necessary property of a substance. The substance he has in mind is God. "The idea of the absolute, with reference to space," Leibniz writes, "is just the idea of the immensity of God and thus of other things" (2.17.3, A6.6:158, G5:145). This is a comparatively rare glimpse into the theological underpinnings of Leibniz's signature relationalism: "[S]pace is no more a substance than time is[.] [...] It is a relationship: an order, not only among existents, but also among possibles as though they existed. But its truth and reality are grounded in God, like all eternal truths" (2.13.17, A6.6:149, G5:136). All finite substances are created by God. Leibnizian space is the order not only of the substances God actually creates (all "existents") but of all the substances God has the power to create (all "possibles as though they existed"). To a first approximation, then, space is an order among finite substances, actual and possible. But more fundamentally, it is an attribute of God: specifically, it is a feature of God's power to create co-existent substances.

Kant, of course, rejects just this sort of account of space and time as "only determinations, or even relations of things, yet such as would still pertain to them even if they were not intuited" (A23/B37.19–22). Indeed, ME3 opens by targeting the familiar Leibnizian position: "Space is no [...] concept of relations of things in general" (A24f./B39.1–3, my underlining). But this difference about the ontological status of space and time does nothing to undermine the similarity between the holistic mereological structure that marks out the Leibnizian "absolute" and that, for Kant, makes something "essentially unitary" (A25/B39.10–11). In both cases, a composition out of prior or independent parts is impossible precisely because those parts are first determined by introducing limits into "the true infinite".

Another telling difference is that Leibniz insists "the infinite cannot be a true whole" (2.17.8, A6.6:159, G5:146) and accordingly claims that we have a positive idea of infinite duration or infinite extension only "provided that it is conceived not as an infinite whole but rather as an absolute, i.e. as an attribute without limits" (2.17.18, A6.6:159, G5:146). This may appear to conflict with Kant's claim that space is "essentially unitary", but the conflict is only apparent. Leibniz and Kant are each concerned with oneness, both in these texts and throughout their corpora. But Leibniz's focus is the unity characteristic of *substance*, whereas Kant is principally interested in the unity characteristic of *knowledge.*[14] So the question whether space or other continua are "true wholes" does not have the same sense or urgency for Kant that it does for Leibniz.

Leibniz and his followers adhere to the Scholastic "unity principle", *omne ens est unum*: all that is, is one.[15] This is an ontological principle, setting a necessary condition on all real existents. Among its prominent consequences, for Leibniz, is that anything *real* must be either (i) simple, i.e. metaphysically indivisible and thus devoid of separable parts, or (ii) composed of simples concatenated according to a determinate principle or rule. Leibniz argues that both continua and infinite collections violate this principle. The case against continua is more straightforward and more relevant to our purposes.[16] A continuum is neither simple, since it is divisible, nor composed of simples, since it is divisible without end.[17] So it violates the unity principle and is therefore not a real thing. But to deny the reality of continua is not to deny they exist tout court. Instead, Leibniz classifies them as ideal things, *entia rationis*, that we conceive either by *abstracting* from concreta or by *con-fusing* their elements, which must

[14] For Kant, the unity of knowledge is, I take it, the sort of "qualitative unity" manifested in "the unity of a theme in a play, a speech, a fable" (B114.7). This is a unity that is only possible "by means of an **idea of the whole**" (A64/B89.17). As such, it differs from substantial unity, inter alia, in being essentially self-conscious. Because critique is concerned with the unity of knowledge before the unity of substance, Kant contends that "the proud name of ontology [. . .] must yield its place to the modest [name] of a mere analytic of the pure understanding" (A247/B303.18–23). Kant does have a place for Leibniz's notion of a "true whole" in the category of <totality>, which applies to compound substances. Notice, however, that in the context of Leibniz's substance metaphysics (as in Kant's pre-critical works *Physical Monadology* and *Inaugural*) the composition of the continuum represents one of the central questions of first philosophy, whereas the *Critique* can treat it as but one of many Antinomies of Reason.

[15] Leibniz appeals to the principle freely. See his *New System of Nature* (G 4:478 f., AG 139); or his letter to Arnauld, 30 April 1687 (G 2:97, AG 86). See also Wolff, *German Metaphysics* §§ 75–81; *Ontologia* §§ 328–329, 333–334; Baumgarten, *Metaphysica* §§ 73–77. It is no accident that the majority of Kant's *Reflexionen* about infinity and continuity pertain to the "unum" sections of Baumgarten. The principle has its roots in Aristotle, *Metaphysics* IV.2 (1003b23–1004a9). See also Aquinas's discussion in *ST* I, q.11. a.1; cf. *ST* I, q.3. a7 and *De Veritate* q.1, a.1, acd4.

[16] Leibniz's diagnosis of the problem with infinite wholes seems to evolve as his account of substantial unity shifts – that is, as he reconceives the principle of organization that distinguishes a compound substance, qua true whole, from a mere aggregate. On the problem of infinite wholes in Leibniz, see the conversation initiated between Carlin (1997), Brown (1998, 2000), and Arthur (1998, 1999, 2001), continuing in Levey (2012) and Harmer (2014).

[17] Points are simple, but Leibniz denies that they can aggregate to compose continuous magnitudes. Interestingly, his rationale is not based on metrical concerns – about how elements of zero measure can "add up" to something with non-zero measure – but on considerations of ontological dependence (Levey 1998, 57, 64). The problem is not their size but the *sort* of thing they are. Points are mere limits of magnitudes, not magnitudes in their own right. It is incoherent, not just mathematically unsound, to try to compose a magnitude out of something that is a mere property of magnitudes. It involves a category error, like proposing to write a sentence consisting of just the spaces between words, or to compose a tune out of the silences between notes.

ultimately be discrete. A dense but lucid statement of this position appears in Leibniz's 1696 response to Foucher, who had criticized his *New System* in the *Journal des Savants.*[18]

> Extension or space and the surfaces, lines, and points one can conceive in it are only relations of order or orders of coexistence, both for the actually existing thing and for the possible thing one can put in its place. Thus they have no bases of composition, any more than does number. A number divided, ½ for example, can be further divided into two fourths or four eighths, etc. to infinity, without our being able to arrive at any smallest fractions or to conceive of the number as a whole that is formed by the coming together of ultimate elements. It is the same for a line, which can be divided just as this number can. Also, properly speaking, the number ½ in the abstract is an entirely simple ratio, in no way formed through the composition of other fractions [. . .]. And it is the same for the **abstract** line. Composition is only in **concretes.** [. . .] And since everything is indefinite in the abstract line, we are dealing with everything that is possible, as in the fractions of a number, without having to bother with divisions actually made [. . .]. But, in actual substantial things, the whole is a result or coming together of simple substances, or rather of a multitude of real unities. It is through the confusion of the ideal with the actual which has muddled everything and caused the labyrinth of **the composition of the continuum**. (G4:491, AG 146, emphases in original)

Leibniz's starting point in this passage is that continua have no "bases of composition", since they can be divided without end. Accordingly, continua are not "formed by the coming together of ultimate elements": They do not have what we have called an atomic containment structure. Leibniz then applies the unity principle as a sort of axiom: "But, in actual substantial things, the whole is a result or coming together of simple substances, or rather a multitude of true unities." It follows that continua are not actual, substantial things, since they do not have the requisite atomic structure. This is a merely negative characterization. But Leibniz also provides positive characterizations of the mode of existence continua do enjoy: They are *abstract* rather than concrete, *possible* rather than actual, and *ideal* rather than real.

[18] Leibniz's mature account of continua is prominent in his correspondence with de Volder: for example, 30 June 1704 (G 2:268, AG 178); 1704 or 1705 (G2:276, AG 182); and 19 January 1706 (G2:282, AG 185). Important aspects of this view are also evident in some of his early writings on the continuum problem, such as *Pacidius Philalethei* (November 1776); see Levey (1998) for discussion. I am focusing on texts to which Kant might plausibly have had access – namely, published writings and, especially, texts included in Raspe's 1765 edition of Leibniz's writings or Dutens's 1768 edition.

The thought is that we begin with the representation of a concrete whole: an extended thing, such as a tree. This whole consists of a determinate plurality of discrete parts – leaves, buds, seeds, bark, roots, cells, and so forth – that are actually divided by topological gaps, differences in motion, coefficients of cohesion, and so forth. We then abstract from the parts into which the whole is actually divided and consider instead all the parts into which it could possibly be divided. This abstract representation of the possible parts of the whole cannot, Leibniz argues, have something *real* as its intentional object, but only something *ideal*, an *ens rationis*. This is not simply because we are engaged in abstraction. It is because it violates fundamental ontological principles governing the nature of reality. Different aspects of the passage suggest different ways to approach this thought.

First, Leibniz argues that "everything is indefinite in the abstract line" (G4:491, AG 146, my underlining). This is because we abstract from any actual divisions into parts that may obtain in the whole. So it is indeterminate what parts (if any) the continuum, so represented, divides into. It is, however, a common metaphysical assumption that reality abhors indeterminacy. What is real is maximally determinate, never indefinite. The thoughts of finite creatures, by contrast, are rife with indeterminacy. I may desire to eat a piece of fruit, for instance. But fruit simpliciter is never what I eat: I eat a particular peach, a certain pear, an individual mango. The determinacy of reality typically outstrips the determinacy of thought. Accordingly, the continuum, with its fundamentally indefinite mereology, cannot be real and must be an *ens rationis*.[19]

Another way to approach Leibniz's thought that continua are unreal and ideal focuses on modal considerations. In order to be possible, something need only agree with itself. But to be real, it must also harmonize with everything else that is real. Reality is constrained not just by possibility but by *com*possibility. Thought, by contrast, can embrace the incompossible, even if it cannot comprehend the impossible. This is a standard feature of Leibniz's account of contingent truths. The Caesar who does not cross the Rubicon is just as possible as the one who does. This is what makes it a contingent truth, not one that can be proved via the principle of contradiction. But the timid Caesar is not compatible with *the rest of the reality* we know. He is not just a different man; he belongs to a different world.

[19] Recent interpretations of the mathematical Antinomies have identified a similar rationale for Kant's own idealism about continua. See Marschall (2019) and Chaplin (MS). See also R5844, 5845, 5846 (early 1780s?) 18:367 f.

(And, on Leibniz's optimistic assessment, a less perfect world.) Yet this does not impede our ability to *think* about the timid Caesar in relation to aspects of our own reality – even aspects that are, in the final analysis, incompossible with him. Such thoughts are coherent *as thoughts*; they are merely false (or fictional). Something similar applies to our thoughts about continua. We conceive a continuum by abstracting from any actual divisions into parts and considering instead all the parts into which it could possibly be divided. But not all partitionings are compossible – a division into thirds is incompatible with a division into quarters, for instance. So, even though we are representing all and only possible divisions and possible parts, these partitionings are not *com*possible.[20] Thus, what we are representing cannot be real: The object of our thought cannot really exist *as represented*. For we represent it as divided in all the ways it can be divided, yet nothing real could be divided in all those ways at once. The continuum is therefore not a real thing but an *ens rationis*, a useful fiction.

But we get closer to the heart of Leibniz's idealism about continua, I think, by focusing on *unity* rather than on determinacy or compossibility. The unity principle, *omne ens est unum*, dictates that anything real must ultimately consist of simples. Yet the continuum is not simple, nor is any of its parts. Though such disunity (i.e. such a lack of true unities) cannot exist *in reality*, it can exist *in thought*, for better and for worse. The thoughts of finite creatures, for instance, often involve confusion, in that the true unities that make up reality are not represented distinctly in their own right but are agglomerated and smeared together without determinacy or differentiation. The intentional content of such thoughts does not consist of simple thought-elements. It is irremediably disunified – a confusion that is not just blooming and buzzing but benumbed and blurry – unlike the discrete and maximally determinate reality to which it strives to be adequate.[21] Such disunity is a constitutive possibility for (finite)

[20] Recall that actualizing all possible divisions would dissolve the continuum into a "powder of points". And Leibniz denies that points are the sort of thing that can compose a magnitude (see note 17). A thoroughgoing division of the continuum is not a possible partitioning of it.

[21] There is a sense in which thought, too, must bottom out in simple elements, for Leibniz. Every perceptual state in a monad represents the entire universe in its infinite complexity. Presumably, then, simple substances are represented by simple representations that concatenate into this infinitely complex representational content. Nevertheless, no finite creature can become *conscious* of such infinitely complex thought contents, as such. So, even if the basic content of all thought consists of simple representations ("*petites perceptions*" *par excellence*), its emergent, intentional content (i.e. what we can become conscious of) cannot always bottom out in simples, as reality must. See Jorgenson (2009); Jauernig (2019, 2022).

thought and a constitutive impossibility for reality.[22] Thus, anything that exhibits such disunity, as continua do, cannot be a real thing but must be an *ens rationis*.

I belabor the Leibnizian distinction between the real and the ideal because it is crucial to understanding the specific sort of holistic, whole-before-part dependence that he attributes to continua. Continua exhibit a holistic containment structure *because* they are ideal. And their ideality, their status as thought entities, is reflected in the *kind* of dependence that obtains between the whole and the part:

> [T]he total ratio ½ is prior (in the sign of reason, as the Scholastics say) to the partial ratio ¼, since it is by the subdivision of the half that we come to the fourth, when considering the ideal order; and it is the same for the line, in which the whole is prior to the part because the part is only possible and ideal. But in realities in which only divisions actually made enter into consideration, the whole is only a result or coming together, like a flock of sheep. (G4:492, AG 147, my underlining)

While it is true that Leibnizian realities exhibit an atomic mereological structure and Leibnizian continua a holistic one, this is not the full story. It is not merely the *direction* of dependence that is different in these two cases: The *type* of dependence is different in kind. This is easy to miss, but it should not be wholly surprising, since the relata involved are also quite different sorts of thing – real substances versus *entia rationis*. In the case of realities, true unities "come together" to form a whole, as sheep come together to form a flock.[23] This is the sort of *ontological* dependence that obtains between a collection and its elements or a set and its members. But "when considering the ideal order", Leibniz writes, the whole is prior to the part "in the sign of reason". That is to say, it is *conceptually* prior: The *concept* of the part depends on the *concept* of the whole. The part depends on the whole not (or not just) for its existence but for its intelligibility – its most basic sortal identity and conceivability.

[22] Monads are not flawless mirrors of the universe. Indeed, each monad is distinguished from the rest by the distinctive way in which it *con-fuses* the *petites perceptions* through which it represents the infinite complexity of the universe (Jauernig 2019, 2022). In this sense, finite minds are creative, for Leibniz, since their representational powers give rise to novel contents that no reality can bear out. But this sort of creativity is a mark of our *im*perfection just as God's power to create ex nihilo is a mark of divine perfection. A more perfect, but still finite, mind would be less creative.

[23] A flock of sheep, of course, is not a true unity (i.e. a compound substance) but a plurality (i.e. an aggregate or collection). My point is only that the ontological dependence of a flock on its constituent sheep is of the same sort as the ontological dependence of a compound substance on the simples that constitute it.

5.3.3 Kant's Leibnizian Conception of Holistic Structure

It is this sort of holistic dependence "in the sign of reason" that Kant has in mind in ME3. Recall that a metaphysical exposition is a special sort of analysis of a concept – in this case, the concept <space>. And ME3 is specifically a reflection on "what one means" "when one speaks of many spaces". It is thus an analysis of the relation *in the sign of reason* between the parts of space ("many spaces", A25/B39.5) and the whole ("the unitary all-encompassing space", A25/B39.7–8). And though it is easy to miss, Kant's language indicates that he is concerned with a *conceptual* dependence: "These parts can [. . .] only be thought **in it** [sc. the unitary all-encompassing space]" (A25/B39.7. . .10, my underlining).[24]

Kant's claim is not merely that the parts of space depend on the whole for their existence, nor even that they depend on the whole for their identity and individuation as the particular parts they are. His claim is that the parts of space depend for their *intelligibility*, for their very *think-ability*, upon the whole of space – or, rather, upon our concept of the whole.[25] It may well be that finite portions of space are ontologically dependent on the whole, in the sense that they are *given* only in and as part of that whole, relative to which they are determined via "limitations [*Einschränkungen*]".[26] But I cannot see how Kant is yet in a position to make this ontological claim – not before he has established the ideality of space and outlined his theory of figurative synthesis and magnitude construction. And it may well be that the numerical identity and difference of finite spaces is only secured by their co-membership as parts of one unitary space, so that the parts depend on the whole for their particular identity and individuation.[27] But this sort of individuation-dependence is clearly secondary to the sort of intelligibility-dependence we have identified. In claiming that parts of space can only be *thought* as in the whole of

[24] Though Kant often leaves the relation of dependence unspecified, saying merely that the whole "precedes" the parts, when he does specify it, he typically characterizes it as a form of conceptual dependence: "Hence not every whole is composite [*Zusammengesetzt*], e.g. space, because the unity here precedes the multiplicity or the multiplicity presupposes the unity in order to be thought in it" (R5299, 1776–1778, 18:147.21–24, my underlining). See also *On Kästner* 20:419.15–18; R5844–5846 (early 1780s) 18:367 f.; R5879 (late 1780s) 18:375; R5962 (late 1780s) 18:402.19–22.

[25] Kant's focus on this relation of conceptual dependence may further contribute to his slippage between talk of space and talk of <space>. This is another reason I consider such slippage to be innocuous.

[26] For readings along these lines, see Messina (2014) and Chaplin (2022).

[27] For a reading along these lines, see Melnick (1973, 9); cf. R5908 (1783–1784) 18:381; R6290 (1783–1784) 18:558.19–21.

space, Kant is claiming that it is in virtue of being (represented as) situated within the whole of space that its parts are (represented as) *spatial* in the first place. Questions of numerical identity and individuation can arise only once this more fundamental question of sortal identity and homogeneity has been settled. It is only once the parts of space have been cognized *as spatial* and thus as (many) spaces that we can subsequently cognize them as identical or different.

Now, it may be surprising that Kant should seize upon Leibniz's solution to the labyrinth of the continuum, when Leibniz's followers – notably, Wolff, Meier, and Baumgarten – were so unconcerned with the problem, much less its solution. Yet Kant's pre-critical writings are clearly animated by the continuum problem, which Kant associates with Leibniz. Kant's 1756 *Physical Monadology* is explicitly Leibnizian not only in its title but in its motivation: "How can metaphysics be married geometry", Kant asks, when metaphysics insists that all compounds bottom out in simples and thus "peremptorily denies that space is infinitely divisible, while the latter [sc. geometry], with its usual certainty, asserts that it is infinitely divisible" (1:475.22–26). This is the problem of how extended substances are possible – that is, how anything continuous could be a true unity. The same dialectic opens, and thus presumably motivates, Kant's 1770 *Inaugural*, which begins with an "exposition" of the concept <compound substance> (2:387.7). This exposition is supposed to show that all composition must bottom out in true unities (i.e. the simple) and top out in complete totalities (i.e. the world) (2:387.4–6). The challenge, Kant writes, is how to reconcile this analysis with the existence of *continuous* magnitudes, such as space and time (2:388.6–11). Here, too, the problem is to explain how anything continuous could be a true unity – and, if continua cannot exhibit the "form and principles" of real substances, to characterize the sort of unity, the "form and principles", proper to them.

In light of Kant's decades-long engagement with the metaphysics of continuous magnitudes, framed in recognizably Leibnizian terms, it is less surprising that continuity should feature prominently in Kant's critical account of space. What remains surprising is that the metaphysical premises about the nature of substance and the structure of reality that make the continuum problem urgent for Leibniz are conspicuously absent from the Aesthetic.[28] Kant is under no pressure to determine whether space is a

[28] By contrast, I take Kant's proto-critical idealism about space and time in *Inaugural* to depend on just these sorts of metaphysical assumptions. It accordingly comes much closer to Leibniz's idealism about continua (Smyth 2015, ch. 1). The *Critique* relocates these metaphysical concerns with

"true unity" or a "genuine whole". Yet his claim that parts of space can only "be thought" as limitations of the whole coincides so neatly with Leibniz's mature solution to the continuum problem that I think ME3 must be understood to identify continuity (i.e. dense ordering) as a mark of <space>. Kant retains Leibniz's conception of the structure of extended continua, while dispensing with the substance metaphysics that make the continuum a labyrinthine philosophical problem. He does this by absorbing continuity of mereological structure into the very concepts of space and time.

When Kant identifies <continuity> as a mark of <space>, however, he is not (yet) asserting that space *is* infinitely divisible. For he has yet to establish the objective validity of the concept <space>. The Metaphysical Expositions demonstrate that <space> is a given concept with an a priori origin. It is only in the Transcendental Exposition and the Conclusions that Kant argues for the possibility of objective cognition through <space>.[29] What Kant is concerned to argue in ME3 is that a certain *content* is available to the mind – namely, that we can necessarily frame the *thought* of space as densely ordered and, hence, infinitely divisible, since this is just an elaboration of "what we mean" "when we speak of many spaces".

But how is this supposed to show that <space> originates in *intuition*? The idea, I think, is that <continuity>, which Kant identifies as a mark of <space> by adopting Leibniz's account of its holistic mereological structure "in the sign of reason", involves the idea of infinite complexity. And spontaneous, discursive mental activity can never give rise to, or fully account for, the idea of infinite complexity. If we can indeed entertain the notion of infinite complexity, of an infinite manifold of elements, that notion cannot have a spontaneous, discursive origin. It must therefore be originally given to us receptively and in intuition. To discern this line of argument, however, we must turn to ME4 – not because ME3 and ME4 are interchangeable or make the same point but because they are, as

simples and totalities to the mathematical Antinomies in the Dialectic. The argument for the ideality of space and time in the Aesthetic proceeds on quite different grounds. Kant's critical turn marks a significant transposition in the nature of his idealism: from what he calls a "material" idealism, of the sort advanced in *Inaugural*, to the "formal" idealism of the *Critique* (see B519n.28–30; letter to Beck, 4 December 1792, 11:395.21–24). I flesh out this account in Smyth (2015, ch. 2).

29 On this distribution of argumentative labor, see Merritt (2010). Establishing the objective validity of <space> – that is, providing its transcendental deduction – is easy: Kant merely observes that the concept necessarily applies to appearances insofar as space is the form of outer sense (A27/B43). See note 39.

moments of a single exposition, "mutually dependent [*an einander hängend*]" reflections (L-Jäsche 9:143.1–2; see Section 4.3).

5.4 Infinitary Intuitions, Finite Concepts

My interpretation of ME3 requires that we read it together with ME4, rather than treating it as a self-standing argument. This is less objectionable than it may initially seem. For the text of ME3 does not mention any criteria for discursive or intuitive representation, yet it must clearly rely on some such criteria to support its central claim that "space is no discursive [...] concept [...] but a pure intuition" (A24/B39.1–3). So *any* reconstruction of ME3 as an argument is obliged to reach beyond the confines of the numbered paragraph. And my interpretation does not have to reach as far as most.[30] For I locate the relevant criteria of form, receptivity, and intuition in the Preliminaries (see Sections 3.3 and 3.4) and the relevant criterion of discursive representation in ME4: "no concept, as such, can be thought as if it contained an infinite plurality [*Menge*] of representations **in itself**" (B40.1–3). I propose that this premise about the finitude of discursive representation "bleeds up" into the foregoing reflections of ME3.[31]

The fourth ME runs:

> Space is represented as an infinite **given** magnitude. Now one must admittedly think every concept as a representation that is contained in an infinite plurality [*Menge*] of distinct possible representations (as their common mark) and that hence contains these **under itself**; but no concept, as such, can be thought as though it contained an infinite plurality of representations **in itself**. Yet this how space is thought (for all parts of space into infinity are simultaneous). Therefore the original representation of space is [an] **intuition a priori** and not [a] **concept**. (B39–40)

Kant's central claim here is twofold: (i) the content of an intuitive representation can be infinitely complex but (ii) the content of discursive concepts cannot be. This is somewhat puzzling on its face. If finite minds are capable of entertaining infinite contents *at all*, why should this cognitive feat be credited to certain sorts of representations but not others? We must first understand in what sense a Kantian intuition "contain[s] an

[30] Interpretations that turn on the singularity of intuition typically appeal to the *Stufenleiter* or *L-Jäsche*. Alternative readings that focus on the allegedly atomic containment structure of discursive representations typically appeal to works on logic, which I think they misread (see Sections 5.2 and 5.4.2).

[31] My thanks to Clinton Tolley for insisting on this aspect of my reading.

infinite plurality of representations **in itself**" (B40.2–3). We then have to explain why discursive contents cannot do this. What finitude of mind allows for infinitary intuitions but only finite discursive contents?

5.4.1 *Infinitary Intuitions*

There are, for Kant, two important senses in which "space is represented as an infinite given magnitude" (B39.21–22; cf. A25.34–35). First, we represent space to be continuous. This, I've argued, is the pivotal observation of ME3. The continuity of space implies that it is infinitely complex, i.e. that spaces are densely ordered within it. The manifold of distinct spaces contained in all-encompassing space is, therefore, at least countably infinite.[32] Infinitely many distinct spaces are given in and with the whole of space. Space is an infinite given magnitude in this first sense in that it constitutes (or contains) an infinite multiplicity: an infinite collection of distinct elements, all of which are given with and through the whole.

The second sense in which we represent space to be infinite is that we represent it to be boundless in extent. Every space is surrounded by more of the same. Now, any space is strictly greater than the spaces contained within it. Accordingly, all-encompassing space must be strictly greater than any finite space, since all finite spaces are contained in it. But to be strictly greater than any finite value is to be infinite in measure. So we represent all-encompassing space as infinite in extent.

This account of the twofold infinity of space invites several objections. First, Parsons (1983 [1964]) objects that the open-endedness of space – that is, the fact that every subspace is surrounded by a strictly greater one – does not, by itself, entail that all-encompassing space is infinite. One must additionally assume that there is no limit on the size of subspaces. Otherwise, the whole of space could remain finite and serve merely as the limit (or "horizon") toward which subspaces converge as they grow more and more capacious. That is, space might have the structure of a convergent series, such as, $\frac{1}{2} + \frac{1}{4} + \ldots + 1/2^n$. Each partial sum of the series (e.g. $\frac{1}{2} + \frac{1}{4}$) "contains" and is strictly greater than the previous partial sum (e.g. $\frac{1}{2}$). Yet these ever-increasing partial sums still converge to a finite value and therefore the whole series does as well, since it is just the totality of those partial sums. Space might be like that: with every subspace

[32] That is, it has the cardinality of the naturals. Since Kant fails to distinguish denseness from true continuity, he cannot claim that it contains an uncountable infinity of spaces, i.e. a manifold with the cardinality of the continuum.

surrounded by a strictly greater space, even though the whole of space is finite in extent. To secure the metrical infinity of space, one must show that there is no limit on the size of these "partial sums", i.e. no limit on the size of the finite spaces contained in all-encompassing space.

It is interesting to observe that Parsons's objection itself presupposes that space is infinitary in the first sense: that is, that it contains a countable infinity of distinct spaces, just as the convergent series mentioned earlier contains a countable infinity of elements. But this might inspire a second objection.[33] What, after all, does it mean to claim that space contains "distinct" subspaces within itself? It is not as though space is given to us pre-sliced into parts that we can then count (all the way up to Aleph-nought). Kant is quite explicit about this: "the manifold in it [sc. all-encompassing space] [. . .] rests solely upon limitations" (A25/B39.11–13). Space contains a multiplicity of subspaces only insofar as these are generated through acts of limitation (and related acts of figurative synthesis through the categories of quantity). Prior to or independent of the limitations that we impose on it, space is "essentially unitary" (A25/B39.10–11): an undivided one. The multiplicity of subspaces is thus comparable in cardinality to the set of limitations we place on the whole of space. But we can never impose infinitely many limitations, since each would require a distinct act and it is uncontroversial that we cannot complete an actual infinity of distinct acts. So space cannot contain an actual infinity of subspaces, countable or otherwise. When Kant talks about the infinity of space, then, he is either wrong – and, worse, betraying his own insights into the constructive character of mathematical cognition – or else he means that space is *potentially* infinite in its manifoldness. There is no limit on the ways we can slice up space by imposing limitations. But the fact that there are infinitely many possible limitations we might impose on space does not imply that it is possible to impose infinitely many limitations on it. What it implies is that all-encompassing space is intrinsically *indeterminate* in magnitude and multiplicity, when considered as the pure given form of outer sense. Determinate spaces, as grounded in limitations, are necessarily finite in

[33] For a version of this objection, see Guyer (2018). I elaborate beyond Guyer's own presentation both to avoid interpretive niceties and to articulate what I take to be a widespread assumption that Kant is hostile to actual infinity. See, for instance, Koriako (1999, 182, 229, 280); Tait (2016); Sutherland (2017, 180n.38). For readings that resist this assumption and emphasize Kant's embrace of actual infinity, see Kemp Smith (1992 [1918], 486); Büchel (1987, 185–220); Carson (1997); Friedman (2000, 2012, 2020); Onof and Schulting (2014, 2015); Tolley (2016); Smyth (2023 [2021]); and Winegar (2022).

both size and multiplicity, though these values can be made arbitrarily large or small.

This second objection is not new. It was first voiced by Kant's contemporary, Abraham Kästner, in Eberhard's *Philosophisches Magazin*.[34] In considering Kant's response to Kästner (the second objection), we will see that it also serves to answer Parsons (the first objection).[35]

Kästner observes that Euclid's second postulate – about extending line segments – places no limit on the magnitude of the lines it enables us to construct. Yet it does not enable us to construct infinite lines.[36] The same applies to the all-encompassing space discussed in the Aesthetic. It is admittedly unbounded, but that does not make it "an infinite given magnitude", as Kant claims.

Kant grants Kästner's point about Euclidian constructions but distinguishes "the different use of the concept of infinity" in geometry and in metaphysics (*On Kästner* 20:418.1–2) In geometry, <infinite> does indeed signify the standing potential for varying magnitudes *ad libitem* (20:420.1–2; cf. *Critique* A511/B539.4–28). It is potential infinity we have in view when we are concerned with geometrical space(s). But the task of metaphysics, Kant argues, is to "show how one can **possess** the representation of space, whereas geometry teaches how one can **describe** a [space]" (20:419.1–2) The discussion of all-encompassing space in the Aesthetic is part of an explanation of how geometry is so much as possible. And this involves explaining the standing potential for extending (or dividing) line segments that Kästner highlights. The potential infinity of geometrical construction is not philosophical bedrock for Kant; it is a datum that stands in need of transcendental explanation. Why is it *true* (and how can we *know* it is true) that every line segment can be extended further, as Euclid's second postulate implies? Here is Kant's answer:

> [T]hat a line can be extended into infinity means as much as: the space within which I describe the line is larger than any line that I may describe in it. Thus the geometer grounds the possibility of his problem [*Aufgabe*] of enlarging a

[34] Kästner (1790, 407–411, 418).

[35] Here, as elsewhere, I appeal to passages outside the Aesthetic in order to clarify Kant's arguments, not to shore them up by providing additional premises. The reply to Kästner is a borderline case, since it answers an objection to his account in the Aesthetic. But his answer, I take it, consists in emphasizing a distinction that is already implicit in the Aesthetic's distinction between metaphysical versus transcendental expositions.

[36] Though these are not licensed by the second postulate itself, Mendell (2015, 47–53) argues that Euclid and Apollonius "were not bothered" by infinite lines. But the mainstream reception of Euclidean geometry by early modern thinkers was resolutely finitistic.

> space (of which there are many) into infinity upon the original representation of a unitary [*einigen*], infinite, **subjectively given** space. (20:420.7–13)

Kant follows tradition in grounding potentialities in actualities. He departs from tradition in arguing that the potential infinity of constructible geometrical magnitudes must be grounded in something that is not just actual (given) but actually *infinite.*[37] In order for it to be true – and necessarily true – that I can extend a line segment to whatever length I please, Kant reasons, there must be some guarantee that I will, so to speak, never run out of space into which I can extend it. Thus, the space that grounds the possibility of all geometrical construction must necessarily be greater than any space that can be constructed in it. But according to Euclid's second postulate, there is no limit on the magnitude of line segments that can be constructed in geometry. So the space that grounds their construction must be strictly greater than any finite magnitude: It must be actually infinite. This answers both objections.

Parsons is, of course, correct that, by itself, the open-ended structure of space does not secure its metrical infinity. But Kant's account of the open-endedness of space in ME3 is not an isolated observation. It is part of a transcendental explanation of a particular datum – namely, the possibility of Euclidean geometry as a synthetic a priori science. And this science includes Euclid's second postulate, which implies that there is no limit on the size of spaces we can construct.[38] So the premise that Parsons thinks is

[37] See also *Prolegomena* 4:285.1–9; R4428 (1770–1775) 17:542; R5896 (1780s?) 18:378. The idea that any potential infinity must be grounded in an actual infinity recurs a century later in Cantor's "domain argument":

> If there is namely no doubt that we cannot do without **variable** quantities in the sense of the potential infinite, this also allows a proof of the necessity of the actual-infinite along the following lines: In order that such a variable quantity can take a value [*verwertbar sei*] in a mathematical inquiry, the "domain [*Gebiet*]" of its variability must strictly be known in advance through a definition; yet this "domain" cannot itself be variable, since otherwise every firm foundation for the inquiry would be lacking; therefore, this "domain" is a determinate actual-infinite set of values [*Wertmenge*]. Thus, every potential infinity, if it is to be strictly mathematically applicable, presupposes an actual infinity. (Cantor 1966[1888], 410–411; cf. 391, 393)

[38] Euclid's second postulate entails this only in conjunction with the notorious fifth postulate about parallels not intersecting. Otherwise, parallels may form a finite closed figure when extended, as in elliptic geometry. The parallel postulate was a research focus for several of Kant's interlocutors, such as Lambert (1786 [composed 1766]) and Schultz (1784, 1786), as well as some of his near contemporaries, such as Leibniz (see De Risi 2016) and Saccheri (2014 [1733]). Heis (2020) argues, however, that Kant and his contemporaries regarded the principle as an axiom, not a postulate proper. And to demand proof for an axiom is tantamount to denying that it is axiomatic (R11 (1800) 14:52); indeed, it risks introducing something empirical into what is properly an a priori science. This is, in effect, just what Parsons does in treating the human life span inter alia as a limiting factor on what is constructible (1983 [1964], 104ff.).

missing from Kant's argument is, in fact, its implicit starting point: It is the explanandum for which holistic mereological structure is (part of) the explanans. It is precisely in order to account for the fact that we can construct line segments of any arbitrary (though finite) size – a fact Kant presumes we already know a priori as a tenet of geometry – that Kant spells out the holistic mereological structure that Parsons wants to consider in isolation. We can always extend a segment further *because* there is always a greater space surrounding it into which it can be extended. And since the whole of all-encompassing space is presupposed by and strictly greater than any subspace we can construct, we represent space as actually infinite in extent after all.[39]

Turning now to the second objection, note that Kant's response to Kästner is epistemological as well as metaphysical. It is not merely that geometrical lines can *be* arbitrarily large or small. We also *know* this – and know it a priori. Kant argues that we can enjoy such knowledge – of Euclid's second postulate, for instance – only if we have a knowledge-enabling, a priori *representation* of a space that is actually infinitary, for only such a space can ground the possibility of arbitrarily large constructions:

> [T]he geometer must admit, in accord with the metaphysician, that [the spaces constructed in geometry] can only be thought as parts of the unitary original space, in keeping with the fundamental representation [*Grundvorstellung*] of space. [...] Thus the geometer, just as much as the metaphysician represents the original space as infinite and, specifically, as infinite-given [*unendlich-gegeben*]. (*On Kästner* 20:419, my underlining)

Kant agrees with Kästner, Guyer, and other advocates of potential infinity that, so far as geometrical cognition is concerned, space is merely potentially infinite in magnitude and manifoldness. We can extend a line arbitrarily far but not infinitely far; and we can divide a segment into arbitrarily many parts but not infinitely many.[40] But they fail to appreciate that, as a point of critical metaphysics, these potential infinities must be

[39] Recall, however, that our representation of space as actually infinite is not yet vindicated as an objective cognition by ME3 or ME4. The MEs merely analyze our concept <space>, without demonstrating its objective validity. The TE of <space> presumes the objective validity of geometry as a body of synthetic a priori knowledge and, thus, the objective validity of <space> and our representation of space as a continuous and boundless given magnitude. This presumption is then vindicated in the Conclusions, which offer a (remarkably quick and easy) transcendental deduction of the concept <space> around A27/B43. See Merritt (2010, esp. 19 and 24–29).

[40] Indeed, the infinite manifoldness of space can be inferred from its infinite extent, as Daniel Sutherland pointed out to me and as Kant himself observes in R5901 (1783/84, 18:379.2–7) in discussing his preferred proof of the infinite divisibility of space, due to Keill (1739 [1702], 30–31,

grounded in actual infinities: a manifold that is densely ordered and strictly boundless. Consequently, they fail to appreciate that, as a point of transcendental epistemology, our mathematical cognition of these potential infinities must be grounded in a cognition of the actual infinities that ground them. This cognition is our *Grundvorstellung* of space, which "the geometer, just as much as the metaphysician, represents" (20:419.13–14, my underlining) and which she represents "as infinite and, specifically, as infinite-given" (20:419.14–15).

Now, the geometer may not *realize* that she enjoys such a representation "until long practice has made [her] attentive to it and adept at separating it out" (B2.24–26). But this is no more remarkable than that psychologists have failed to appreciate the pervasive role of the imagination in sense perception (cf. A120n.28–29), despite the fact that psychologists are themselves perceivers as well as theorists of perception and despite the fact that the imagination's role in perception is, according to Kant, knowable through a priori reflection (in the form of a transcendental deduction). Indeed, it is the "most difficult of all [reason's] occupations" to cultivate self-knowledge of this transcendental sort (Axi.20–21). It is particularly difficult in the case of infinitary representations such as space and time, because their complexity outstrips our capacities for conscious, phenomenological discrimination. One cannot appreciate the infinitary character of our *Grundvorstellung* of space simply by shifting the spotlight of one's attention to the relevant feature(s) of one's conscious representations. Infinitary structure is, as such, not the sort of thing we can be directly aware of.[41] This is doubtless part of what motivates the objections mooted previously. But it is no part of Kant's conception of sensible intuitions that we must be conscious of their contents, as he makes clear in response to Eberhard:

> If, however, the word [sc. "sensibility"/"*Sinnlichkeit*"] is used in its proper sense, it is obvious that, if no simple part of an object of the senses is sensible [*empfindbar*], the latter [sc. the object] cannot itself be sensible [*empfindbar*] as a whole, and conversely, if something is an object of the

which Kant owned). Like many such proofs, Keill's involves drawing lines to increasingly distant points in order to cut a perpendicular at ever-smaller increments, thus basing the infinite divisibility of space on its (assumed) infinite expanse. This order of argumentation reflects the fact that the extensibility of segments is a fundamental principle of geometry (namely, a postulate) while their infinite divisibility is a theorem.

[41] *Critique* A431n./B459n.15–22; *Discovery* 8:222.17–19; R4673 (1774) 17:638.22–639.05. I agree with Sutherland (2021b, 126) that "continuity is a property that cannot be directly represented", since "to know this requires concept-employing reflection on the conditions for the representation of parts of space".

> senses and of sensation, all simple parts of it must be as well, even if clarity in their representation may be lacking; and [it is obvious] that this obscurity in the partial representations of a whole, insofar as the understanding alone discerns [*einsieht*] that they nevertheless must be contained in it [sc. the object of the senses] and its intuition, cannot place them beyond the sphere of sensibility and make them into beings of reason [*Verstandeswesen*]. (*Discovery* 8:205.4–13)[42]

Kant is not admitting here that sensible objects have simple parts – a view he consistently opposes. His point is rather that, when it comes to representing sensible objects in intuition, one represents a whole *by* representing its parts: "All parts must necessarily be objects of the senses, if the whole is supposed to be" (8:205.22–23). Whatever the mereological microstructure of sensible objects may be – discrete or continuous – an intuition of a sensible whole intrinsically involves the intuitive representation of all its parts. Thus, even if sensible objects consisted of simple parts (*per* Eberhard) those simples would, of necessity, be objects of sensible representation (*pace* Eberhard), not supersensible noumena. It makes no difference to their sensible status that "the understanding alone discerns" that these (alleged) simples must be given in intuition (8:205.11, my underlining) and that they cannot be immediately perceived on their own. The question is simply whether they *are* given to the mind in sensible intuition, not how we *know* that they are so given. If the whole is given, the parts are, too, regardless of whether we have an independent and clear (i.e. conscious) sensible representation of those parts as such.[43]

Indeed, on Kant's account, there will *always* be sensible objects that escape our powers of immediate sensory perception but that we nonetheless represent in sensible intuition. For there are obviously finite limits on the scope and acuity of our senses. Technological aides, such as microscopes and telescopes, can extend the limits of what we can immediately and clearly perceive, according to Kant, but they cannot remove them altogether. There will always be sensible objects so large and so small that we cannot attain a clear (i.e. conscious) sensible representation of them on their own (using current technology). But while it is natural to wistfully speculate about what we might perceive "if our senses were finer" – Kant mentions the "magnetic material that pervades all bodies" (A226/B273.20), "Newton's small lamellae, that constitute the color-particles of

[42] See also *Discovery* 209.12–210.07, 212.23–30, 217.1–13 and Kant's 19 May 1789 letter to Reinhold (11:45 f.).

[43] For further argument that phenomenological awareness is not a constraint on intuitive givenness, see Chaplin (2022). See also Rosefeldt (2022).

bodies" (*Discovery* 8:205.13–14), and the wave-structure of color (*Judgment* 5:224.22–31) – it is crucial to recognize "their [sc. the senses'] coarseness has nothing at all to do with the form of possible experience" (A226/B273.27–29; cf. A522/B550.3–8). Technological refinements of our perceptual faculties, as Kant understands them, merely bring to light what is *already given* to us in sensible intuition, though we may not yet be aware of it:

> [W]e are not conscious that the Milky Way consists merely of small stars when we observe it with the naked eye, but through a telescope we see this. Now we infer that since we have seen the whole Milky Way, we must also have seen all the individual stars. For if that were not so, then we would have seen nothing. But what we have seen, we must have represented. Since we know nothing of these representations, they must be obscure. (M-Mr 29:879.25–31)[44]

This same point applies to the infinitary structure of our *Grundvorstellung* of space. Infinitary structure is not something we can enjoy an immediate awareness of in sensible intuition, pure or empirical; it is not something that can be phenomenologically present to the mind. Rather, just as we "infer" (29:879.27) that we really represent all the individual stars of the Milky Way, even when we do not consciously perceive the discrete stars that make it up, we must likewise infer that space has an infinitary structure and that we represent it (albeit unconsciously) as having this structure. For we know a priori that we can construct line segments of arbitrary magnitude, by Euclid's second postulate. And we cannot know this unless we have a knowledge-enabling a priori representation of an actually infinite space within which alone segments of arbitrary length can be produced.

This clarifies the sense in which "[s]pace is represented as an infinite given magnitude" (B40.21–22, my underlining). Its infinity, I've argued, is twofold: It is continuous in its manifoldness and boundless in its magnitude. What is now clear is that we do not (cannot) represent this infinitary structure as a datum of quasi-perceptual awareness. For the infinite, as such, lies outside our phenomenological ambit. We rather represent space

44 In his lectures, Kant repeatedly argues that, when we see far-away objects (his favorite examples are the Milky Way, the moon, and people in the distance), we necessarily see and thus sensibly represent their parts. He often follows this with the comparison of the mind to a map, only dimly illuminated – his point being that the parts of distant objects are already "on the map" of the mind (i.e. given in sensible intuition), despite being inadequately "illuminated" by consciousness. See L-Jäsche 9:35.14–20; *Anthropology* 7:135.3–136.13; A-Menschenkunde 25:867.25–268.07; A-Mrongovius 25:1221.7–14.

to be infinite on the basis of an *inference* premised on our potentially knowledgeable uses of the concept <space> – including its uses in Euclidean geometry. When Kant claims that we represent space to be infinite, he is not calling on the reader to introspectively verify that she harbors representations of infinite complexity among the contents of her conscious mind. He is demanding that the reader acknowledge a transcendental (and likely unexpected) implication of her own competent use of the concept <space>.

Ironically, then, the boundlessness of sense, the infinitary character of sensible intuition, is something that cannot be known to us sensibly but only through the intellect. This is the claim at the heart of my "top-down" approach to Kantian intuition. The ratio cognoscendi of intuitive representation, in the MEs, is the twofold infinity of space (and time). This is the mark that enables us to recognize that spatiotemporal representation has an origin that is intuitive as well as a priori. Yet this mark is – and can only be – grasped *intellectually*, through apperceptive, analytical reflection on our use of the relevant concepts. Kant's core argument for the intuitive status of space and time is not based on phenomenological considerations or the description of the intrinsic properties of introspectively available representations. For it is based on a property – namely, infinitary complexity – that could never be present to our consciousness in a quasi-perceptual fashion.

We can now consider this argument itself. Why is the twofold infinity of space and time a mark of *intuitive* origin? The answer Kant must give is obvious; the rationale behind it much less so. The concepts <space> and <time> must have an intuitive origin because a discursive intellect cannot possibly be the source of infinitely complex representations. It is hardly controversial that discursive contents are intrinsically finite, but it is important to pinpoint why Kant thinks they must be. For this will set the basic terms in which one understands the intuition/concept contrast in finite minds.

5.4.2 *Finite Concepts*

Consider a prominent account of why Kant thinks discursive concepts can have only finitely complex contents.[45] Concepts are formed through the synthesis of marks (as *Teilvorstellungen*). This synthesis is successive:

[45] See, in particular, Jauernig (2019; 2021, 93–94) and McLear (2015, 89–93). But these are just the most fulsome expressions of a view I take to be widespread.

It involves "running through" and then "taking together" the various marks that constitute the content of the concept. The key claim here is that discursive synthesis is *successive*, proceeding from part to part, and consequently *piecemeal*, proceeding from part to whole.[46] Indeed, advocates of this reading often take the discursivity of human cognition to *consist* in its successive or piecemeal character.[47] This would indeed imply that discursive contents are intrinsically finite. For an infinitely complex content contains infinitely many *Teilvorstellungen* – in this case, infinitely many marks (*Merkmale*). Yet it is impossible to complete a successive synthesis of infinitely many elements – and not because of any cognitive infirmity on our part, nor because we lack world enough and time (though we do). Not even a divine intellect could complete such a synthesis: It is intrinsically impossible. To complete the synthesis, some element must be the last, in that it has no successor. But on any total ordering of an infinite collection, every element has a successor. So there is no last element. Accordingly, no successive synthesis of its elements can be complete.

The problem with this account, as I see it, is that not all discursive synthesis is successive in this sense. Even syntheses that Kant explicitly calls "successive" are not always successive in a sense that would entail the finitude of synthesized contents. I will focus on three examples, though there are others: (i) judgmental synthesis, (ii) the synthesis underlying the synthetic unity of apperception, and (iii) the figurative synthesis in the construction of continuous magnitudes.[48]

(i) Judging, for Kant, involves a synthesis of concepts in a particular truth-evaluable form.[49] But the *form* of the judgment cannot be produced

[46] This account is often advanced to support the view that discursive contents have an atomic rather than holistic containment structure. I've argued that this is not true of given concepts (Section 5.2). My argument here focuses on the allegedly successive and piecemeal character of synthesis, rather than the atomic versus holistic structure of the resulting contents.

[47] Jauernig suggests this is part of the very meaning of the term: "The Latin '*discurrere*' literally means 'to run through.'" (2019, 36) This is not quite right. *Discurrere* means to run *about*, to wander to and fro, to roam. Running *through* would be *percurrere* or *transcurrere*. This suggests that the discursivity of our intellect manifests itself not in its manner of processing contents – its "running through" a manifold of representations – but in its dependence on objects – its need to "roam about" the world to acquire contents (matter) to process in the first place. Engstrom (2006, 12–13) heeds this etymology more closely.

[48] To this list, I am pleased to add the "decomposing synthesis" involved in representing determinate spaces as parts of the all-encompassing whole, which is the focus of Rosefeldt (2022). I had avoided this example so as not to appear to beg the question, but I gladly endorse the thrust Rosefeldt's admirably detailed account.

[49] See Land (2014, 527–530) for a different argument for the holistic character of judgmental synthesis.

successively. Consider a disjunctive judgment: for example, <*the world has a beginning in time, or else it is temporally infinite*> (cf. A426f./B454f.). The disjunction is affirmed in the assertoric mode, but its disjuncts are affirmed merely problematically. Now if judgmental synthesis were successive, it should be possible to "interrupt" the act of judging after the first disjunct: <*the world has a beginning in time*>. What would the modal status of that partial judgment be: assertoric or problematic? Neither option is plausible.

Suppose it is initially asserted. The completion of the act of judging must then involve a retraction of this premature assertion, since it is not asserted in the final judgment. On this option, the act of judgmental synthesis might be temporally extended, but it would not be successive in the sense that counts. For, properly speaking, the *asserted* proposition, <*the world has a beginning in time*>, turns out *not* to be a part of the final judgment. Accordingly, framing that proposition cannot count as a stage in the piecemeal production of the whole judgment from its constituent parts. For it is not the representation of a part of the judgment. Rather, the judgmental synthesis proceeds holistically, since it is in light of the sense of the whole judgment that this first step (or, rather, misstep) is corrected and thereby incorporated into the judgment.

Suppose, then, that the first disjunct is initially mooted problematically. How does the final judgment (the disjunction) become assertoric? Does the mind first moot multiple scenarios and subsequently realize (and therefore assert) that they exhaust the sphere of real possibilities? That is implausibly haphazard – as though the mind were surveying possibilities at random, in the hope of hitting upon a cognitively significant combination. No, the disjuncts are put forward *in the first place* with the expectation that they express mutually exclusive and jointly exhaustive scenarios. The disjunctive form of the judgment holistically governs each stage of the synthesis. In this sense, the whole of the judgment (viz. its form) precedes and determines its parts. The problematic mode of the first disjunct is not the expression of a cognitive tentativeness that subsequently, with suitable qualifications, gains in assertiveness. It is already put forward as a condition for a complex assertion.

I take analogous points to hold for the modality of the antecedent and consequent in a hypothetical judgment and for the order of concepts in a categorial judgment. The general moral is that the form of a judgment, though it is realized through synthesis, cannot be produced piecemeal but must precede and determine (in the order of explanation and semantics) all parts of the judgment, as such.[50] Not all discursive synthesis is successive or piecemeal.

(ii) Consider now the synthetic unity of apperception. Kant holds that "the 'I think' must **be able** to accompany all my representations" (B131.4–5). It follows that "all manifold of intuition has a necessary relation to the 'I think' in the same subject in which this manifold is to be met with" (B132.10–12). For if the intuition is "mine", the manifold in it must be "mine" as well, i.e. something I think. Kant then argues that "this thoroughgoing identity of apperception of a manifold given in intuition contains a synthesis of representations and is only possible through the consciousness of this synthesis" (B133.1–4). This move from the analytic unity of apperception to the synthetic unity cannot detain us here. What I wish to highlight is the implication Kant draws from it:

> Therefore, this relation [sc. of the manifold given in intuition to the identity of the subject, or the "I think"] does not yet arise [*geschieht*] through my accompanying each representation with consciousness, but rather by my **adding** [*hinzusetze*] one [representation] to the other and being conscious to myself of the synthesis of them. (B133.7–10)

This talk of "adding" one representation to another sounds very much like a successive synthesis. But it is clear, on reflection, that it cannot be successive in any sense that would restrict it to finitely complex contents. For the manifold of intuition is infinitely complex, as the Aesthetic asserts (B39.21–B40.4; B48.22–23; cf. B136n.23–24). So if a successive synthesis of an infinite collection is impossible – as Kant himself emphasizes in the Antinomies (A432/B460.27–29) – then the synthesis underlying the synthetic unity of apperception cannot be successive. It is surely too uncharitable to suppose that Kant, having carefully reconceived the Transcendental Deduction, begins it by asserting the necessity of a synthesis he knows to be impossible. Perhaps empirical apperception proceeds piecemeal, as I successively accompany one representation after another with consciousness. But the synthesis that makes possible such piecemeal empirical consciousness must encompass *all* my representations, including the infinitely complex manifolds of my intuitings. And no successive synthesis can survey all my representations: There are simply too many of them. So the

[50] Similar points hold for the form of inferences and for the architectonic form of a body of knowledge qua science, though I cannot argue the point here. Discursive knowledge certainly accumulates piecemeal with respect to its content (its matter). Yet its rational form – as it is articulated in judgments, inferences, and theories – cannot be produced piecemeal, but conditions and precedes every item of knowledge in a holistic manner.

synthesis at the heart of Kant's transcendental epistemology – the synthesis underlying the synthetic unity of apperception – cannot be successive in any sense that would entail the finite complexity or multiplicity of the manifolds it comprehends. Not all discursive synthesis is successive or piecemeal in the finitistic sense.

(iii) This issue arises in more pointed fashion in the Axioms of Intuition, where Kant argues that all appearances are extensive magnitudes. He claims this on the grounds that all appearances "as intuitions in space or time must be represented through the same synthesis as that through which space and time themselves are determined" (B203.20–23). Now Kant is quite happy to call this synthesis "successive": "I can represent no line, however small it may be, without drawing it in thought, i.e. generating all parts gradually [*nach und nach*] from a point, and thereby first sketching [*verzeichnen*] this intuition" (A162f./B203.26–29). Accordingly, extensive magnitudes "can be cognized in apprehension only through successive synthesis (from part to part)" (A163/B204.5–7). Indeed, the piecemeal nature of this synthesis is what constitutes such magnitudes as extensive: "I call an extensive magnitude one in which the representation of the parts makes possible the representation of the whole (and thus necessarily precedes the latter)" (A162/B203.24–25). Kant thus generalizes that: "It is upon this successive synthesis of the productive imagination, in the generation of figures, that the mathematics of extension (geometry) is grounded" (A163/B204.12–14).

A synthesis that is successive in this sense cannot, however, be restricted to finite manifolds. For the manifold of parts in a line segment is *not finite*, as Kant insists just a few pages later (A165/B206.8–9; A169f./B211f.16–06). "All appearances *überhaupt* are continuous magnitudes," Kant writes, "with respect to their intuition, as extensive [magnitudes]" (A170/B212.3–4). And in a continuous extensive magnitude, "no part is the smallest possible" (A169/B211.16). So when one "generates all the parts [of the line] gradually from a point" (A162f./B203.27–28, my underlining), one is not aggregating a finite number of pre-given linear *minima*, as units. One is rather drawing (continuously) a continuous line: a line in which an infinite manifold of parts is contained, and each part of which is *itself* a continuous line. While there is clearly a sense in which such a synthesis is successive and piecemeal – since, in drawing the line, one will have drawn some parts before others and before one has drawn the whole – it is just as clearly *not* successive in any sense that would restrict it to a finite multiplicity of elements (parts, *Teilvorstellungen*). The synthesis is successive and piecemeal in that the parts are generated and represented before the whole is. But if one has succeeded in drawing *any* part of the line, one has already succeeded in generating *infinitely many* parts of it, since each part of a continuous line is itself continuous.[51]

The figurative synthesis that generates continuous extensive magnitudes is surely "successive" in some sense, just as there is surely a sense in which acts of judging unfold successively over time and can be interrupted partway through. But these syntheses are not successive in a sense that would restrict them to finite manifolds. Here, the continuity of the final product – and, thus, its infinite multiplicity – must already be present at each stage of its production, even if that production unfolds gradually (*nach und nach*) over time. Similarly, the form of a judgment must be represented as a guiding principle of synthesis at every stage of its articulation, even if elaborating its content takes time. And, of course, the synthesis underlying our unity of apperception is the antecedent and constant condition of all objectively valid cognition, including the infinitely complex manifolds of our intuitings. Each of these cases undermines the standard rationale for holding that conceptual contents must be finite because discursive synthesis is successive and cannot accommodate infinitary manifolds.

But if synthesis is not always successive for Kant and, in particular, if the discursive synthesis of infinite manifolds is not impossible, what is to prevent discursive contents from being infinitely complex? The answer, I think, lies in the essentially classificatory nature of discursive concepts.

The contents of discursive concepts are marks (*Merkmale*). A mark arises "1. in that something is regarded as [*betrachtet als*] a partial representation that can be common to several [representations], e.g. the red color; 2. when I regard the partial representation as *notam* [i.e. a mark], as a ground of cognition of a thing, e.g. [when I] cognize blood, a rose, etc. through **red**".[52] Marks are intrinsically general. To regard something "as a partial representation that can be common to several" is to represent it as a

[51] For a detailed discussion of this issue, see Sutherland (2021b, 98–119). Sutherland argues that the generation of continuous extended magnitudes requires a synthesis that, though successive, is itself continuous. The result of such synthesis, Sutherland maintains, is a determinate representation of a whole (continuous magnitude) in which the parts are represented only indeterminately, i.e. as merely determinable through a subsequent synthesis that would delineate them *as parts* of the magnitude. On this account, too, it is not the case that successive synthesis proceeds as the successor function does in arithmetic, moving from one determinate element to another – a view Sutherland dubs "intuitive atomism". This likewise undermines the standard rationale for holding that products of discursive synthesis are necessarily finite.

[52] L-DW 24:753.18–22, cited by Sutherland (2021b, 129); cf. L-Jäsche 9:58; see also B39.22–40.1, B133.24–134.35; A320/B377.30–33; *Progress* 20:273.33–274.5; *Judgment* 20:211.30–33; R2280–2286 (mid-1770s) 16:298–300, and Section 3.3.

dimension of possible comparison, a respect in which things may be the same or different.[53] Marks enable us to classify things by comparing them and sorting them into classes of similarity and difference.

This implies that discursive representations are intrinsically finite in complexity. We represent common features, and thus entertain certain marks, only insofar as they are made salient by comparing and contrasting possible *instances*. Our concepts can only be as fine-grained as the distinctions between instances we can make. Because we can only ever make a finite number of comparisons, we can only ever note a finite number of similarities or differences.[54] Now the objects we cognize and the features we recognize them to share may, in fact, be infinitely complex.[55] But our concepts of them can never be. Had we but world enough and time we might refine our concepts ad infinitum. But their comparison-based, classificatory character means that no discursive concept – no concept whose content is determined and refined by "running about" from object to object, instance to instance, comparison to comparison – can ever have an infinitely complex content.[56]

[53] See *Teleological* 8:178.3–9; R1689 (1770?) 16:84; R2875 (late 1770s) 16:554 f.; R2883 (1776–1789) 16:558; M-Mr 29:888.17–20; L-Wien 24:834.3–8, 909.19–34; L-Blom (early 1770s) 24:106.14–17, 136.26–34, 266.1–10; L-Pö 24:533; L-DW 24:725.20–30; L-Ph (1772) 24:407.3–7. Kant often characterizes discursive generality in terms of the acts of (i) comparing particular objects with an eye to their commonalities, (ii) reflecting upon (i.e. representing with clarity) the similarities they exhibit, and (iii) abstracting from the remaining differences. See L-Jäsche 9:94–95; R2876 (late 1770s? or 1780s) 16:555 f.; L-Wien 24:909; L-Pö 24:566; L-Bus 24:654; for discussion, see Longuenesse (1998, 111–127). These acts are not supposed to explain our acquisition of marks, but to indicate what their generality consists in: It is the generality of comparison and reflection – a generality that involves "roaming about" from instance to instance. In *Judgment* § 76, Kant entertains the notion of a kind of non-discursive generality exhibited by the "synthetic-universal" representations of an intuitive intellect (5:407). This discussion is a key inspiration for post-Kantian Idealists such as Hegel, who theorize non-discursive forms of generality, such as the concrete universal that is *der Begriff*. For discussion, see Förster (2002b, 2018).

[54] R2352 (late 1760s or early 1770s) 16:330; L-Wien 24:920.20–26, cf. 911.2–7; L-Jäsche 9:97.24–29.

[55] L-Blom (early 1770s) 24:109.1–15; L-Pö 24:533.6–7; L-Wien 24:834.26–29, 927.29–928.02.

[56] The finitude of discursive representations also follows from the fact that any concept can be represented as a node in a genus-species tree. Though there is no lowest species, there is a highest genus. Every concept is thus finitely many steps (specific differentiations) from this highest genus and therefore contains a finite number of marks (as specific differentiae). See, for instance, A290/B34628–05; A658f./B686f.22–30; L-Jäsche 9:59.17–21, 97; L-DW 24:754.30–755.21; L-Wien 24:912.1–10. For discussion, see Anderson (2004, 507–14; 2015, chs. 1–4). I think this account is correct, but do not consider it explanatory bedrock. The reason there must be a highest genus is because the act of abstracting from all differences among conceivable objects yields a unique discursive content – namely, what everything conceivable has in common. Similarly, the reason every concept is only finitely many differentiae removed from this common genus – an assumption that is not argued for in traditional logic – is because we can perform and reflect on only finitely many comparisons.

For example, *being a muskrat* may be an infinitely subtle matter, involving the compresence of innumerable distinct and distinguishable properties and relations. Now, we can compare muskrats with each other and with other objects as much as we would like and along as many different dimensions as we please and thereby develop the impressively complex concept <*ondrata zibethicus*>. But we can know in advance that this concept will never be infinitely complex, whatever may be the case with its intended object. For it owes its content to a finite number of encounters with a finite number of particulars, subject to a finite number of comparisons along a finite number of dimensions.

Nor is this point limited to empirical concepts. Consider the concept <virtue>, one of Kant's favorite examples of an a priori given concept. We analyze this concept and thus render its content distinct by considering particular instances in which we would use it. Such casuistical reflections may enrich our concept of <virtue> by inducing us to reflect on marks such as <freedom>, <self-determination>, <overcoming the resistance of disincentives>, and so forth. The nature of virtue may be such that it rewards endless reflection – so that we would require an eternal afterlife not just to become virtuous but to fully comprehend what this involves. Yet at every stage of the lifelong and (we may hope) endless project of coming to understand the true character of virtue, our concept <virtue> will remain finitely complex so long as our intellect remains discursive. For we will only ever have considered finitely many instances of virtue and vice and compared them along finitely many dimensions.

The discursivity of our intellect thus consists in its ineluctable reliance on *instances* (on particulars) as occasions for the comparison and reflection that jointly account for the determinacy (specificity) and the generality of our concepts. The finite complexity of discursive contents is thus a reflection of the ontological finitude of our minds. The reason we are cognitively beholden to instances, the reason our universal *Erkenntnis* is valid only so far as our *Kenntnisse* of particulars can extend, is because our thoughts are not ontically creative: They do not generate the objects we seek to know.

5.5 The Boundlessness of Sense

Having now established (i) that, and why, discursive contents are intrinsically finite in complexity, and having earlier established (ii) that, and in what sense, we represent space to be infinitely complex in content, we can appreciate Kant's argument for the intuitive status of spatial representation in ME3.

It is a mark of <space> that space is doubly infinitary: boundless and continuous. It follows from this that we have a representation with an infinitely complex content, namely our original representation (*Grundvorstellung*) of space. But the theory of discursive marks, which is based on the essentially classificatory character of discursive concepts, implies that no discursive representation can be infinitely complex. So our original representation of space cannot be discursive. Moreover, because it has a content that no act of discursive intellect could possibly account for, it must be *given* to the mind in order to be thinkable at all, for it cannot be an expression of the mind's spontaneity.[57] It is therefore an *intuitive* and, what is more, a *receptive* representation.[58]

But does this not assimilate ME3 and ME4? I do not think so. It is true that a contrast between the infinitary structure of intuition and the finite complexity of discursive contents is central to both reflections. Yet they make distinct points. ME3 emphasizes the *oneness* of all-encompassing space: the holistic containment structure that is the mark of its continuity and boundlessness. ME4 emphasizes the *manyness* of subspaces: the "infinite collection of representations" (B40.02), contained within that "infinite **given** magnitude" (B39.21–22). This is more than just a difference in emphasis. ME3 directs our attention to the *cardinality* of the manifold in

[57] Our pure intuitions of space and time therefore "give" us "objects" in the sense of developed in Section 2.3: They provide us cognitive access to grounds of truth for synthetic propositions (e.g. the theorems of geometry). But these "objects" are quite different from the causally efficacious *Dinge* given in empirical intuition. Kant is adamant that space and time are *not* intuitively given to us as objects in the latter sense (A39/B56.26–29; A291/B347.26–32 and R6324, 1790–1793, 18:647.17–27.

[58] This line of thought bears some similarity to Descartes's so-called "causal" argument for the existence of an infinite being (namely, God) in the third *Meditation* (AT 7:40ff.). Descartes maintains that (i) we have an idea of an infinite being, (ii) we could not have derived this idea from anything but an infinite being, and (iii) since we know ourselves to be finite beings, we cannot have derived the idea from ourselves, therefore, (iv) there must be an infinite being that is distinct from us and from which we have derived this idea. Accordingly, Descartes and Kant face structurally similar objections. Yet, while it is plausible for Descartes's critics to argue (against (i)) that we do *not* in fact have a genuine idea of an infinite being, and (against (ii)) that an idea an infinite being *can* be derived from our ideas of finite beings, these challenges lose much of their force against Kant. For it is not similarly plausible to contend (against a Kantian analogue of (i)) that we do not represent space as boundless and continuous (see Section 5.4.1). Moreover, if I am correct in arguing the holistic structure of space is a mark of its continuity, then it is false to claim (against a Kantian analogue of (ii)) that our idea of the infinite complexity of space can be derived from an idea of finitely complex space(s). Thus, Kant's responses to these objections – relying as they do on our a priori conception of the holistic infinitary structure of space – are different from and arguably stronger than any responses available to Descartes. If Kant's argument is to be overturned, it must be on the grounds that human spontaneity can indeed account for the infinitary structure of space and time. This, I take it, is the strategy pursued by Hegel, who credits *Geist* with a non-discursive form of intellection.

space, whereas ME4 directs our attention to the kind of *relations* that hold among the elements of that manifold. In ME3, the implicit contrast is between the infinitely many elements contained, as *Teilvorstellungen* in an intuitive content and the finite number of elements that a discursive representation can contain as *Teilvorstellungen*. In ME4, the implicit contrast is between the mereological relation of composition that articulates the internal structure of intuitive contents, on the one hand, and the information-theoretical relation of classification that articulates the internal structure of discursive contents, on the other.[59]

To appreciate the contrast at issue in ME4, recall the essentially classificatory nature of discursive representations. The content of a concept expresses itself in the distinctions among instances that it enables us to draw – that is, the similarity and difference classes it enables us to induce. This implies that discursive marks cannot iterate or compose in the way that intuitive *Teilvorstellungen* can. A certain space (figure, construction) can be iterated to generate a larger or more complex one: Distinct but homogeneous spaces can be joined (com-posed) to form greater wholes. Not so with discursive marks. Marks are information-theoretical in that they consist in the classificatory information they convey. Once a mark has served its classificatory purpose – once it has cloven the class of conceivable instances into like and unlike – there is no more cognitive work left to be done by "iterating" it or by "adding" a qualitatively identical mark. A would-be "iteration" or "addition" of homogeneous marks is not just otiose; it is incoherent. The concept <reasoning rational animal> is not the supersaturated sibling of the concept <rational animal>: They are one and the same. For once the mark <reasoning> has done its classificatory work, there is no more classificatory work for the "second" mark <rational> to do. And if has no classificatory work to do, it is not a mark after all.

This contrast between mereological relations, which allow for homogeneous elements to compose to form greater wholes, and information-theoretical relations, which do not, is especially vivid in the infinite case. For the mereological relation places no limit on the size of the wholes that can be composed through the iteration of homogeneous elements (as we see in Euclid's second postulate). And Kant argues that this open-endedness is possible (and knowable) only if we represent an actually infinite whole, within which (and as limits on which) all finite wholes

[59] A version of this contrast is central to Wilson (1975); see also Sutherland (2004) and Anderson (2015). See also note 7.

are constructed (through iteration). By contrast, the nature of instance-based comparison entails that we will only ever possess a finite amount of classification-inducing information.

The contrasts highlighted in ME3 and ME4 establish that our original representation of space must be receptive and intuitive. But they also do something more: They enrich our conception of what receptive intuition is. As we have seen, ME3 argues that space is represented as "essentially unitary". This implies that there is a single space and that any diversity of spaces should be understood as a diversity of particular parts within that singular whole. So, if we accept Kant's "Conclusions" that space is the form of outer sense, it follows that our outer intuitions are intrinsically singular representations. Provided the analogous case can be made for the representation of time, it follows that sensible intuitions are intrinsically singular representations – in humans anyway. And ME4 adds a further layer to this notion of singular representation. For it argues that spaces are articulated by a mereological relation of composition. This entails that each part of space is a singular individual just as much as the whole of space is. Assuming, again, that the case for the formality of space goes through and that an analogous case can be mounted for time, we now have a very rich notion of singular representation. Sensible intuitions not only refer to a single object, as such, they also represent all the *parts* of their object as themselves individuals.

This is what enables Kant to claim in the B-Deduction that "Space and time and all their parts are **intuitions**, hence singular [*einzelne*] representations with the manifold that they contain" (see Transc. Aesthetic) (B137n., my underlining). It is a *consequence* of Kant's arguments in the Metaphysical Expositions that receptive, intuitive representation is, for us, the singular representation of individuals in their infinite particularity. This is not, as some commentators suggest, an initial premise of his reasoning but a significant advance in his "synthetic" unfolding of the "original seeds" of reason (*Prolegomena* 4:374.27–35). Spatial representation is intuitive because its content, as infinitely complex, must be given to us – a fact that holds regardless of whether we can become fully conscious of this content by making its infinitary structure an object of quasi-perceptual awareness. Kant's critical conception of intuition demands nothing less than our full openness to the infinite complexity of the knowable world – an ability to represent particulars and their parts in their rich individuality. Yet the source of this insistence, I have argued, is an apperceptive appreciation of the cognitive needs of our finite, discursive intellect combined with analytical reflection on the marks of concepts that are given to us a priori. That spatial representation must be object-giving because its contents outstrip in complexity every possible product of our discursive spontaneity – this is something we establish not through phenomenological introspection but through conceptual analysis. It is reason alone that reveals the boundlessness of sense, the infinity of receptive intuition.

6

Prolegomena to a Stufenleiter *of Kantian Intuition*

A central claim of this book is that Kant conceives receptive intuition as the cognitive complement of discursive understanding. A discursive understanding is spontaneous with respect to its acts of representing (its form) but not with respect to the objects that serve as truth makers of those acts (its matter). Discursive acts of thought are not guaranteed to agree with their objects. It follows that discursive thought is not intrinsically veridical, since truth consists in the agreement of a thought with its object. Nor is it intrinsically knowledgeable, since knowledge requires not just truth but a consciousness of truth. Even if one's discursive thoughts were to agree with their objects as a matter of necessity – for example, in a "preformation system of pure reason" (B167) – such thought would not constitute knowledge if that agreement obtained only behind the back of the understanding. An infallible understanding afflicted with intellectual blindsight would not constitute a faculty of knowledge (an *Erkenntnisvermögen*) for Kant. In order to qualify as an *Erkenntnisvermögen*, then, a discursive understanding must be complemented by a capacity that "gives" objects to thought in the twofold sense of (i) securing the existence of objects of thought so that acts of thinking can dispositively agree or disagree with them and (ii) making these objects, as agreeing or disagreeing with thought, available to cognition. This twofold criterion, *givenness*, is the defining function of intuition, as a cognitive capacity. If this function is performed spontaneously, then the intuition is intellectual. But we have already seen that the spontaneity of a discursive intellect is not intuitive. So, in order for a discursive intellect to constitute a faculty of knowledge, it must be paired with a capacity for intuition that is not spontaneous but receptive.

Kant frequently summarizes this line of thought by arguing that intuition (whether receptive or spontaneous) "gives" objects to the mind, which a discursive intellect is incapable of doing. My interpretive contribution consists, first, in a new conception of what "giving" objects to the mind consists in: namely, securing (i) truth evaluability for the intellect's representations as well as (ii) its cognitive access to that truth. My second interpretive intervention comes in arguing that the receptivity of our intuition and the discursivity of our intellect must be understood together. Specifically, I argued that Kant's grounds for attributing a capacity for intuition to the human mind, and for characterizing this intuitive capacity as receptive, lie in his conception of the discursive understanding and its specific cognitive limitations – a conception that is available to us in virtue of the essentially apperceptive nature of the intellect. On this conception, the spontaneous thoughts of a discursive understanding secure neither agreement with their intended objects, since these may fail to exist, nor a consciousness of such agreement, since it may fail to obtain. On the assumption that knowledge of objects is indeed possible for discursive intellects such as our own – that is, in order to conceive the discursive intellect as a faculty for *knowledge* – we must suppose that these necessary conditions on knowledge are instead fulfilled by a cognitive capacity distinct from the understanding, since they are specifically *not* fulfilled by discursive thought. Receptive intuition is this distinct cognitive capacity. Kant introduces and characterizes receptive intuition, qua cognitive capacity, as remedying the epistemic shortcomings of discursive intellection: "**without intuition there can be no object** [*Objekt*] with respect to which the logical function [of judgment] could be determined as category and thus no knowledge of any object [*Gegenstand*] whatsoever" (*Prolegomena* 4:475n.21–24, Kant's emphasis).

The aim of these concluding chapters is to take a broader view of how this reading of receptive intuition, as the cognitive complement of discursive understanding, is situated within Kant's general theory of intuition *überhaupt*. Givenness is the defining criterion of intuition *überhaupt*, for Kant. But Kant says a great deal more about intuition than merely that it is a capacity for giving cognizable objects to the mind, just as he says a great deal more about intellect than merely that it is a capacity for spontaneous thought. Kant's further characterizations differ not only in the particular properties they attribute to our cognitive capacities and their associated representations (e.g. singularity vs. generality; immediacy vs. discursive mediation) but also in the level of abstraction from which those properties are considered. For example, the B-edition Transcendental Deduction considers intuition merely as receptive in §§ 15–21, but thereafter considers its specific spatiotemporality.[1] And Kant sometimes presents our

[1] Likewise, Kant characterizes the understanding as a faculty of spontaneity (A51/B75), at other times as a faculty of pure apperception (B134n.), or as a faculty of judgment (A69/B94). One might view

human modes of intellect and intuition as particular species within broader genera, suggesting that other kinds of cognizers might have non-sensible modes of receptive intuition (A254/B310.24–04) or non-spatiotemporal forms of sensible intuition (A27/B43.29–04; A42/B59.30–03); that other intellects might cognize through different categories (B145.16–146.22), and that a divine mind might intuit objects through its spontaneous acts of thinking (B138.6–139.13). To clarify how these various characterizations relate to the fundamental criterion of intuitive representation, givenness, I will organize them into a *Stufenleiter* of species of Kantian intuition, presenting them as so many ways in which this fundamental cognitive function can be realized.

The benefit of this *Stufenleiter* is that it enables us to better track the different levels at which Kant pitches his arguments about the nature of the cognitive faculties and, according, the sorts of evidence that are relevant to prosecuting those arguments. For example, phenomenological reflections on our own mode of spatiotemporal experience do not, in the absence of further considerations, count as evidence about the essential properties of receptive intuition, much less intuition in general. Conversely, if the evidence Kant relies on in characterizing our spatiotemporal intuition (as "essentially unitary", say, or as "an infinite given magnitude") does not turn on any parochial features of space and time, we may fairly expect this feature to hold of non-spatiotemporal forms of intuition as well. By thus discriminating the levels of specificity and abstraction at which Kant's arguments are pitched and the sorts of evidence appropriate to these levels, we can better appreciate how the various features Kant attributes to the cognitive capacities (and to their signature representations, concepts and intuitions) are supposed to relate. This will offer us a new vantage on some long-standing questions – such as the debate about the relative priority of singularity and immediacy as criteria of intuitive representation – in addition to raising new questions about features of intuition that have enjoyed less attention in the literature.

But before I present my own *Stufenleiter* of Kantian intuition, in Chapters 7 and 8, it is important to clarify what a *Stufenleiter* is and how I intend mine to be understood.

these as three distinct features of our intellect, but this is not the only option. For one might instead regard them as three increasingly determinate specifications of a single property – viz. the discursive cognitive activity of our intellect. On this reading, apperception is not distinct from spontaneity but a more determinate form in which spontaneity can be realized in the human mind (pure willing being another). Similarly, judgment is not distinct from apperception but is a more determinate mode of apperception.

6.1 Peculiarities of Porphyrian Trees

The ubiquity of Porphyrian trees (or *Stufenleiter*) in medieval and early modern philosophical texts can lull us into a false sense of familiarity with their logic. So it is worth highlighting some of their peculiarities that are easily overlooked.

The *locus classicus* for Porphyry's eponymous "tree" (or "scale" or "ladder") is § 2 of *Isagoge*. The aim of *Isagoge* is to clarify some technical terms that Aristotle employs in presenting his account of the categories or forms of predication. These technical terms came to be known as the *quinque voces*, the "five words" – namely, "genus", "difference", "species", "property" (i.e. "*propria*", meaning attribute), and "accident". It is to illustrate the senses of "most generic", "generic", "specific", and "most specific" that Porphyry indicates how the traditional definition of *human* as *rational animal* relates to the genus *substance* through a series of subordinated specifications:

> Substance is itself a genus. Under it is body, and under body animate body, under which is animal; under animal is rational animal, under which is human; under human are Socrates and Plato and particular men. Of these items, substance is the most generic and is only a genus, while human is the most specific, and is only a species. Body is a species of substance and a genus of animate body. [...] Every item which is proximate before the individuals will be only a species and not also a genus. Thus just as substance, being highest in that there is no genus before it, was the most generic item, so human, being a species after which there is no other species nor indeed anything which can be split but only individuals (for Socrates and Plato are individuals), will be only a species and the last species and, as we said, the most specific item. The intermediate items will be species of the items before them and genera of the items after them. (Porphyry 2003, 6; *Isagoge* § 2, 4.22–5.6)

Porphyry's aim here is not to defend a particular account of human essence but to clarify the relational properties, *being-a-genus-of* and *being-a-species-of*. So he does not explicitly indicate the differentiae (another of the *quinque voces*) that divide the genera into species. Nor does he mention any species or genera other than those under which *human* falls, as another classification might if it were interested, say, in how humans relate to plants, or to angels. Moreover, no diagrammatic representations or illustrations appear in extant ancient editions of Porphyry's *Isagoge* or Boethius's Latin translation of it, through which it was mostly known in Europe. Ancient texts abound with carefully ordered, classificatory *language* articulating genus–species hierarchies, but tree *diagrams* only begin to appear in medieval texts – either in discussions of dialectic in the tradition of Porphyry (e.g. John of Damascus's *Dialectica* or in Peter of Spain's *Tractatus*) or as illuminations and marginalia in editions of Boethius's translation of Porphyry.[2] In Porphyry's original text, then, there is no tree (no image, no diagram) and, if we *were* to translate his discursive classification into a diagram, it would be a tree without any branches (Figure 6.1).

As Porphyrian classification gets absorbed and adapted in the medieval period, this tree grows branches as it is supplemented in several ways. First, the differentiae that divide each genus into species are made explicit, as are their respective contradictories. Thus, in Figure 6.2, it is made explicit that *body* is defined as a species of the genus *substance* through the differentia *material*. Second, with the representation of the contradictories of the specific differentiae (e.g. *immaterial*), the diagram begins to gesture in the direction of coordinate species that are the logical complements of the kinds Porphyry explicitly names. Thus, by indicating that *immaterial* is the specific contradictory of the differentia *material*, the diagram suggests that, in addition to *material substances* (bodies), there is at least the notional possibility of *immaterial substances* (spirits).

It is a natural next step to make these notional possibilities explicit by representing each genus as branching into two coordinate species. We can do this by merging, into a single node, each specific differentia with the species it defines. This is a natural move, since a species is defined through its immediately superordinate genus plus its specific differentia: *body* $=_{\text{def.}}$ *material substance*. So we do not really need separate nodes, one representing the species and another its specific differentia. Once we combine the species with its specific differentia in a single node, and provide a node for the contradictory differentia (with the coordinate species it defines), we get a more familiar, though conspicuously asymmetrical, branching pattern (Figure 6.3).

It is in this way that the traditional Porphyrian tree develops as a dichotomous branching structure, which is the canonical form it takes in early modern works of logic and metaphysics. Nodes (genera) divide into exactly two exclusive and exhaustive species through the respective affirmation and negation of a single specific differentia.[3]

[2] On this history, see Verboon (2014; 2010, ch. 2) and Hacking (2007).

[3] On the logic of Porphyrian trees and their place in eighteenth-century German philosophy, see de Jong (1995, 2010); Anderson (2005; 2015, chs. 3 and 4).

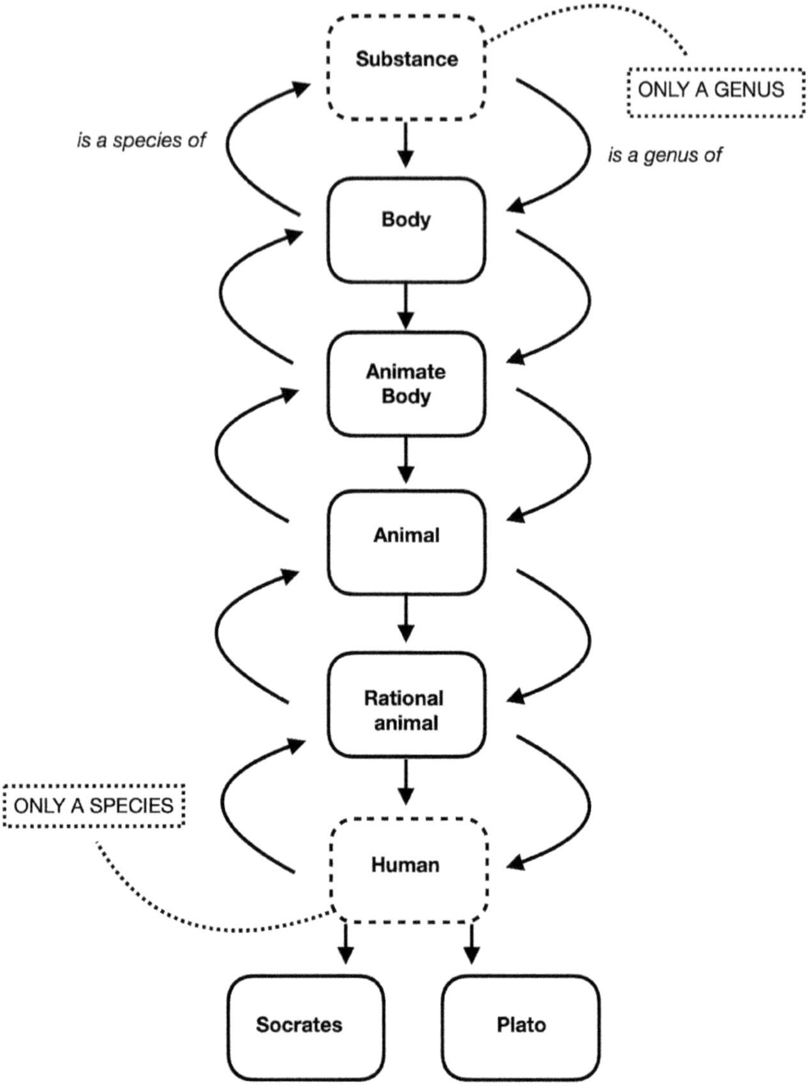

Figure 6.1 Diagram of Porphyry *Isagoge* § 2.
All features correspond to Porphyry's words.

Now, it is sometimes observed that Kant's distinctions display a suspicious tendency to trichotomy.[4] To accommodate this, Anderson (2015, 60–61) has suggested that the logical division of a genus, as Kant conceives

[4] Kant attempts to allay suspicion about this tendency at B110f.12–04 and *Judgment* 5:197n.18–27.

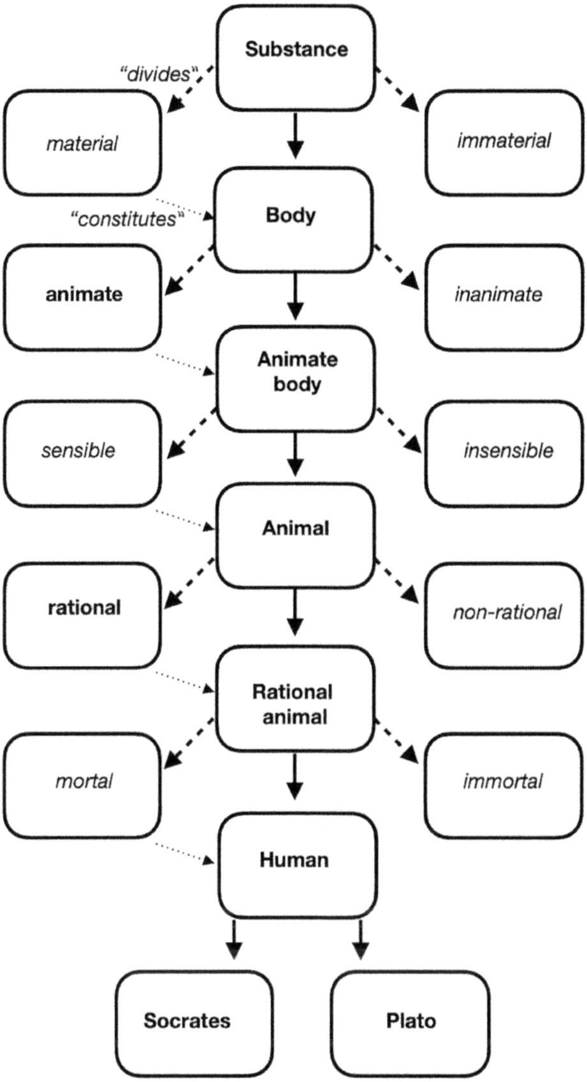

Figure 6.2 Traditional supplements to Porphyry *Isagoge* § 2. Words in bold appear in Porphyry, the rest do not.

it, can induce more than two coordinate species, citing Kant's trichotomy of judgments into *categorical*, *hypothetical*, and *disjunctive* as a case in point. Kant certainly allows that genera may have more than two species. But polytomous specific differentiations count as *logical* divisions only if they

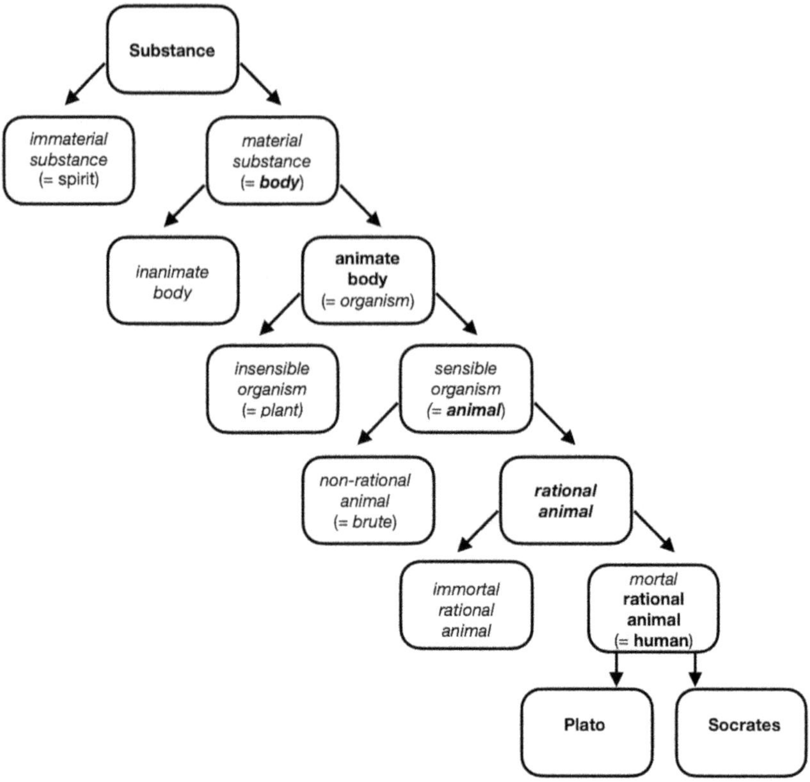

Figure 6.3 Asymmetrical tree with traditional elaborations and collapsed differentiae and species.
Words in bold in Porphyry, others not.

are reducible to dichotomies.[5] We might, for instance, divide the genus *judgment* into *molecular* judgments (i.e. judgments that consist of further judgments) and *atomic* judgments (i.e. judgments that do not contain any judgments among their constituent elements) (cf. A73/B98.19–22). Categorical judgments are atomic. The genus *molecular judgment* divides, in turn, into *hypothetical* judgments, which involve an asymmetrical grounding relation among their judgmental elements, and *disjunctive judgments*, which involve a symmetrical dependence among their judgmental elements. (Molecular judgments that involve no dependence between their judgmental elements reduce to concatenations of atomic

[5] For instance: L-Wien 24:928.3–22; L-DW 24:761.2–15, 762.10–23; L-Jäsche 9:147.19–148.2.

judgments.) In this manner, polytomous divisions can be reduced to nested dichotomies.[6] Dichotomy is not just the form that Porphyrian trees traditionally take; it is the structure that must obtain in any hierarchy where species are induced through logical division – that is, through the truth-functional negation of a single differentia.

Now, one reason it might seem desirable to allow for polytomous divisions, in addition to apologizing for Kant's tendency to trichotomize, is that restricting ourselves to dichotomy requires abandoning the ambition of uniting all conceptual hierarchies into a unique, privileged tree. For there are usually multiple ways to reduce polytomy to dichotomy. The strategy behind such reductions is to represent contraries through a series of nested logical contradictories. And it is typically possible to order the nestings differently, with suitable adjustments to the differentiae. For example, the contraries *isosceles*, *scalene*, and *equilateral* can be represented through two steps of dichotomous division. First, divide the genus *three-sided figure* into the species *all sides equal* and *not all sides equal*. Then, divide the genus *not all sides equal* into the species *no sides equal* versus *some (but not all) sides equal*. This would make *isosceles* and *scalene* coordinate species of a common genus, namely *not all sides equal*. But the order of these steps could obviously be reversed. One might first divide *three-sided figure* into *no sides equal* versus *some sides equal* and subsequently divide the genus *some equal sides* into the species *all sides equal* and (*some but*) *not all sides equal*. Now *isosceles* is not coordinate with *scalene* under a common genus, but rather with *equilateral* under the common genus, *some sides equal*.

[6] The above treatment of the relational forms of judgment is merely illustrative. I am, in fact, skeptical that Kant intends the relational forms of judgment to be coordinate species, but neither do I think Kant conceives of this distinction as logical in the strict sense. Kant claims that, in his table of categories, "the third category in each class always arises [*entspringt*] from the combination of the second [category] with the first" (B110). This suggests that an analogous claim may hold of the functions of judgment, which provide the "Clue" ("Leitfaden") to the discovery of the categories. In that case, *disjunctive* judgment would not be coordinate with *categorial* and *hypothetical* judgment but derivative from and subordinate to them. And it is implausible that the third form "arises" from the other two in a purely *logical* manner. In *Judgment* Kant characterizes such trichotomies as conceptual but nevertheless "synthetic" divisions, in contrast to "analytic" divisions of the form "*est aut A aut non A*". Synthetic conceptual divisions, Kant says, identify "(1) a condition, (2) something conditioned, (3) the concept that arises from the unification of the conditioned with its condition" and therefore "the division must necessarily be a trichotomy" (*Judgment* 5:197n.; cf. L-Jäsche 9:147.30–148.2; L-DW 24:762.20–25). Kant's thought here is difficult to grasp but seems to imply that only analytic divisions are logical, since only they are governed merely by the principle of contradiction (*Judgment* 5:197n.21; L-Jäsche 9:147.1–3; cf. L-DW 24:762.15–20). At any rate, trichotomies can be represented in *Stufenleiter* only if they can be represented as series of dichotomies.

To hold that there is a uniquely correct tree that captures all genus–species relations (even within a particular domain) is to claim that all contraries can not only be *represented as* logical contradictories (dichotomies) but also that they fundamentally *are* logical contradictories, so that there is ultimately only one consistent way to reduce polytomies to dichotomies. This is why Wolff's commitment to the existence of such a unique and comprehensive conceptual hierarchy goes hand-in-hand with his view that all truths are grounded in the principle of contradiction.[7] But this is clearly a controversial assumption and, more to the point, one that Kant emphatically rejects. Thus, Porphyrian trees, insofar as they are structured by dichotomous logical divisions, do not, in themselves, make any claim to provide a privileged classification. A Porphyrian tree is not a diagram magnifying some portion of the Great Chain of Being.

Nor is exhaustiveness an ambition of Porphyrian classification. This is evident from their structure alone. The branching diagrams that adorn medieval and early modern texts in the Porphyrian tradition do not have the fully branched-out, arboreal structure familiar from charts of genealogy and consanguinity, much less the unevenly metastasizing structure of Linnaean classifications or the Encyclopedists' notorious "system" of human knowledge.[8] Rather, they display the verticality of a stalk, or a ladder with a single central pole (Figure 6.1), with truncated offshoots or rungs on either side (Figure 6.2). Even in a Porphyrian tree that does divide into distinct branches (Figure 6.3), only one species of each genus is subjected to further division. Half the species identified in the tree are merely placeholders for notional possibilities that are tangential to the current investigation – concepts that are mentioned solely for the sake of contrast. Only half the species are represented as branching in turn; the other half are dead-end stubs.

A Porphyrian tree is fundamentally concerned with just a *single* species that it sets in relation to an ordered series of genera under which that species falls. Porphyry's example in *Isagoge* § 2 targets the concept *human* and relates it to the substance-genera under which it falls: namely, *rational animal*, *animal*, *animate body*, *body*, *substance*. Porphyrian trees are not schemata for the privileged or exhaustive classification of kinds, but tools for displaying the content of a single concept that one has targeted for logical analysis. Porphyrian trees (both diagrammatic and discursive) retain

[7] See Anderson (2015, ch. 3).

[8] Hacking (2007, 255–258). On Diderot and D'Alembert's system of knowledge in the *Encyclopédie* in relation to the those of Bacon and Chambers, see Darnton (1984).

this targeted, asymmetrical form well into the nineteenth century, though they are increasingly replaced by rectilinear charts and tables. (This shift reflects the rise of printing, since tables are easier to typeset than tree-diagrams, which are easier to draw. See Hacking 2007, 249–253, 256.) Also, the layout of rectilinear tables suggests quite a different mode of inquiry from an asymmetrical branching structure – namely, an aspiration to synoptic completeness and global determination, rather than a local elucidatory exercise.

Understanding Porphyrian trees as instruments of local, targeted conceptual analysis reveals that, although the language of logical division suggests a movement from genus to species, there is an important sense in which Porphyrian trees "grow" from the bottom up and not from the top down. For the logical divisions represented in a Porphyrian tree display a marked bias for the species in which the tree terminates. A *Stufenleiter* is typically not concerned to chart *all* the speciating paths that descend from a certain genus – that is, its full logical "sphere" of species and subspecies – but only the path that leads to a particular species that is of interest (e.g. *human*). Though this species is the *terminus ad quem* of the tree's logical divisions, it is the *terminus a quo* of the analysis and, in that sense, the "root" from which the tree grows.

Further, the nature of one's interest in this target concept is what recommends a certain category of genera – substantial determinations, say, rather than relational or qualitative characteristics – as especially relevant to the inquiry and, thus, as worth representing in a tree. A Porphyrian tree explicates the content of a particular concept by mapping a principled route, via logical division, from a certain genus, through various relevant marks (as specific differentiae), to the concept under investigation – the concept <human>, say, or the idea of a metaphysics of morals, or of synthetic a priori knowledge, or the concept of an idea of reason.

6.2 Porphyrian Classifications in Kant

This traditional asymmetry or targeted analytical attention is conspicuous in Kant's own classifications of genera and species. These classificatory schemes tend to appear when Kant is introducing a topic or clarifying the nature of an inquiry he is about to undertake. A prominent example is the opening of the *Groundwork*:

> Ancient Greek philosophy was divided into three sciences: physics, ethics, and logic. This division is perfectly suited to the nature of the topic and there is no need to improve upon it apart from also providing its principle,

> partly in order to assure oneself of its completeness and partly to be able to correctly determine the necessary subdivisions. (*Groundwork* 4:387)

This passage at first seems to contravene all the conventions I have just associated with Porphyrian trees. First, it outlines a trichotomy, not a dichotomy. Second, it announces an aspiration to completeness, rather than a partial and local analysis. And third, it suggests that the subdivisions are necessary, yielding a privileged hierarchy that does not admit the legitimacy of alternative re-orderings. Yet, when Kant spells out his "principled" account of this received division of philosophy, his discussion embodies traditional Porphyrian analysis rather than the encyclopedic and necessary system he advertises:

> All rational cognition is either material and considers some object or other, or formal and concerns itself merely with the form of the understanding and reason itself [. . .]. Formal philosophy is **logic**, but material philosophy, which has to do with particular objects and the laws to which they are subject, is, in turn, twofold. For these laws are either laws of nature or of freedom. The former science is called physics, the other ethics. (*Groundwork* 4:387, Kant's emphasis)

Here Kant reduces the announced trichotomy to a series of dichotomies. Rational cognition is either formal or non-formal – or, if one prefers, non-material or material. And material cognition is concerned, in turn, with laws of freedom (ethics) or laws of nature (physics).[9] Just as clearly as Kant's discussion replaces trichotomy with dichotomies, his further elaboration of this division of philosophy abandons any pretense of completeness. Having identified logic with formal rational cognition, Kant says nothing more about it, despite the fact that he is elsewhere quite concerned to subdivide logic into a variety of species (such as special vs. general, as well as pure vs. applied) and to identify within these species of logic distinct branches of inquiry (such as a doctrine of elements vs. doctrine of method, as well as an analytic vs. a dialectic). Similarly, Kant mentions but does not name or discuss the empirical and pure branches of physics, much less their proper subdivisions (cf. *Metaphysical Foundations* 4:467–470), whereas he devotes the rest of the Preface (4:387–392) to clarifying and contrasting the notion of practical anthropology (empirical

[9] The dichotomy between nature and freedom may seem to involve contraries rather than logical contradictories. But Kant's discussion of transcendental freedom in the Antinomies suggests that he understands this distinction in terms of the truth-functional affirmation or negation of the possibility of spontaneous causality – that is, of a cause that is not determined in its causality by prior causes. That would make it a logical division in the strict sense.

Table 6.1 *Analytic/Synthetic orthogonal to a priori/a posteriori*

Judgments	**Synthetic**	**Analytic**
A Priori	*<7 + 5 = 12>;* *<every event has a cause>*	*<bodies are extended>*
A Posteriori	*<the sun warms the stone>*	X

ethics) and the idea of a metaphysics of morals (pure rational cognition of laws of freedom).[10]

It must be admitted that Kant does seem to regard this division of philosophy as necessary or, at least, privileged, since he repeats it in many places.[11] But this necessity reflects, as he says, "the nature of the topic [*Sache*]" (*Groundwork* 4:387). It is not an intrinsic feature of such classifications. We can see this by considering that most iconic of Kantian classifications: the distinction of judgments into analytic, synthetic, a priori, and a posteriori. Anyone who has taught the *Critique* has, at some point, drawn a rectilinear table on the board with analytic/synthetic along one axis and a priori/a posteriori along the other (Table 6.1).

Whenever one draws this table, one is forced to immediately modify it – typically by drawing a large *X* through one of its four cells – in order to indicate that *analytic a posteriori* is not a genuine class of judgments (cf. B11f. and Section 2.2). The need for this correction is one reason the table is pedagogically effective: One must understand the distinctions to see why this cell must be blank. But this kludge also indicates that we have departed from the native structure of Kant's thought. When Kant pursues this classification, the entire discussion is aimed at introducing and clarifying a single notion – namely, *synthetic a priori judgment*. The table, with its matrix of homogeneous cells, obscures this asymmetrical focus by presenting all four combinatoric variants as though they were on a par – as though the nonsensical category of *analytic a posteriori* judgment merited equal billing alongside Kant's signature innovation, *synthetic a priori* judgment. Kant's classification does not aspire to such combinatoric completeness or evenhandedness. It is a targeted elucidation of a quite specific kind of judgment that raises a particular philosophical problem. Nor does Kant

[10] It might be objected that by "complete", Kant does not mean the exhaustive enumeration of all subspecies – which may well be an impossible task – but only that, whenever a genus is divided, none of its species are omitted. In this sense, however, every Porphyrian classification is trivially complete, since all dichotomy is exhaustive.

[11] For instance, Bix-x.16–11 and the First Introduction to *Judgment* (20:195.10–22).

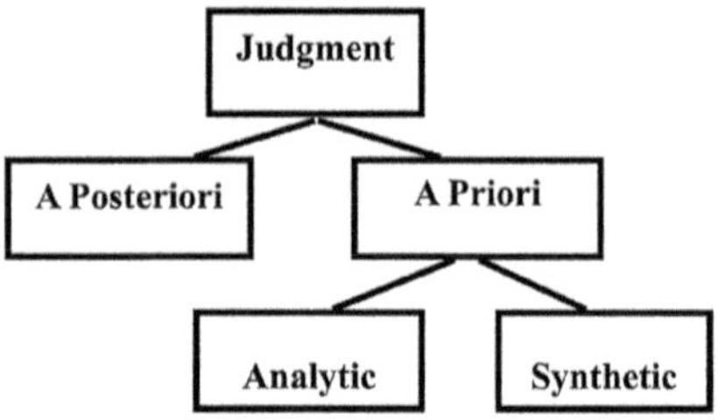

Figure 6.4 *Stufenleiter* of Synthetic A Priori Judgment.
(Critique B1–3, B10–14; Prolegomena 4:265–267)

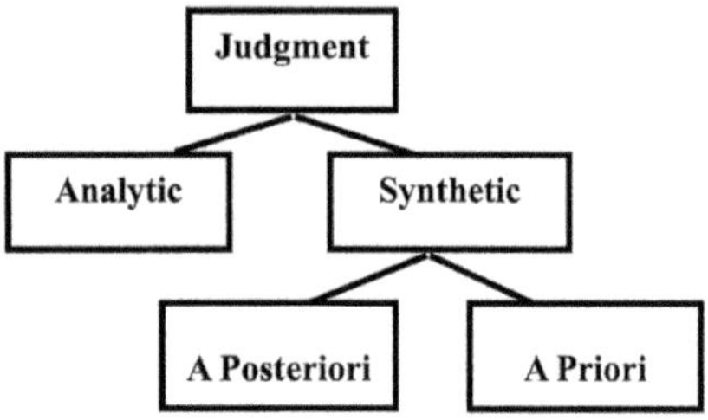

Figure 6.5 Alternate *Stufenleiter*.
(Prolegomena 4:275; Discovery 8:228–230)

seem to think there is a necessary or privileged order in which these divisions ought to be presented. (This is one reason why the table's orthogonal layout is such an inviting representational strategy.) Indeed, Kant's own presentation varies. Sometimes he begins by dividing judgments into *a priori* and *a posteriori* and then divides a priori judgments into *analytic* and *synthetic* (as in *Critique* B1–3, B10–14, or *Prolegomena* 4:265–267; Figure 6.4). Elsewhere he proceeds in the reverse order, first dividing judgment into *analytic* and *synthetic*, and then dividing *synthetic* judgment into *a priori* and *a posteriori* (as in *Prolegomena* 4:275 or *Discovery* 8:228–230; Figure 6.5).

In no text does Kant present the analytic/synthetic and a priori/a posteriori distinctions as orthogonal or offer a table or some other synoptic overview of the combinatoric possibilities. He always pursues a targeted and selective Porphyrian analytical structure, because the focus of his interest is invariably the category of synthetic a priori judgment.[12]

[12] Though diagrams are rare in Kant's corpus (cf. R3370, 18:601), discursive *Stufenleiter* abound – and their peculiarities can usually be explained by reference to the Porphyrian tradition I have

6.3 The *Stufenleiter* Passage (A320/B376)

I belabor these points about Porphyrian classification because they are so often neglected in discussions of Kant's classification of types of representation commonly known as "the *Stufenleiter*". This passage from the first section of the Transcendental Dialectic is often mined for choice phrases and preferred formulations – especially characterizations of intuitive and conceptual representation – but it is rarely quoted in full. Here is the beginning of the passage, from which most quotes are drawn:

> The genus is **representation** überhaupt (*repraesentatio*). Under it stands representation with consciousness (*perceptio*). A **perception** that refers solely to the subject, as a modification of its state, is **sensation** (*sensatio*), an objective perception is **cognition** (*cognitio*). This [sc. cognition] is either **intuition** or **concept** (*intuitus vel conceptus*). The former relates immediately to the object [*Gegenstand*] and is singular [*einzeln*]; the latter [relates to the object] mediately, by means of a mark that can be common to several - things. (A320/B376f.24–33, Kant's emphases)

Note that, in identifying *perception* as a species of the genus *representation*, Kant does not bother to mention the other coordinate species of that genus – namely, *representation without consciousness* – even though he elsewhere claims that most of our representations belong to this species (e.g. *Anthropology* 7:136 f.). Similarly, after identifying *sensation* and

sketched. Particularly interesting is Kant's division of logic in the introduction to the Transcendental Logic (A52–55/B76–79). He first divides logic into general and special, and then divides general logic into pure and applied. This classification does not pursue any further speciation of special logic – for example, into pure and applied – and the text does not explicitly associate *transcendental logic* with any of these species. Yet interpreters (and teachers) regularly present the general/special and pure/applied distinctions as orthogonal and classify transcendental logic as a pure special logic. The substance of this suggestion is quite plausible, but it is textually awkward, since it holds that the principle function of the passage is to classify something that Kant does not mention (transcendental logic) under a heading that Kant does not mention (pure special logic). Attention to the peculiar norms of Porphyrian classification opens up an alternative interpretation. The purpose of the classification is just to clarify the idea of pure general logic, which is the *terminus ad quem* of Kant's divisions. This is desirable because PGL is not just one sort of logic among others: It is, so to speak, logic *au naturel*, logic in its unadulterated, autonomous form. By clarifying the nature of PGL, then, we clarify the nature of "Logik überhaupt", which is the title of the subsection where Kant discusses the general/special and pure/applied distinctions (A50/B74.7). Particular types of logic count *as logic* precisely insofar as they resemble or relate to PGL. Accordingly, the next subsection introduces "The Idea of a Transcendental Logic" (A55/B79.14) – which is also the aim of the supersection overall (A50/B74.5) – by relating it to PGL (A55–56/B79.15–80.10). Kant does this *not* by locating TL as a species within the foregoing classificatory scheme – which has, by that point, completed its elucidatory task of introducing PGL as the paradigm of logic *überhaupt* – but by spelling out an altogether different sort of relation between PGL and TL. This provides a further textual rationale for the sort of reading defended by Tolley (2012). See also Section 1.2.1 and Lu-Adler (2018a, ch. 3.3).

cognition as the two species of *perception*, Kant pursues further specific divisions within the genus of *cognition*, but does not distinguish any species of *sensation*. The reason for this uneven treatment is not that Kant considers *sensation* and *unconscious representation* to be uninteresting or epistemically irrelevant notions, or primitives that admit of no further elucidation. For he says quite a bit about the nature and epistemological significance of both kinds of representation in other contexts.[13] The reason Kant's *Stufenleiter* traces only one path of speciation descending from *representation überhaupt* is because the central aim that governs its organization is to elucidate the concept <idea of reason> and thereby to set up the Transcendental Dialectic. The types of representation Kant mentions are introduced for the sake of shedding light on what an *idea of reason* is. Accordingly, any representational genera that are not superordinate to this species, *idea of reason*, are of merely tangential interest and serve only as placeholders. This becomes obvious when one considers the passage in full, rather than cherry-picking phrases about topics of interest. Here is its immediate continuation:

> A concept is either an **empirical** or a **pure concept**, and the pure concept, insofar as it has its origin solely in the understanding (not in a pure image of sensibility), is called *notio*. A concept consisting of notions, which exceeds the possibility of experience, is the **idea**, or concept of reason. Once one has become accustomed to this differentiation [*Unterscheidung*], it must strike one as intolerable to hear the representation of the color red called an idea. It is not even to be called a notion (concept of the understanding). (A320/B376–377.33–05, my underlining, other emphases Kant's)

It is not simply that Kant continues the classification beyond the concept/intuition distinction, on which most commentators focus. It is that his prosecution of the classification evinces a single-minded interest in a particular *terminus ad quem* – namely, his preferred account of *ideas* or *concepts of reason*. What one "becomes accustomed to [through] this differentiation" is a certain use of the term "idea". The function of the *Stufenleiter* is to clarify the notion <idea of reason> by tracing its conceptual lineage. For this elucidatory project, only its direct analytical forebears are relevant; conceptual cousins are only curiosities, serving as formal placeholders to mark possible continuations of the structure, which is why Kant does not explore them (except when he cannot help himself).

[13] For Kant on unconscious (i.e. obscure) representations, see La Rocca (2008a, 2008b) as well as the essays by Crone, Heidemann, Kitcher, Rockmore, and Schulting in Giordanetti et al. (2012). For Kant on sensations, see George (1981) and Falkenstein (1990).

This is one reason why it is quite misleading to cite the *Stufenleiter* passage as providing a "definition" of *intuition*, as so many commentators do. If Kant's *Stufenleiter* pursues any sort of definition, the *definiendum* is <idea of reason> and the definition is an Aristotelian-cum-Porphyrian classification that presents this *definiendum* as resulting from a series of logical divisions – namely, the increasingly specific genera *representation, perception, cognition, concept, pure concept*, and *notion*. These genera are not themselves the focus of the analytical excursus; they rather serve as *definientia* of the target concept <idea of reason>, to which they are superordinated. Now these *definientia* are, of course, also presented as super- and subordinate to one another. So it might be argued that Kant's *Stufenleiter* provides, in a secondary sense, partial definitions or contextual elucidations of these terms by exhibiting their interrelations. Note, however, that *intuition* is not one of these *definientia*. It is one of undeveloped offshoots of the tree that form no part of either the target *definiendum* or its *definientia*. It would be obviously wrongheaded to look to Kant's *Stufenleiter* for a definition of <unconscious representation> (which he does not even mention), or of <sensation>, <empirical concept>, or <category> (which is also omitted but which is presumably coordinate with <idea of reason> under the genus <notion>). These headings, where they appear at all, are mere signposts for analytical paths not taken. But then it is no less wrongheaded to cite the *Stufenleiter* passage as providing a definition, or even a privileged account, of <intuition>. The notion of intuition figures in Kant's *Stufenleiter* only as a negative placeholder for an analysis that has not been prosecuted.[14]

[14] Another reason it is misleading to cite the *Stufenleiter* as providing a "definition" of intuition is because Kant denies that philosophy is capable of providing definitions in the strict sense (A727–732/B755–760). In a looser sense of "definition", Kant does suggest that, in philosophy, definitions "must rather conclude the work than begin it" – in contrast to mathematics, where definitions ought to precede all argumentation (A731/B759.13–15; *Practical* 5:9n.33–37). Situated as it is at the outset of the Dialectic – and thus "conclud[ing]" the Analytic's "**analysis of the cognitive faculty itself**" (A65/B90.11–12, Kant's emphasis) – it is prima facie plausible to expect the *Stufenleiter* to offer definitions of <concept>, <intuition>, and so forth, in the loose sense appropriate to philosophical inquiry. But it does not go without saying that the *Stufenleiter* actually provides such definitions. Kant surely intends to be stating truths – even significant truths – about concepts, intuitions, and so forth, in the *Stufenleiter*. But not all true characterizations are definitions, and, anyway, a truth about *X* (e.g. about intuition) may be significant not because it illuminates the essence of *X* but because of the light it reflects onto *Y* (e.g. onto ideas of reason), to which *X* stands in some determinate relation. Despite all this, it could be that Kant does intend to offer definitions of *intuition* and *concept* in the *Stufenleiter*. But this cannot be taken for granted: It must be argued for.

6.4 *Stufenleiter* as Targeted Analytical Tools

Kant presents his various classifications in prose, with minor exceptions, but they generally adhere to the Porphyrian tradition I have sketched. Kant's *Stufenleiter* are analytical tools for displaying the content of a particular concept. Because of their analytical function, *Stufenleiter* are well-suited for presenting definitions of concepts or similarly privileged accounts of the essence of some object of inquiry. Kant frequently puts *Stufenleiter* to this sort of essence-specifying use – for instance, in outlining the branches of philosophy or in distinguishing the cognitive faculties and their associated representations. That they lend themselves to such a use does not, however, imply that every *Stufenleiter* constitutes a definition of the concept that is the focus of its analytical attention. For, as we have seen, different orderings of the same classificatory differentiae can produce distinct but functionally equivalent *Stufenleiter* – particularly when polytomous distinctions are represented via nested dichotomies.

There can, moreover, be considerable degrees of freedom in the selection of classificatory differentiae, not just in their ordering. For a given analysand will typically fall not just under various genera but under various different categories of genera. The differentia *rational* is, on the traditional account, a determination of *human* in the category of substance. It expresses a survival condition on one's continuing to exist – on preserving one's identity as a human – through various sorts of changes. Yet *human* also falls under the genus *biped*. And this is no less a determination of human essence, no less part of "the what it was to be [*to ti en einai*]" a human. But *rational* and *bipedal* are not merely different determinations; they are determinations belonging to different Aristotelian categories. Rather than indicating what it takes for a human to persist (in being human) through change, *bipedal* characterizes what Aristotle would call a *quality* of human beings. Even if one holds the analysand *human* constant, it is easy to imagine circumstances in which *bipedal* might be a more relevant or more interesting classification than *rational*. So one might construct a Porphyrian tree in which *bipedal* figures as a genus of *human*, but *rational* does not appear at all. To draw or endorse such a tree need not involve rejecting the traditional definition of *human* as *rational animal*. For the analysis in question may not be concerned to characterize the analysand qua substance and, indeed, may not aim to provide a definition at all.

If a *Stufenleiter* does not, as such, purport to define the focal concept in which its logical divisions terminate, then it a fortiori does not offer definitions of the concepts "upstream" from this analysand. For instance, in traditional elaborations of Porphyry's tree (Figures 6.2 and 6.3), *rational* is represented as a genus of the analysand *human* and also as a species of *animal*. This should not be taken to imply that, if our interest shifts to analyzing the concept <rational>, we should expect *animal* to figure as a differentia. It might, of course. But it need not. And with respect to conceptual cousins – that is, species that are not superordinate to the analysand – all bets are off. If, for instance, we shift from analyzing <human> to analyzing the concept <emu>, we might well construct a tree in which *human* is represented through the determinations *featherless biped*. This clearly does not commit us to rejecting the traditional definition, *rational animal*, when our focus returns to the concept <human>.

To be sure, Porphyrian classifications are rooted in an Aristotelian tradition that accords a central place to definitions and to real essences. And Kant's *Stufenleiter* self-consciously participate in this tradition. But such classifications are not themselves tantamount to definitions. Indeed, when we come to appreciate their dichotomous logic and their function as targeted and local tools of analysis, it becomes clear that, in the absence of supplementary considerations, no *Stufenleiter* can function as a definition of *any* of the concepts it invokes. Even when a tree does aspire to be definitive, none but the focal concept of the tree is a candidate for *definiendum*.

Still more relevant, for our purposes, is the way that the nature of the inquiry, of which the classificatory analysis is part, can influence the selection of differentiae. Conceptual analysis is rarely pursued as an end in itself. And even if it were, one would still have to choose between a variety of alternative differentiae and ways of ordering them. In practice, however, the selection of differentiae is (quite appropriately) informed by the epistemic aims of the overall inquiry, the types of features it is particularly interested in, its judgments about what is salient or probative, the sorts of evidence it treats as admissible, and so on. Nor can we always take for granted that the differentia at one level will reflect the same sort of characteristic or consideration as differentiae at other levels. Returning to Porphyry's tree, it certainly seems natural to think that the differentia *living*, which divides *body* into *animate* and *inanimate*, is the same kind of determination and reflects the same kinds of considerations as the differentia *perceiving*, which divides *animate* into *plant* and *animal*. For both are determinations of soul. But are these two differentiae (life, perception) of the same sort as the differentia *material*, which is the specific differentia of the genus *substance*? After all, life and perception concern the *form* of the substance, whereas materiality concerns, well, its matter. Similarly, to judge that something is *rational* seems to require not just more evidence but evidence of a different sort from what is required to judge that something is material or that it is alive. In sum, different considerations and forms of evidence might be deployed at different levels within the same *Stufenleiter*.

One cannot expect and one should not demand that the specific differentiae invoked at different levels in a particular Porphyrian classification will all have the same evidentiary status, or belong to the same category of determination, or reflect the same sorts of considerations. In practice, conceptual analysis is always somewhat messier than an abstract account of its normative principles can make it sound. The practice of Porphyrian classification, as an analytical tool, reflects this. The central purpose of a Porphyrian classification is to clarify the content of a particular concept that is its *terminus ad quem*. But "clarify" here means "clarify sufficiently for the purposes of the present inquiry". And a key consideration in deciding what is "sufficiently" clear is extensional adequacy – that is, the ability of the classification to capture (or exclude) certain paradigm cases that are of special concern. Thus, the author prosecuting the analysis will often have one eye on the logical *extensions* of the species – that is, instances that exemplify them – even though the classification itself properly concerns the *intension* of the concept. Indeed, extensional adequacy is sometimes the primary rationale for selecting a particular differentia or effecting a particular division. When this is the case, certain specific divisions, which do not seem well motivated by mere reflection on the analysand, may come to seem inevitable once a new comparison class of instances is treated as relevant.

We see this in one of the traditional elaborations of Porphyry's tree. In Porphyry (Figure 6.1), for instance, *human* falls directly under *rational animal*. Medieval authors (Figure 6.2), however, insert a further division at this point: *Rational animal* divides into *immortal* and *mortal*, with *human* falling under *mortal*. One might, of course, attempt to explain this shift in terms of changing views about the intensions of the concepts. One might argue that, for Aristotle, death is not a change that flows from the form (the soul) of an animal but rather from the inevitable breakdown in the matter that the animal depends on to live. To that extent, mortality is not part of the *essence* of humans but something accidental, despite being a predictable, materially necessary, and (in that sense) natural part of human life. Perhaps medieval Aristotelians, influenced no doubt by Christian and Islamic dogma, came to regard death as a more essential and formal aspect of human nature. Perhaps. But it is at least as plausible to suppose that the medievals became concerned with a certain class of *instances* that had to be excluded as non-human, which Aristotle and Porphyry would not have had in view – namely, angels. Once angels are on the classificatory horizon, they have to be excluded either through higher differentiae (e.g. if one takes them to be *immaterial*) or through ad hoc divisions closer to the *terminus ad quem* (as with *immortal rational animal*). In that case, there need not have been any shift in the understanding of the intension (the content) of the concept <human>. Rather, new extensional concerns have shifted what it means to "sufficiently" clarify this concept and have thereby motivated the introduction of a differentia that was, for Porphyry, superfluous.

By the same token, an inquiry that principally aims to characterize the essence of something may introduce logical divisions and differentiae that are quite superfluous from the perspective of extensional adequacy. Kant's division of logic in the introduction to the Transcendental Logic (A52–55/B76–79) is a good illustration. It is clearly important to Kant to argue that logic *überhaupt* – logic in its essence – is both *general* and *pure*. To make this point, he distinguishes PGL from special logics and from applied general logic (see note 12). But in terms of the extensions of the concepts, it is not clear that he needs the general/special distinction at all. Kant's chief complaint about the logics of his day was that they failed to distinguish pure principles from empirical (psychological) ones.[15] There simply was no significant tradition of *special logics* with which a general logic such as PGL might possibly be confused. Kant's motivation in drawing the special/general distinction cannot be to contrast two live currents in the actual practice of logic. His aim is rather to highlight an important further feature of a practice that he has already been sufficiently distinguished from neighboring disciplines.

I emphasize the messiness and strangeness of Porphyrian classifications not in order to denigrate them but to highlight the plasticity that we must take into account if we are to understand the use Kant makes of them, and if we are to make use of them to understand Kant. A Porphyrian tree offers a targeted and local analysis of a single concept – an analysis that is framed within a broader inquiry, whose guiding aims and constraints influence both the selection and the ordering of differentiae. And it is with this sense of their flexibility and analytical function that I will now propose my own *Stufenleiter* to analyze Kant's conception of human sensible intuition.

[15] See Lu-Adler (2018a, chs.4 and 5.5).

7

A Stufenleiter *of Kantian Intuition, Part I*

Intuition überhaupt *and Spontaneous Intuition*

In this chapter and Chapter 8, I will present my own *Stufenleiter* of Kantian intuition, i.e. of intuition as Kant conceives it. Despite their familiarity, *Stufenleiter* have, as I argued in Chapter 6, a number of peculiar and often misunderstood features. So before walking through the details of my diagram (Figure 7.1), I want to make several general points about how I mean it to be understood and to outline the interpretive payoffs I think it can deliver.

My commentary on this diagram is extensive enough that I have divided it into two chapters. The present chapter contains general remarks on my *Stufenleiter* (Section 7.1) and discussion of its highest genus, intuition *überhaupt* (Section 7.2), the differentia of that genus, *spontaneity* (Section 7.3), and the species induced by that differentia, spontaneous and non-spontaneous intuition (Sections 7.3.1–7.3.3). Chapter 8 considers the species of receptive intuition and their respective differentiae.

7.1 A Targeted Analysis of Human Intuition

Like traditional Porphyrian trees and Kant's own genus–species classifications, my proposed *Stufenleiter* is a targeted analytical tool. Just as Kant's famous *Stufenleiter* at A320/B376 targets the concept <idea of reason> and pursues only those logical divisions that ultimately lead to this notion (see Section 6.3), my own *Stufenleiter* targets <human intuition> and does not further determine species of intuition that are not superordinate to this focal analysand. This asymmetrical focus is not just a hat-tip to tradition. It also reflects Kant's view that we can have no positive conception of faculties of intuition different from our own. There is, from a Kantian perspective, little to be gained from discussing species of intuition that are not part of our own human lineage.

Because it is a targeted analytical tool with a single analysand, a *Stufenleiter* does not, as such, claim that the analysis it presents is uniquely

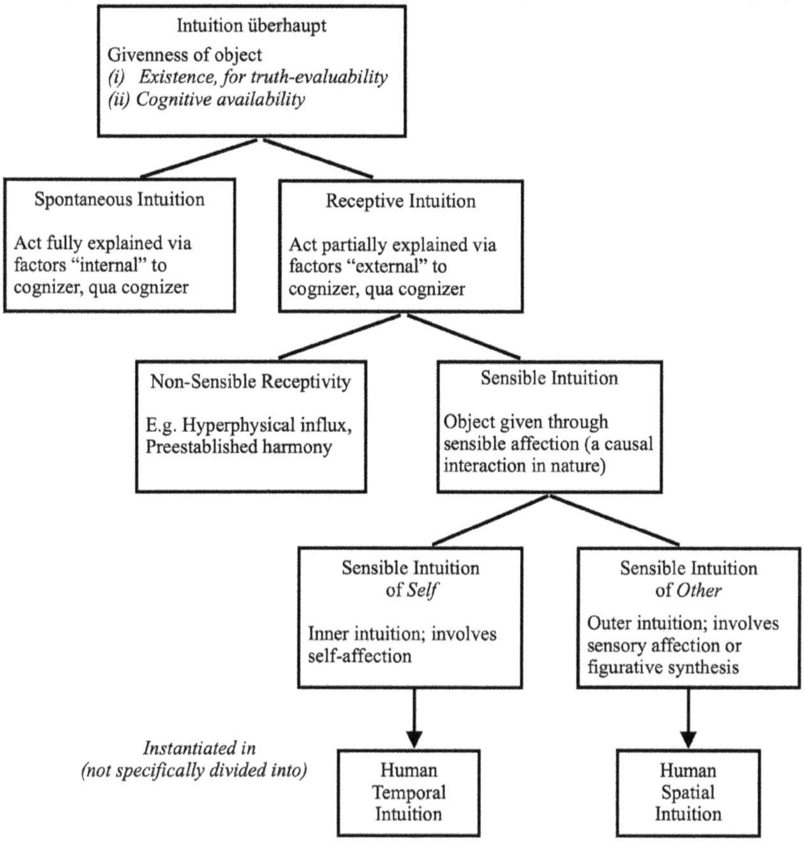

Figure 7.1 My *Stufenleiter* of Kantian Intuition in Humans

correct or even privileged among other possible classifications (see Sections 6.2 and 6.4). Anyway, I make no such claims for my proposed *Stufenleiter*. What I do claim is (i) that its divisions and differentiae track important aspects of Kant's transcendental epistemology and (ii) that they are well grounded in specific texts.

Any such classification will reflect the general explanatory ambitions, interests, and evidentiary constraints of the broader inquiry to which its analysis contributes. This influence is particularly evident in the selection of differentiae. Though logical divisions are induced through the affirmation and negation of a single differentia, species may in fact differ in multiple irreducible respects. Which differences, and which sorts of differences, one wishes to track in a *Stufenleiter* can depend on a variety of considerations – some of them neutral matters of arbitrary preference, others more contentious matters of philosophical dispute.[1]

It is important to note, then, that my own interests, explanatory ambitions, and evidentiary constraints in constructing this *Stufenleiter* are not quite the same as Kant's in the *Critique*, though they are closely related. Kant introduces intuition and invests it with certain attributes in order to explain how synthetic a priori knowledge is possible for us, thereby revealing the possibility and the limits of human knowledge. My explanatory project, by contrast, is to make sense of Kant's texts as the expression of a philosophical system that seeks to discharge this transcendental task.

So the distinctions that limn my *Stufenleiter* have a hybrid status. In one sense, the differentiae are Kant's own, since I only invoke features Kant explicitly discusses. In another sense, however, I am responsible for selecting and ordering the criteria and for elevating them to the status of specific differentiae. The concepts that serve as differentiae call for philosophical clarification and support; their selection calls for textual argumentation. Kant is ultimately on the hook for the former; I'm responsible for the latter. Some differentiae – such as <spontaneity>, or <sensible affection> – implicate us in philosophical difficulties whose resolution would take us much too far afield. This renders the logical divisions they induce philosophically problematic. I will attempt to clarify such problems as they arise, but I will ultimately pass the buck to Kant. My aim is not to resolve all the philosophical problems with Kant's conception of intuition but to discover where they lie. I will, however, offer a textual defense of my classification – not one that establishes its unique correctness but one that shows it to be licensed by key passages.

Another subtle but significant difference between Kant's *Stufenleiter* and the present one is that Kant's distinguishes types of *representation* (*Vorstellungsarten*, A319/B376.18, 21) – i.e. different kinds of mental *acts* – whereas mine concerns cognitive *capacities* for intuition. Of course,

[1] Kant himself emphasizes this point. Kant distinguishes, for example, between the "metaphysical" conception of sensibility, as receptivity, and the "logical" conception, as a capacity for intuition (L-Jäsche 9:36). Now, human sensibility is both receptive and intuitive, so both conceptions are correct and consistent. But one conception may be preferable in the context of a particular explanatory project. Nor are metaphysics (i.e. transcendental philosophy) and PGL the only explanatory enterprises in which Kant deploys the notion of sensibility. A rather extensive discussion also occurs in Kant's *Anthropology*, which bears the significant qualification "*in pragmatischer Hinsicht*". One might hope to integrate these various discussions into a comprehensive account. But such integration is a non-trivial task: One must always attend to the specific interests and explanatory aims that inform each discussion.

capacities are often characterized in terms of their acts, so this may seem like a distinction without a difference.[2] But the potential to contribute to cognition resides with the capacity, not with its acts. If one is only characterizing a certain type of representation – that is, a class of token representings that share specific features – then the failure of one token to contribute to cognition may raise a question about the cognitive significance of all the other tokens of that type. For if one member of the class fails to contribute to cognition, despite manifesting the features that typify the class in question, then it is plausible that no member of the class contributes to cognition – or, at least, not in virtue of manifesting those shared features. And this threatens to undermine the cognitive significance of the entire type of representation, leaving it an open question whether the ability to produce such representations is an intrinsically *cognitive* capacity at all.[3]

My approach here, by contrast, presumes that the question of cognitive significance is already settled in the affirmative. For the conception of intuition I am investigating is introduced precisely in order to explain the possibility of synthetic cognition (see Sections 2.3 and 2.5). Receptive intuition, I have argued, is the cognitive complement of discursive understanding. To call into question the cognitive significance of receptive intuition is to lose touch with the relevant conception altogether. To conceive intuition as the cognitive complement of intellection, which itself is conceived as a cognitive faculty, is to approach intuitive representings as intrinsically capable of contributing to contentful human knowledge. This is not to deny the value of casuistic analysis of token misfires or paradigm cases. But such considerations are downstream from the present investigation of the essential characteristics of intuition as a cognitive *capacity*. Token misfires do not, merely as such, threaten the cognitive significance of their conspecifics. They instead raise questions of the form, "What prevented *this* token from enjoying the cognitive significance that such representations *typically* enjoy as exercises of a cognitive capacity?"

Though the capacity of intuition I examine here is an intrinsically cognitive capacity, I have endeavored to remain neutral on the intellectualism/sensibilism debate, to adopt the labels recommended by McLear (2014). My account does presuppose an anodyne form of intellectualism,

[2] Cf. *De Anima* II.4, 415a20–22, where Aristotle suggests that capacities are posterior in definition to their characteristic activities and that such activities, in turn, are posterior to their proper objects.

[3] Even approaches that present themselves as "capacities first" often fall prey to this slippage by focusing too exclusively on the acts of the capacities they aim to characterize. See Section 2.4, note 21.

inasmuch as I regard discursive understanding and receptive intuition to be mutually implicating as cognitive capacities. But this only amounts to claiming (i) that receptive intuitings cannot, on their own, suffice for cognition, (ii) that acts of discursive thought cannot, on their own, suffice for cognition, but (iii) that cognition is possible for a mind with both capacities. My classification is silent on more contentious aspects of the debate. It is neutral about whether or how token intuitings may involve certain intellectual activities, such as acts of categorial synthesis, figurative synthesis, and so forth.

Because my *Stufenleiter* limns the genus of intuition qua cognitive capacity, its nodes represent, at varying levels of abstraction, cognitive capacities that perform the defining function of intuition in specifically different ways. But there is nothing in the logic of the diagram to prohibit a cognizer from possessing multiple species of intuition – for example, a capacity for inner intuition as well as a capacity for outer intuition. Indeed, further considerations (presented in the Refutation of Idealism) might reveal such dual possession to be necessary. Similarly, there may be compelling reasons to hold that it is impossible for a single mind to possess certain combinations of intuitive capacities – for example, sensible as well as spontaneous. But any such argument must turn on one's grounds for attributing specific intuitive capacities to a specific (type of) mind. None of this is, as far as I can see, baked into my *Stufenleiter*.

For the same reason, my illustrations of these conceptual distinctions may sometimes be tendentious. It is one thing to argue that there is a notional distinction between an intuition that depends on external affection and one that depends on self-affection. It is quite another to argue that a certain representation (type or token), such as an experience of double vision, is an instance of the one or the other capacity at work. We must distinguish between the conceptual considerations that discriminate various notions (genera and species) of intuition, on the one hand, and the grounds for predicating these notions of particular (types of) minds or identifying particular (types of) mental states as their exercises, on the other. I will unavoidably pursue both lines of argument in exfoliating my *Stufenleiter*, since I will illustrate conceptual points with concrete examples. But my main concern is to outline a conceptual framework that captures both the unity and the diversity of Kant's various claims about intuition. If particular examples offend, the reader is encouraged to supply her own. My reconstruction is threatened only if there are no clear examples of the species I distinguish, or if paradigm cases of intuiting cannot plausibly be subsumed under any of my species.

Finally, a word about the interpretive payoff of this *Stufenleiter*. Part of my argument here is that when Kant makes claims about human intuition – or when, as is more often the case, he simply does not specify whether his claims concern only human intuition or intuition in some more general sense – we need to ask at what level of abstraction his claims are pitched. Kant's arguments and terminology tend to focus on human cognition, since his central aim is to establish the possibility and the limits of *our* knowledge. But that does not mean that the claims and concepts he develops in prosecuting the critical project are restricted to the human case. For instance, Kant repeatedly claims that intuition is immediate. Surely he does not consider this a parochial feature of human intuition, as though a non-spatiotemporal intuition or the intellectual intuitings of a divine mind might be mediate. Indeed, I will argue that immediacy is essential to all intuition, including intellectual intuition. Immediacy, in the relevant sense, is just about as abstract a characterization of intuition as one can frame without losing one's grip on the notion. I will put this point by saying that immediacy is a feature of intuition *überhaupt* or that it pertains to intuition at the most generic level. By contrast, when Kant attributes chiral orientability to human intuition, I will suggest, his claim holds at most for all *sensible* intuition and need not hold for all *receptive* intuition, much less for intuition *überhaupt*. One of the chief benefits of this *Stufenleiter* is that it enables us to tease apart Kant's various characterizations of intuition – distinguishing the levels of abstraction at which they are pitched, the sorts of evidence they rely on, and the relative priority or fundamentality of the features they invoke.

This provides us with a principled analytical tool (though not the only possible one) for parsing interpretive debates – for example, about whether singularity (Hintikka) or immediacy (Parsons) is more fundamental to Kantian intuition. It reveals, for instance, that parties to these debates are prone to talk past one another inasmuch as they take different types of evidence, different sorts of considerations, to be relevant.

7.2 Givenness as Criterion of Intuition *überhaupt*

The highest genus in my proposed *Stufenleiter* is a capacity for intuition that contributes to cognition by giving knowable objects to the mind, where "object" signifies a ground of truth for synthetic judgment. As I argued in Chapters 2, 3, and 5, it is in just this capacity that intuition functions as the cognitive complement of a discursive understanding, supplying those cognitive requirements that a discursive intellect cannot itself secure. This does not mean that any mind with a capacity for intuition *überhaupt* must possess a discursive intellect. Rather, any mind with a discursive intellect must have a capacity for intuition *überhaupt*, if that intellect is to qualify as an *Erkenntnisvermögen*. The cognitive shortcomings of discursive thought reveal entirely general requirements on knowledge of objects. Any mind capable of knowledge of objects must be endowed with a capacity for intuition *überhaupt*, regardless of the character of its intellect.[4] For truth consists in the agreement of thought with its object, whether such thought is discursive or not.[5]

Genuine knowledge, however, requires not just the truth of a thought but its consciousness of its truth. Thought that is discursive cannot, of itself, secure either the truth of its judgments or consciousness of such truth: Discursive thought depends, for its cognitive significance, on the givenness of knowable contents. Intuitive givenness thus involves two things: (i) the possibility of thought's agreeing with an object (truth evaluability) and (ii) the possibility of its recognizing such agreement (cognitive availability). Securing these conditions is the defining function of intuition *überhaupt* as a cognitive capacity. The species of intuition I will discriminate share these generic features and differ only in the specific ways they realize them.

Though I find it helpful to distinguish two conditions within the criterion of givenness – namely, truth evaluability and cognitive availability – Kant clearly regards givenness as a single, indissoluble property of representations. So we must not treat the securing of the object's existence as a separate act from the act that makes the object available to cognition.[6] To do so would be, in effect, to split intuition into two distinct capacities, each with its own distinctive exercise. Kant rather takes these conditions to

4 The epistemic shortcomings of a discursive intellect thus reveal that it is not itself a capacity for intuition. It is conceivable that the cognitive activity of a non-human mind might intrinsically fulfill *both* the criteria of intuition *and* the criteria of intellection. For such a mind, there is, in the terminology of Suárez, a merely *rational* distinction between its intuitive and its intellectual capacities, not a *modal* distinction, as in the case of a discursive intellect paired with a receptive intuition.

5 Kant reserves the term 'thought' and its cognates for acts of *discursive* intellection (B71.2–5; B145.9–15; M-Mr 29:888.5–16). I find it more convenient to use the term for all acts of intellection, discursive or otherwise. Insofar as the acts of an intuitive intellect issue from an *intellect*, I will persist in calling them "thoughts", though I acknowledge that Kant's considered position may be that non-discursive intellects do not think *stricto sensu*.

6 By separating the existence condition from the cognitive-availability condition, we invite the sort of "hybrid" conception of intuition discussed in Section 7.3.2, where one condition is satisfied spontaneously, the other receptively. Watkins and Willaschek (2017, 89–90) helpfully distinguish these aspects of intuitive givenness but do not explain why they should be inseparable.

be distinguishable but inseparable aspects of a single act. We might express this by saying that it is *in* securing the existence of the object that intuition renders it available to cognition. The object's availability to cognition involves its existence.[7]

These two aspects of givenness point up two senses in which intuitions must be *immediate*. First, intuitions cannot be mediated through discursive marks. For, as I argued in Section 3.3, mediation through discursive marks enables conceptual representations to refer to objects that do not exist. So no discursively mediated representation can, merely as such, satisfy the existence condition. Accordingly, any representation that satisfies the existence condition must be immediate in the sense of not relating to its object via discursive marks. Second, the cognitive-availability condition points in the direction of a sort of cognitive immediacy, or direct awareness. I think we should be circumspect about characterizing this cognitive immediacy as *phenomenological* presence to mind (cf. Parsons 1992 [1969]) – certainly while our investigation remains at such a high level of abstraction. For the present characterization must be valid for *all* forms of intuition, including the productive intuitings of a divine mind. And it is not obvious, to me at least, that the divine mind has a phenomenological character or first-person point of view. We should not assume that there is something "that it is like" to be the divine mind or to enjoy its intuitive cognitions. Nevertheless, it is certainly arguable that, *for us humans*, cognitive availability in intuition takes the form of phenomenological presence to consciousness – though I have raised difficulties for this view in light of the infinitary structure of intuition (Section 5.4.1).

I will also note in passing that the criterion of cognitive availability is the locus of the most intense debates between intellectualist and sensibilist accounts of intuition. Both parties agree that an essential feature of intuition is to make knowable contents available to the mind for cognition. They disagree about what this cognitive availability consists in and whether it can be secured through sensible receptivity alone, or whether it must instead draw on intellectual resources, such as categorial or figurative synthesis. My classification is intentionally neutral on this point. A sensibilist can point to the fact that, on this account, it is intuition itself

[7] This is not to say that hallucinations, imaginings, and other cases of apparent reference failure cannot count as intuitive. First, recall that I am characterizing the capacity, not offering an exceptionless generalization about its acts. Second, if we stipulate that a particular hallucination (etc.) *is* an intuiting, it is not obvious what its *object* is qua intuitive representation. It does not go without saying that the object it makes available for cognition (and whose existence it secures, qua intuition) is the intentional object it purports to be a perception of. See Section 2.4.

that is responsible for rendering knowable objects available to cognition. And this remains true, the sensibilist will insist, when we descend to the level of *receptive* intuition. This allows room for the sensibilist to argue that acts of intuiting make the Given available to cognition independently of any exercises of spontaneity on the part of the intellect. On the other hand, an intellectualist will be able to observe that my classification analyzes intuition as an intrinsically *cognitive* capacity. It is presumed throughout that intuition is here complemented by an intellectual faculty, both of which are essential aspects of a unified faculty of knowledge. We cannot, therefore, assume that the features attributed to intuition obtain *independently* of the contributions of intellectual spontaneity, or that a capacity for sensible representation might exhibit such features in the absence of a complementary intellectual faculty. This allows room for the intellectualist to argue for an exercise-level dependence of intuition on intellection.

One interpretive benefit of the present *Stufenleiter* is to show that, although the intellectualism/sensibilism debate tracks illuminating aspects of and ambivalences in Kant's account, it is far from exhausting the interesting features of Kant's conception of intuition.

In sum, then, givenness of knowable objects is the essential characteristic of intuition *überhaupt*. A cognitive capacity is intuitive just insofar as it presents the mind with knowable objects and, in so doing, puts it in a position to cognize the (dis)agreement of its thoughts with those objects.

7.3 Cognitive Spontaneity as Differentia

Species of intuition *überhaupt* differ in how each fulfills its cognitive role of giving knowable objects to the mind for cognition. I propose to divide this genus via the specific differentia *spontaneous*. Insofar as a capacity is not spontaneous, it is, in that respect, receptive.[8] To a first approximation, a spontaneous faculty is one whose exercises are acts of self-determination, whereas a capacity is receptive insofar as its exercises are determined from without – insofar as they are suffered rather than performed.

Kant says remarkably little in his published writings to elucidate the notion of spontaneity, despite its centrality to his account of discursive

[8] I follow Kant in reserving the term 'faculty' ('*facultas*', '*Vermögen*') for spontaneous capacities. A receptivity (*receptivitas, Empfänglichkeit*) is a passive capacity, i.e. a capacity for being affected. I use 'capacity' in the neutral sense of *potentia* and *Fähigkeit*, which can accommodate either spontaneity or passivity. See R3588 (1773–1778) 17:75; cf. Engstrom (2006, 22n.9).

understanding and, especially, to his theories of synthesis and transcendental apperception. In the *Critique*, Kant says little more than that "**spontaneity** of cognition" is "the faculty for bringing forth representations of itself [*das Vermögen, Vorstellungen selbst hervorzubringen*]" (A51/B75.4–5; cf. A68/B93.15–21). Kant is more expansive in his discussions of the spontaneity involved in free will. But the explanatory burden of all his discussions is mostly borne by the use of reflexive pronouns and metaphors of internality and externality. Spontaneity is, in a characteristic formulation, "self-activity out of the **inner principle**" (M-Pö/L$_1$ 28:267.28, my underlining).[9]

A good first step, then, is to couch the spontaneity/receptivity distinction in terms of an inner/outer distinction. A capacity is spontaneous when the sufficient ground of its exercises is internal to the subject possessing the capacity; otherwise it is (to some degree) receptive.[10] One benefit of framing *spontaneity* and *receptivity* in terms of *inner* and *outer* is that it explains why they are not just contraries but contradictories. For it is analytic that the sufficient ground of a given determination lies either wholly within the thing whose determination it is, or partly outside it. In the first case, the determination expresses spontaneity; in the latter, some degree of receptivity.

This account treats spontaneity as a particular kind of relation; one that holds between the exercise of a capacity and something else – something *inner*. But "inner" in what sense? What is the thing whose boundaries we are marking? What are its identity conditions? Answers to these questions will determine what kind of spontaneity one has in view. A thief, Kant writes, may act out of a principle that is "internal" in the sense that her action is not the result of compulsion or coercion, but rather determined by her own avowable psychological states, such as her desires, inclinations, and personality traits. Kant admits that it is customary to call such actions "free" or "spontaneous" when they are caused by "inner representations produced by our own powers" – namely, "desires occasioned by the circumstances" – and are therefore "actions caused [*bewirkt*] in accordance with our own discretion [*Belieben*]" (*Practical* 5:96.12–15). This yields a conception of *psychological* spontaneity and receptivity. For we are here

[9] Cf. M-Pö/L$_1$ 229.23–24, 275.11–12, 285.20; *Prolegomena* 4:344.8; M-Mr 29:800.12–13, 877.32–33, 881.35–36, 913.28–29.

[10] This account of spontaneity, which invokes the principle of sufficient reason/ground as well as a particular conception of inner/outer, is most evident in Kant's marginalia in *Metaphysica* §§ 216–222, where Kant criticizes Baumgarten's accounts of action, passion, faculty, and power; see R3582–3590 (17:72–76). I hope to discuss this in future work.

fixing the boundaries of inner/outer by conceiving the agent through the concept of the soul that is central to empirical psychology – that is, through the concept of an individual human mind with a particular personality, life history, more or less stable character traits, and so forth. Actions that can be sufficiently accounted for by reference to such features of the agent count as *psychologically* spontaneous; and to the extent that they cannot be thus accounted for, they are psychologically receptive.

Alternatively, we might fix the boundaries of inner/outer through the biological concept of the human organism. This yields a conception of *organic* or *physiological* spontaneity, on which an action (or behavior) is spontaneous just in case it can be sufficiently accounted for by reference to biological features of the agent. Operating with this conception might lead us to reclassify an act of theft, which psychologists characterize as a compulsive and hence non-spontaneous expression of kleptomania, as a spontaneous expression of an underlying biological condition (e.g. of the dopamine, serotonin, and opioid systems).

Yet the conception of spontaneity we want is not psychological or biological but *cognitive*. Cognitive spontaneity comes into view when we mark the boundaries of inner/outer through the mere concept of a (practical or theoretical) cognizer. A faculty is spontaneous in this sense just in case its acts can be sufficiently accounted for by reference to features and capacities that a subject possesses merely qua cognizer, i.e. qua rational being.[11] It is, of course, a matter of extensive philosophical debate what it means to conceive a subject merely as a cognizer, and what features and capacities we must attribute to a mind thus conceived. Kant has much to say on these matters.[12] But our purposes do not require us to fill in those details. Indeed, it is an interpretive advantage of the present classification

[11] From this we can derive Kant's signature ethical doctrine that an action is free just in case it has its determining ground in the mere form of practical reason – that is, just in case it can be accounted for solely by reference to those features and capacities that an agent possesses merely in virtue of being a practical reasoner.

[12] Kant famously argues, for instance, that representing an agent as a practical reasoner involves representing her as a thing in itself – that is, as a mind outside of time (e.g. *Practical* 5:94–98, esp. 94.22–95.23). For only in this way can we make room for a kind of causal connection between agent and act that is not the mechanistic determinism of natural causality. Psychological, physiological, and other such notions of practical spontaneity yield only "a **comparative** concept of freedom", Kant argues, for the determining grounds they identify as "inner" still belong to the natural causal order (5:96.3–5). Even if these senses of "inner" meant that "the determining grounds of my causality, or even my entire existence, were not at all external to me, this would not in the least transform such natural necessity into freedom" (5:95.1–3). For I still would not have control over any of these elements, since each is determined by its temporal predecessor (5:94.30–95.9; cf. 96.19–35). For discussion, see Kitcher (2011, ch. 14). On the spontaneity involved in apperception and judgment, see Pippin (1987); Kitcher (2011, chs. 9 and 10); Boyle

that it remains neutral on such questions. The concept of cognitive spontaneity is clear enough to function as differentia, even if debates remain about how to flesh it out and about which particular faculties and acts count as instances of cognitive spontaneity. A faculty is spontaneous when its exercises are determined "from within" the mind to which the faculty belongs, where the boundary between inner and outer is fixed by the concept of a rational cognizer, merely as such.

7.3.1 Spontaneous Intuition

The first thing to emphasize about spontaneous intuition is that Kant denies that humans possess such a faculty. Indeed, he holds that we cannot even frame a positive conception of what such a capacity would be like.[13] The point of spelling out the defining criteria of spontaneous intuition is to clarify, through contrast, our conception of the sort of intuition that we do in fact possess. Such characterizations are part of a targeted analysis of human intuition; they are not descriptions of a form of mindedness that we conceive to be really possible. In *Judgment*, for example, Kant prefaces his discussion of the intuitive understanding by saying that "[t]his reflection [. . .] may enter in here only for elucidation (not for proof of what is presented)" (§ 76, 5:401). Rather, Kant writes, it is in order to appreciate "a peculiarity of our (human) understanding" that:

> the idea of a possible understanding other than the human must be presupposed [*zum Grunde liegen*] here (just as in the *Critique of P*[*ure*] *R*[*eason*] we had to think of another possible intuition, if our own [intuition] was going to be considered a particular species [*besondere Art*], namely the sort for which objects only count as appearances)[.] (*Judgment* § 77, 5:405)

Though we cannot cognize them as really possible, we must be able to think about such alternative cognitive constitutions without contradiction. Describing alternative modes of cognition is just an indirect way of highlighting peculiarities of our own cognitive constitution. Like Kant's, my account of spontaneous intuition does not aspire to describe a form of mindedness that is really possible. My aim is not to give an account of the divine mind or any other non-human mode of cognition.[14] The examples I discuss serve solely to elucidate the concept of spontaneous intuition; and

(2015); Ellis (2017); and Choi (2019). Callanan (2017) provides a fresh perspective on spontaneity that complements the interpretation sketched here.

[13] For example, B139.13–19; *Judgment* 5:406.24–25, 408.18–23; M-Mr 29:857.19–24.

[14] For a thoughtful engagement with Kant's conception of the divine mind, see Brewer (2022).

the concept of spontaneous intuition serves solely to elucidate the concept of receptive intuition and, ultimately, the concept of *human* intuition.

With that disclaimer in mind, we can turn to the case of spontaneous intuition that Kant terms "intellectual intuition".[15] To understand this label, we must recall Kant's rationale for distinguishing intellect from intuition in the human case. Human thought is not intrinsically veridical, nor are our veridical thoughts intrinsically knowledgeable. Intuition is introduced as the capacity that compensates for these cognitive shortcomings. A spontaneous intuition, then, would be a faculty that makes thoughts true and knowledgeable and that does so spontaneously – that is, by drawing solely on those features and capacities (whatever they may be) that the subject possesses merely in virtue of being a cognizer. This spontaneity is what earns the faculty the title "intellectual". Yet it also deserves the name "intuition" because its defining function is still to *give* objects to the mind.

Because it thinks objects into existence, intellectual intuition is commonly ascribed to God qua rational creator: "**originary** [intuition] is one through which the existence of the object of intuition is given (and which, so far as we can see, can only belong to the originary being [Urwesen])" (B72.16–19). This yields a picture of God as *intellectus archetypus*: as a mind whose ideas are self-realizing blueprints that generate the objects they represent.[16] This would be "an understanding that itself intuits (such as a divine [understanding] that would not represent given objects but through whose representation the objects themselves would at once be given or produced)" (B145.4–7).

These discussions of intellectual intuition are implicitly informed by specific theological assumptions. Kant assumes, in particular, (i) that there

[15] Kant does not invariably use the label "intellectual intuition" for the faculty I discuss here; he sometimes calls it an "intellect that intuits" (cf. B135.24–26, 138.6–8, 145.3–4), a "non-sensible intuition" (B149.26–27), an "*intellectus archetypus*" (A695/B723), or even "an intuition (that is [. . .] intellectual and can be given through the understanding itself)" (B159.17–18). It is not clear to me that Kant has the same faculty in view every time he uses the term "intellectual intuition" (cf. *Practical* 5:99.21). Especially when discussing non-human cognitive capacities, Kant's labels are not the most reliable indicators of the cognitive functions he has in mind. That can only be settled by considering the surrounding text.

[16] Our mind, by contrast, is an *intellectus ectypus* that traffics in copies (*ectypa*) that derive from the objects they represent – objects that exist independently of being so represented (A578/B606.21–30; cf. Kant's letter to Herz, 21 February 1772, 10:130). Kant discusses *intellectus archetypus* in more detail in *Judgment* § 77 (5:405–410), but I will focus on his account of intellectual intuition in the *Critique* (e.g. A695/B723.28–32), which bears more directly on his epistemology of human intellect and intuition. For an interpretation that contrasts the account of intellectual intuition in *Judgment* with that in *Critique*, see Förster (2002a, 2002b).

is only one *Urwesen*, (ii) that intellectual intuition constitutes its entire *Erkenntnisvermögen*, and (iii) that all knowable objects are created by its acts of intuiting. If we instead suppose a plurality of divine minds, each generating its own stream of objects, or if we simply suppose that some knowable objects have a different provenance (i.e. are not created through intellectual intuitings of the mind in question), then a power of intellectual intuition is no longer a fully general *Erkenntnisvermögen*. For intellectual intuition is only a power to know objects that are generated in the very acts of knowing them. Objects with a different genesis would have to be known (if at all) in some other way – namely, through exercises of *receptive* intuition. By the same token, the continued existence of objects known through intellectual intuition depends on the continuous intellectual activity of knowing them.[17] For if the *esse* of the knowable object is not *concipi* (to be conceived) but merely *conceptum esse* (to have been conceived), then the divine mind must additionally possess a capacity for receptive intuition in order to cognize what it *has done* in addition to what it *is doing*. It is an act of receptive intuition, not intellectual intuition, that is described in Genesis 1:31, when "God saw all that He had done and, look, it was very good."

Now, the idea of a mind whose entire *Erkenntisvermögen* consists in intellectual intuition makes sense only under certain theological assumptions.[18] On my account, our most fundamental conceptions of intuition, intellect, and cognition are our first-personal conceptions of our own forms of intuition, intellect, and cognition.[19] It is central to my interpretation, however, that what is thus first-personally accessible to us is not limited to our specifically *human* forms of mindedness but also extends to more generic aspects of our cognitive constitution – for example, the sensibility and, more generic still, the receptivity of our intuition. Inasmuch as our fundamental conceptions of cognition are first personal, they comprise only the species and genera of cognition that actually apply

[17] This picture belongs to a traditional conception of God as continuously "concurring" with the existence of all things. See, for instance, Descartes, *Meditations* (AT 7:14, 48–49); *Fifth Replies* (AT 7:369–371); *Principles* I § 51 (AT 8:25). For an intellectual intuition, such ontological concurrence is realized through acts of cognition, thus integrating God's omniscience into God's role as creator.

[18] These theological assumptions are not, however, written into the concept of intellectual intuition itself. This is one reason I disagree with Engstrom's (2006, 23n.14) suggestion that the idea of an *intellectus archetypus* (which I identify with intellectual intuition) is more fundamental than the idea of a discursive intellect paired with a receptive intuition. It is also why the concept is able to enjoy such a rich afterlife in the work of post-Kantian idealists (see Förster 2018).

[19] I further argue that these first-personal conceptions of our cognitive capacities are available through pure apperception. It is plausible that inner experience provides a further, empirical source for such first-personal conceptions of our mindedness; see Kraus (2020).

to our own case. To the extent that we can form cogent ideas of specifically different sorts of cognition, such as the idea of an intellectual intuition, those ideas are derivative. I take this to be one of Kant's fundamental breaks with the rationalist tradition of epistemology – exemplified in Descartes and Leibniz – which treats divine cognition as the fundamental standard against which human cognition is to be understood and evaluated.[20]

It is therefore instructive to observe that many – but, importantly, not all – of the terms we employ to characterize cognition begin to break down when applied to intellectual intuition, particularly under the theological assumptions just outlined. Where it is possible for something to be knowable yet unknown, it is natural to describe the agent and patient of cognition in terms that are not mutually implicating. We speak, as Kant does, of the act of knowing as a *representation* and we characterize truth as a *relation* (e.g. of correspondence or agreement) of that representation to an *object* that is conceived to be at least modally (if not really) distinct from the representation of it. For an intellectual intuition, however, such terms lose their footing, since unknown knowables are impossible by definition, as are acts of knowing that are not fully borne out in their "objects". What is knowable is an inseparable aspect of the act of knowing it, not an independent or even independently conceivable element to which intellection merely corresponds – not even if we suppose such correspondence to be metaphysically necessary. Thus, as Kant argues in *Judgment* § 76, it is not quite right to say that the thoughts of an intellectual intuition are *necessarily* true; it is more apt to say that modal determinations of necessity, possibility, and actuality have no application. Truth, here, consists not in a relation of correspondence but in something like emanation, fruition, or self-realization. If it is a relation at all, it is a peculiar sort of *self*-relation. This confounds the standard schema of *representation – correspondence relation – object*. And this may help to explain Kant's apparent hesitancy to characterize the acts of an intellectual intuition as *thoughts*.

[20] For instance, in M-Vi/K_3 (1794/95) we read:

> One admittedly says that God's understanding is sheer intuition, yet all this is words without [a] concept, which [sc. concept] of an intuiting understanding we humans at least cannot make for ourselves, and through which [sc. concept] one only wants to set the operation of the divine being into relation with the human faculty of thought; yet with God not even an analogous [mode of] thinking can be assumed. (29:954.4–10)

See also *Progress* 20:267.23–37. See Section 3.2. Jauernig (2019) sees greater continuity between Leibniz and Kant on the relation of human to divine cognition.

Significantly, however, this terminological breakdown is not total. Even in the case of intellectual intuition, one can still make out a rational (notional) distinction between act and object, agent and patient, of cognition. Act and object are inseparable aspects of a single unity and cannot be conceived except in relation to one another. But they are nevertheless distinguishable and, indeed, asymmetrically related: The act determines the object, not vice versa. This is the sort of distinction that the language of hylomorphism is perfectly suited to capture. As Pollok aptly puts it, the divine *intellectus archetypus* "creates real matter in an ideal form" so that "the objective world is the content of God's ideas" (2017, 222). Though the entanglement of agent and patient confounds the traditional representationalist model of cognition, the language of hylomorphism registers that act and object are distinguishable yet mutually implicating and asymmetrically related aspects of an essential unity – a unity in which *matter* is determined by *form*.

The form/matter distinction is, in this respect, a more fundamental (more generic) characterization of intuition than talk of representations and their objects.[21] The idea of intuition *as representational* comes into view only at a lower level of specification: namely, with the idea of an intuition that is *receptive* – that is, one whose exercises are at least modally (if not really) distinct from their contents. The content of intuition is conceivable not merely as *matter* but as *object of representation* only on the assumption that the intuit*ed* exists independently of our intuit*ing*: as something that can "stand against" us (a *Gegen-stand*) or that we find "cast before" us (an *Ob-ject*). But this etymological presumption that objects are independent of acts of intuiting holds only if intuition is receptive in securing the existence and cognitive availability of its content. Thus, the content of intuition is determinable merely as *matter* at the level of intuition *überhaupt* and becomes a knowable *object* only at the level of *receptive* intuition. Further specification will yield *concrete* (i.e. causally efficacious) *particulars* at the level of *sensible* intuition; and determinate *spatiotemporal* individuals at the level of *human* outer sense (see Section 8.3.1).

It is tempting to align this form/matter distinction with the two conditions of givenness: the matter of intuition corresponds to the existence

[21] I do not mean to suggest that Kant's account of intellectual intuition provides the primary rationale for his hylomorphic characterizations of intuition or cognition. But the aptness of such concepts for characterizing intellectual intuition does reveal how fundamental they are when used to characterize *human* intuition.

condition, the form of intuition to the cognitive availability of that matter.[22] Certainly, when Kant deploys hylomorphic language to characterize acts of intellectual intuition, what he juxtaposes (as form) to the manifold (the matter) of intuition is the *unity of consciousness* that unites the manifold.[23] And it is attractive, in the case of human intuition, to be able to say that space and time are the forms in which the manifold of sensation is made available to cognition, but are not existents (*entia*) in their own right that are given with, or in, or as that manifold.[24] As I observed previously (Section 7.2), however, the cognitive-availability condition is the site of the most contentious debates about intellectualism/sensibilism. And I do not see a way to pursue this suggestion about the form/matter distinction without prejudicing that issue.

One final point about Kant's account of intellectual intuition. Kant invokes intellectual intuition both in the Aesthetic, to serve as a conceptual foil for sensible intuition (B68, B72), and in the Transcendental Deduction, to serve as a conceptual foil for discursive understanding (B135, B138–139, B145, B149, B153, B159). This indicates that the idea of a discursive understanding and the idea of a sensible (or, properly speaking, receptive) intuition, which may seem quite distinct, are in fact inseparable. If possessing a non-discursive understanding entails having an intellectual intuition, yet possessing a non-receptive intuition also entails having an intellectual intuition, then any mind capable of cognition but lacking intellectual intuition must have *both* a discursive understanding *and* a receptive intuition. The conceptions of discursive understanding and of receptive intuition must be elaborated in concert or not at all. This lends support to my "top-down" approach to human intuition as a cognitive capacity. For it suggests that the cognitive character of our receptive intuition may be explicable in terms of our apperceptive grasp on the nature of our discursive intellect.

7.3.2 *Hybrid Conceptions of Spontaneous Intuition*

I have argued that intuitive givenness involves two conditions. Intuition must, first of all, secure the truth evaluability of thought – that is, the

[22] I owe this suggestion to Jess Tizzard.

[23] See, for instance, B68.30–34, B138–139.6–13; compare also his characterizations of an apperception that does *not* generate the manifold of cognition, B135.20–21.

[24] See especially A291/B347.26–32 and R6324 (1790–1793) 18:647.17–27. Kant distinguishes actuality (and actualities) from existence (and existents) and explicitly identifies space and time as actualities that are not existents proper, but mere forms of existents.

possibility of a thought's agreeing or disagreeing with its intended object.[25] This (dis)agreement can obtain only if the object exists. So intuition enables the truth evaluability of thoughts by guaranteeing the existence of the object. Acts of intuition are, in that sense, object involving.[26] Knowledge, however, requires not just truth but consciousness of truth. So, in addition to ensuring the existence of thought's object, intuition must make this object cognitively available, as agreeing (or disagreeing) with thought. Kant conceives these conditions, we noted in Section 7.2, as distinguishable but inseparable aspects of a unified act. It is *in* securing the existence of the object that intuition renders it available to cognition. The object's availability to cognition involves its existence.

It is nevertheless tempting to view these conditions as distinct differentiae. And doing so invites the question whether one condition might be satisfied receptively, the other spontaneously. Förster (2002a, 178n.12) has suggested that emanation theories of vision, such as one finds in Plato, describe a quasi-spontaneous intuition: one that is receptive with respect to the existence of visible objects but spontaneous in making them available to cognition.[27] It is instructive to consider such theories from a Kantian perspective, in order to vindicate the criterion of givenness as a single, unified differentia and, thus, to confirm the division of intuition *überhaupt* into exactly two species: one wholly spontaneous, the other not.

Plato's Socrates argues that the eye emits an intraocular fire that coalesces with the fire of ambient light to form a "single homogeneous body" that acts as a visual sensorium, which "transmits the motions of whatever it comes into contact with" (*Timaeus* 45b–d; cf. 67c–e). We cannot see in the dark because there is no ambient light to mix with the fire emanating from our eyes. Vision, on this account, functions like touch, except that the medium of visual perception is forged afresh through the interaction of the eyes' fire with the ambient fire radiating

[25] Here and throughout, "object" means *knowable* object in the sense of *ground of truth for synthetic judgment*, as outlined in Chapter 2. We cannot simply assume that objects of intuition are material, spatiotemporal particulars without begging important questions about the character of truth makers. A question that I do not take up here but hope to pursue in future work is, how objects must be structured in order to be able to serve as truth makers for thought. That is, what formal features must *intuitive* contents exhibit in order to be capable of dispositively confirming and disconfirming *judgments* of specific forms? Answering this question is tantamount to offering a Metaphysical Deduction of the formal features of receptive intuition.

[26] I say "object involving" rather than "object dependent", because the dependence relation can run in either direction: The intuiting may depend on the object (receptive intuition), or the object on the intuiting (spontaneous intuition).

[27] On ancient emanation theories of vision and their later reception, see Lindberg (1976).

from luminous bodies. The sighted person uses this lightsaber as a blind person uses a white cane.

What is interesting about this account, for our purposes, is its structure. Vision is obviously a paradigm case of outer intuition. Yet here the act of vision seems to unite a *receptivity* to existing visible objects with a *spontaneous* activity that makes them available to cognition. On reflection, however, these moments must be distinct acts of different capacities.

First, if we grant that the spontaneous emission of intraocular fire is responsible for the cognitive availability of visibilia, we must also accept that it secures their existence: "the eye and some other thing [i.e. a visible object] [...] generate both whiteness and the perception which is by nature united with it [sc. whiteness] (things which would never have come to be if it had been anything else that eye or object approached)" (*Theaetetus* 156d, my underlining). What the soul perceives of visible objects are their visible qualities – for example, their colors. These *perceptibilia* simply do not exist in the absence of the soul's activity of emitting intraocular fire. So, if we credit the spontaneous aspect of vision (i.e. the emission of intraocular fire) with making perceptual content cognitively available, we must also credit it with securing the existence of that content.

On the other hand, if we insist that the soul is receptive with respect to the existence of what it sees – since the soul's activity does not, after all, determine *what* is seen (e.g. white rather than green) but only *that* it is seen – then we must also grant that the soul is receptive in making this available to cognition. For what determines the specific quality that is seen is the visible object – namely, its disposition to produce certain motions in the "single homogeneous body" that coalesces out of intraocular fire and ambient light. This visible object, with its dispositions to produce certain motions, exists independently of the soul's spontaneous emission of intraocular fire (cf. *Timaeus* 67d–e). By the same token, however, it is not the soul's spontaneity in emitting intraocular fire that makes the object (and its dispositions) available to cognition, but rather the soul's *receptive* capacity to become conscious of (i.e. to be affected by) the motions transmitted through the resulting medium.

In these cases, then, we have either a single capacity that is spontaneous with respect to *both* existence and cognitive availability, or one that is receptive in both respects. It would, of course, be hasty to conclude from this that a unified cognitive capacity for intuition cannot, as a matter of conceptual necessity, satisfy the givenness criterion in a hybrid fashion. But the present argument does highlight a general line of response that is available to a defender of Kant. For the manner in which the existence condition is satisfied must be quite intimately related to the way that the cognitive availability condition is satisfied, in order for the capacity to count as both *single* (unified) and *cognitive*. Thus, a Kantian will always be able to argue (i) that the conditions are satisfied so independently that we are left with distinct acts of different capacities, or (ii) that their connection is so intimate that they must be realized in the same fashion (spontaneous or receptive), or not at all.

The second move is conspicuous in my sketched interpretation of Plato. For it argues that, insofar as the emission of intraocular fire is both spontaneous and cognitively significant, the object it renders available to cognition (the whiteness that is perceived) depends, for its existence, on that same spontaneous activity. Insofar as the soul is receptive with respect to the existence of what is seen (the visible object), however, it must be likewise receptive in cognitively accessing that content (in being affected by the motions transmitted through the visual medium). The acts and their contents are too intimately connected to be realized in a hybrid fashion, partly spontaneously, partly receptively. And the interpretation implicitly makes the first move as well. For it effectively claims that the soul's receptivity with respect to the existence condition (the visible object) is not intimately enough related to its spontaneity with respect to cognitive availability (emission of intraocular fire) for the two to constitute unified aspects of a single capacity's exercise. Insofar as either of these activities is to be conceived as belonging to a single, intrinsically cognitive capacity, it must satisfy the other givenness condition in just the same (receptive or spontaneous) fashion that it does the first.

This argument is far from decisive. But it gives us reason to defer to Kant in treating givenness as a single criterion with distinguishable but inseparable aspects.

7.3.3 Receptive Intuition

Since Chapter 8 provides positive and increasingly specific characterizations of the receptivity of human intuition, the most important point to register here is how very abstract the bare notion of receptivity is. It does not yet involve the idea of causal affection, still less the idea of sensation. It merely signifies an intuition that is not productive in the manner an intellectual intuition is. It denotes a cognitive capacity for intuition, where the sufficient grounds of its respective exercises do not lie *wholly* within the mind in question, considered merely qua cognizer or rational being. Acts of receptive intuition, merely as such, are determined by factors external to the mind merely as knower. Both the character of these external factors and the nature of the determining relation are left entirely unspecified. The external factor could be a real universal (a Platonic Form), a concrete spatiotemporal particular, or the hand of God in bestowing a particular individual nature on the mind. The determining relations in which these factors stand to the mind are as varied as the factors themselves. Likewise, the sorts of contents that can be intuited via these determining relations vary considerably. Although the mystical intuition of a Platonic Form is, in some sense, determined by a unique and singular "object", that object is a universal: something that can be common to many individuals.[28] So we should be leery about assuming that receptive intuition must be a kind of *singular* representation, and should certainly resist the idea that receptive intuitions intrinsically refer to concrete (causally efficacious) particulars or maximally determinate individuals (see Section 8.3.1).

To further underscore the diversity that this abstract notion of receptivity allows for – with respect to the character of the (external) determining ground, the relation of determination, and the type of representational content – we might briefly consider the practical analogue of our reflections on intuition as a capacity that contributes to theoretical cognition.[29] Kant famously writes, for instance, that respect (*Achtung*) is a "feeling not **received** through influence but **self-actuated** [*selbstgewirktes*] through a rational concept" (*Groundwork* 4:401n.20–21; cf. 435.17–24). This might initially suggest that respect is an expression of the spontaneity of practical cognition, inasmuch as its sufficient determining ground (viz. "a rational concept") is internal to the mind in question. Yet Kant goes on to argue:

> The immediate determination of the will through the law and the consciousness of this [determination] is called **respect**, so that it [sc. respect] is regarded as the **effect** of the law on the subject and not as its **cause**. (*Groundwork* 4:401n.25–28)

[28] On the individuation of Platonic Forms as unique but essentially relational abstract objects, see Irani (2022).

[29] Kant invites such an analogy in *Practical* (5:89–90), where he aligns intuition, as the sensible capacity relevant to theoretical cognition, with feeling, as the sensible capacity relevant to practical cognition. He even suggests that his account of moral feeling is a sort of "Aesthetic of pure practical reason" (*Practical* 5:90.14–15), on analogy with the Transcendental Aesthetic in the *Critique*. The crucial disanalogy in the case we are considering is that respect (like all feeling) is a merely subjective state and thus does not involve the existence of any object, however else it may contribute to practical cognition. Tizzard (2018) offers a trenchant exposition of the analogy between respect as the formal aspect of practical sensibility and spatiotemporality as the formal aspect of theoretical sensibility.

Insofar as respect is to be viewed as the effect of the moral law on us, through our rational concept of that law, it is ultimately an expression of our receptivity, our susceptibility to external determination, even if this external influence also involves our cognitive spontaneity – namely, our ability to frame "a rational concept" of the law. A few years later, in *Practical*, Kant appears to walk back the idea that respect is "a particular species of feeling" in its own right, in the sense of having a distinctive phenomenology and inner psychological character (5:74.30–75.5; cf. 72.32–34). Yet he argues that it is nonetheless appropriate to call respect "**moral feeling**" (5:75.18) because it is still to be understood as an influence on the inclinations (*Neigungen*) of the subject:

> Now since everything that is found in self-love belongs to inclination, and all inclination rests on feelings, what abjures all inclinations collectively in self-love thus necessarily has, in just that respect, an influence on feeling[.] (*Practical* 5:74.30–33, my underlining)

What Kant is most concerned to retain, even as he seems prepared to concede that respect is not a feeling proper, is the idea that respect manifests the *receptivity* of the practical subject. Even if respect is to be understood as a mere privation of all self-interested inclination, not as a full-fledged feeling in its own right, it belongs to the agent not as a mere practical reasoner but as "rational and affected [afficirten] by inclinations" (*Practical* 5:75.11, my underlining). A holy will – an agent whose inclinations (if they have any) necessarily align with the moral law – could not experience respect any more than an intellectual intuition could experience sensation (or its privation):

> It must be remarked that, since respect is an effect on feeling and hence on the sensibility of a rational being, it presupposes this sensibility and thus also the finitude of such beings on whom the moral law imposes respect, and that respect for the **law** cannot be attributed to a supreme being or even one free from all sensibility, one for whom it [sc. sensibility] thus cannot be a hindrance to practical reason. (*Practical* 5:76.8–15)

It is an indication of just how thin the present notion of receptivity is that the feeling of respect would still qualify as receptive. The fact that respect "is effected [*bewirkt*] solely through reason" and thus through our spontaneous cognition of the moral law is not enough to make it an expression of spontaneity (5:76.16–17; cf. 90.6–9). By the same token, intuitions of my own mental states are not made spontaneous by the fact that "what determines the inner sense is the understanding and its original faculty for combining the manifold of intuition" (B153.4–6). Nor is respect any less receptive in virtue of the fact that nothing is, properly speaking, *received*, since "no feeling at all [*gar kein Gefühl*] for this [moral] law takes place", but only the "clearing away [*Wegräumung*]" of self-interested feelings (5:75.13–15). For neither would any sensations be received if, "as one can very well conceive [*ganz wohl denken kann*], no objects [*Gegenstände*] [were] to be met with in [space]"; yet space itself would remain as a form for *receiving* sensations (A24/B38f.19–20).

The conception of receptivity that comes into view at this high level of abstraction is inordinately thin: It admits everything that fails to exhibit the unconditional cognitive spontaneity outlined in Section 7.3. If the exercises of a capacity cannot be fully accounted for by reference to features and capacities that the subject possesses merely qua cognizer, then it is receptive. Differentiating the specific character of human receptivity amid the wild variety of intuitive capacities that fit this description is the task of Chapter 8.

8

A Stufenleiter *of Kantian Intuition, Part II*

Receptivity and Sensibility

Chapter 7 concluded by emphasizing how very abstract the notion of cognitive receptivity is. The class of receptive intuitive capacities is broad and motley and can, accordingly, be sorted into species in a variety of ways. There are a few cases of receptive but non-human intuition that Kant repeatedly discusses. But apart from denying that we possess them, Kant does not indicate how they specifically differ from human intuition. So the next specific differentia in our *Stufenleiter* is motivated partly by extensional adequacy and partly by an account of what features matter to the human case.[1] Thus, I aim (i) to exclude the cases Kant excludes at roughly the level of abstraction where he excludes them and (ii) to exclude them for reasons that Kant would recognize and that illuminate interesting and important features of human intuition.

8.1 Sensible-Affection Dependence as Differentia

I propose to divide the genus, *receptive intuition*, into species via the differentia, *dependence on sensible affection*. Sensible affection is a causal relation in which one of the relata is a representational act/state in a mind (*Gemüt*). A paradigm case might involve a physical object impinging on my sense organs so as to occasion an empirical perception. It is important to note, however, that not all sensible affection involves the physical stimulation of our sense organs. If it did, (i) all sensible intuition would be empirical, since it would essentially involve sensation and (ii) inner intuition would be impossible, since we have no dedicated organ of "inner sense" nor a distinctive manifold of "inner sensations" analogous to our

[1] It is not uncommon for extensional considerations to inform *Stufenleiter* in this way. As I suggest in Section 6.4, *mortal* may well have been introduced into Pophyry's eponymous tree to distinguish human rational animals from a newly salient class of angelic ones. As targeted analytical tools, *Stufenleiter* only take account of contrasts that are relevant to the explanatory project they subserve.

"outer" sensations – for example, of pink, cold, or the pitch A440. Kant must therefore distinguish merely *sensible* affection from *sensory* affection – that is, a modification of our physical sensorium that gives rise to an array of sensations.

The challenge, then, is to characterize a relation of determination that is more specific than mere affection (cognitive receptivity to determination from without) but more generic than sensory affection (physical stimulation of the sense organs). Charting this middle course raises a number of interesting questions about Kant's idealism (Section 8.1.2) as well as his views on natural causation (Section 8.2.1) and the mind–body relation (Section 8.2.2).

8.1.1 Receptive but Non-Sensible Intuition

Kant offers only scattered remarks about modes of receptive intuition that do not involve sensible affection. These are usually designed to contrast his own account of human mindedness with some conception of cognition drawn from the history of philosophy. Kant is particularly concerned with two types of case, both of which figure in his famous 1772 letter to Herz:[2]

(1) The "hyperphysical influx" that he takes to be involved in the Platonic theory of recollection and in Malebranche's doctrine that we "see all things in God"; and
(2) The "preestablished harmony" that Kant attributes to Crusius (a different version of which could also be attributed to Leibniz and Wolff).

The principal rationale behind my proposed differentia, *sensible-affection dependence*, is that it explains why these cases are salient alternatives to human receptivity, while also emphasizing an aspect of human intuition that is interesting and important in its own right.

Now, in the 1772 letter to Herz, Kant admittedly discusses hyperphysical influx and preestablished harmony as competing accounts of how "intellectual representations" might relate to their objects (10:130.25–131.01, my underlining). But it is apparent, on reflection, that the modes of representation he describes also satisfy our twofold "givenness" criterion of intuition. They (i) secure the existence of their represented objects (ii) in making them cognitively available. This makes them intuitions, on the functional conception we are working with,

[2] See also R4859 (1776–1778) 18:12.2–4; M-Mr 29:796.38–797.18.

despite the fact that the representational contents "given" through them have a logical form that we customarily associate with the intellect.[3] And indeed, Kant consistently describes the "hyperphysical influx" he attributes to Malebranche and (more frequently) to Plato as an "*Anschauen*".[4] According to Kant, Plato takes this intuiting to occur prior to the incarnation of the soul, whereas Malebranche thinks it is "still ongoing and ever-present" in ordinary experience (10:131.25). But both take our cognition of first principles and privileged universals (10:131.24) to result from a special kind of non-physical affection by a non-sensory object – the Forms, for Plato; God, for Malebranche.

This affection clearly qualifies as the sort of external determination that defines cognitive receptivity. After all, Kant's guiding question in the 1772 letter to Herz is: "Upon what ground does the relation rest of that in us which is called representation to the object?" (10:130.7–8, my underlining). The grounding relation proposed by Plato and Malebranche involves a relatum external to the mind, conceived merely qua cognizer. So the determining relation here, the grounding, involves cognitive receptivity on the part of the cognizer. Moreover, the grounding is "hyperphysical" – i.e. non-natural and, hence, non-sensible.[5] We thus have a case of intuition that is both receptive and non-sensible. Our differentia neatly captures Kant's discussion of these cases.[6]

[3] Here it helps to recall the principles of our "capacities-first" approach to the mind. The term 'intuition' does not track *acts* of representation that exhibit this or that property (e.g. singularity of content). Rather, 'intuition' is the title of a cognitive capacity, whose contribution to knowledge is specified in functional terms.

[4] 10:131.23, 25; cf. M-Vi/K_3 (1794/95) 29:950.25–29, 953.36–954.18, 957.25–29; R4449 (around 1771) 17:555.18–20; R4446 (1771?) 18:554.1; M-Pö/L_1 28:232.23–27, 241.15–24. The intuitive status of representations on the preestablished-harmony view is less obvious and will be addressed presently.

[5] Kant characteristically understands "*physisch*" and its cognates in the etymological sense of "having to do with nature". See, for instance, his division of material philosophy into ethics, which concerns *freedom*, and physics, which concerns *nature* (*Groundwork* 4:387).

[6] One can easily contrive further cases of "hyperphysical influx". Prophetic and divine revelations seem to fit the bill, for instance, as does the "spirit seeing" Kant dismantles in *Dreams* (cf. M-Pö/L_1 28:300.4–19; M-Pö/L_2 28:593.28–34). It also fits Kant's speculations about the disembodied human soul. After death, Kant muses, "when the sort of sensibility should cease through which transcendental and, for now, wholly unknown objects appear as [the] material world, that need not annul all intuitions of them [sc. those objects], and it is quite possible that these very unknown objects continue to be cognized by the thinking subject, albeit no longer in the quality of bodies" (A393.14–394.30, my underlining). Such non-sensible intuitings would presumably remain receptive, since it is hardly plausible that death should elevate us to the status of gods, endowing us with spontaneous, productive intuition. In his metaphysics lectures, Kant repeatedly suggests that "the separation of the soul from the body consists in the change of sensible intuition into spiritual intuition" (M-Pö/L_1 28:297.37–39), i.e. a receptive but non-sensible intuition of things-in-themselves. See M-Mr 29:919.23–30; M-Vo 28:445.18–446.18; M-Pö/L_2 28:592.34–593.16.

The non-sensible character of the determining relation is even more evident in the case of "preestablished harmony".[7] Being created is clearly not a case of being sensibly affected. For it is only in being created that a creature first comes to possess a capacity for sensible affection. Any "*anerschaffene*" dispositions that God implants in a creature in the very act of creating it – for example, "certain implanted rules for judging and concepts" (10:131.27) – cannot result from sensible affection. Yet finite creatures are obviously passive – that is, receptive – vis-à-vis God's act of creating them. Finite beings do not spontaneously bootstrap themselves into existence. Neither do they self-generate their own natures and innate capacities. Thus, according to our differentia, the possession of such innate capacities – and their subsequent exercise – manifests a non-sensible receptivity just as Kant claims.

Now, one may want here to separate the question, whether a certain capacity is receptively *acquired*, from the question, whether the *exercises* of the capacity, once acquired, are receptive. Surely, one might object, the fact that certain "rules for judging" are innate or implanted does not preclude the judgments one makes in accordance with those rules from being spontaneous.

But recall that, for Kant, the central question is: "Upon what ground does the relation rest of that in us which is called representation to the object?" (10:131.7–8) On the conception of cognitive spontaneity developed in Section 7.3, the ground of the relation between representing and object must be *internal* to the subject, considered merely qua cognizer, for the representing to count as spontaneous. This condition is not satisfied in Crusius's system of preestablished harmony.[8] In a system of preestablished harmony, the relation between representation and object

[7] Kant later describes this view as "a preformation system of pure reason" (B167.27), by which he likely has in mind not just Crusius but also an objection raised by Johann Schultz in his review of Ulrich's *Institutiones Logicae et Metaphysicae* (Schultz 1785, 299; Sassen 2000, 214). That Schultz is Kant's target at B167 is suggested by Kant's footnote in *Metaphysical Foundations* (4:474n.–476n.; see Allison 2015, ch. 7 section II). Kant's criticism applies equally to Leibniz's account of preestablished harmony (see note 8). It is also worth observing that, in the context of discussing embryology and the epigenesis/preformationism debate, Kant labels the preformationist view "hyperphysical" (*Judgment* 5:423.12–36). For Kant's extension of the idea of epigenesis into epistemological contexts, with special reference to the Herz letter, see Mensch (2013, ch. 4).

[8] This holds a fortiori for Leibniz's preestablished harmony. Whereas Crusius claims that only "certain [...] rules for judging and [certain] concepts" are implanted in us by God at creation, Leibniz holds that *every* state of a substance is determined by an innate internal principle: "We also see that every substance has a perfect spontaneity (which becomes freedom in intelligent substances), that everything that happens to it is a consequence of its idea or of its being, and that nothing determines it, except God alone." (*Discourse on Metaphysics* § 30; cf. §§ 13–14, 31, 32; see also *New System of Nature* (G 4:484–485; AG 143–144); *Theodicy* § 400; *Monadology* §11 and § 15)

obtains (if it does) through the grace of God, not on account of the subject's own powers as a rational being. Now one might argue, as a point of theodicy, that it is metaphysically necessary for the appropriate relation between representation and object to obtain. But this necessity would still be due to the nature of God, not the cognitive powers of the mind entertaining it.[9] Such representations remain cognitively receptive in the relevant sense.

Kant elaborates this position in later critical works, such as his colorful objection that Leibniz's system of preestablished harmony affords us only "the freedom of a turnspit" (*Practical* 5:97.19; cf. M-Pö/L$_{I}$ 28:267–271). Kant grants that there is "comparative" spontaneity in the representations and actions of a creature when they spring from its internal powers and dispositions. But he argues that issuing from an "internal" determining ground is not, of itself, sufficient for genuine spontaneity and freedom:

> When it comes to the question of the sort of freedom that must underlie all moral laws and responsibility in accordance with them, it is wholly irrelevant whether the determining grounds lie **within** the subject or **outside** it, if the causality is determined according to a natural law[.] (*Practical* 5:96.19–23)

For if the causality operates according to natural necessity, then each state is determined by the ones preceding it, regardless of whether those states are inner or outer, psychological or physiological, spiritual or material. Because its every action is predetermined by prior states, to exercise such a power is to behave as an automaton:

> Here we look only to the necessity of the connection of events in a temporal series, as it unfolds in accordance with the natural law, and one can call the subject in which this process [*Ablauf*] takes place *automaton materiale*, where the machinery is driven by matter, or with Leibniz [*automaton*] *spirituale*, where it is driven by representations, but if the freedom of our will were none but the latter (e.g. psychological and comparative not simultaneously transcendental, i.e. absolute), then it would be

Though this determining ground may be *in* the Leibnizian substance, it is crucially not *of* it. From a Kantian perspective, there is only a difference of degree between Crusius's and Leibniz's systems of preestablished harmony, for "with such a hypothesis one can see no end to how far one might carry the presupposition of predetermined dispositions for future judgments" (B167.28–30). Kant explicitly associates Leibniz and Crusius on this point in M-Mr 29:761.20–24.

9 By the same token, Kant need not deny that we are creatures of God nor that many of our cognitive capacities are innate in the sense of being determined to exist in us through God's act of creation. What Kant denies is that it is *in virtue of* this act of creation that our representations *relate to objects* in the sense relevant for cognition. Kant aspires to a theology-free epistemology.

> fundamentally no better than the freedom of a turnspit, which also executes its movements of itself, once it is wound up. (*Practical* 5:97.11–20)[10]

It is tempting to read Kant's objection to Leibniz's spiritual automata as motivated by his desire to preserve so-called "liberty of indifference": the counterfactually robust freedom to do or forebear. And Kant does indeed hold that "the assessment [*Beurteilung*] of the moral law" "presupposes that [an immoral act] could indeed have been omitted [*unterlassen*]" (*Practical* 5:95.32–34). Yet I think this captures only part of Kant's complaint. The problem is not merely that Leibniz offers us necessity where the moral law demands liberty but that Leibniz, like Crusius, offers a necessity of the wrong sort.[11] Kant's objection is that systems of preestablished harmony can deliver only a *subjective* necessity, whereas genuine cognition – whether of the moral law or of synthetic truths – demands a form of *objective* necessity.

From a Kantian perspective, when a Leibnizian agent acts freely, the ultimate reason why she acts as she does is because it is her subjective constitution so to act: Her action is determined by the individual nature that she is created possessing.[12] If that action accords with the moral law (either contingently or as a matter of necessity), that is a separate fact, which obtains through the grace of God. Such accord is not due to the agent's own cognitive powers as practical reasoner. Preestablished harmony makes it strictly impossible to act *on the objective ground* that the moral law demands such action. One can only ever act on the *subjective* ground that one cannot help but *represent* an action as demanded by the moral law.[13] It is then up to God to arrange the universe so that this subjective appearance is actually (or even necessarily) valid. This makes the action receptive, according to the criterion of cognitive spontaneity sketched earlier (Section 7.3). For the agent's action, as morally valid, cannot be understood or accounted for by reference to features and capacities that the agent possesses merely qua practical reasoner. An elaborate theodicy must be appended in addition.

[10] Leibniz speaks of the mind as a "spiritual automaton" at *Theodicy* § 87; *Monadology* § 18; *New System of Nature* (G 4:485; AG 144).

[11] After all, Kant's own view is that true freedom, genuine autonomy, involves the "necessitation" of the will by the moral law. See *Groundwork* 4:413.2–8; *Practical* 5:32; *Metaphysics of Morals* 6:223. The ability to do what the law forbids, or to omit what the law commands, is not a freedom worthy of the name.

[12] Tellingly, this is also the ultimate reason why a Leibnizian agent acts as she does when her action is *not* free.

[13] Accordingly, Leibniz characterizes freedom as the power to seek what *appears* to be good (e.g. *Discourse on Metaphysics* § 30).

By contrast, the ultimate reason a Kantian agent acts as she does, when she acts freely, is because the rational form of her will, which finds expression in the moral law, objectively requires that she so act. Her action, her practical cognition, is spontaneous because we do not need to appeal to anything other than the nature of the agent as a practical reasoner to explain why she does what she does and why this necessarily coincides with what the moral law demands.[14]

The B-edition Transcendental Deduction applies the same line of argument to the case of theoretical cognition. Kant claims that there are just two ways of explaining a "**necessary** agreement of experience with the concepts of its [sc. experience's] objects: Either experience makes these concepts possible, or these concepts make experience possible." (B166.3–7) Kant, of course, has just argued for the latter option in lieu of the empiricist alternative. But he observes that "a sort of preformation system of pure reason" (B167.27) might seem to offer "a middle course" (B167.20). The categories, on this view:

> would be neither **self-thought** first principles a priori of our cognition, nor derived from experience, but subjective dispositions for thinking [*Anlagen zum Denken*] implanted in us with our existence, which are so contrived [*eingerichtet*] by our creator that their use exactly agrees with the laws of nature according to which experience proceeds. (B167)

What Kant finds objectionable in such an account is obviously not that it fails to make room for libertarian freedom in theoretical cognition. For there is no such freedom: We are not free to refrain from applying the categories to experience.[15] Kant's objection is rather that the necessity by which we are compelled to apply the categories to objects of experience must be of the right sort. A preformation system of pure reason yields only a "subjective necessity" (B168.3).[16] On this view, we think as we do on account of inborn dispositions implanted in us at creation. We can at most

[14] This account of the spontaneity of moral action may appear to conflict with my characterization of respect (*Achtung*) as receptive (Section 7.3.3). For the feeling of respect is likewise grounded in features of the agent that belong to her merely as a practical reasoner. I think we should conceive respect as analogous to pure sensible intuition. The latter is sensible (and a fortiori receptive) rather than spontaneous because it rests on self-affection. Yet it remains pure, despite involving sensible affection, because the affection issues from the merely formal aspects of the relevant spontaneous cognitive faculty – the understanding in the case of formal intuitions; the will (i.e. practical reason) in the case of respect. See Section 8.1.2.

[15] A point rightly emphasized by Callanan (2017); cf. Boyle (forthcoming-b).

[16] Somewhat counterintuitively, genuine spontaneity of cognition requires an objective necessity, in order to ensure the objective validity of synthetic a priori judgments. See, for instance, Shaddock (2015).

claim that "I am so constituted [*eingerichtet*] that I cannot think this representation except as so connected" (B168.6–8). If such thinking agrees (actually or necessarily) with the objects we represent, that is a separate fact, which obtains through the grace of God or some other structural feature of the preformation system in which the mind is caught up. The agreement is, in that sense, due to a factor external to the mind, considered merely qua cognizer.[17] Such a capacity would be cognitively receptive, according to our criteria. So an intuition governed by a preestablished harmony would be a receptive but non-sensible cognitive capacity, like cases of hyperphysical influx.[18]

8.1.2 Sensible Intuition

Human intuition essentially involves sensible affection. It is for this reason that Kant speaks of inner and outer "sense" and calls time and space "forms of sensibility" (A41/B58.26–27 *et passim*). But not all sensible affection involves sensory affection, i.e. the material stimulation of a sense organ that gives rise to a manifold of sensations. How should we conceive of affection that is sensible but non-sensory? Here we confront some of the

[17] Because the ground of this agreement is so very external to the mind, one might question whether *any* representation governed by a preestablished harmony could fulfill the twofold givenness criterion of intuition. Even if such a representation were, in fact, necessarily correlated with the existence of its intentional object, it is doubtful whether that fact is made cognitively available to the subject through that very act of representing. Genuine knowledge involves consciousness of the truth of one's judgments. Here, such consciousness would seem to require knowledge of the preestablished harmony that guarantees the agreement of representation and object. But such knowledge does not appear to be contained in the mere act of representing an object. This is one important sense in which Leibniz "intellectualized appearances" (A271/B327.10–11): A system of preestablished harmony seems to preclude the possibility of Kantian intuitings. This would not threaten our classification. It would merely mean that preestablished harmony cannot be used to illustrate the heading, *receptive but non-sensible intuition.*

[18] Another case that arguably involves a preestablished harmony is Aquinas's picture of angelic cognition (e.g. *ST* I, q.54–58). On the one hand, Aquinas holds that angelic cognition is exclusively intellectual (*ST* I, q.54, a.5) and that angels' intellects are neither passive nor active, since that modal distinction obtains only for minds like ours, which can understand something potentially yet not actually (*ST* I, q.54, a.4). On the other hand, the knowledge angels enjoy is not due to their mere substance or essence, as divine knowledge is (*ST* I, q.55, a.1). Rather, angels cognize through "species" (*ST* I, q.55, a.1) – that is, through discrete mental representations of intelligible things, as finite minds do (*ST* I, q.84, a.2). The intelligible species through which angels cognize, however, are not acquired via sensation or affection by external things, since angels have no bodies: They are instead "connatural" to the angel (*ST* I, q.55, a.2; unlike in the human case: *ST* I, q.84, a.3). That is to say, they are implanted in the angel with or through its nature. Angelic cognition of mundane things is, in that sense, an instance of a preformation system of pure reason. If it is reasonable to assume that angelic cognitive "species" satisfy the twofold givenness criterion, then Aquinas's angels would possess a kind of receptive but non-sensible intuition, in Kant's terms (see also note 24). To my knowledge, Kant never discusses angelic cognition.

murkiest and most contentious issues in Kant's transcendental epistemology, namely his doctrines of figurative synthesis and self-affection.

Figurative synthesis is supposed to account for the possibility of intuitions that are sensible yet pure (not empirical). Any intuiting that involves *sensory* affection is empirical by definition, since sensation just is "the effect [*Wirkung*] of an object on the capacity for representation, insofar as we are affected by it" (A19/B34.23–24) and a representation is pure just in case it contains "nothing that belongs to sensation" (A20/B34.18). By contrast, pure intuitions, such as the formal intuitions we appeal to in geometry, involve "an effect [*Wirkung*] of the understanding on sensibility" (B152.5–6; cf. A119.10–14, A120.20–24). As Kant famously declares, "we cannot think a line without **drawing** it in thought, a circle without **describing** it" (B154.5–7; cf. A102.22–34).[19] Here it is not an external object that affects the mind so as to occasion an intuitive representation but the mind's own spontaneity of understanding, operating as a "power of imagination", "a faculty for determining sensibility a priori" (B152.1–2).[20]

At the heart of this account is the difficult notion of self-affection, which Kant himself regards as paradoxical: "we intuit ourselves only as we are internally **affected**, which seems to be contradictory, insofar as we would have to relate to ourselves passively [*leidend*]" (B153.22–23, Kant's emphasis; cf. 156.21–22, 156n.).[21] The apparent contradiction arises, I take it, because such affection is a *causal* relation. Causal interactions seem to require some sort of "gap" between the agent exercising a causal

[19] As Friedman (2000, 2012) observes, drawing a line and describing a circle are the two fundamental rigid motions in Euclidean geometry, which are jointly sufficient to ground all constructible figures. Figurative synthesis likewise accounts for formal intuitions of time: "Motion, as the action of the subject (not determination of an object) and hence [as] the synthesis of the manifold in space, first produces the concept of succession, when we abstract from this [manifold in space] and attend merely to the action through which we determine **inner sense** according to its form." (B154.15–155.20, my underlining)

[20] Note that the present discussion remains neutral on the intellectualism/sensibilism debate (cf. McLear 2014). Even if one holds that formal intuitions involve figurative synthesis and that figurative synthesis is an intellectual activity, one might still argue that such intellectual activity merely "brings to concepts" the intrinsic structure of human outer intuition, which obtains independently of such intellectual synthesis though it cannot, of course, be cognized independently of it (see Falkenstein 1995, 98–100, 245–252) .

[21] Note that self-affection does not always produce pure intuitions. All our inner intuitings, including empirical ones, involve self-affection (B68, B153.22–23, B156.21–22; B156n.). Pure intuition results, I take it, just in case the mental activity that affects our sensibility is itself pure (cf. B154.3). My aim here is merely to distinguish the notion of sensible affection from the idea of mere cognitive receptivity, on the one hand, and the idea of sensory affection, on the other. Valaris (2008) offers an illuminating discussion of self-affection and inner sense; see also Schmitz (2013), Indregard (2017), and Laywine (2020). On Kant's related notion of inner experience, see Emundts (2007) and Kraus (2020).

power and the patient suffering its effect. So it is unclear how one and the same subject could serve as both agent and patient in a causal transaction. This puzzle would not arise if self-affection were a mere grounding relation or a relation of logical determination. For these relations can be unproblematically reflexive: All spontaneous faculties involve self-determination – as when I make up my mind to judge that *p*, to draw the inference *p entails q*, or to subordinate my maxim to the moral law, and so on. But Kant rejects the idea that self-affection is mere self-determination. For that would render our pure, formal intuitings spontaneous, since they would then be fully accounted for by features the mind exhibits merely qua cognizer. And this would elide the distinction between apperception and inner sense (B153.25–03; cf. B154.22–30; *Progress* 20:270).

Kant is grappling with some unappealing options here. To assimilate sensible affection to sensory affection would render all intuition empirical. But to conceive self-affection as mere self-determination would collapse the distinction between inner sense and apperception. Kant's proposed middle course is to treat sensible affection, including self-affection, as an irreducibly causal relation and to simply embrace the agent/patient paradox. Here we hit philosophical bedrock and our spades are turned:

> How it is possible that I, who think, can be an object (of intuition) to myself, and thus distinguish myself from myself, is absolutely impossible to explain, although it is an undoubted fact[.] (*Progress* 20:270; cf. B67.18–69.13, B155.23–156.4)

What we are running up against here is our ignorance of things-in-themselves – in particular, our ignorance of the character of the grounding relation between things-in-themselves and the appearances to which they give rise. If sensible affection is a causal relation, then both its relata (agent and patient) must be phenomena, denizens of nature. The production of an inner intuition (pure or empirical) is a clockable event in the phenomenal realm, as is the state of mind (*Gemütszustand*) that brings it about and that it sensibly represents. Now, that state of mind (the agent in the affection relation) is the phenomenal counterpart of some thing-in-itself, which Kant variously calls "the logical I", "the subject of apperception", "the I who thinks" (*Progress* 20:270) or "I as intelligence and thinking subject" (B155.27–28). What we cannot comprehend, I suggest, is how the phenomenal mental states that we perceive through inner sense and that we cognize as natural events subject to deterministic causal laws can nevertheless be expressions of an absolute spontaneity of intellect.

The idea of sensible affection as a causal but non-sensory relation invites further discussion. For present purposes, however, we can content ourselves that Kant carves out a place for a conception of sensible affection that is more specific than mere cognitive receptivity, yet more generic than sensory affection.[22] Any intractable philosophical problems with these notions must ultimately fall to Kant and do not count against the present classification as an interpretive analytical tool.

8.1.3 *Why the Receptive/Sensible/Sensory Distinction Matters*

The reason I have argued at such length to distinguish receptivity from sensibility from sensory sensitivity is because I think different features of human intuition come into view at these different levels of abstraction. Relatedly, different levels of abstraction may demand different types of evidence and modes of argumentation. Attending to these distinctions can help us navigate interpretive disputes.

For instance, phenomenological considerations clearly bear on intuition insofar as it is *sensory* and perhaps also insofar as it is *sensible* but not insofar as it is merely *receptive*. This is not simply because we sensible beings cannot know "what it is like" to possess a non-sensible intuition. It is because there is no fact of the matter about "what it is like" to possess a merely receptive intuition. The phenomenological character of a mode of representation fades from view at that level of abstraction.

Suppose, as seems plausible, that the phenomenology of our outer intuitings essentially involves a figure/ground distinction. In any outer intuiting, attention will focus upon part of the manifold, as figure. Yet one will also represent that figure as embedded within, or as standing out from, an encompassing background or "horizon", of which one is but dimly aware. What is ground in one intuiting can become figure in another. And every outer intuiting exhibits both figure and ground.

[22] Cases of sensible yet non-sensory affection are quite numerous in Kant's corpus. Prominent examples include our feeling of respect for the moral law (*Practical* 5:76; cf. Section 7.3.3), our pleasure in the beautiful (*Judgment* 5:217f.), and our thrill at the sublime (*Judgment* 5:257.20–32, 265.1–9). These typically involve sensory stimulation as an occasioning cause, but the resulting feeling is determined not by the sensation but by a spontaneous activity of the mind in response to sensation: respect by practical reason's determination of the will, pleasure in the beautiful by the free play of the cognitive faculties, the thrill of the sublime by our consciousness of the supremacy of reason over sensibility. Further cases are discussed in the contributions to Williamson and Sorensen (2017). A full account of sensible affection would have to take account of all these cases, not just the sensible affection involved in human intuition. I again recommend Tizzard (2018) as an illuminating comparison of respect with spatiotemporality as the respective forms of our practical and theoretical sensibility.

Such considerations might form the basis for an argument that space, as the form of outer sense, is "essentially unitary", i.e. that every space is represented as a mere part of a larger space encompassing it (cf. A25/B39).[23] Such an argument, if sound, would imply only that *sensible* intuition has a holistic containment structure. Or, rather, it would imply that human intuition is holistic in virtue of being sensible. It would not show, for instance, that merely receptive intuition must be holistic, or that human intuition is holistic in virtue of being receptive.[24]

To characterize human intuition at the more abstract level of mere receptivity would require a different kind of argument – one that appeals to the sort of conceptual and metaphysical considerations that bear on the notion of cognitive spontaneity (see Section 7.3). These include, *inter alia*, considerations of grounding, sortal identity, types of representational content, and distinctions between potentiality versus actuality or self versus other. Features of intuition that can be supported by such abstract metaphysical and epistemological considerations deserve to be considered more fundamental to human intuition than properties that are demonstrable only at lesser levels of abstraction and on the basis of more specific argumentative resources, such as phenomenological considerations.

Or consider a feature of Kantian intuition that began attracting commentators' attention in the later twentieth century. Human intuitings are orientable: They enable us to represent chiral properties and incongruent counterparts (enantiomorphs).[25] Spatial intuition, for instance, enables us to distinguish, and demonstrate the incongruity of, objects such as right

[23] For arguments along these lines, see Parsons (1983 [1964]); Aquila (1994); Carson (1997); McLear (2015, 95–97); Rosefeldt (2022).

[24] Here, too, the Angelic Doctor supplies an interesting foil. Aquinas argues that "in the cognitive act by which angels understand things through the Word, they know all things through a single intelligible species, viz. God's essence. And so far as this cognitive act is concerned, they know all things at once" (*ST* I, q.58, a.2, co.). So angelic cognition of things through the divine essence admits of no figure/ground distinction or any analogous sort of division or uneven distribution of consciousness. By contrast, angelic cognition of mundane things does involve an analogue of the figure/ground relation, according to Aquinas. For although an angel is never in a state of mere potentiality (i.e. ignorance) with respect to cognition, "it is not always actually considering all the things that it knows by its natural cognition" (*ST* I, q.58, a.1, co., my underlining). Note, however, that this line of thought does not involve *phenomenological* considerations. It rather turns on a particular application of the potentiality/actuality distinction, an account of the content of cognition, cognitive grounds, and so forth. My point here is that an argument would have to be mounted in similarly abstract, non-phenomenological terms in order to show that human intuition, as Kant conceives it, is holistic in virtue of being *receptive*.

[25] An excellent overview of Kant on incongruent counterparts is Rusnock and George (1995). On the role of chirality in the development of Kant's idealism, see Buroker (1981), Hogan (2021), and Smyth (MS). On chirality as a distinguishing feature of intuition, see Severo (2005) and Bernecker (2010).

and left hands, or helices that wind in opposite directions. Kant highlights chirality not just as a mathematical curiosity but as an important feature that distinguishes human intuition from discursive, conceptual representation. Yet this gives us no reason to think that orientability is a necessary feature of intuition *überhaupt*, for nothing in the character of mere givenness suggests that what is given must admit of chirality.

Nor does orientability appear to be essential to every conceivable mode of receptivity. Enjoying orientable representations involves, at the very least, occupying a point of view on things distinct from oneself. Though Leibniz likes to claim that every monad represents the universe from its own point of view, it is not obvious that this follows as a necessary feature of his system of preestablished harmony.[26] Nor is the idea of a point of view essential to Platonic or Malebranchean hyperphysical influx. To have a point of view is, minimally, to be situated within a frame of reference so that one is "closer" to some things than others. Yet it seems quite compatible with the hypothesis of preestablished harmony, and that of hyperphysical influx, that a mind with a receptive capacity for intuition could be, as it were, equally distributed across the entire frame of reference. For such an isotropic cognizer there would be no *near* or *far*, much less *up* or *down*, *front* or *back*, *left* or *right*. So it is far from obvious how considerations available at the level of merely receptive intuition could account for the orientability of human intuition.

By contrast, it is eminently plausible that possessing a point of view is essentially tied to sensibility. For sensible affection involves standing in, and representing oneself as standing in, causal relations. And this arguably involves representing oneself as occupying a particular location within the relevant frame of reference, precisely unlike the isotropic consciousness just mooted. Indeed, Kant suggests that differences in direction and orientation are apparent for any *embodied* mind, any rational creature possessed of *sensory* consciousness. For sensation is integrated with one's first-personal

[26] Leibniz assumes, naturally enough, that our representations grow more confused as we represent more distant objects and events. He therefore argues that spatiotemporal properties – including relations of distance and chiral orientation – are emergent upon properties of representations (see Jauernig 2019). But his system of preestablished harmony does not explain why each monad must be associated with a determinate, circumscribed location – that is, a particular body that "belongs" to it (cf. B416n.23–417n.10). He gives no reason why all my representations could not be afflicted by an equal degree of confusion, so that every object and event would be equally "proximate" to me and I would not refer my representations to one particular object (as my *body*) against all others. Nor does he explain why a monad could not occupy multiple points of view, but must be limited to a single situs.

sense of animal locomotion, which first imbues orientational terms such as *front/back* and *left/right* with their sense (*Directions* 2:378–381; *Orient* 8:134 f.).

Examples could be multiplied. A notion of immediacy that rests on phenomenological considerations pertains to intuition qua sensible and is not the same as a notion of immediacy that rests on semantic considerations, which arguably pertains to intuition *überhaupt*. A notion of singularity that is motivated by the metaphysics of causation pertains to intuition qua sensible (or sensory) and should not be confused with a conception that arises from logical reflections on the type/token distinction. My purpose in raising these examples is not to argue for a particular account of the features of Kantian intuition – the holistic structure of human intuition, say, or its essential orientability. My point is the receptive/sensible/sensory distinction is helpful in weighing arguments about these matters. Certain features of our intuition arguably obtain in virtue of its mere receptivity, whereas others are grounded in the specifically sensible, or the concretely sensory character of our intuitings. Features that first come into view at levels of greater specificity are less fundamental than those that can be established on the basis of more generic considerations. Distinguishing these levels of abstraction has the further merit of directing us toward the appropriate argumentative resources for making and adjudicating these attributions.

8.2 Self-Representation as Differentia

Because our *Stufenleiter* classifies *capacities*, and a mind can possess multiple specifically different capacities, there is no principled reason why a mind could not possess all the intuitive capacities discussed thus far: spontaneous, receptive but non-sensible, and sensible. Nevertheless, the implicit presumption throughout has been that each of these divisions contrasts human intuition with variants that we do not possess. The present logical division, however, revokes this presumption. I propose that we divide sensible intuition into *intuition of one's own states* and *intuition of things distinct from oneself* – that is, into inner intuition and outer intuition.

Though this division differs from the others, in that both species appertain to the human mind, it is textually uncontroversial. Kant consistently characterizes inner sense as that "by means of which the mind [*Gemüt*] intuits itself or its inner state" (A22/B37.10–11; cf. A33/B49.9–11). There are, of course, questions about how, precisely, this characterization should be understood. What are the identity conditions of "the mind" (A19/B33.11) or "the soul" (A22/B37.12, 14) or "the self" (A33/B49.10) that determine the inner/outer boundary?[27]

As with other gnarly interpretive issues, my classification is neutral. All can agree on paradigm cases of inner sense and on the principal criteria that make these cases paradigms. Intuitions of one's occurrent thoughts, desires, or feelings, for instance, are inner intuitions. And they count as "inner" for the same reasons: They represent one's mental states as one's own and they do so on account of being sensibly receptive to those very states in a manner that involves their (the states') existence and cognitive availability.

8.2.1 Inner Intuition and Sensible but Non-Sensory Self-Affection

Inner sense involves sensible self-affection: a causal transaction in nature, the realm of phenomena. A philosophical advantage of conceiving sensible affection, including self-affection, as a causal relation of natural necessitation is that it captures the sense that our intuitings are "wrung" from us. But the account also raises philosophical challenges.

First, conceiving inner intuitings as phenomena subject to causal laws implies that the Analogies apply to the phenomenal mind. And this suggests that the phenomenal mind, as the site of alternating and interacting mental states, is a substance – an abiding substratum in which these changes inhere. Now Kant argues in the Paralogisms that rational psychology, based on pure apperception, cannot demonstrate the substantiality of the rational mind (the thinking subject). But if self-affection is a causal relation, it would appear that *empirical* psychology does provide evidence for the substantiality of the mind qua phenomenon. And if the phenomenal mind is a substance, one would like to know what sort of substance it is.

This is the second philosophical challenge posed by inner sense. Sensible but non-sensory affection is an odd sort of natural causality: one that does not involve any material interaction or mediation. It is physical (natural) but not material (sensory). If this is right – if self-affection does not involve material interaction – then empirical psychology delivers on yet another promise that rational psychology cannot, according to the

[27] In what follows, I will refer to the subject whose inner states are intuited through inner sense as "the mind". On Kant's related uses of the notions "I", "mind", "self", and "soul", see Longuenesse (2017, 102–112). On Kant's conception of "the soul" as an encompassing mental notion and the topic of rational psychology, see Dyck (2014).

Paralogisms. For it points to the immateriality of the mind qua phenomenon. This, of course, leads one to wonder what other immaterial substances may lurk in Kant's phenomenal realm. But more importantly, it raises the notorious problem of mind–body interaction, to which we now turn.

8.2.2 Outer Intuition and Sensible Affection from Without

The contradictory complement of *intuition of one's own mental state(s)* is *intuition not of one's own mental state(s)* or, more naturally, *intuition of things distinct from one's mind and its states.* At this level of abstraction, the "outer" in *outer intuition* has the significance "other than" and not the sense "spatially external to". The distinction between inner and outer sense, as species of sensible intuition, tracks a logic of identity and difference, of self and other, and not (yet) a logic of topological or spatial containment.[28]

The philosophical challenge posed by outer sense is to understand how the mind can be causally affected by things distinct from itself. When posed in such abstract terms, the problem appears quite tractable. But it becomes trickier once we consider that outer affection is paradigmatically *sensory,* not merely sensible. For then we must explain how material substances can "[affect] the mind [*Gemüt*] in a certain manner" (A19/B33.11–12) so as to produce sensation – that is, "the effect of an object on the capacity for representation [*Vorstellungsfähigkeit*] insofar as we are affected by it" (A19/B34.23–24). Kant offers few explicit, positive characterizations of the sort of thing the phenomenal mind is supposed to be. But his doctrine of self-affection, as we just saw, suggests it must be immaterial. And Kant explicitly denies that it is material.[29] So Kant needs

[28] Recent commentators have convincingly argued that the first moment in Kant's Metaphysical Exposition of <space> employs an irreducibly spatial sense of "*außer*" (A23/B38.6). See Falkenstein (1995, 163–165); Warren (1998); Friedman (2000, 190–193 and associated notes). But this poses no threat to our classification. For the Expositions analyze the concept <space>, not the mere concept of outer sense. Spatiality is not baked into the concept of outer intuition. The Metaphysical Expositions aim to show, by analyzing the concept <space>, that space instantiates the concept <form of sensible intuition>. That is, certain marks of the concept <space> are sufficient for applying the concept <form of sensible intuition>. (*Mutatis mutandis* for time and inner intuition.) This is why my *Stufenleiter* (Figure 7.1) uses vertical lines to subsume *spatial intuition* as an instance of *outer sensible intuition,* rather than the sloped lines that divide genera into species – just as Porphyry subsumes Plato and Socrates under *human* as instances, not as species. One might conceivably want to treat *human spatial intuition* as a species, but only if there is a salient contrast case that it is important to distinguish (e.g. *non-Euclidean spatial intuition*).

[29] For instance, B409.18–22, A357.11–22; *Prolegomena* 4:363.5–11, 25–30; see Ameriks (2000, ch. 2). Of course, Kant argues in the Paralogisms that rational psychology, grounded in pure apperception, provides no support for the view that the mind enjoys an immaterial existence

to explain how a material object can causally interact with something that is not material.

Kant's doctrine of outer sense runs headlong into the problem of mind–body interaction, in the modern guise it assumes following Descartes.[30] It is difficult to ascertain Kant's views here, since his pre-critical interest in mind–body interaction, which was never especially intense anyway, seems to all but vanish in his published critical writings.[31] Indeed, the most extensive critical discussion of mind–body interaction, in the A-edition Paralogisms, culminates in what Sellars dubs Kant's "*ignorabimus*" (1970, 12). Kant first suggests that his transcendental idealism mitigates the most troubling aspects of the problem, before finally declaring it insoluble.

The problem, according to Kant, lies in the supposed heterogeneity of cause (material object) and effect (mental state): "[W]hat appears as matter cannot, through its immediate influence, be the cause of representations, as effects of a wholly heterogenous sort" (A390.27–30).[32] Material agents can interact with material patients, and immaterial representations with other immaterial representations. But they cannot mix. Kant's proposed solution is to distinguish the object as thing in itself from the object as appearance. If we consider the object as thing in itself, no heterogeneity is discernible between cause (object) and effect (intuiting), since we are ignorant of the nature of things in themselves and a fortiori of whether they are homogeneous or heterogeneous with any appearances or representations (A360.20–25; B427.4–428.10). On the other hand, if we consider the object as appearance, it is ideal and thus a representation. And then there can be no problematic heterogeneity between cause and effect, agent and patient, since both are representations (A385.30–386.29).

(B409.31–04). But so long as Kant does not positively affirm that the phenomenal mind is *material*, there is a prima facie puzzle about how material things can causally affect it.

30 That is to say, the problem Elisabeth of Bohemia presses on Descartes – namely, how the soul, which is not material, can possess "the capacity to move a body and to be moved by it" (AT 3:685). In his pre-critical period (1766), Kant admits puzzlement, calling it "mysterious" how "an immaterial substance [is] supposed to lie in the path of matter so that it [matter] can collide [*stoße*] with a spirit" (*Dreams* 2:327.12–328.02). Pre-critical Kant appears to be an avowed immaterialist about the mind, which lands him with the modern problem of mind–body interaction.

31 Erdmann (1878, 226); cited by Kemp Smith (1992 [1918], 471) and by Powell (1990, 199). On the mind–body problem in pre-critical works, see Carpenter (1998). For discussion of Kant's critical views on mind–body interaction, see Powell (1990, ch. 5) and Ameriks (2000, ch. 3).

32 It was widely assumed in the period that causal interaction requires agent and patient or cause and effect to be homogeneous in some fundamental sense. See A385.5–386.25, 386.1–6, 387.29–32; B427.30–04; M-Vi/K_3 (1794/95) 28:831.29–832.20.

This proposal is unsatisfying on both counts. First, it renders the homogeneity or heterogeneity of agent and patient unknowable, whereas our causal claims presume that their homogeneity is known. Second, it fails to resolve the manifest heterogeneity between material agents and immaterial patients. By identifying a different respect in which agent and patient are homogeneous – namely, in being appearances and therefore ideal representations – Kant simply relocates the problem into the realm of appearances. In the phenomenal world, some things are material (objects) and others are immaterial (minds and their states). And Kant offers no explanation of how these things can causally interact. As if sensing the inadequacy of his proposed idealistic solution, Kant concludes that no explanation is possible:

> The notorious question of the community [*Gemeinschaft*] of thought and extension, once one has separated out everything illusory, would therefore come to this: **how in a thinking subject überhaupt outer intuition is possible**, namely [intuition] of space (a filling of its shape and movement). To this question, however, it is not possible for any human to find an answer, and one can never fill this gap in our knowledge but only mark it by ascribing outer appearances to a transcendental object which is the cause of this kind of representations, but with which we are utterly unacquainted and of which we can never acquire any concept. (A392f.; cf. M-Pö/L_1 28:280)

The notion of outer affection at the core of Kant's conception of human outer sense is, by his own lights, inscrutable. However unsatisfying this may be, it is an important datum in any account of Kantian outer sense.

8.2.3 Human Outer Sense and Spatial Location

As we descend from sensible outer intuition to the particular case of human, spatial outer sense, the mind–body problem takes on a new dimension – namely, the spatial *location* of the mind vis-à-vis material objects.[33] In the first Metaphysical Exposition of the Concept of Space, Kant writes that I "refer certain sensations to something outside me (i.e. to

[33] It is worth noting that these two dimensions of the problem are effectively collapsed in Descartes, since he equates materiality with extension (*Rules* AT 10:444–448; *Principles* II § 4 AT 8a: 42; cf. 23, 25). Descartes sometimes seems to distinguish materiality in the sense of impenetrability from extension in the sense of non-zero spatial expanse, but he maintains that the two are necessarily coextensive if not conceptually identical (cf. Descartes to More 15 April 1646, AT 5:342). Kant clearly distinguishes the question of mind–body interaction from the question of the mind's location vis-à-vis the body; see M-Pö/L_1 28:280–282.

something in a different place [*Ort*] in space from the one in which I find myself)" (A23/B38.5–8). Note here that "I find myself" "in [. . .] a place in space". The *I* here must be the mind that is subject to outer affection. For it is only insofar as it is subject to sensory affection that the *I* possesses "sensations" in the first place, which it can then refer to "something outside me". So Kant holds that the mind, as the subject of outer affection, is located in space.

It is natural to assume that it is in virtue of having a *body* that I "find myself" in a particular place in space. Yet the mind that finds itself in that location is not identical to the body. Indeed, Kant later writes that "it is an analytic proposition that I distinguish my own existence as a thinking being from other things outside of me (to which my body also belongs)" (B409.18–20). When I refer my sensations to things outside of me, I may indeed be referring them to parts of my own body, as when I feel tingles spreading through my foot. But in referring these sensations to parts of my body, I am, curiously enough, referring them to something "outside of me". The irreducibly spatial sense of "outer" in *human outer sense* is not complemented by a spatially "*inner*" realm: "Space [cannot be intuited] as something in us" (A23/B37.17–18). Everything in space, including every atom of one's own lived body, is represented through outer sense and, hence, represented as "outside me".

How, then, can the mind occupy a location in space if everything we represent in space is, *ipso facto*, non-identical with the mind? At least early in his career, Kant explains this by appealing to the doctrine of "virtual location", which he likely borrows from Euler.[34] On this account, something can be present in a location in the sense of exercising causal influence there. Such presence is "virtual" in the sense of the post-classical Latin "*virtualis*": having to do with the expression of a power. Thus the mind is virtually present in the lived body in the sense that it acts on or through the body. Like the simple substances of Kant's *Physical Monadology* (§ V, 1:480), the mind can remain unextended and non-spatial in itself, even as it is virtually present over a non-zero spatial expanse through its sphere

[34] See Euler (1768, vol. I, Letter LXXX, dated 19 November 1760, and Letter XCII, dated 10 January 1761). Kant claims in *Inaugural* that "the presence of immaterial things in the corporeal world is a virtual not a local presence" (2:414.8–9, my underlining) and shortly thereafter praises Euler's *Letters to a German Princess*. See also R177 (1769?) 15:66.11–14. Kant appeals to the theory of virtual presence as late as his 1795 response to Sömmerring (12:32; cf. 13:399.7–14), which he allowed Sömmerring to publish (12:30) as a critical postscript to his *Über das Organ der Seele* (1796, 81–86). This suggests Kant retained the view throughout his career.

of activity.[35] It is because the mind is only virtually present in the body that the spatial sense of "outer" does not admit of a complementary "inner" realm. Although external objects are "outside me" by being outside my body, it does not follow that what is inside my body is "inside me". Rather, things outside my body are "outside me" because they are outside my sphere of activity, while things within my body are merely inside (the current boundaries of) my sphere of activity, but not within *me* (my mind). For something to be inside *me* would either mean that it is spatially contained in my mind, which makes no sense, or that it is identical with some part of my mind, which is not true of anything in space.[36]

Note, however, that while the theory of virtual presence offers an elegant solution to the problem of the *location* of the mind vis-à-vis the body, this solution presupposes that the problem of mind–body *interaction* has already been solved. For such interaction is central to the notion of a sphere of activity. So Kant's conception of sensible outer intuition still faces grave challenges.

8.3 Levels of Abstraction, Types of Evidence, and Features of Kantian Intuition

On the basis of the classification of human intuition presented here and in Chapter 7, we can draw up the following chart that aligns (i) the levels of abstraction marked out in our *Stufenleiter*, (ii) the kinds of evidence and argumentation appropriate to those levels, and (iii) the particular features of human intuition that come into view at those levels and in light of that evidence.

I offer this table not to defend *en detail* these characterizations of Kantian intuition but to illustrate the interpretive benefits of my *Stufenleiter*. So I will not argue for my attributions of particular features to Kantian intuition, nor my assignment of those features to particular levels of abstraction, nor my association of them with certain types of

[35] Kant himself draws this comparison in *Dreams* 2:323.19–324.6.

[36] This helps clarify the dispute between Allison, Falkenstein, and Warren about how to characterize outer sense. Allison (1983, 83; 2004, 100–104) distinguishes inner and outer sense at the level of mere sensibility, where the inner/outer distinction neatly tracks the self/other distinction. Falkenstein (1995, 163–165) and Warren (1998) observe that this abstract notion of outer sense (as the intuitive representation of what is numerically distinct from the subject) does not capture Kant's reasoning in the first Metaphysical Exposition. That requires a more concrete and explicitly spatial notion of "outer". The "inner" complement of outer sense, viewed at this level of specifically *human* intuition, is not the intuition of things *spatially internal* to me, but the intuition of *temporally successive* states of my mind.

Table 8.1 *Correlation between levels of abstraction, features of human intuitions, and types of evidence*

Level of Abstraction	Differentia	Features of Intuiting	Types of Evidence
Intuition *überhaupt*	Givenness	† immediacy # form/matter	epistemological, semantic
Receptivity	Lack of Cognitive Spontaneity	† actuality (vs. possibility) # act/object (of representation) * singularity quantitative manifoldness	metaphysical
Sensibility	Sensible Affection	† perspicuity * concreteness ‡ infinity in kind qualitative manifoldness mereology holistic containment structure	phenomenological
Human Intuition	[Instantiation] Space/Time	* individuality ‡ metrical infinity	mathematical practice, empirical observation

evidence and modes of argument. My aim is just to show that my classification provides a useful framework within which to pursue such debates. And the table can do that illustrative work so long as its various attributions are sufficiently plausible. If particular attributions offend, the reader is invited to provide her own. Indeed, the reader's ability to make such substitutions bolsters my claim that the proposed *Stufenleiter* (Figure 7.1) and associated table (Table 8.1) provide a framework for articulating and adjudicating interpretive disputes.

I take it to be plausible, for instance, that human intuition presents a manifold of different *qualities* to the mind and that these should, in the first instance, be understood as *sensory* qualities – sensations of flavor, texture, temperature, pitch, timbre, and so forth.[37] Accordingly, the qualitative manifoldness of intuition is a feature that obtains at the level of sensibility (or lower). This makes it appropriate to appeal to

[37] Though inner sense does not have a qualitative manifold of its own, it still involves a manifold of sensory qualities: It just inherits them from outer sense (Bxxxixn.24–26; A34/B50.14–15; B67.5–7). See Valaris (2008) and Newton (2019).

phenomenological evidence in order to justify claims that human intuition, as sensible, is qualitatively manifold. It is hard to see why receptive but non-sensible intuitings would have to exhibit a diversity of distinctive qualities.

It is, by contrast, eminently plausible that a receptive but non-sensible intuition would still exhibit, if not qualitative diversity, at least *quantitative* manifoldness, in representing contents as numerically distinct. Any mind endowed with receptive intuition must at least distinguish itself (its own states) from things distinct from it. It must possess both inner and outer sense. Accordingly, its intuitings must exhibit this minimal degree of quantitative manifoldness: It must represent the content(s) of its inner intuitings as numerically distinct from the content(s) of its outer intuitings. Such numerical diversity is essential, even if we suppose that all its outer intuiting consists in a constant and unchanging representation of a single, internally undifferentiated content and all its inner intuitings consist in a commensurately unitary representation of its own state. Thus, intuition is capable of representing quantitative plurality in virtue of being receptive. And just as quantitative manifoldness is a more abstract feature than qualitative diversity, so too, the considerations that support this attribution (of quantitative manifoldness to *receptive* intuition, as such) are more abstract than those that establish the qualitative manifoldness of *sensible* intuition, as such. In particular, the line of argument just mooted involves no phenomenological considerations. Rather, it invokes quite abstract metaphysical principles concerning identity and difference, sortal identity, as well as semantic considerations about representational contents (cf. Section 8.1.3).

Note that, though I just appealed to semantic considerations in attributing quantitative manifoldness to receptive intuition, my table (Table 8.1) lists "semantic considerations" not at the level of receptivity but rather at the higher level of intuition *überhaupt*. This is only to keep the table tidy and avoid repetitions. In fact, I expect types of evidence to "cascade" downward. Any type of consideration or form of evidence that is pertinent at one level remains pertinent at lower levels. The converse, however, does not hold. Phenomenological considerations, for instance, have no place in determining the character of merely receptive intuition (cf. Section 8.1.3).

Something similar holds for the features listed in the chart. Features of intuition also cascade downward, but, as they do so, they take on more concrete and determinate shapes. Receptive intuition does not merely inherit, unchanged, all the abstract features of intuition *überhaupt*, as though we could just repeat the same words in the same sense throughout the column. Rather, the same feature that first comes into view at the abstract level of intuition *überhaupt* can reappear in more concrete forms at lower levels. This is a significant but sometimes counterintuitive effect of shifting between levels of abstraction and concreteness. For instance, the classical Porphyrian tree classifies *animal* as a species of *substance*. Now, existence is, of course, one of the primary features of *substance*. But this does not mean that we should simply list *existence* as one of the features of *animal* alongside its other, more specific features, such as *locomotion* and *perception*. As Aristotle memorably writes, "for living things, to be is to live".[38] The feature that appears as *existence* at the abstract level of *substance überhaupt* reappears at the more concrete level of *animate substance* in the determinate form of *animal life*. This is the very same feature, viewed from different levels of abstraction.

In the same manner, features of intuition that come into view at abstract levels of consideration reappear in more determinate forms lower down the table. I have used special characters (asterisk, hashtag, dagger, double dagger) to track features as they cascade down the table in ever-more concrete guises. By way of conclusion, then, I will sketch how the most widely discussed feature of Kantian intuition – namely, singularity – takes on ever more concrete forms as we descend my *Stufenleiter*.

8.3.1 Singularity, Concreteness, and Individuality of Kantian Intuition

Singularity appears in three guises in this table: most abstractly as *singularity*, less abstractly as *concreteness*, and most concretely as *individuality*. An asterisk accompanies each term in order to indicate that we are dealing with the same property, viewed from different levels of abstraction.

Singularity, as I understand it, is the logical complement of multiple instantiability (discursive generality). Something is singular (*einzeln*) just in case it is non-repeatable. By extension, a representation is singular insofar as it represents something *as* non-repeatable. Singularity is, in this sense, a logical or semantic notion and it is common for commentators to invoke semantic considerations in order to establish or explain that intuition is singular in this sense. Hintikka, for example, invokes chiefly semantic considerations in arguing that: "Kant's notion of intuition is not very far from what we would call a singular term. An intuition is for Kant a 'representation' – we would perhaps rather say a symbol – which refers

[38] *De Anima* II.4, 415b13.

to an individual object or which is used *as if* it would refer to one" (Hintikka 1969, 43, original italics).[39] Such lines of argument yield a clear and attractive conception of singular representation. And there is considerable force to the idea that a system of representation that employs discursive, general representations must *also* employ singular representations.

But this line of argument, as it stands, has equally obvious disadvantages as an interpretation of Kant. For the relevant notion of singularity is too thin to adequately distinguish intuitive from intellectual representations. As we have seen, many intellectual representations satisfy this singularity criterion. Kant admits a variety of concepts and ideas of reason that purport to represent particulars, as such – for example, <coldest known temperature>, <even prime number>, <natural world>, or <*ens realissimum*>.[40] Even the Platonic Forms intuited through hyperphysical influx are singular in the relevant sense: There is a unique and non-repeatable Form of Beauty, for instance, even if there is an indefinite plurality of beautiful things.[41]

Though Hintikka fails to consider the counterexamples posed by intellectual representations with non-repeatable contents, he does recognize the central problem for his "logical" interpretation: namely, to explain why intuition, as representation of particulars, would have anything to do with *sensibility*.

> What is the relation of this notion [sc. *Anschauung*] to sensibility? If there is sometimes no connection between the two, how did Kant at other times come to relate them to each other? Of all the occasions on which Kant employs the notion of intuition, when are we entitled to assume a connection with *Sinnlichkeit* and when not? (Hintikka 1969, 38, cf. 45–46, 49–50)

Whereas Hintikka finds himself forced to claim that intuition, as representation of particulars, is "sometimes" connected with sensibility and "sometimes" not, we can instead recognize a unified account of human intuition that employs multiple levels of abstraction. It is not that intuition, as singular representation, has "no connection" with the notion of sensibility. It is that human intuition, which is ineluctably sensible, is singular insofar as

[39] Strawson holds a similar view, though he emphasizes that this sort of particularity can be established by metaphysical, epistemological, or semantic considerations (1966, 47).

[40] See Sections 5.2, and 3.3, note 18; as well as Thompson (1972).

[41] It is perhaps tempting to regard Platonic Forms as repeatable, insofar as an indefinite plurality of things *participate* in a given Form. But it is at least as plausible to read Plato's Socrates as attempting to *explain* the repeatability, the multiple instantiability, of general properties and concepts by positing a privileged particular (the Form) to which all these instances bear a special relation (of participation). On the individuation of Platonic Forms, see Irani (2022).

it serves as the cognitive complement of discursive intellection, with its characteristic mode of generality. And intuition is the cognitive complement of discursive intellection insofar as it is *receptive* (as opposed to spontaneous). So the singularity of human intuition obtains at the level of *receptivity*. That is why "a connection with *Sinnlichkeit*" is not immediately apparent when one is considering intuition qua singular representation.

In order to elevate singularity into a sufficient condition of intuitive representation – one that distinguishes intuitings from *all* intellectual representations, even those with non-repeatable contents – one must introduce more concrete considerations. This, I take it, is the source of Parsons's complaint that Hintikka treats the immediacy criterion as "non-essential" (Parsons 1992 [1969], 45). Parsons understands the immediacy of intuition to mean "that the object of an intuition is in some way directly present to the mind, as in perception" (Parsons 1992 [1969], 44). This direct presence to mind is what I have termed "perspicuity" in my table (Table 8.1). It is a feature Parsons associates with sense perception and that he characterizes in phenomenological terms. So we can understand Parsons's objection as claiming that one cannot provide an adequate account of Kantian intuition while remaining at the level of mere receptivity – that is, while relying on merely semantic ("logical"), epistemological, and metaphysical considerations. One must descend to the level of sensibility where phenomenological considerations become relevant.

In our *Stufenleiter*, descending to the level of sensibility involves specifying that the receptivity of human intuition is irreducibly *causal*. This specification enables us to similarly enrich our conception of the singularity of human intuition. Abstract entities such as tropes, sets, numbers, or Platonic Forms qualify as singular, since they are non-repeatable. But on most accounts, including Kant's, they cannot exercise causal powers or enter into causal relations (Watkins 2004, ch. 4). So they cannot be objects of sensible affection. By descending from the level of mere receptivity to the level of sensibility, the singularity of intuition takes on a more determinate character: Its objects are no longer mere non-repeatables, but singular *things* (*Dinge*, *res*) endowed with causal powers.[42] This is what I have called "concreteness" in my chart: representing something as a non-repeatable *Ding* capable of entering into causal interactions and, in particular, capable of sensibly affecting the mind. At this lower level of abstraction, where causal affection becomes relevant, the singularity of intuition *does* entail its

[42] On Kant's use of the term '*Ding*' as the German equivalent of the Latin scholastic term '*res*', see Smit (2000, 240–242).

non-intellectual character. For to represent particulars in virtue of being *causally affected* by them is to manifest a kind of cognitive *receptivity*. Such intuition is therefore non-intellectual, because non-spontaneous.

If we descend still further, to the level of spatiotemporal intuition, we can supplement, and even partly supplant, this causally individuating mode of singularity qua concreteness. Whereas we rely on the metaphysics of causation to single out objects of intuition at the level of mere sensibility, the determinately spatiotemporal form of human intuition provides us with a still richer notion of singularity that I call "individuality". Minimally, space and time enable us to individuate objects by associating each with a unique spatiotemporal location.[43] But recall that space and time are represented as continuous. The objects we locate in space and time inherit this infinite complexity in their mereological structure. It is not merely that anything occupying a particular region of space is singular: all its *parts* are as well. Spatiotemporal objects are individual in all their parts. They are infinitely particular: singular all the way down.[44]

It is one and the same property that we have in view at these various levels of abstraction. Singularity, as mere non-repeatability, obtains at the level of *receptive* intuition, since receptive intuition is the complement of discursive intellection, which traffics in general (repeatable) representations. The concreteness of intuition, as the representation of unique *things* (*Dinge, res*), obtains at the level of *sensible* intuition, where the metaphysics of causal affection ensure that only particular substances endowed with causal powers can serve as objects of intuition. And the individuality of intuitive content, as uniqueness of spatiotemporal location and mereologically dense particularity, obtains only at the level of specifically human intuition.

One of the generative implications of my proposed classification is that similar inquiries could be mounted into other key features of Kantian intuition and their interpretation in the literature. It also gives us reason to hope that these inquiries will complement one another and coalesce into a unified account of intuition as a cognitive capacity. My aim in this book has not been to deliver such an account but to indicate its possibility, while emphasizing the richness of Kant's conception of intuition and the plurality of interpretive approaches it invites.

[43] In one respect, spatiotemporal individuality is thinner than causal concreteness, for geometrical figures will count as spatiotemporally individual though they are not causally concrete. The representation of such figures remains sensible, not because the represented figures affect the mind (they cannot: they are causally inert) but because the mind sensibly affects itself through figurative synthesis. See Section 8.1.2.

[44] See B137n. as well as Section 5.5; cf. Jauernig (2021, 207–209).

Bibliography

Adelung, Johann Christoph. 1793. *Grammatisch-kritisches Wörterbuch der hochdeutschen Mundart*. Leipzig: Breitkopf.

Allais, Lucy. 2009. "Kant, Non-Conceptual Content and the Representation of Space." *Journal of the History of Philosophy* 47(3): 383–413.

2015. *Manifest Reality: Kant's Idealism and His Realism*. Oxford: Oxford University Press.

Allais, Lucy, and Callanan, John (eds.) 2020. *Kant and Animals*. Oxford: Oxford University Press.

Allison, Henry. 1983. *Kant's Transcendental Idealism: An Interpretation and Defense*. New Haven, CT: Yale University Press.

2004. *Kant's Transcendental Idealism: An Interpretation and Defense*. Revised and expanded edition. New Haven, CT: Yale University Press.

2015. *Kant's Transcendental Deduction: An Analytical-Historical Commentary*. Oxford: Oxford University Press.

Alter, Robert. 2004. *The Five Books of Moses: A Translation and Commentary*. New York: Norton.

Ameriks, Karl. 2000. *Kant's Theory of Mind: An Analysis of the Paralogisms of Pure Reason*. 2nd ed. Oxford: Clarendon Press.

Anderson, R. Lanier. 2004. "It Adds Up After All: Kant's Philosophy of Arithmetic in Light of the Traditional Logic." *Philosophy and Phenomenological Research* 69(3): 501–540.

2005. "The Wolffian Paradigm and Its Discontents: Kant's Containment Definition of Analyticity in Historical Context." *Archiv für Geschichte der Philosophie* 87(1): 22–74.

2015. *The Poverty of Conceptual Truth: Kant's Analytic/Synthetic Distinction and the Limits of Metaphysics*. Oxford: Oxford University Press.

Aquila, Richard. 1994. "The Holistic Character of Kantian Intuition." In *Kant and Contemporary Epistemology*, edited by Paolo Parrini, 309–329. Boston, MA: Kluwer.

Aquinas, Thomas. 1994. *Truth*. 3 vols. Translated by Robert Mulligan, James McGlynn, and Robert Schmidt. Indianapolis, IN: Hackett. [Abbreviated "*De Veritate*".]

2022. *Summa Theologiae*. Translated by Alfred J. Freddoso. www3.nd.edu/~afreddos/summa-translation/TOC.htm [Abbreviated "*ST*"].

Aristotle. 1984. *The Complete Works of Aristotle*. 2 vols. Translated by Jonathan Barnes. Oxford: Oxford University Press.

Arthur, Richard T. W. 1998. "Infinite Aggregates and Phenomenal Wholes: Leibniz's Theory of Substance as a Solution to the Continuum Problem." *The Leibniz Review* 8: 25–45.

1999. "Infinite Number and the World Soul: In Defence of Carlin and Leibniz." *The Leibniz Review* 9: 105–116.

2001. "Leibniz on Infinite Number, Infinite Wholes, and the Whole World: A Reply to Gregory Brown." *The Leibniz Review* 11: 103–116.

Baumgarten, Alexander Gottlieb. 2013 [1757]. *Metaphysics: A Critical Translation with Kant's Elucidations, Selected Notes and Related Materials*. Translated and edited by Courtney D. Fugate and John Hymers. London: Bloomsbury.

Beck, Jacob Sigismund. 1796. *Grundriß der critischen Philosophie*. Halle: Renger.

Beck, Lewis White. 1965 [1955]. "Can Kant's Synthetic Judgments Be Made Analytic?" In his *Studies in the Philosophy of Kant*, 74–91. Indianapolis, IN: Bobbs-Merrill.

Berkeley, George. 1948–1957. *The Works of George Berkeley, Bishop of Cloyne*. 9 vols. Edited by A. A. Luce and T. E. Jessop. London: Thomas Nelson and Sons.

Bernecker, Sven. 2010. "Kant on Spatial Orientation." *European Journal of Philosophy* 20(4): 519–533.

Blecher, Ian. 2018. "Kant's Principles of Modality." *European Journal of Philosophy* 26(3): 932–944.

Boghossian, Paul. 2014. "What Is Inference?" *Philosophical Studies* 169(1): 1–18.

Boyle, Matthew. 2011. "Transparent Self-Knowledge." *Proceedings of the Aristotelian Society* 85: 223–241.

2015. "Die Spontaneität des Verstandes bei Kant und einigen Neokantianern." *Deutsche Zeitschrift für Philosophie* 53(4): 705–726.

Forthcoming-a. "Kant's Hylomorphism and the Thing-in-Itself." In Gobsch and Land (eds.).

Forthcoming-b. "Kant on Categories and the Activity of Reflection." In *The Palgrave Handbook of German Idealism and Analytic Philosophy*, edited by James Conant and Jonas Held. London: Palgrave Macmillan.

Brandt, Reinhard. 1998. "Transzendentale Ästhetik, §§1–3 (A19/B33-A30/B45)." In *Immanuel Kant: Kritik der reinen Vernunft*, edited by Georg Mohr and Marcus Willaschek, 81–106. Berlin: Akademie Verlag.

Brewer, Kimberly. 2022. "Kant's Theory of the Intuitive Intellect." *History of Philosophy Quarterly* 39(2): 163–182.

Brittan, Gordon. 1978. *Kant's Theory of Science*. Princeton, NJ: Princeton University Press.

Brown, Gregory. 1998. "Who's Afraid of Infinite Numbers? Leibniz and the World Soul." *The Leibniz Review* 8: 113–125.

2000. "Leibniz on Wholes, Unities, and Infinite Number." *The Leibniz Review* 10: 21–51.

Büchel, Gregor. 1987. *Philosophie und Geometrie: zum Verhältnis beider Vernunftwissenschaften im Fortgang von der Kritik der reinen Vernunft zum Opus postumum*. Berlin: De Gruyter.

Buroker, Jill Vance. 1981. *Space and Incongruence: The Origins of Kant's Idealism*. Dordrecht: Springer.

Callanan, John. 2013. "Kant on Nativism, Scepticism and Necessity." *Kantian Review* 18(1): 1–27.

2017. "Kant on the Spontaneous Power of Mind." *British Journal for the History of Philosophy* 25(3): 565–588.

Cantor, Georg. 1966 [1888]. "Mitteilungen zur Lehre vom Transfiniten." In his *Gesammelte Abhandlungen mathematischen und philosophischen Inhalts*, edited by Ernst Zermelo, 378–439. Hildesheim: Olms.

Carlin, Laurence. 1997. "Infinite Accumulations and Pantheistic Implications: Leibniz and the 'Anima Mundi'." *The Leibniz Review* 7: 1–24.

Carpenter, Andrew. 1998. Kant's Earliest Solution to the Mind/Body Problem. PhD dissertation. University of California, Berkeley.

Carson, Emily. 1997. "Kant on Intuition in Geometry." *Canadian Journal of Philosophy* 27(4): 489–512.

Cassam, Quassim. 2016. "Knowledge and Its Objects: Revisiting *The Bounds of Sense*." *European Journal of Philosophy* 24(4): 907–919.

Chaplin, Rosalind. 2022. "Kant on the Givenness of Space and Time." *European Journal of Philosophy* 30(3): 877–898.

MS. "Idealism, Infinity, and Indeterminacy: Kant's Solution to the Second Antinomy."

Chignell, Andrew. 2007a. "Kant's Concepts of Justification." *Nous* 41(1): 33–63.

2007b. "Belief in Kant." *Philosophical Review* 116(3): 323–360.

2014. "Modal Motivations for Noumenal Ignorance: Knowledge, Cognition, Coherence." *Kant-Studien* 105(4): 573–597.

2017. "Kant on Cognition, Givenness, and Ignorance." *Journal of the History of Philosophy* 50(1): 131–142.

Choi, Yoon. 2019. "Spontaneity and Self-Consciousness in the 'Groundwork' and the B-*Critique*." *Canadian Journal of Philosophy* 49(7): 936–955.

Code, Alan. 2008. "Aristotelian Colors as Causes." In *Festschrift for Julius Moravcsik*, edited by Dagfinn Føllesdall and John Woods, 235–242. London: College Publications.

Coope, Ursula. 2013. "Aquinas on Judgment and the Active Power of Reason." *Philosophers' Imprint* 13(20): 1–19.

Darnton, Robert. 1984. "Philosophers Trim the Tree of Knowledge: The Epistemological Strategy of the *Encyclopédie*." In his *The Great Cat Massacre and Other Episodes in French Cultural History*, 191–214. New York: Basic Books.

de Jong, Willem. 1995. "Kant's Analytic Judgments and the Traditional Theory of Concepts." *Journal of the History of Philosophy* 33(4): 613–641.

2010. "The Analytic–Synthetic Distinction and the Classical Model of Science: Kant, Bolzano, and Frege." *Synthese* 174(2): 237–261.

De Risi, Vincenzo. 2016. *Leibniz on the Parallel Postulate and the Foundations of Geometry: The Unpublished Manuscripts*. New York: Birkhäuser.

Descartes, René. 1897–1910. *Oeuvres de Descartes*. Edited by Charles Adam and Paul Tannery. 11 vols. Reprint: Paris: Vrin. [Abbreviated "AT".]

Domski, Mary. 2008. "Kant's Argument for the Infinity of Space". In *Recht und Frieden in der Philosophie Kants. Akten des X. Internationalen Kant-Kongresses*, vol. 2, edited by Valerio Rohden, Ricardo Terra, Guido de Almeida and Margit Ruffing, 149–159. Berlin. Walter de Gruyter.

Dyck, Corey. 2014. *Kant and Rational Psychology*. Oxford: Oxford University Press.

2017. "The Principles of Apperception." In *Immanuel Kant: Die Einheit des Bewusstseins*, edited by Udo Thiel and Giuseppe Motta, 32–46. Berlin: De Gruyter.

Forthcoming. "The 'Aristotle of Königsberg'?: Kant and the Aristotelian Mind." In Gobsch and Land (eds.).

Ellis, Addison. 2017. "The Case for Absolute Spontaneity in Kant's *Critique of Pure Reason*." *Con-Textos Kantianos* 6: 138–164.

Emundts, Dina. 2007. "Kant über innere Erfahrung." In *Was ist und Was sein soll. Natur und Freiheit bei Immanuel Kant*, edited by Udo Kern, 189–205. Berlin: De Gruyter.

Engstrom, Stephen. 2006. "Understanding and Sensibility." *Inquiry* 49(1): 2–25.

2009. *The Form of Practical Knowledge*. Cambridge, MA: Harvard University Press.

2013. "Unity of Apperception." *Studi Kantiani* XXVI: 37–54.

2016. "Self-Consciousness and the Unity of Knowledge." In *Consciousness – International Yearbook of German Idealism*, edited by Dina Emundts and Sally Sedgwick, 25–47. Berlin: De Gruyter.

2017. "Knowledge and Its Object." In *Kant's "Critique of Pure Reason": A Critical Guide*, edited by James O'Shea, 28–45. Cambridge: Cambridge University Press.

Forthcoming. "Truth, Falsity, and the Capacity to Judge." In Gobsch and Land (eds.).

Erdmann, Benno. 1878. *Kants Kriticismus in der ersten und in der zweiten Auflage der Kritik der reinen Vernunft*. Leipzig: Leopold Voss.

Euler, Leonhard. 1768. *Lettres à une princesse d'Allemagne sur divers sujets de physique & de philosophie. Tome premier*. Saint Petersburg: Imprint of the Imperial Academy of Sciences.

Falkenstein, Lorne. 1990. "Kant's Account of Sensation." *Canadian Journal of Philosophy* 20(1): 63–88.

1995. *Kant's Intuitionism: A Commentary on the Transcendental Aesthetic*. Toronto: University of Toronto Press.

Ferrarin, Alfredo. 2019. "Method in Kant and Hegel." *British Journal for the History of Philosophy* 27(2): 255–270.

Förster, Eckart. 2002a. "Die Bedeutung von §§76, 77 der *Kritik der Urteilskraft* für die Entwicklung der nachkantischen Philosophie [Teil 1]." *Zeitschrift für philosophische Forschung* 56(2): 169–190.

2002b. "Die Bedeutung von §§76, 77 der *Kritik der Urteilskraft* für die Entwicklung der nachkantischen Philosophie [Teil II]." *Zeitschrift für philosophische Forschung* 56(3): 321–345.

2018. *Die 25 Jahre der Philosophie. Eine systematische Rekonstruktion.* 3rd improved ed. Frankfurt am Main: Klostermann.

Friedman, Michael. 1992. *Kant and the Exact Sciences*. Cambridge, MA: Harvard University Press.

2000. "Geometry, Construction, and Intuition in Kant and his Successors." In *Between Logic and Intuition: Essays in Honor of Charles Parsons*, edited by Gila Sher and Richard Tieszen, 186–218. Cambridge: Cambridge University Press.

2012. "Kant on Geometry and Spatial Intuition." *Synthese* 186: 231–255.

2020. "Space and Geometry in the B Deduction." In Posy and Rechter (eds.), 200–228.

Gava, Gabriele. 2015. "Kant's Synthetic and Analytic Method in the *Critique of Pure Reason* and the Distinction between Philosophical and Mathematical Syntheses." *European Journal of Philosophy* 23(3): 728–749.

2018. "Kant, Wolff, and the Method of Philosophy." *Oxford Studies in Early Modern Philosophy* 8: 271–303.

George, Rolf. 1981. "Kant's Sensationism." *Synthese* 47(2): 229–255.

Giordanetti, Piero, Pozzo, Riccardo, and Scarbi, Marco (eds.) 2012. *Kant's Philosophy of the Unconscious*. Berlin: De Gruyter.

Gobsch, Wolfram, and Land, Thomas (eds.). Forthcoming. *The Aristotelian Kant*. Cambridge: Cambridge University Press.

Goethe, Johann Wolfgang. 1987. *Schriften zur Morphologie*. Edited by Dorothea Kuhn. Frankfurt am Main: Deutscher Klassiker Verlag. [Abbreviated "FA 24".]

Golob, Sacha. 2020. "What Do Animals See? Intentionality, Objects, and Kantian Nonconceptualism." In Allais and Callanan (eds.), 66–88.

Gomes, Anil, and Stephenson, Andrew (eds.). 2017. *Kant and the Philosophy of Mind*. Oxford: Oxford University Press.

Graubner, Hans. 1972. *Form und Wesen: ein Beitrag zur Deutung des Formbegriffs in Kants "Kritik der reinen Vernunft"*. Bonn: Bouvier.

Grüne, Stephanie. 2017. "Are Kantian Intuitions Object-Dependent?" In Gomes and Stephenson (eds.), 67–85.

Guyer, Paul. 1987. *Kant and the Claims of Knowledge*. Cambridge: Cambridge University Press.

2018. "The Infinite Given Magnitude and Other Myths about Space and Time." In Nachtomy and Winegar (eds.), 181–204.

Haag, Johannes. 2007. *Erfahrung und Gegenstand: Das Verhältnis von Sinnlichkeit und Verstand*. Frankfurt am Main: Klostermann.

Hacking, Ian. 2007. "Trees of Logic, Trees of Porphyry." In *Advancements of Learning: Essays in Honour of Paulo Rossi*, edited by John L. Heilbron, 219–261. Florence: Olschki.

Hanna, Robert. 2005. "Kant and Nonconceptual Content." *European Journal of Philosophy* 13(2): 247–290.

2008. "Kantian Non-Conceptualism." *Philosophical Studies* 147: 41–64.

Harmer, Adam. 2014. "Leibniz on Infinite Numbers, Infinite Wholes, and Composite Substances." *British Journal for the History of Philosophy* 22(2): 236–259.

Heidegger, Martin. 1995. *Phänomenologische Interpretation von Kants "Kritik der reinen Vernunft" (Wintersemester 1927–28)*. Edited by Ingtraud Görland. Frankfurt am Main: Klostermann. [Abbreviated "GA 25".]

2010 [1929]. *Kant und das Problem der Metaphysik*. Edited by Friedrich-Wilhelm von Herrmann. Frankfurt am Main: Klostermann. [Abbreviated "GA 3".]

Heis, Jeremy. 2020. "Kant on Parallel Lines: Definitions, Postulates, and Axioms." In Posy and Rechter (eds.), 157–180.

Hintikka, Jaakko. 1969. "On Kant's Notion of Intuition (Anschauung)." In *The First Critique: Reflections on Kant's Critique of Pure Reason*, edited by T. Penelhum and J. MacIntosh, 38–53. Belmont, CA: Wadsworth.

Hoeppner, Till. 2021. *Urteil und Anschauung: Kants metaphysische Deduktion der Kategorien*. Berlin: De Gruyter.

Hogan, Desmond. 2013. "Metaphysical Motives of Kant's Analytic-Synthetic Distinction." *Journal of the History of Philosophy* 47(3): 267–307.

2021. "Handedness, Idealism, Freedom." *The Philosophical Review* 130(3): 385–449.

Hume, David. 2000 [1748]. *An Enquiry concerning Human Nature*. Edited by Tom L. Beauchamp. Oxford: Clarendon Press. [Abbreviated "Enquiry".]

2007 [1739]. *A Treatise of Human Nature*. 2 vols. Edited by David Fate Norton and Mary J. Norton. Oxford: Clarendon Press. [Abbreviated "Treatise".]

Indregard, Jonas Jervell. 2017. "Self-Affection and Pure Intuition in Kant." *Australasian Journal of Philosophy* 95(4): 627–643.

Irani, Tushar. 2022. "Perfect Change in Plato's *Sophist*." *Oxford Studies in Ancient Philosophy* 60: 45–93.

Jacquette, Dale. 2001. *David Hume's Critique of Infinity*. New York: Brill.

Jauernig, Anja. 2019. "Finite Minds and Their Representations in Leibniz and Kant." *Internationales Jahrbuch des Deutschen Idealismus* 14: 47–80.

2021. *The World according to Kant: Appearances and Things in Themselves in Critical Idealism*. Oxford: Oxford University Press.

2022. "Kant on the (Alleged) Leibnizian Misconception of the Difference between Sensible and Intellectual Representations." In Look (ed.), 177–210.

Jesseph, Douglas. 1993. *Berkeley's Philosophy of Mathematics*. Chicago: University of Chicago Press.

1999. *Squaring the Circle: The War between Hobbes and Wallis*. Chicago: University of Chicago Press.

Jorati, Julia (ed.). 2021. *Powers: A History*. Oxford: Oxford University Press.

Jorgenson, Larry. 2009. "The Principle of Continuity and Leibniz's Theory of Consciousness." *Journal of the History of Philosophy* 47(2): 223–248.
Kant, Immanuel. 1901–. *Gesammelte Schriften*. Edited by Deutsche Akademie der Wissenschaften. Berlin: De Gruyter.
1998. *Kritik der reinen Vernunft*. Edited by Jens Timmerman. Hamburg: Meiner.
Kästner, Abraham. 1790. "Ueber den mathematischen Begriff des Raumes." *Philosophisches Magazin* 2(4): 403–419.
Keill, John. 1739 [1702]. *Introductio ad veram physicam et veram astronomiam*. Leyden: Verbeek.
Kemp Smith, Norman. 1992 [1918]. *A Commentary to Kant's "Critique of Pure Reason"*. Atlantic Highlands, NJ: Humanities Press.
Kern, Andrea. 2017. *Sources of Knowledge: On the Concept of a Rational Capacity for Knowledge*. Translated by Daniel Smyth. Cambridge, MA: Harvard University Press.
Kitcher, Patricia. 2011. *Kant's Thinker*. Oxford: Oxford University Press.
Kitcher, Philip. 1992 [1975]. "Kant and the Foundations of Mathematics." In Posy (ed.), 109–131.
Koriako, Darius. 1999. *Kants Philosophie der Mathematik. Grundlagen. Voraussetzungen. Probleme*. Hamburg: Meiner.
Kraus, Katharina. 2020. *Kant on Self-Knowledge and Self-Formation: The Nature of Inner Experience*. Cambridge: Cambridge University Press.
Kripke, Saul. 1982. *Wittgenstein on Rules and Private Language*. Cambridge, MA: Harvard University Press.
Kuehn, Manfred. 2001. *Kant: A Biography*. Cambridge: Cambridge University Press.
La Rocca, Claudio. 2008a. "Der dunkle Verstand. Unbewusste Vorstellungen und Selbstbewusstsein bei Kant." In *Recht und Frieden in der Philosophie Kants. Akten des X. Internationalen Kant-Kongresses*, vol. 2, edited by Valerio Rohden, Ricardo Terra, and Guido de Almeida, 447–458. Berlin: De Gruyter.
2008b. "Unbewußtes und Bewußtsein bei Kant." In *Kant-Lektionen. Zur Philosophie Kants und zu Aspekten ihrer Wirkungsgeschichte*, edited by Manfred Kugelstadt, 47–68. Würzburg: Koenigshausen Neumann.
Lambert, Johann Heinrich. 1786. "Theorie der Parallellinien." *Magazin für reine und angewandte Mathematik*, 13–64 and 325–358. Reprinted in *Die Theorie der Parallellinien von Euklid bis auf Gauss*. Edited by Friedrich Engel and Paul Stäckel, 152–207. Leipzig: Teubner, 1895.
Land, Thomas. 2014. "Spatial Representation, Magnitude and the Two Stems of Cognition." *Canadian Journal of Philosophy* 44(5–6): 524–550.
2021 [2018]. "Epistemic Agency and the Self-Knowledge of Reason: On the Contemporary Relevance of Kant's Method of Faculty Analysis. *Synthese* 198 (Suppl. 13): 3137–3154.

Langton, Rae. 1998. *Kantian Humility: Our Ignorance of Things in Themselves*. Oxford: Oxford University Press.

Laywine, Alison. 2020. *Kant's Transcendental Deduction: A Cosmology of Experience*. Oxford: Oxford University Press.

Leibniz, Gottfried Wilhelm. 1765. *Œuvres philosophiques latines et françaises de feu Mr de Leibnitz, tirées des ses Manuscrits qui se conservant dans la Bibliothèque royale à Hanovre et publiées par M. Rud. Eric Raspe*. Amsterdam: Jean Schreuder.

1768. *Opera omnia nunc primum collecta in Classes distributa praefactionibus & indicibus exornata*. Edited by Ludovici Dutens. 6 vols. Geneva: Fratres de Tournes.

1875–90. *Die philosophischen Schriften von Gottfried Wilhelm Leibniz*. Edited by C. I. Gerhardt. Reprint. Hildesheim: Georg Olms. [Abbreviated "G".]

1923–. *Sämtliche Schriften und Briefe*. Edited by Deutsche Akademie der Wissenschaften. Berlin: Akademie Verlag. [Abbreviated "A".]

1989. *Philosophical Essays*. Edited by Roger Ariew and Daniel Garber. Indianapolis, IN: Hackett. [Abbreviated "AG".]

Levey, Samuel. 1998. "Leibniz on Mathematics and the Actually Infinite Division of Matter." *Philosophical Review* 107(1): 49–96.

1999. "Matter and Two Concepts of Continuity in Leibniz." *Philosophical Studies* 94(1–2): 81–118.

2012. "On Unity, Borrowed Reality and Multitude in Leibniz." *The Leibniz Review* 22: 97–134.

2021. "The Continuum, the Infinitely Small, and the Law of Continuity in Leibniz." In Shapiro and Hellman (eds.), 123–157.

Lindberg, David C. 1976. *Theories of Vision from Al-Kindi to Kepler*. Chicago: University of Chicago Press.

Longuenesse, Béatrice. 1998. *Kant and the Capacity to Judge*. Translated by Charles T. Wolfe. Princeton, NJ: Princeton University Press.

2017. *I, Me, Mine: Back to Kant and Back Again*. Oxford: Oxford University Press.

Look, Brandon. 2022. "Kant's Leibniz: A Historical and Philosophical Study." In *Leibniz and Kant*, edited by Brandon C. Look, 1–26. Oxford: Oxford University Press.

Lu-Adler, Huaping. 2013. "The Objects and the Formal Truth of Kantian Analytic Judgments." *History of Philosophy Quarterly* 30(2): 177–193.

2018a. *Kant and the Science of Logic: A Historical and Philosophical Reconstruction*. Oxford: Oxford University Press.

2018b. "Epigenesis of Pure Reason and the Source of Pure Cognitions." In *Rethinking Kant*, vol. 5, edited by Pablo Muchnik and Oliver Thorndike, 35–70. Newcastle upon Tyne: Cambridge Scholars Publishing.

MacFarlane, John. 2002. "Frege, Kant, and the Logic in Logicism." *Philosophical Review* 111(1): 25–65.

Marschall, Benjamin. 2019. "Conceptualizing Kant's Mereology." *Ergo* 6(14): 374–404.

Marshall, Colin. 2014. "Does Kant Demand Explanations for *All* Synthetic A Priori Claims?" *Journal of the History of Philosophy* 52(3): 549–576.

Matthews, Gareth B. 2003. "Augustine on the Mind's Search for Itself." *Faith and Philosophy* 20(4): 415–429.

McDowell, John. 2011. *Perception as a Capacity for Knowledge*. Milwaukee, WI: Marquette University Press.

McLear, Colin. 2011. "Kant on Animal Consciousness." *Philosophers' Imprint* 11 (15): 1–16.

2014. "The Kantian (Non-)Conceptualism Debate." *Philosophy Compass* 9(11): 769–790.

2015. "Two Types of Unity in Kant's *Critique of Pure Reason*." *Journal of the History of Philosophy* 53(1): 79–110.

2016. "Getting Acquainted with Kant." In Schulting (ed.), 171–197.

2017. "Intuition and Presence." In Gomes and Stephenson (eds.), 86–103.

2020. "Animals and Objectivity." In Allais and Callanan (eds.), 42–65.

Meier, Georg Friedrich. 1752. *Auszug aus der Vernunftlehre*. Halle: Johann Justinus Gebauer. [Abbreviated "*Auszug*".]

Melamedoff-Vosters, Damian. 2023. "Kant's Argument for Transcendental Idealism in the Transcendental Aesthetic Revisited." *Archiv für Geschichte der Philosophie* 105(1): 141–162.

Melnick, Arthur. 1973. *Kant's Analogies of Experience*. Chicago: University of Chicago Press.

Mendell, Henry. 2015. "What's Location Got to Do with It? Place, Space, and the Infinite in Classical Greek Mathematics." In *Mathematizing Space: Objects of Geometry from Antiquity to the Early Modern Age*, edited by Vincenzo De Risi, 15–64. London: Springer.

Menn, Stephen. 1994. "The Origins of Aristotle's Concept of *energeia*." *Ancient Philosophy* 14(1): 73–114.

1998. *Descartes and Augustine*. Cambridge: Cambridge University Press.

Mensch, Jennifer. 2013. *Kant's Organicism: Epigenesis and the Development of Critical Philosophy*. Chicago: University of Chicago Press.

Merritt, Melissa McBay. 2009. "Reflection, Enlightenment, and the Significance of Spontaneity in Kant." *British Journal for the History of Philosophy* 17(5): 981–1010.

2010. "Kant on the Transcendental Deduction of Space and Time: An Essay on the Philosophical Resources of the Transcendental Aesthetic." *Kantian Review* 14(2): 1–37.

2011. "Kant's Argument for the Apperception Principle." *European Journal of Philosophy* 19(1): 59–84.

2018. *Kant on Reflection and Virtue*. Cambridge: Cambridge University Press.

Messina, James. 2014. "Kant on the Unity of Space and the Synthetic Unity of Apperception." *Kant-Studien* 105(1): 5–40.

2015. "Conceptual Analysis and the Essence of Space: Kant's Metaphysical Exposition Revisited." *Archiv für Geschichte der Philosophie* 97(4): 416–457.

2018. "Kant's Stance on the Relationalist-Substantivalist Debate and Its Justification." *Journal of the History of Philosophy* 56(4): 697–726.

Molnar, George. 1999. "Are Dispositions Reducible?" *The Philosophical Quarterly* 49(1): 1–17.

2003. *Powers: A Study in Metaphysics*. Oxford: Oxford University Press.

Mumford, Stephen. 2009. "Causal Powers and Capacities." In *The Oxford Handbook of Causation*, edited by Helen Beebee, Christopher Hitchcock, and Peter Menzies, 265–278. Oxford: Oxford University Press.

Nachtomy, Ohad. 2011. "A Tale of Two Thinkers, One Meeting, and Three Degrees of Infinity: Leibniz and Spinoza in 1675–78." *British Journal for the History of Philosophy* 19(5): 935–961.

Nachtomy, Ohad, and Winegar, Reed (eds.) 2018. *Infinity in Early Modern Philosophy*. Berlin: Springer.

Newton, Alexandra. 2019. "Kant and the Transparency of the Mind." *Canadian Journal of Philosophy* 49(7): 890–915.

Nunez, Tyke. 2018. "Logical Mistakes, Logical Aliens, and the Laws of Kant's Pure General Logic." *Mind* 128(512): 1149–1180.

Oberhausen, Michael. 1997. *Das neue Apriori: Kants Lehre von einer "ursprünglichen Erwerbung" apriorischer Vostellungen*. Stuttgart: frommann-holzboog.

Onof, Christian, and Schulting, Dennis. 2014. "Kant, Kästner, and the Distinction between Metaphysical and Geometric Space." *Kantian Review* 19(2): 285–304.

2015. "Space as Form of Intuition and Space as Formal Intuition: On the Note to B160 in Kant's *Critique of Pure Reason*." *Philosophical Review* 124(1): 1–58.

Parsons, Charles. 1983 [1964]. "Infinity and Kant's Conception of the 'Possibility of Experience'." In his *Mathematics in Philosophy: Selected Essays*, 95–109. Ithaca, NY: Cornell University Press.

1992 [1969]. "Kant's Philosophy of Arithmetic." In Posy (ed.), 43–80.

2012 [1992]. "The Transcendental Aesthetic." In his *From Kant to Husserl: Selected Essays*, 5–41. Cambridge, MA: Harvard University Press.

Paton, H. J. 1936. *Kant's Metaphysic of Experience*. 2 vols. New York: MacMillan.

Patton, Lydia. 2011. "The Paradox of Infinite Given Magnitude: Why Kantian Epistemology Needs Metaphysical Space." *Kant-Studien* 102(3): 273–289.

Perler, Dominik (ed.). 2015. *The Faculties: A History*. Oxford: Oxford University Press.

Pippin, Robert. 1982. *Kant's Theory of Form*. New Haven, CT: Yale University Press.

1987. "Kant on the Spontaneity of Mind." *Canadian Journal of Philosophy* 17 (2): 449–475.

Plato. 1997. *Complete Works*. Edited by John M. Cooper. Indianapolis, IN: Hackett.

Pollok, Konstantin. 2017. *Kant's Theory of Normativity: Exploring the Space of Reason*. Cambridge: Cambridge University Press.

Porphyry, 2003. *Introduction*. Translated with an Introduction and Commentary by Jonathan Barnes. Oxford: Clarendon Press.

Posy, Carl (ed.). 1992. *Kant's Philosophy of Mathematics: Modern Essays*. Dordrecht: Kluwer Academic.

2008. "Intuition and Infinity: A Kantian Theme with Echoes in the Foundations of Mathematics." *Royal Institute of Philosophy Supplement* 63: 165–193.

Posy, Carl, and Rechter, Ofra (eds.). 2020. *Kant's Philosophy of Mathematics, Volume 1: The Critical Philosophy and Its Roots*. Cambridge: Cambridge University Press.

Powell, C. Thomas. 1990. *Kant's Theory of Self-Consciousness*. Oxford: Clarendon Press.

Quine, Willard van Orman. 1980 [1951]. "Two Dogmas of Empiricism." In his *From a Logical Point of View*, 20–46. 2nd revised ed. Cambridge, MA: Harvard University Press.

Rosefeldt, Tobias. 2022. "Kant on Decomposing Synthesis and the Intuition of Infinite Space." *Philosophers' Imprint* 22(1): 1–23.

Rosenkoetter, Timothy. 2008. "Are Kantian Analytic Judgments about Objects?" In *Recht und Frieden in der Philosophie Kants*, vol. 5, edited by Valerio Rohden, Ricardo Terra, Guido de Almeida, and Margit Ruffing, 191–202. Berlin: De Gruyter.

Rusnock, Paul, and George, Rolf. 1995. "A Last Shot at Kant and Incongruent Counterparts." *Kant-Studien* 86(3): 257–277.

Saccheri, Gerolamo. 2014 [1733]. *Euclid Vindicated from Every Blemish*. Edited by Vincenzo De Risi. Translated by G. B. Halsted and L. Allegri. New York: Birkhäuser.

Sassen, Brigitta. 2000. *Kant's Early Critics: The Empiricist Critique of the Theoretical Philosophy*. Cambridge: Cambridge University Press.

Schafer, Karl. 2019. "Kant's Constitutivism as Capacities-First Philosophy." *Philosophical Explorations* 22(2): 177–193.

2020a. "Transcendental Philosophy as Capacities-First Philosophy." *Philosophy and Phenomenological Research* 103(3): 661–686.

2020b. "A System of Rational Faculties: Additive or Transformative." *European Journal of Philosophy* 29(4): 918–936.

2021 [2018]. "A Kantian Virtue Epistemology: Rational Capacities and Transcendental Arguments." *Synthese* 198(Suppl. 13): 3113–3136.

2022. "Kant's Conception of Cognition and Our Knowledge of Things in Themselves." In *Sensible and Intelligible Worlds*, edited by Nicholas Stang and Karl Schafer, 248–278. Oxford: Oxford University Press.

2023. "Practical Cognition and Knowledge of Things-in-Themselves." In *The Idea of Freedom: New Essays on the Kantian Theory of Freedom*, edited by Dai Heide and Evan Tiffany, 83–109. Oxford: Oxford University Press.

Schechtman, Anat. 2018. "The Ontic and the Iterative: Descartes on the Infinite and the Indefinite." In Nachtomy and Winegar (eds.), 27–44.

2019. "Three Infinities in Early Modern Philosophy." *Mind* 128(52): 1117–1147.

Schmitz, Friederike. 2013. "On Kant's Conception of Inner Sense: Self-Affection by the Understanding." *European Journal of Philosophy* 23(4): 1044–1063.

Schmucker, Josef. 1976. "Was entzündete in Kant das große Licht von 1769?" *Archiv für Geschichte der Philosophie* 58(4): 393–434.

Schulting, Dennis (ed.). 2016. *Kantian Nonconceptualism*. London: Palgrave Macmillan.

Schultz, Johann. 1784. *Entdekte Theorie der Parallelen*. Königsberg: Kanter.

1785. "Philosophie: Rezension von *Institutiones Logicae et Metaphysicae*." *Allgemeine Literartur-Zeitung* 295(December 13, 1785): 297–299.

1786. *Darstellung der vollkommenen Evidenz und Schärfe seiner Theorie der Parallelen*. Königsberg: Hartung.

Sellars, Wilfrid. 1970. "…this I or He or It (The Thing) which thinks…" *Proceedings and Addresses of the American Philosophical Association* 44 (1970–1971): 5–31.

Setiya, Kieran. 2004. "Transcendental Idealism in the 'Aesthetic'." *Philosophy and Phenomenological Research* 68(1): 63–88.

Severo, Rogério Passos. 2005. "Three Remarks on the Interpretation of Kant on Incongruent Counterparts." *Kantian Review* 9: 30–57.

Shabel, Lisa. 2010. "The Transcendental Aesthetic." In *The Cambridge Companion to the "Critique of Pure Reason"*, edited by Paul Guyer, 93–117. Cambridge: Cambridge University Press.

Shaddock, Justin. 2015. "Kant's Transcendental Idealism and His Transcendental Deduction." *Kantian Review* 20(2): 265–288.

Shapiro, Stewart, and Hellman, Geoffrey (eds.). 2021. *The History of Continua: Philosophical and Mathematical Perspectives*. Oxford: Oxford University Press.

Smit, Houston. 1999. "The Role of Reflection in Kant's *Critique of Pure Reason*." *Pacific Philosophical Quarterly* 80(2): 203–223.

2000. "Kant on Marks and the Immediacy of Intuition." *Philosophical Review*. 109(2): 235–266.

2009. "Kant on Apriority and the Spontaneity of Cognition." In *Metaphysics and the Good: Themes from the Philosophy of Robert Merrihew Adams*, edited by Sam Newlands and Larry Jorgensen, 188–251. Oxford: Oxford University Press.

Smyth, Daniel. 2014. "Infinity and Givenness: Kant on the Intuitive Origin of Spatial Representation." *Canadian Journal of Philosophy* 44(5–6): 551–579.

2015. Infinity and Givenness: Kant's Critical Theory of Sensibility. PhD dissertation. University of Chicago.

2023 [2021]. "Kant's Mereological Account of Greater and Lesser Actual Infinities." *Archiv für Geschichte der Philosophie* 105(2): 315–348.

MS. "The Sinister Dexterity of Kant's Idealism: Chirality and Embodiment."

Sömmerring, Samuel Thomas. 1796. *Über das Organ der Seele*. Königsberg: Friedrich Nicolovius.

Spinoza, Baruch. 1925–. *Spinoza Opera*. Edited by Carl Gebhardt. Heidelberg: Carl Winters. [Abbreviated "G".]

2002. *The Complete Works*. Edited by Michael Morgan. Translated by Samuel Shirley. Indianapolis, IN: Hackett. [Abbreviated "SM".]

Stang, Nicholas. 2016. *Kant's Modal Metaphysics*. Oxford: Oxford University Press.

Stephenson, Andrew. 2015. "Kant on the Object-Dependence of Intuition and Hallucination." *The Philosophical Quarterly* 65(260): 486–504.

2017. "Imagination and Inner Intuition." In Gomes and Stephenson (eds.), 104–123.

Strawson, P. F. 1966. *The Bounds of Sense: An Essay on Kant's "Critique of Pure Reason"*. London: Methuen.

Sutherland, Daniel. 2004. "Kant's Philosophy of Mathematics and the Greek Mathematical Tradition." *Philosophical Review* 113(2): 157–201.

2017. "Kant's Conception of Number." *Philosophical Review* 126(2): 147–190.

2021a. "Continuity and Intuition in Eighteenth-Century Analysis and in Kant." In Shapiro and Hellman (eds.), 158–186.

2021b. *Kant's Mathematical World: Mathematics, Cognition, and Experience*. Cambridge: Cambridge University Press.

Tait, William. 2016. "Kant and Finitism." *Journal of Philosophy* 113(5/6): 261–273.

Thompson, Manley. 1972. "Singular Terms and Intuitions in Kant's Epistemology." *The Review of Metaphysics* 26(2): 314–343.

Tizzard, Jessica. 2018. "Kant on Space, Time, and Respect for the Moral Law as Analogous Formal Elements of Sensibility." *European Journal of Philosophy* 26(1): 630–646.

2020. "Why Does Kant Think We Must Believe in the Immortal Soul?" *Canadian Journal of Philosophy* 50(1): 114–129.

Tolley, Clinton. 2007. Kant's Conception of Logic. PhD dissertation. University of Chicago.

2012. "The Generality of Kant's Transcendental Logic." *Journal of the History of Philosophy* 50(3): 417–446.

2016. "The Difference between Original, Metaphysical and Geometrical Representations of Space." In Schulting (ed.), 257–285.

2021. "The Metaphysics of Powers in Kant and Hegel." In Jorati (ed.), 243–270.

Tonelli, Giorgio. 1974. "Leibniz on Innate Ideas and the Early Reactions to the Publication of the *Nouveaux Essais* (1765)." *Journal of the History of Philosophy* 11(4): 437–454.

Vaihinger, Hans. 1881. *Kommentar zur Kritik der reinen Vernunft*. Vol. I. Stuttgart: Spemann.

1892. *Kommentar zur Kritik der reinen Vernunft*. Vol. II. Stuttgart: Union Deutsche Verlagsgesellschaft.

Valaris, Markos. 2008. "Inner Sense, Self-Affection, and Temporal Consciousness in Kant's *Critique of Pure Reason*." *Philosophers' Imprint* 8(4): 1–18.

2020. "Reasoning, Defeasibility, and the Taking Condition." *Philosophers' Imprint* 20(28): 1–16.

Vanzo, Alberto. 2018. "Leibniz on Innate Ideas and Kant on the Origin of the Categories." *Archiv für Geschichte der Philosophie* 100(1): 19–45.

Verboon, Annemieke. 2010. Lines of Thought: Diagrammatic Representation in the Scientific Texts of the Arts Faculty, 1200–1500. PhD dissertation. Leiden University.

2014. "The Medieval Tree of Porphyry: An Organic Structure of Logic." In *The Tree: Symbol, Allegory, and Mnemonic Device in Medieval Art and Thought*, edited by Pippa Salonius and Andrea Worm, 95–116. Turnhout: Brepolis.

Vetter, Barbara. 2015. *Potentiality: From Dispositions to Modality*. Oxford: Oxford University Press.

Warren, Daniel. 1998. "Kant and the Apriority of Space." *Philosophical Review* 107(2): 179–224.

Watkins, Eric. 2004. *Kant and the Metaphysics of Causality*. Cambridge: Cambridge University Press.

Watkins, Eric, and Willaschek, Markus. 2017. "Kant's Account of Cognition." *Journal of the History of Philosophy* 55(1): 83–112.

2020 [2017]. "Kant on Cognition and Knowledge." *Synthese* 197: 3195–3213.

Willaschek, Marcus. 2001. "Affektion und Kontingenz in Kants transzendentalem Idealismus." In *Idealismus als Theorie der Repräsentation?*, edited by Ralph Schumacher and Oliver Scholz, 211–231. Paderborn: mentis.

2018. *Kant on the Sources of Metaphysics: The Dialectic of Pure Reason*. Cambridge: Cambridge University Press.

Williamson, Diane, and Sorensen, Kelly (eds.). 2017. *Kant and the Faculty of Feeling*. Cambridge: Cambridge University Press.

Wilson, Catherine. 1995. "The Reception of Leibniz in the Eighteenth Century." In *The Cambridge Companion to Leibniz*, edited by Nicholas Jolley, 442–474. Cambridge: Cambridge University Press.

Wilson, Kirk Dallas. 1975. "Kant on Intuition." *The Philosophical Quarterly* 25 (100): 247–265.

Winegar, B. Reed. 2022. "Kant's Three Conceptions of Infinite Space." *Journal of the History of Philosophy* 60(4): 635–659.

Wolff, Christian. 1730. *Philosophia prima sive ontologia methodo scientifica pertractata qua omnis cognitionis humanae principia continentur*. Frankfurt. [Abbreviated "*Ontologia*".]

1965 [1754]. *Vernünftige Gedanken von den Kräften des menschlichen Verstandes und ihrem richtigen Gebrauche in Erkenntnis der Wahrheit*. Edited by H. W. Arndt. Hildesheim: Olms. [Abbreviated "German Logic".]

1983 [1751]. *Vernünftige Gedanken von Gott, der Welt und der Seele des Menschen, auch allen Dingen überhaupt*. Edited by Charles Corr. Hildesheim: Olms. [Abbreviated "German Metaphysics".]

Wolff, Michael. 1995. *Die Vollständigkeit der kantischen Urteilstafel*. Frankfurt am Main: Klostermann.

Wuerth, Julian. 2014. *Kant on Mind, Action, and Ethics*. Oxford: Oxford University Press.

Index

For EU product safety concerns, contact us at Calle de José Abascal, 56–1°,
28003 Madrid, Spain or eugpsr@cambridge.org.

www.ingramcontent.com/pod-product-compliance
Ingram Content Group UK Ltd.
Pitfield, Milton Keynes, MK11 3LW, UK
UKHW020659060925
462614UK00020B/396

* 9 7 8 1 0 0 9 3 3 0 2 8 2 *